CRITICALLY MODERN

Critically Modern

Alternatives, Alterities,

Anthropologies

Edited by Bruce M. Knauft

INDIANA
University Press
Bloomington & Indianapolis

This book is a publication of
Indiana University Press
601 North Morton Street
Bloomington, IN 47404-3797 USA

http://iupress.indiana.edu

Telephone orders   800-842-6796
Fax orders   812-855-7931
E-mail orders   iuporder@indiana.edu

The paper used in this publication meets the minimum requirements of American National
Standard for Information Sciences—Permanence of Paper for Printed Library Materials,
ANSI Z39.48-1984.

Manufactured in the United States of America

Library of Congress Cataloging-in-Publication Data
Critically modern : alternatives, alterities, anthropologies / edited by Bruce M. Knauft.
p.   cm.
Revisions of papers presented at a special session held at the 2000 meeting
of the American Anthropological Association in San Francisco.
Includes bibliographical references and index.
ISBN 0-253-34125-6 (cloth : alk. paper) — ISBN 0-253-21538-2 (pbk. : alk. paper)
1. Social change—Cross-cultural studies. 2. Civilization, Modern—Cross-cultural studies.
3. Acculturation—Cross-cultural studies. I. Knauft, Bruce M.
GN358 .C75 2002
303.4—dc21
2001008306

1 2 3 4 5   07 06 05 04 03 02

Contents

Contents

vi

Preface

Some ideas germinate for a long time, while others develop quickly. Though concern with "modern society" has been robust for well over a century, an explicit concern with "modernity" seems to have mushroomed in the human sciences, especially since the mid-1980s. Yet more recently, during the late 1990s, issues of alternative or vernacular modernity have come to the fore. The present book acknowledges a debt to all these strands of social thought, while being most immediately impacted by the last. The differentiation of modernity has stimulated anthropologists as well as other scholars to think both more carefully and more critically about what it means (and does not mean) to become "modern" in various cultural and world area contexts. These issues provide the core concerns of the present book.

For me as the editor of this volume, a concern with the alternatively modern arose most forcefully not from academic writing but from fieldwork—when I returned to the Gebusi of Papua New Guinea after an absence of sixteen years. Though all the contributors to this volume have their debts to acknowledge, my own stem especially from Gebusi —specifically, from their willingness to share the remarkable transformations of their lives with me. As I returned from fieldwork in late 1998, the comparative dimension of what it meant to be or become modern was especially poignant to me. But when I started perusing the manuscripts, articles, and books that had been accumulating during my absence in the rainforest, it became quickly obvious that notions of alternative, vernacular, or "other" modernity were emerging almost explosively through independent invention and reinvention across a range of disciplinary and world area perspectives.

After inaugurating and assuming the leadership of a Ford Foundation–funded program at Emory University on "Vernacular Modernities," it became possible, in 2000, to return to a plan I had deferred since returning from the field: to organize a session on alternative modernities at the annual meetings of the American Anthropological Association (AAA). By this time, the literature on the subject had swelled to such a size that the task was as much to take critical stock of this intellectual endeavor as it was to propose or push it forward. The resulting session, "Inflections of Modernity," was held at the annual AAA meetings in San Francisco on 16 November 2000. The presentations of that session were so productive and acute—in both ethnographic perception and historical sweep—that it seemed fitting for us to revise our papers and collect them into an edited volume. The contributions to the present volume were all originally presented at the AAA "Inflections of Modernity" session. Jonathan Friedman's chapter in this book and my own introduction both stem from our participation as discussants on this panel.

Though it is commonplace for session organizers to tout the collective success of their enterprise, the participants in the present collection deserve special note. Both at the session itself and during our ensuing discussions and revisions, this project has had a strong sense of intellectual dialogue. The value of this dialogue stemmed from our differences; we do not all agree concerning the issues that swirl about the modern and the alternatively modern, nor even on the exact terms of this discussion. But it seemed to us (and is, I hope, self-evident in the chapters herein) that we have been wrestling deeply and concretely, from our complementary vantage points, with a key problematic in contemporary cultural anthropology. The present volume is an acknowledgment, appreciation, and extension of recent interest in modernity and, in equal proportion, its critical reevaluation.

Given our spontaneous sense that we were engaged in a larger collective enterprise, it was especially pleasing to us that Rebecca Tolen, anthropology editor at Indiana University Press, took keen interest in having our efforts revised for publication. Beyond the usual shepherding and logistics, Rebecca has been a source of creative planning, timely advice, and effective management for the prompt production of this volume. In an academic world where edited books often languish for many years before emerging in print, great thanks are owed to Rebecca, as well as to all the contributors, for a publication process that has maximized quality while also enabling swift completion.

We also extend warm and sincere thanks to our two external manu-script reviewers, who have generously made their identities known to us: Edward LiPuma and Charles Piot. The penetrating comments of these scholars have been invaluable to the contributors, and especially to me as editor, during the process of revising the book's manuscript.

The remaining debts of this volume are more intellectually diffuse in nature. As editor, I have benefited greatly from the scholarly and aca-demic environment of the Vernacular Modernities Program at Emory. This program, which is funded in significant part by the Ford Founda-tion's "Crossing Borders" initiative, has brought a wide range of speak-ers to Emory and supported an interdisciplinary cadre of graduate stu-dents in our Vernacular Modernities Seminar. The students, scholars, and colleagues of the Vernacular Modernities Program have had a major impact on my intellectual development and hence on the conceptualiza-tion of the present volume. The Vernacular Modernities Program has it-self been importantly supported, in a variety of ways, by Emory's Insti-tute for Comparative and International Research, the Emory Graduate School of Arts and Sciences, Emory College, and Emory's anthropology department. Warm thanks are extended to all these organizations.

My final thanks is for the powerful engagement and ongoing stimu-lus provided by the contributors to this volume. Their work has strongly influenced me. More generally, they have refreshed my belief that criti-cal dialogue and sustained intellectual effort can illuminate key features of cultural change and inequality in a contemporary world.

Bruce M. Knauft
Atlanta, Ga.
August 2001

CRITICALLY MODERN

Critically Modern

An Introduction

Bruce M. Knauft

What is entailed by the process of being or becoming modern? This question has been important for Western societies since the late eighteenth century, if not before. But it takes on new dimensions in a contemporary world. Modernity has become global in new ways. Or has it? What does it mean to be or to resist being modern in world areas and locales that have different cultural histories? In recent years, these questions have generated vigorous debate across the social sciences and humanities. Especially among anthropologists and critical theorists, standards of social advancement and progress are seen to differ depending on cultural and historical conditions. The process of becoming modern is contested and mediated through alter-native guises. It has been increasingly suggested that modernity is importantly regional, multiple, vernacular, or "other" in character.[1]

Despite its highly equivocal and uneven outcomes, economic and social development has often been associated with aspirations for a better style of life, including a hope that living standards will eventually approximate those of Western countries. In the process, it has often been suggested, customary practices are relinquished or transformed; social relations are dislodged, disrupted, or disembedded by market forces and by new institutions and aspirations. But what new social formations arise? What forms of subjectivity and subordination are incited? What new diversities are generated, and how do these draw on local history as well as on regional connections or international influences?

Anthropologists have often questioned the homogeneity of so-called global developments. On one hand, our strong appreciation of cultural

1

diversity pointedly questions the ostensible convergence of the world's peoples to a single global culture. On the other hand, anthropologists' concerns with power and domination—how and why some people become disenfranchised and disempowered relative to others—make us skeptical about claims of global progress and collective improvement. Along with other critical theorists, then, anthropologists have questioned the attempt to view modernity as a singular or coherent development. Indeed, the divergent responses of the world's peoples arguably maintain or increase their cultural diversity at the same time that they become more deeply entwined with capitalist influences, institutions, and impositions. Hence the paradox that people in different world areas increasingly share aspirations, material standards, and social institutions at the same time that their local definition of and engagement with these initiatives fuels cultural distinctiveness.

In contemporary cultural anthropology, this view of modern diversity has, in various permutations, become important and influential.[2] Amid this growing interest, however, the question of how modernity becomes "different"—and how we should conceptualize this process—bears further scrutiny. Is the current interest in modernity and its alterities sufficiently clear? Do recent approaches unwittingly adopt the biases of earlier modernization theories and of eurocentric assumptions that we hope to have left behind? Or does an emphasis on being modern and its inflections lever fields such as anthropology to important new insights concerning culture and power in a contemporary world? At issue is whether our understandings of modernity and its alternatives are critically flawed, or if instead they are critically important to anthropology and to the people we study with. It is time to take stock of these issues.

The goal of the present book is to gain critical purchase on the central problematic of modernity and its multiples through a strongly presented range of anthropological perspectives. Constituent chapters combine ethnographic and theoretical interventions authored by established and developing anthropological scholars. Rather than being pinned to a single viewpoint, contributors adopt complementary perspectives on a shared problematic. These perspectives draw variously on theories of capitalism and political economy, history, subjectivity, and aesthetics. The contributors' empirical engagements articulate in important ways with the contemporary study of gender, language use, labor, commodification, public culture, nongovernmental organizations (NGOs), political upheaval, imperial ideology, and governmentality. World area perspectives range from Africa and Oceania to the Caribbean, Euro–America, and interareal connections more generally.

Instead of presenting a single dogma, the chapters of this book pursue a sustained critical dialogue on the problematic of modernity. These treatments are "critical" in three senses. First and most generally, they provide a powerful critique of the notion that being or becoming modern betokens the global triumph of Euro-American economic, social, or cultural development. Second, they reflect critically on recent notions of the alternatively modern—the understanding of modernity as a differentiated or variegated process. Third and more reflexively, the perspectives are critical in a positive sense; their compass of perception is critically important for a self-consciously current anthropology. In this respect, a key shared goal is to combine ethnographic and historical engagements with trenchant theorization to better understand trajectories of culture and power in a contemporary world.

Anthropology that is critical for current understanding needs itself to be critically theorized. In the present case, some of the contributors suggest that relativized views of modernity give short shrift to larger patterns of power and domination. In this critique, an emphasis on the plural modern sheds insufficient light on the deeper and longer impact of political economy—the historical forces of capitalism that shape contemporary globalization and undergird the sense of being or desiring to become modern. On the other hand, viewing modernity as multiple raises thorny questions of ethnographic application. How do we characterize different inflections of modernity relative to each other, or with respect to practices that cannot be considered modern at all? Unless it is clarified to be an analytic perspective rather than an empirical grid for mapping the world, the differentiation of modernity still presents us with dichotomous categories and choices. Which cultural features fit one or another mode of being modern, and which are left behind as backward-looking or traditional? Faced with this question, analysis easily subsumes nuances of subjectivity and cultural belief into one or another variant of a modern world—that is, to save them from being relegated to backwardness or put in a "savage slot" (see Trouillot 1991).

Stated more generally, long-standing ideologies of the modern—which have typically incorporated the West and excluded the Rest—can be unwittingly recapitulated in contemporary approaches. As we relativize our sense of what is alternatively modern, there remains a lingering danger of reinscribing older views, bequeathed from the European Enlightenment, in which people are judged and ranked according to the extent they have achieved—as Immanuel Kant put it in 1784, an "exodus . . . by their own effort from a state of guilty immaturity."[3] Even as they are relativized, concepts of modernity can imply a creeping shared totality, a global standard of improvement against which others are judged. In this respect, modernity and even its plurals can become an omnibus assumption—a new black box of unexamined ideology in the social science of late capitalism.

Nevertheless, it remains true that aspirations for economic development and for associated institutional if not cultural progress are, if anything, stronger than ever in much of the contemporary world. Nations and local communities push energetically to become more economically and institutionally "developed." Notions of being and becoming modern are not simply an academic projection; they are a palpable and potent ideology in many if not most world areas. Ideologies of becoming modern are commonly hitched to the aspirations, programs, and propaganda of the nation-state, where they alternatively inform and juxtapose against notions of national authenticity and cultural or religious history. Even when expectations for national improvement are sorely disappointed, they easily inform continuing desires for a style of life associated with economic development and Western-style material betterment. Relatedly, the values that attend modern aspiration interact powerfully with the construction of selfhood and social or material endeavors in diverse world areas. These processes may alternatively resist or reinforce the imposition of Western-style institutions, policies, and initiatives—as variously pursued by state or local governments, businesses, international corporations, NGOs, and development agencies. However much these forces may be disagreed with, they can seldom be ignored.

Whatever terms are used to describe it, the way people engage the ideologies and institutions of a so-called modernizing world provides a valuable vantage point for understanding contemporary articulations of culture and power. So, too, the ethnography, theorization, and critique of alternative or vernacular modernities provide a stimulating point of departure to address these issues while also rendering a productive target for reflexive examination and critique. In diverse circumstances across the world, local notions of value, worth, and success articulate with escalating desires for economic development or social progress to redefine longer-standing practices and orientations. These dynamics are mediated by cultural history and by the economic and political realities of what it means locally to be developed or experience progress. Considering these trajectories and their relationship is crucial for an engaged and contemporary anthropology.

Acknowledging this importance, the present book addresses the issues that surround the process of being or becoming differently modern in different world areas. This issue is analyzed and made problematic through a combination of local, national, and regional understandings. In what ways does the multiplication of modernity capture current dynamics of power and culture? In what ways does it go beyond the over-generalizations for which previous master narratives of modernity have been critiqued? Reciprocally, in what ways do recent conceptualizations of modernity neglect key dimensions of political economy on one hand, or local culture on the other? Yet more fundamentally, how do we tease apart the issues in this debate without devolving into old-fashioned relativism or global reductionism? Addressing these questions is crucial for confronting one of anthropology's central current challenges—namely, to critically understand the ways in which people engage images of progress and institutions of development at the same time that they become more culturally diverse, unequal, and disempowered.

Inflections of Modernity: A Genealogy

A critical understanding of being or becoming modern can hardly be developed without an historical perspective. As part of this history, we need to consider how modernity has emerged as a problem in Western thought and connect this problem to trajectories of sociocultural change or transformation. Besides adding historical perspective, tracing the problematic of modernity provides a vantage point from which current views can be more clearly analyzed and reformulated. The goal is not to promote a hegemony of Western thought. It is rather to provide grounds for critical scrutiny and alternative lines of intervention.

In one respect, modern life is associated with the appreciative search for new meaning in the daily features of a differentiated social world. This conceptualization of "modernity" as can be dated at least as far as back as Charles Baudelaire's essay "The Painter of Modern Life," written in 1859–1860 and published in 1863 in *Le Figaro* (Baudelaire 1964). Baudelaire emphasized the rendering and seeking of artistic significance in daily experience, epitomized by the mannered explorations of the man-about-town and the impressionistic drawings of Constantin Guys, a "passionate lover of crowds and incognitos" (1964:5). As Trouillot (this volume) notes, Baudelaire's experience was also profoundly affected by his travels to the Indian Ocean and by his long-term liaison with a Caribbean mulatto woman—though the impact of these experiences on his work has often been neglected by literary scholars. Quotidian sensibilities were also explored during the last half of the nineteenth century in the novels of Flaubert and in French impressionist painting. These portrayed the daily images and perspectives of unadorned contemporary life in France at the time. Such developments were complemented by the increasing growth of travel literature, memoirs, and experiential accounts of life in non-Western areas.

In a deeper and more general sense, modern notions of selfhood have often been associated with an affirmation of ordinary life, a secular or instrumentalist orientation, and a heightened sense of autonomous individuality, self-fashioning, and inwardness (see Taylor 1989). In Europe and other areas, these aspects of modern identity often went hand in hand with increasing desire for personal or collective progress based on new ways of daily living—and frequently at the expense of previous ways of life. These trends drew fundamentally on mercantile and incipient capitalist exploitation of non-Western areas. During the late eighteenth and the nineteenth centuries, these trends intensified and melded with the powerful growth of industrial capitalism, technological innovation, and increasing desires for manufactured commodities. In both developments, much of Western economic success ultimately derived from the exploitation of non-Western areas. In ideational and ideological terms, correspondingly, non-Western areas typically served as the primitive Other against which European Enlightenment and colonialism were elevated and justified. This rank ordering of humanity informed the "civilizing mission" of Western intrusion and exploitation of non-Western peoples.

During much of the nineteenth and twentieth centuries, desire for progress had a pronounced political side—including the groundswell to create new forms of government that superseded monarchies, aristocracies, and eventually colonial regimes in the hope of creating better and more equitable national societies. These features were highlighted in the watershed transformation of the French Revolution, which is often seen—from a Western political perspective—to inaugurate the beginning of the modern era at the end of the eighteenth century. As Benedict Anderson (1991) has noted, however, the modern nation as a collectively imagined community also arose in the Americas during the late eighteenth and nineteenth centuries, including in Latin America as well as in the United States.

New modes of temporality also appear to have developed during the late eighteenth century. Reinhart Koselleck (1985:279, 285) suggests that a growing disjunction between future expectations and present experiences developed in Europe during this period. Among the results was a burgeoning belief in progress. Economically and politically, this "progress" was related to the growth of industrial capitalism at home and the global intensification of Western colonial exploitation. In the midst of these developments, the civilizing mission of Europe was complemented by struggles among creole populations for recognition and status against escalating standards of European superiority. Both in Europe and its colonies, the growing discrepancy between aspirations and realities increased a sense that the passage of time should expectably be marked by progress and improvement vis-à-vis the past. As Foucault (1984:39) notes, "Modernity is often characterized in terms of consciousness of the discontinuity of time: a break with tradition." These assumptions appear so ubiquitous today that it is important to realize how distinctive and even unusual they are in the context of alternative cultural orientations and earlier phases of Western history. These often emphasized allegiance to the beliefs and orientations of the past rather than plans for a newly different and hopefully better future. The increasing Western emphasis on progress was complemented by the notion that "history" was not so much an index of authenticity or propriety as it was an undeveloped past against which the march of progress should be asserted.

As discussed by Foucault (1984:32 ff.; cf. 1970), notions of Enlightenment changed correspondingly during the latter half of the eighteenth century—as illustrated in the work of Immanuel Kant. These developments reflected the increasing desire for self-conscious improvement through new forms of knowledge, action, and understanding. More darkly, Foucault exposed how the modern will to knowledge incited new forms of classification and power during the nineteenth century. National states used new types of knowledge and forms of knowing to stigmatize, discipline, and punish their subjects—in the name of improving society. This same process informed the subjugation, racialization, and stigmatization of colonial subjects abroad (Stoler 1995). More generally, the enumeration, classification, and codification of subjects into social categories inculcated new forms of moral onus while making persons more "legible" to authorities and hence more controllable by the state (Scott 1998). Correspondingly, modern institutions of legal, penal, medical, and educational imposition made the process of becoming a subject problematic in new ways. The incitement to search for value in daily life—to heroize the present while avoiding the stigma of being backward or depraved—was paralleled by a mandate to reinvent oneself as a newly ascetic and disciplined modern subject (Foucault 1984:41–42; cf. Weber 1958).[4]

Though these trends have usually been attributed to European and colonial life since the late eighteenth century, they had important precursors before this time. Max Weber (1958) suggested that the motivational spirit of capitalism developed from an ethic of this-worldly asceticism associated with Calvinism and related branches of puritanical Christianity during and after the Protestant Reformation. Further, as Trouillot (this volume) emphasizes, Anglo and Germanic views of Western history tend to neglect the earlier relationship of Spain and Portugal to the projective geography of modern imagination and domination, as reflected in the Iberian exploitation of the Caribbean, Latin America, and other areas during the sixteenth century (cf. Dussel 1993).

Even apart from the reciprocal impact of non-Western areas back on the development of European modernity, an emphasis on advancement through inventive self-fashioning had earlier permutations in the European Renaissance and, much earlier, in ancient Greece.[5] Fredric Jameson (n.d.:1) suggests that the concept of being modern—per the Latin word *modernus*—was used as far back as the fifth century A.D. to distinguish the contemporary from the ancient or antique. In a yet deeper historical perspective, Jonathan Friedman (this volume; cf. 1994:39) suggests that civilizational empires have often been characterized by a period of modernism when they have been at the height of their political centralization and cultural hegemony.

Building on these earlier strains and precedents, however, the various strands of Western and colonial modernity braided together in powerful new ways during the late eighteenth and especially the nineteenth and early twentieth centuries. It was during this period that industrial capitalism most dramatically transformed life in European towns and cities—while displacing and disrupting local communities of peasants, artisans, landowners, and clergy. These processes were recursively linked to several developments: the increasing activities of Europeans overseas; the exploitation of non-Western areas in a global network of exploitation and commodity production; disruption and movement of non-Western peoples; the growing development of creole populations, including in Europe; and the hybridization of Western values, sensibilities, and institutions among subaltern populations.

These developments are not unique to the modern Western world, as Jonathan Friedman (this volume) suggests. Permutations of them can be found in expansionist development of other civilizational systems, including ancient Roman and Chinese empires and the Old World prior to European hegemony (Abu-Lughod 1989; see Held et al. 1999). But the scale and intensity of *global* connections after 1500 was unprecedented. By the late nineteenth century, these worldwide connections were firmly linked to Western forms of industrial commodity production on one hand, and to globally intense forms of Western colonialism on the other. These two developments—capitalism and colonialism—became increasingly connected to each other. In the process, the threatened influence of *non*-Western areas rebounded back on Europe. This counterforce intensified the needs of the Europeans to construct themselves as superior to and different from non-Westerners and from subaltern groups within Europe itself. In this sense, the ideological as well as social disruptions that Europe visited on the New World and elsewhere came home to roost in a newly modern key.

Classic Social Theory

In the latter part of the nineteenth and the early twentieth centuries, the destructive and yet potentiating developments of "modern society" in the West became a central problematic for thinkers such as Marx, Durkheim, Simmel, and Weber—figures who have since become classic or foundational for social and cultural theory. These scholars were deeply concerned by the advent of full-blown capitalism, the spread of wage labor, the uprooting of people from European communities, and the bustling growth and great risks of life in modern Western cities and towns. Their perspectives were strongly influenced by a desire for progress based on critical inquiry. Bequeathed from the Enlightenment, their approaches employed documentation and reason to understand social developments and, optimally, enable their improvement. As such, classic social theorists critically analyzed the present of their day against the possibilities of the future and the lost benefits of the past. In the process, they drew heavily from Enlightenment notions of improvement through critique. In the formulations of Marx, Durkheim, Simmel, Weber, and others, modern Western society was viewed —depending on the theorist—as an engine of economic inequity and oppression, a specialized division of labor threatened by alienation, an arena for monetary dehumanization, or an iron cage of bureaucracy and rationalization. At the same time, these views also accorded modern society powerful potentials for more efficient organization, technological progress, and moral or humanistic improvement.

The insights of classic social theorists continue to provide important perspective for understanding more recent developments—including those that have taken place during the last half of the twentieth century. Before the 1960s, however, classic social theory was infrequently used to consider or analyze patterns of exploitation in *non*-Western areas. This is a huge shortcoming that has been addressed, with varying degrees of critical success, in more recent decades.

It is perhaps significant that while the problems and potentials of modern society were central to classic social theorists, the term "modern" was typically used in their works as a casual modifier rather than as a central concept. Correspondingly, the notion of "modernity" appears only rarely in their writings. It has only been much more recently —since the mid-1980s—that "modernity" has emerged explicitly as a core problematic in the human sciences.[6] A quick example illustrates this trend. Emory University's ample but by no means exhaustive research library includes a whopping 545 books published between 1991 and 2000 that have the word "modernity" in the title. A full 145 of these volumes were published during 1999 or 2000 alone. By contrast, only a handful of volumes that used "modernity" as a title concept were published before the mid- and early 1980s.

This semantic shift reflects deeper issues. Classic social theory— including the work of Marx, Durkheim, Weber, and Simmel—emphasized a close and interactive relation between the subjective features of what we now generally refer to as culture and the more ostensibly objective features of politics and economy. These theorists, along with others, were strongly committed to a *combined* analysis of mental and material factors—a critical consideration of how economic and political features were reciprocally or dialectically related to values, beliefs, and subjective experiences. During the succeeding decades of the twentieth century, however, the disciplinary interests of the social sciences and humanities became increasingly specialized and atomized. In the process, they have been prone to a widening split between models of social change based on economic or political determinism on one hand, those that stress beliefs and cultural values on the other.

Against the backdrop of this academic history, the more recent emphasis on "modernity" reflects an attempt to bring the two sides of this issue back together in the study of contemporary social and cultural change. Whereas empiricist social scientists often stress the economic or political determinism of modernization and globalization, a range of critical theorists, broad-based intellectuals, and social scientists now emphasize the interactive importance of cultural and material influences in the development of alternative modernities. As the Canadian philosopher and cultural activist Charles Taylor (1989, 1992, 1999) has suggested, the moral values and beliefs that attend modernity are not reducible to dominant assumptions of economic determinism and its ostensible relation to social and political "progress." At the same time, the analysis of modernity does not reject material forces and economic or political factors. Rather, studies of alternative modernities provide a productive middle ground for analyzing these features in relation to cultural and subjective orientations. As such, they connect the social and material emphases of sociology and political science with the evocative but often unsystematic presentations of representational analysis, literary criticism, and cultural studies.

From POMO Back to MO

From the perspective of the 1970s and 1980s, the split between the social sciences and humanities was galvanized by a newly contentious, influential, and transdisciplinary movement: postmodernism. Since the
postmodern impetus has, with some irony, informed and provoked the
mushrooming recent interest in modernity, it is worthwhile to consider
postmodernism as a predisposing context. As Harvey (1989) suggests,
the radical questions posed by postmodernism dovetailed with the economic stagnation and institutional rigidity that plagued Western capitalism during the 1970s. Skeptical of uniform standards of truth and
knowledge, postmodern sensibilities rejected rational modernism and
all that it implied. This radicalism was important to question the conservative assumptions and ideologies associated with Western reason
and progress (which could certainly not be legitimately imparted to all
of humanity). Third-wave feminism, subaltern studies, cultural studies, black cultural criticism, and other initiatives drew on postmodern
sensibilities to trouble Western assumptions across a wide variety of
gendered, sexual, racial, ethnic, and national fronts. That European
modernity had disrupted, impoverished, and killed so many people—
producing two world wars, racism, crushing colonization, violent decolonization, and then neocolonial domination through postcolonial
capitalism that undercut subsistence production and made people in diverse world areas dependent on the strictures of a market economy—
made Western modernity highly suspect as a model for general improvement and world progress.

During the 1980s, postmodern perspectives drew variously on French
deconstruction, poststructuralism, surrealism, the literary and artistic avant-garde, and pop culture to deconstruct master narratives of understanding and grand theories of development and progress. Full of
pastiche, playfulness, hybridity, and experimental forms of expression,
postmodern sensibilities made problematic not only the canons of Western description, reason, and explanation but also the means and styles
by which these were pursued and expressed. Beyond an intellectual enterprise, postmodern perspectives claimed to ride an emergent wave of
contemporary and popular culture—a public world of discordant images
and mass-mediated idioms that accelerated in dizzying patterns of possibility and parody. They also foregrounded what Foucault (1980) called
subjugated knowledges and helped energize queer theory, postmodern
feminism, critical cultural studies, and postcolonial studies, among
other initiatives. Many of these perspectives privileged evocation and

impression—a cutting edge of irony, insinuation, and protest—as opposed to systematic demonstration by means of detailed documentation, empirical analysis, or logical explanation.

If postmodern sensibilities refused standards of declarative logic and universal truth, they were effective in criticizing assumptions of Western thought, the structures of its social and political economy, and its understanding of historical and contemporary "progress." By the late 1980s, the "post" in postmodernity became an exclamation point of rupture, refusal, and disconnection from rational or historical understanding. Though full-blown postmodernists were few in number, they were highly provocative.[7] Postmodern sensibilities had great transdisciplinary influence during the late 1980s, including through the loosening of assumptions and the responses they provoked—not to mention the defenses they engendered among scholars who felt threatened.

From the beginning, postmodern sensibilities were critiqued as thickly as they were asserted or expressed. Many if not most of the interlocutors with postmodernism—including Jean Baudrillard, Fredric Jameson, Gayatri Spivak, Judith Butler, Douglas Kellner, Mike Featherstone, and the early Lyotard—had themselves been strongly influenced by Marxism.[8] The same was true of the greatest defender of Western reason against the poststructural and postmodern critique: the German philosopher Jürgen Habermas.

A characterization of Habermas's large opus is beyond our present concerns. But his treatment of modernity is relevant. In 1981, Habermas published his voluminous *Theory of Communicative Action* (translated in 1984). Committed to maintaining reason and rational discourse in contemporary society, Habermas reanalyzed the use of reason in the works of Weber, Lukács, Adorno, Mead, Durkheim, and Parsons. In the process, he developed a theoretical model of communicative action that critiqued functionalist reason and promoted rational discourse. Through this discourse, Habermas suggested, communicational action could integrate different aspects of the modern experience or "lifeworld." For Habermas, analyzing and understanding proper communication allows us to appreciate the accomplishments and cultivate the unrealized potentials of Western modernity.[9] He thus maintains that rational communicative action can be developed for the good and proper progress of society through a public sphere of reasoned understanding (Habermas 1987; cf. Calhoun 1992).

Habermas is often considered to be the arch philosophical champion of contemporary Western modernity. In his perspective, modernity is the positive fruit of rational discourse bequeathed from the European Enlightenment. By the mid-1980s, however, the poststructural and postmodern critique of Western reason was near its height. In the context of these critiques, Habermas's ideas were considered out-moded by many; he seemed to be adopting an antiquated model of Western rational superiority. In 1985, Habermas counterattacked with the twelve lectures of his *Philosophical Discourse of Modernity*. These launched a frontal assault on figures such as Bataille, Foucault, Derrida, and Castoriadis—while asserting Habermas's own stance that moder-nity continued, and should continue, as a preeminent project of rational communication based on general truth derived from universal reason. This perspective was alternately ignored and responded to with cri-tiques that further undermined pretensions to rational progress. The writings of Foucault—who emphasized how Western regimes of truth operated as instruments of domination and oppression—were especially important in this respect (Foucault 1980, 1984; see in Kelly 1994). It was out of these debates—and their deeper historical precursors[10]—that contemporary concerns about modernity and its multiples have since emerged. In the process, the legacy of the Foucault–Habermas debate has expanded to consider how people in different world areas have been impelled to engage the progressivist project of Western modernity—and how they resist or countermand it. Subaltern and postcolonial stud-ies have been especially important in this regard.[11]

During the early 1990s, the radical impetus of postmodernism began to burn itself out. Indeed, the explicit influence of postmodernism sub-sided almost as quickly as its initial rush had been intense. As early as 1992, the question became, as Michael Rosenthal put it in *Socialist Re-view*, "What *Was* Postmodernism?" But if the claims of postmodern sensibility were inflated, they highlighted key problems in the perspec-tives they had attacked—including the Western project of progress through rational development. Though Habermas has continued to be influential—and prolific—he is increasingly seen by many scholars, and even by some of his acolytes, as a classic or anachronistic apologist for master narratives of rational reason in a world that is rife with compet-ing standards of truth and rationality.[12] In the mix, however, the asser-tion of postmodernity has paved the way for a complementary question: If the asserted break with modernity has been overblown, what new un-derstandings of modern life now become necessary to comprehend the intense trajectories of contemporary change? In what ways have post-modern sensibilities themselves been a symptom of late modern cultural disjunctions? If the "post" in postmodernity was excessive, what is a better way to understand "modernity" to begin with? During the 1990s, then, the excursus of postmodernism led many scholars back in a sig-nificantly new key to the study of "modernity."

14

From Philosophy to Social Theory:
The Reemergence of Modernity as a Social and Cultural Problematic

For reconsidering the relation between modernity and postmodernity, the work of David Harvey during the late 1980s has been particularly important (see Harvey 1989, cf. 1982, 1996, 2000). A scholar of Western urban geography, political economy, and culture, Harvey brings a distinctly Marxist and historical perspective to the question of what dynamics of modernity—economic, political, and cultural —were disrupted and thrown into crisis during the 1970s and 1980s to produce the cultural symptoms associated with postmodernity. In Harvey's view, high industrial capitalism—earlier termed "Fordism" by Antonio Gramsci— was brought into global crisis during the early 1970s due to corporate rigidity, difficulties of further expansion, and falling profit margins. The capitalist response to this crisis, according to Harvey, was increased reliance on "flexible accumulation." Flexible accumulation goes hand in hand with the speeding up and decentralization of transactions and profit-seeking across time and space, including through electronic transmission of ideas, information, and financial transactions. These patterns drew on new electronic technologies while compressing social and cultural experience across time and space. For Harvey, time–space compression is diagnostic of the social and cultural fragmentation of "the condition of postmodernity."

From an anthropological perspective, Harvey's work has major shortcomings that echo those of Habermas and also Foucault. Among other things, all of these approaches sideline the economic and political histories of non-Western peoples—including their engagements with and resistances against capitalism. Harvey's perspective further downplays the motivating force of cultural values, idioms, and ideologies in their own right; they become, on balance, a reflection of economic and political forces. Since the so-called electronic age arguably makes the dissemination of ideas and information one of its prime arenas of production, profit making, and consumption, it needs to be seriously considered if the old Marxist infrastructure and superstructure now have a transformed causal relationship. There is ample evidence that cultural and subjective orientations have been dynamic forces in Western development, including—as Max Weber (1958) emphasized—in the Protestant asceticism that helped spawn a capitalist ethos to begin with. In a contemporary world, subjective orientations exert an obviously huge impact. The events of 11 September 2001 and the aftermath of U.S. bombing that began the following 7 October have sadly underscored that cultural diversity in the developing world system is, if anything, more important than ever to understand. All this runs against the singular weight that Harvey affords to "time–space compression" as a relatively undifferentiated and implicitly globalizing condition. Harvey's characterization of contemporary time and space ultimately draws more from hoary assumptions and categories of Western intellectualism than it does from evidence concerning how time and space are in fact experienced and constructed in different parts of the world (cf. Greenhouse 1996; Miller 1994; Birth 1999).

This said, Harvey's argument has, within its restricted Western frame, been highly important as well as influential. First, his work is rich in detail, critical in Western cultural perspective, and breathtaking in economic and historical scope. As such, it has provided an important example of how critical scholarship need not sacrifice evidential rigor or strength of argument to be evocative and important.[13] Second, Harvey put our understanding of contemporary cultural developments squarely back in play with economic and political factors. Even if culture emerges as something of an infrastructural reflection in his analysis, he opens the door for more dynamic articulations between cultural sensibilities and trajectories of political economy, including in world areas he does not consider. Third, Harvey appreciates the distinctive nature of urban Western developments while also contextualizing them with larger historical processes. His deep appreciation of Marxist thought (see Harvey 1982) gives his analysis an important critical edge even as he also strives to understand the dynamics of Western cultural experience.

Alongside other works and critical reassessments, Harvey's analysis foreshadowed an increasingly explicit consideration of modernity during the early and mid-1990s.[14] Among others, Anthony Giddens's books *The Consequences of Modernity* (1990) and *Modernity and Self-Identity* (1991) have been particularly influential. Giddens amalgamated and elaborated on classic social theorists such as Ferdinand Tönnies (1957) to contrast "traditional" social relations—based on customary regularities within relatively stable communities—with modern ones fraught with disjunction and decontextualization across social contexts (cf. Appadurai 1991). Drawing on this basic contrast, Giddens describes modernity as emerging historically through four related features: capitalism, industrialism, surveillance (especially political control by the nation-state), and the growing organization of military power. For Giddens, these four features link directly to modernity's global spread and have corresponding results in the world capitalist economy, the international division of labor, the nation-state system, and the world military order.

On Giddens's analysis, changes wrought by modernity have a distinct impact on human social relations. People are increasingly uprooted, displaced, engaged in wage labor, and enmeshed in an ever more complex and differentiated social world. According to his argument, stable individual identity based on affiliation with a physical *place* has transformed into *variable* identities across *space*. Modernity as such disconnects space from place. In the process, social relations become increasingly disembedded; they are differentiated and lifted out of traditional contexts. Interactions based on symbolic tokens, such as money (à la Simmel), become more impersonal. According to Giddens, this both requires and makes problematic new patterns of trust in social relations. As social actors grapple with and reflect on their relation to a complicated social world, their identities become more fragmented, individuated, and inward. Individuation and reflexivity come to permeate the social disembeddedness of a modern world. According to Giddens, these patterns have been evident for well over a century but have now intensified and spread with the globalization of modernity throughout the world. For Giddens, then, the modern epoch has been foundational—and becoming hegemonic—since the mid-nineteenth century. Conversely, the contemporary features associated by some with postmodern distinctiveness and rupture are in his analysis a continuation and extension of long-standing trends.

Giddens's notion of modernity is certainly diffuse; it combines features of economy, politics, social organization, and personal identity in a generalized, schematic, and abstract model. Modernity is here a pervasive but largely undifferentiated process that is global in scope even as it contrasts diametrically to traditional patterns that are historical in the West and presumably cultural in the lingering pockets of a nonmodernized world.

As might be expected, Giddens's view of modernity has been subject to critique while also being influential by virtue of its scope, generality, and the ability of researchers to isolate, refine, and transform particular components of his model. Like Harvey, but even more than him, Giddens is open to charges that he neglects the importance of cultural and symbolic influences. These include the values that attend mass consumer, electronic, and infomatic influences on social life in advanced capitalist countries and also in the rest of the world (cf. Miller 1994, 1995; Breckenridge 1995; Freeman 1999; Mankekar 1999; Spitulnik, in press).

Further, Giddens's model creates a rigid historical and cultural divide that admits little articulation between features of non-Western modernity—economic, political, social, and cultural—and those ascribed as global by virtue of their ostensible origin in the West. In this sense, Giddens and related theorists who champion a homogenous view of modernity reproduce the self-justified excesses of modernization theories that burgeoned during the 1950s, 1960s, and 1970s—that is, the idea that developments in the modern Western world are destined for unaltered export to other areas.[15] Views of an undifferentiated modernity no longer seem tenable amid the complexities, differentiations, and resistances of a contemporary world.

Modernity as Contemporary Problematic and Critique

Against a homogeneous notion of modernity, a range of social theorists and anthropologists have developed approaches that are both more critical and more differentiated during the 1990s. These include an increasing critique of modernity itself as a concept. These treatments problematize and diversity modernity across alternative ranges of time, space, and identity. Against the modern as hegemonic, these views emphasize how different world areas refract the trends of so-called modernity in ways that do not exemplify either Western modernity or non-Western traditions. This perspective pries open our assumptions about how modernity has operated and spread in different contexts and world areas. As part of this mix, increasing emphasis is placed on the subjective and cultural dimensions of modernity—the alternatively modern is not just a reflex of infrastructural forces but a force of distinctive identification and subject making.

The interactive nature of modern subjectivity and modern social life was critically emphasized by Marshall Berman in his early work, *All that Is Solid Melts into Air: The Experience of Modernity* (1982). Written as a Marxist interpretation of modern urban experience and Western literary expression, this work has become quite influential. Emphasizing the modern dialectic between destructive creation and creative destruction, Berman described modernity as an orientation of hoped-for progress and renewal through identification with the ostensible triumphs of Western-style economics, politics, material culture, science, and aesthetics (1992:33). Berman's notion of modernity is particularly useful for our present purposes because it incorporates a strong cultural and ideological dimension. It foregrounds powerful aspirations that may nonetheless be inflected quite differently from alternative cultural vantage points and under different socioeconomic and political conditions. In this perspective, the subjective orientations of modernity articulate integrally with economic forces and sociopolitical institutions without becoming their reflex or residuum.

Put more simply for purposes of the present book, *modernity can be defined as the images and institutions associated with Western-style progress and development in a contemporary world.* The images of "progress" and institutions of "development" in this formulation do not have to *be* Western in a direct sense, but they do resonate with Western-style notions of economic and material progress and link these with images of social and cultural development—in whatever way these are locally or nationally defined (cf. Anderson 1991). Reciprocally, modernity in a contemporary world is often associated with either the incitement or the threat of individual desire to improve social life by subordinating or superseding what is locally configured as backward, undeveloped, or superstitious (Berman 1994:3). To paraphrase Trouillot (this volume), modernity is a geography of imagination that creates progress through the projection and management of alterity.

Conceptual Plurality and Threats of Demise

Since the mid-1990s, the issues surrounding modernity have become more complex, both in academic conception and in the objective complexities of a contemporary world. Works such as Arjun Appadurai's *Modernity at Large: Cultural Dimensions of Globalization* (1996) pursued an increasingly globalized and culturalized view of modernity. However, Appadurai and most of those influenced by his work have been quick to emphasize the paradoxical nature of this ostensible modernizing globalization, which is based on experiences of disjunction, difference, and dislocation. Cultural and subjective orientations can become increasingly diverse, differentiated, and fractal through the intensification of cultural modernity, as Appadurai stresses.

It has been only a short step from these sensibilities to the outright pluralization of modernity. The eurocentrism of resurgent interest in modernity was quickly exposed from a Latin American perspective by Enrique Dussel (1993) and pursued from a number of postcolonial perspectives (e.g., Chakrabarty 1992, 2001; Alonso 1998; Canclini 1995). Jean Comaroff and John Comaroff (1993) provoked fresh interest in postcolonial ritual and power in Africa through the lens of "modernity and its malcontents." During the mid-1990s, authors such as Allan Pred (1995) were arguing that Europe itself had been subject to diverse capitalist modernities for well over a century (cf. Pred and Watts 1992). By the late 1990s, the pluralization of modernity became something of an academic industry. Contributions included Partha Chatterjee's *Our Modernity* (1997), Gyan Prakash's "A Different Modernity" (1998), Klaus Lichtblau's "Differentiations of Modernity" (1999), and ethnographic interventions such as Brian Larkin's (1997) consideration of "parallel modernities"—based on the Nigerian penchant for Indian films—and Lisa Rofel's book *Other Modernities* (1999), which plumbed the generational vicissitudes of gendered yearning among female factory workers in China. Casual usages of the plural modern became increasingly common. Fernando Coronil's *The Magical State: Nature, Money, and Modernity in Venezuela* examined "the formation of the Venezuelan state within the context of the historic production of . . . subaltern modernity" (1997:16–17). In *Marxist Modern*, Donald Donham (1999) exquisitely analyzed the Ethiopian revolution in the mid-1970s and suggested that "vernacular modernities" are attempts "to reorder local society by . . . strategies that have produced wealth, power, or knowledge elsewhere in the world" (1999:xviii). Charles Piot's *Remotely Global: Village Modernity in West Africa* (1999) argues that the seeming traditions of the Kabre of northern Togo have in fact been modern for at least three hundred years. The book's conclusion asserts,

> I prefer to see the village as a site—and also, in many ways, an effect—of the modern, one that is as privileged as any other, one that has shaped the modern as much as it has been shaped by it, and one that brings the modern—that always uneven, often discordant, ever refracting, forever incomplete cultural/political project—its own vernacular modernity. (1999:178)

Complementing individual case studies of the alternatively modern have been collectively orchestrated treatments, including conferences, university programs, and issues of major academic journals.[16] Though some of the contributions to these projects have but a tangential relation to the explicit problematic of modernity, the theme of the multiply modern has certainly been strong in the recent academic wind.[17]

For all this attention, major problems quickly arise. The critique of modernity follows close on the heels of its multiple assertions. In a much-discussed article, Englund and Leach (2000) hold forth, from a rather Strathernian point of view, against what they see as the new metanarratives of modernity. Charles Piot (2001) considers the Comaroffs' revealing and revolutionary two volumes and critiques the ease and slipperiness of "modernity" as a faceted concept.[18] Bernard Yack, in his *Fetishism of Modernities* (1997), considers the epochal self-consciousness of contemporary social thought and asks more generally, "Why is it that contemporary intellectuals cannot uncover a new or hidden development without declaring the coming of a new epoch in human experience?" (1997:138). Plagued by a continuation of what he calls "modernity envy," intellectuals now talk, according to Yack, as if developments do not deserve our attention unless they are as epoch-making and pervasive as the ideas and practices of modernity itself.

Though disavowed on the surface, the assumption that modernity is globally hegemonic easily enforces its terminological prevalence. Large swaths of classic social theory are now read through the lens of that thing called modernity, even though the term and its conceptualization are hardly prominent in the works of Marx, Weber, Durkheim, Simmel, and others (Swingewood 1998; contrast Baudelaire 1964). Modernity is sometimes used as a catchphrase for anything that is contemporary in the loosest sense of the term.[19]

The view of modernity as globally diffuse can be troubling for our attempts to comprehend contemporary cultural and subjective diversity. Concern over this problem has become widespread among critical theorists. Indeed, worries over this issue were a prime motive for relativizing our notions of modernity to begin with. More reflexively, as concepts of modernity differentiate and multiply, we may be tempted to agree more than ever with Latour's (1993) assertion, from a structuralist point of view, that we ourselves have never been modern, at least in the ways we might have thought.

Scales of Modern Variation

Amid the burgeoning of modernity and its plurals, we may recognize a continuum of conflicting or what Rofel (this volume) calls "discrepant modernities." At one end of the continuum are more structurally robust assessments that highlight the disjunctions and displacement of modernity at large (Harvey 1989; Giddens 1990, 1991; cf. Appadurai 1996). These perspectives are most open to the relativizing critique that Englund and Leach (2000) have pursued. At the other end of the spectrum are the micromodernities that are so locally and culturally situated that they become practically a synonym for current custom or personal performance. This is modernity written very small. An example is Louisa Schein's (1999) article on "Performing Modernity," in which artful personal enactments among the Chinese Miao minority simultaneously encode, comment on, and ironize a local notion of modernity even as they reinforce it (cf. Schein 2000). This heightened localization increases the ethnographic purchase of modernity while also raising the possibility of neocultural relativism. This is exemplified, for instance, in Marshall Sahlins's (2001:7) assertion that indigenous versions of modernity are basically self-conscious recapitulations and extensions of indigenous culture. In reaction against this general point of view, Arif Dirlik (1999) slams quite hard at what he calls the new culturalism, which he characterizes as the attempt to relativize modernity while downplaying if not ignoring the power and pragmatics of Euro-American capitalism—the larger structures of economic, political, and social as well as cultural power that have underlain it.

Sandwiched between these global and local extremes are analyses that emphasize how modernity is shaped at the national or regional level. The state-based dimension of alternative modernity is prominent in Coronil's (1997) account of oil-glutting Venezuela. Prakash's (1998) depiction of a different Indian modernity is also centered around the state, tied to Nehru's tropes of the historical nation. This path is also pursued more philosophically in Partha Chatterjee's (1997; cf. 1993) *Our Modernity* and made more historically reflexive in the direction Chakrabarty has taken *Subaltern Studies* (cf. Chakrabarty 2001). In Lisa Rofel's book (1999), other modernities are inflected through the state but are locally situated and, of particular import, strongly inflected by gendered and generational differences.[20] Donald Donham's work on the Ethiopian revolution (1999) is perhaps the best so far to articulate the chain of modernities' historical connections, appropriations, and counterreactions all the way up and down the international, state, and local hierarchy. A similar perspective is pursued at a more detailed local level by Edward LiPuma concerning the Maring of Papua New Guinea in his book *Encompassing Others: The Magic of Modernity in Melanesia* (2000)[21] and by Charles Piot in *Remotely Global* (1999), mentioned above.

As these examples and many others suggest, modernity as a concept is itself being relativized. For some, including Jonathan Friedman (this volume), the proclaiming of alternative modernities has become so loose as to encompass almost any development that is not bound within a bell jar of traditional culture. However, the current spate of interest in alternative modernities—like most new developments in anthropology when viewed historically—is yielding significant insights even as it also contains excesses, vague assertions, and tangential arguments. One of the empirical realities that gives most of these analyses significant purchase is the fact that desires to become modern are not simply an academic projection. Images and institutions of so-called progress and development are extremely powerful forces in the world today. This is true internationally, regionally and at the level of the nation-state, and in the construction of local subjectivities. Yet how can we investigate and analyze this impact while avoiding the problems discussed further above?

Bruce M. Knauft

22

The Present Volume in
Contemporary Context

Is the critical understanding of modernity and its inflections a productive project? How can the critiques of modernity extend our awareness of political economy and subjective experience—and the key articulations between them in a contemporary world? The chapters of this book take these questions as their central focus.

All of our contributors agree on two key points. First, modernity as a problematic—regardless of what one thinks of it—has had a major impact on contemporary thought, including in fields such as cultural anthropology. Second, modernity as a concept is fraught with difficulties, especially in the singular. Not only are configurations of modernity slippery and prone to selective guises, they easily reify either as sublime or, I might add, as villainous. The fundamental question that emerges is not whether it is better to singularize or relativize our understanding of modernity. Rather, it is whether relativized notions of modernity go far enough and in the right directions.

For some of this volume's authors—those in part 1, including Robert Foster, Ivan Karp, Holly Wardlow, and me—inflections of modernity can be critically analyzed to reveal the construction and contestation of contemporary subjects in an unequal world. These understandings take the modern as a means of confronting one of the main challenges to contemporary anthropology—that is, how it is that people in the world now share much in common at the same time that they are as differentiated, diverse, and even more unequal than they were before. Modernity in this sense is integrally related to local understandings of what it means to be traditional or progressive. More generally, these contributions explore the "alternativeness" of becoming modern—the ways modernity refracts through different cultural and contextual guises. It is noteworthy that the chapters in this section are concretely ethnographic in focus. As such, they illustrate how research on the process of becoming alternatively modern can put us intimately in touch with the lives and experiences of people in diverse world areas.

The contributors to part 2, Lisa Rofel, Debra Spitulnik, and Michel-Rolph Trouillot, agree with this point of view to a certain extent. But they trouble our views of the modern more deeply. In particular, they suggest that our understandings will be inadequate if we fail to consider non-Western alterity in more fundamental terms. In the process, their expositions contribute to our understanding of matters as diverse as language use, gendered alterity, the groundedness of material relations, and the Western formulation of modernity itself. In this last regard, as Michel-Rolph Trouillot's contribution poignantly suggests, the drive to be modern has always *already* presumed the alterity of Others as the fulcrum point of Western self-elevation. In this sense, modernity has been plural from the start, even if our awareness of its ideological work has not. As such, we have to query more deeply, to critically revisit Kant, how the West configured the exodus of humanity from its *own* state of guilty immaturity through the construction and projection of Others.

Yet more strongly critical of modernity and its inflections are the chapters comprising part 3 of this volume. At the extreme, as suggested by John Kelly, this raises the possibility of a different kind of anthropology altogether. Donald Donham, for his part, is critical of the way that modernity and its alternatives have often been used in academic discourse. He suggests that we restrict our use of "modernity" until we specify more clearly what we mean. Jonathan Friedman critically reviews a range of the chapters in the present volume and uses them as a foil for sharpening his own contrastive perspective. Whereas other contributors question or critique a generalized notion of modernity, Friedman expands the notion of modernity and then internally differentiates it. Kelly carries the critique a step further and suggests that discussions about modernity are not only not a new debate, but the wrong debate to be having at all. These assessments are important in bringing us to the limit point of our problematic. On one hand (from Donham and from Friedman), this limit point comes from a perspective that stresses political economy and the deeper history of capitalism. On the other (from Kelly), it comes from an aesthetic that questions the modernizing tropes and sensibilities that underlie our analysis of modernity to begin with. For Kelly, our assumptions about the modern tend toward the sublime and neglect what is most unsublime and grotesque: the power of the United States since World War II. For Donham, our analyses too easily subsume disparate articulations of capitalism and local history to a single model. And for Friedman, the notion of alternative modernities mixes together disparate features that should be distinguished and then encompassed within a larger structural model. More generally, these contributions push against current assumptions in the understanding of modernity and its alternative inflections.

The element that unites the contributions of this volume is a willingness to engage in focused debate—based on concrete evidence and scholarly analysis—concerning one of the key issues that has emerged in cultural anthropology toward the end of the 1990s. The problematic of modernity and its inflections provides a sharpening stone for the volume's contributors, each of whom reaches important new insights even as she or he adopts or opposes a different stance. Indeed, it is striking to me as the editor that the chapters make contributions in the very areas in which each author finds the conceptualization of modernity to be weakest.

For instance, several of the critiques illuminate larger structures of power in the history of capitalism. The chapters by Michel-Rolph Trouillot in part 2 and Donald Donham and Jonathan Friedman in part 3 are particularly strong in this respect. Other chapters articulate aspects of modernity with fine-grained intricacies of local subjectivity and disposition. This is especially true of the contributions based on Melanesian ethnography—those by Foster, Wardlow, and me—plus Spitulnik's account of modern turns of speech in the town Bemba discourse of urban Zambia.

In larger terms, the present volume links the critique of modernity to greater understanding of how images of progress and institutions of development operate historically and intensify in a contemporary world. Though the contributions may be grouped for heuristic purposes into those that are more appreciative of an alternatively modern perspective, those that stress the deeper significance of alterity, and those that emphasize other anthropological perspectives, their insights crosscut this simple alignment. All the contributors challenge us to consider the problem of modernity and its multiples in new ways. The present volume thus exemplifies a debate between points of view that are stimulating rather than compromising of rigorous ethnographic and theoretical analysis. Against talk that cultural anthropology has become anthropology lite, it is gratifying here to see important issues at the heart of the field contended so richly through acute evidence and critical theorization.

Alternatively Modern: A Critical Appreciation

Our introductory understanding can be rounded off by summarizing the key contributions of an alternatively modern perspective. From the present vantage point, becoming modern entails a core articulation between regional or global forces of so-called progress and the specifics of local sensibility and response. The alternatively modern engages the global with the local and the impact of political economy with cultural orientations and subjective dispositions. A focus on alternative modernities directs our attention to these complementary processes and forces us to analyze them in the direct context of each other. This perspective is highly appropriate for a contemporary anthropology that strives to connect larger features of political economy and regional history with the appreciation of local cultural diversity. More specifically, it encourages us to consider in a new and more concrete way what methods and means of knowing are most appropriate for contemporary anthropology. What modes of inquiry, and what kinds of response, do we take as evidence of social or cultural identities in complex contemporary conditions? How do we combine information gathered from direct observation, discursive revelation, or enacted presentation with the study of regional, historical, and even global dimensions of political economy? Grappling with these questions is facilitated by a distinctively anthropological perspective on the process of modern differentiation in different world areas.

In certain respects, relativized notions of modernity harbor a theory of how modern powers and agents extend their influence. In particular, they suggest that modern images and institutions become forceful through the very opposition and reciprocal definition of progress or development vis-à-vis notions of tradition or national neotradition. These competing tropes and meanings of what indicates authenticity and what indicates development and progress are locally and regionally mediated. They are highlighted as actors negotiate their desire for economic success or development vis-à-vis their sense of value and commitment to longer-standing beliefs and practices. These articulations develop through schism and discontinuity—for instance, as disjunction between of images of economic and material development and those of cultural or historical identification. The alternatively modern thus harbors a dialectical notion of how becoming locally or nationally "developed" occurs through selective appropriation, opposition, and redefinition of authenticity in relation to market forces and aspirations for economic and political improvement. This recursive pattern has been evident since the exploitative expansion of Western political economies during the sixteenth century. But it has intensified under capitalism and more recently during the latter part of the twentieth century.

Focusing on this key relationship, the alternatively modern may be said to address the figure–ground relationship between modernity and tradition as these are locally or nationally perceived and configured. Though these features are often viewed as antithetical to one another, they are in fact intricately and importantly intertwined. We may here paraphrase Donham (this volume) in a slightly different way to say that the alternatively modern is the social and discursive space in which the relationship between modernity and tradition is configured. This configuration is forged in a crucible of cultural beliefs and orientations on one hand, and politicoeconomic constraints and opportunities on

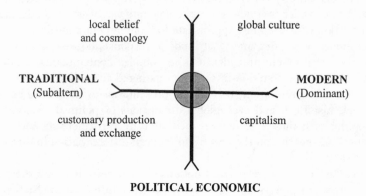

Figure 1.1. The articulatory space of the alternatively modern

the other. In short, the alternatively modern is the articulatory space through which notions of modernity and tradition are co-constructed as progress and history in the context of culture and political economy (see figure 1.1).

The process of becoming alternatively modern juxtaposes and articulates dominant and subaltern notions of propriety and development. As such, it does not divorce our awareness from concrete contestations of belief and practice; to the contrary, it puts us squarely in touch with them. This provides an ethnographically concrete rather than an abstract way to consider the continuing development of capitalism, the local workings of so-called global culture, shared traditions of belief and cosmology, and customary patterns of production and exchange. An emphasis on the alternatively modern is more processual than classificatory, more concerned with specific disempowerments and cultural engagements than with typological differences. It also moves us close to ethnographic and historical specifics, which are often if not typically our best defense against the imposition of Western assumptions and oppositions.

Does this conceptualization still borrow too much from the Western notion of modernity that it attempts to relativize? In practical terms, I think there is a simple way to address this issue. (Practicality is important here, lest we launch into spirals of hermeneutic absorption or reflexive doubt.) The simple reply is to consider if notions of being alternatively modern make sense of specific ethnographic and larger dynamics. Is the problematic of modernity and its alternatives good to think with, or not?

To me, the contributions to this volume suggest that the answer to this question is yes. Robert Foster presents a convincing argument that the weaknesses of modernity theory should not lead us to neglect its insights. Taking the stimulating but unrefined generalizations of Anthony Giddens, Foster shows how local uses of money and responses to state institutions recontextualize Giddens's generalizations in a more concrete manner. In particular, he shows how Giddens's notions of distanciation and disembedding can be productively reconsidered to show how local people reembed and reposition themselves as they bend modern trends to their own objectives. In political terms, Foster shows how the reassertion of personal ties of gift giving and patronage recolonize Melanesian politics from below. These practices contravene the bureaucratic and top-down nature of Western-style political authority.

A striking example of Papua New Guinean's bargaining with modernity comes in Foster's account of the Anganen ritual use of money. Crisp, red twenty-kina currency notes that depict the head of a boar now combine ritual efficacy and financial value. Here is the antithesis of the colonial exotic that projected native people as thinking that money was merely pretty paper. Instead, Anganen play actively and consciously with meanings of money through performative enactment. They directly engage the importance of cash with the importance of ritual. The creative fusion of these divergent "modern" and "traditional" elements does not deny one for the other. Instead, Foster's analysis reveals a capital ritual in which becoming healthy and becoming wealthy in a modern way can hardly be disentangled.

Ivan Karp steps back to analyze the discursive structure and assumptions about personhood that inhere in development discourse. Though the specific terms of development discourse may seem to apply especially to the post–World War II era—and to professional cadres—Karp shows how development discourse is in fact a key ideological feature that reverberates through wide ranges of national, local, and international policy, decision making, assessment, evaluation and—ultimately —stigmata. As Karp suggests, development discourse promulgates hierarchical images of self and other based on social institutions and personal qualities that define the "developed" or "undeveloped" person. Though these images may at one level be contested by national or local respondents, Karp (this volume) illustrates in fine detail how the fragments of this discourse "echo and quote one another, often unknowingly . . . through repetition and reproduction across time, space, and social setting." Starting with an analysis of official promulgations and media reports, he shows how ideologies of development are quite influential in inciting emergent dimensions of personhood. At the same time, development discourse fosters a remarkably similar notion of stigmatized personhood across diverse settings. It is hence not simply a rhetorical imposition but a key means by which a much deeper history of colonial and international domination insinuates itself into national and local subjectivity.

At issue here is the classification of persons into ranked categories by the bleached authority of an ostensibly objective scale of social and moral development. Now as before under colonialism, the local subject is viewed as inert material to be transformed through new forms of discipline. But now, this objective is soft-pedaled under the guise of "social training"—and then effaced from awareness by overweening emphasis on technocratic assessments of material advancement. As Karp insightfully shows, the ideological power of development discourse stems from its ability to treat subjects, in alternative moments, as shared participants on a universal path of progress and yet as "exceptions" who require outside intervention and imposition. His larger point is central for the present volume: even as tropes of development and becoming modern are in danger of being reified by us as academics, they are reified with great cultural, political, and economic power as ideologies of value in a plethora of real-world places. These draw on and perpetuate deep legacies of capitalist and colonial exploitation. As Karp reminds us, "development ideology is one of the constituting features of a global system that is heir to colonial and imperial domination."

My own ethnographic chapter in this volume illustrates how local desires to be modern spiral with the subordinated re-presentations of what it means to be traditional. The Gebusi of south lowland Papua New Guinea were not exposed to colonial influence until the 1960s, and they retained many of their indigenous customs and beliefs into the 1980s. By 1998, however, many Gebusi had relocated next to the government station and oriented their lives around Christian churches, the community school, market, sports leagues, aid post, and government administration. These changes are striking because Gebusi have not been subject to significant land alienation, forced labor, taxation, colonial violence, outmigration, or economic development. This underscores the degree to which the process of becoming alternatively modern is one of subjective and cultural incitement (Knauft 2002).

Among Gebusi, local modernity is marked by the redefinition and reperformance of traditional customs as well as by participation in contemporary institutions and by adopting fundamentalist Christian beliefs. On national Independence Day, indigenous practices are enacted by Gebusi in farcical and buffoonish fashion for a large interethnic crowd. This dynamic reveals how becoming alternatively modern is simultaneously a process of reconstructing tradition through new forms of public culture. For Gebusi, this entails a new sense of historicity and identification with beliefs and practices associated with a more "developed" and "progressive" style of life. In remote areas, the desire to be modern easily becomes acute or "oxymodern" through the redefinition of indigenous practices and beliefs. Reciprocally, the continual threat of backsliding into tradition intensifies aspirations for modern development in the absence of realistic opportunities for economic or political progress. This renders people such as Gebusi receptive to ideologies of material and moral development that subordinate them to externally introduced institutions—including those associated with fundamentalist Christianity. Reciprocally, this dynamic fuels a continued sense of feeling locally "backward." The larger implication is that ideologies of local progress can be stood on their heads to reveal how alternative modernities incite subordination and disempowerment even when political coercion and economic development are only implicit. This underscores the degree to which the subaltern modern is a cultural and subjective as well as a political and economic entailment.

Focusing on a very different Melanesian society, Holly Wardlow exposes the cultural problems raised by modern commodities in a cultural context that accorded high value to prowess in physical labor. In contrast to Gebusi, Huli are a populous and thickly settled people with a history of aggressive expansion against their neighbors, a longer history of colonial contact, and a stronger sense of indigenous cultural propriety. Wardlow shows how the Huli process of becoming modern is radically gendered. The burgeoning growth of criminal theft by "rascals" is strongly associated with men. More generally, the acquisition and public display of commodities and Western clothes are lauded for Huli men but disparaged for Huli women—who are enjoined to occupy a moral place of tradition. One is reminded here of Carol Smith's (1995) work on gendered Mayan economy, in which male capitalization is complemented by the traditionalization of Mayan women. Analogous cases can found in central Asia, as described in Wynne Maggi's (2001) book on Kalasha women of northwestern Pakistan. Of course, women are not universally associated with historical tradition—and such an association may not preclude them from so-called modern pursuits in any event. The feminization of wage labor in Latin America and Southeast and east Asia reminds us of Donald Donham's insistence that the larger capital field is fundamental for understanding the relation between labor and the process of becoming alternatively modern. But how sensibilities of progress and development are locally gendered is distinctively important as part of this mix, as Lisa Rofel emphasizes in her book, *Other Modernities* (1999) and in chapter 5 of the present volume.

Against this background, a gendered perspective troubles any notion of multiple modernity that would assume alternative coherence within a community or society. Gendered issues are not limited to the domestic sphere—nor to ideologies of womanhood or motherhood as they refract at a regional or national level. Rather, gendered relations themselves configure the larger structure of social and political change (Freeman 2001; see Marchand and Runyan 2000; Massey 1994, pt. 3; Felski 1995; Knauft 1997). Wardlow's chapter brings this awareness from a large-scale assertion to a detailed analysis of how Huli gender informs commodity acquisition through labor on one hand, and theft on the other. This vantage point sheds an importantly new light on the contemporary tensions of sociality and exchange in Melanesia. In all, Wardlow's chapter is a model example of how the theoretical analysis and the ethnographic critique of modernity can drive each other to new levels of sophistication in our understanding of contemporary cultural and socioeconomic change.

Lisa Rofel's chapter provides a large-scale theoretical and structural complement to Wardlow's nuanced portrayal of alternatively gendered modernity. In a revealing critique, Rofel exposes the masculinist assumptions that inform our general theories of modernity. These assumptions are ingrained in even the most ostensibly cutting-edge Marxist global analyses. Rofel takes as a detailed case in point Michael Hardt and Antonio Negri's much-discussed recent book, *Empire* (2000). Billed as a Communist manifesto for the twenty-first century,[22] Rofel shows how this important book is in fact flawed to the core not just by its global reification of modern sovereignty but by its inexcusable neglect of subaltern populations, women, and those who are most disempowered. These people are effaced by Hardt and Negri in favor of a more philosophical assessment of Western thought that finds its social complement in the undifferentiated mass of the growing "multitude." As Rofel documents, this undifferentiated multitude is portrayed by Hardt and Negri in unswervingly masculinist and occidentalist terms. As the events of 11 September 2001 have so dramatically shown, opposition to the American-led system of world sovereignty can be powerfully non-Western and poignantly gendered in its own masculinizing terms. It will hardly do to leave these factors as an afterthought; they are obviously central to both the potentials and the perils of globalizing opposition.

In a bitingly playful twist, Rofel reveals how Hardt and Negri's master narrative—of radical Leftists fighting against the system—is itself a very Western masculine account that parallels quite closely the sexist and racist assumptions of George Lucas's *Star Wars* movies. In both cases, the evil and diffusely hegemonic Force is overthrown by a cadre of masculine oppressed who fight against all odds to heroically vanquish the Empire for the blessed good of all. One recalls here, if in a less searing key, the arguments of Catherine Lutz (1995) on "The Gender of Theory": the grander the edifice of theoretical assertion, the more likely its symbolic capital derives from masculinist assumptions. To counter this trend, Rofel encourages alternative narrative strategies that highlight a range of subaltern and postcolonial perspectives. These put us more fully in touch with the gendered, sexualized, racialized, and other stigmatizing ways that the imperial workings of contemporary modernity are actualized in fact—and by means of which they may also be resisted. This can be done without resorting to the crude reactionary violence of masculinist terrorism. Rofel follows a more nuanced track in her monograph on gendered yearnings in postsocialist China (1999). In this sense, she evokes sensibilities that are well-tuned to recuperative work across widely differing contexts. In the present volume, this brings us back to the nuanced insights of Holly Wardlow concerning the gendering of modernity in the southern Highlands of Papua New Guinea, discussed further above. Such perspectives, which consider gender in the context of modern tension, are crucial to our understanding of current developments—global as well as local.

Debra Spitulnik's chapter directs our attention to the specific words and discursive usages that evoke modernity in urban Zambia. Spitulnik shows in detail how vernacular discourse concerning things modern is often cast in the former colonial language (English) and historically informed by the structures and ideologies of colonial rule. Zambian preoccupations with being modern now include usages that gloss as "modern times," "being enlightened," "being European," and "being in a style of affluence." As Spitulnik suggests, these linguistic usages link directly to the Western metanarrative of modernization. She views these specifics in larger linguistic and cultural terms to refine our methodological as well as theoretical sense of how modernities can be concretely studied in ethnographic practice. In the process, she underscores how important it is for anthropologists not to neglect the specifics of local linguistic use amid their desire to reach larger and more sweeping generalizations in the study of contemporary cultural and social change.

Pushing her analysis further, Spitulnik critically questions whether Zambian terms and usages can be easily lumped under the singular banner of "modernity." The postcolonial inflections of so-called modernity take multiple guises in Zambia. Some Zambian usages evoke continuous or quick action. Others emphasize newness or novelty. Still others convey a sense of progress; a concern with consumption, prosperity, and affluence; or conversance with outside forms of knowledge and goods. Some of these usages operate in a referential sense—as social attributions or designations—while others signify that the speaker is him- or herself claiming a modern identity. In short, though images of being or becoming modern constitute an extremely important nexus of cultural reference and identification in contemporary Zambia, they do not cohere easily within a single or simple notion of modernity—as might be analytically or theoretically attributed on a priori grounds. Spitulnik thus asks pointedly, "What is obscured in the cluster of conceptual distinctions and/or ethnographic realities that are grouped together under the shade of the modernity umbrella?" Ultimately, she adopts a notion of modernity that has heuristic value not as a definitional category but as a stimulus for revealing the distinctively Zambian linguistic practices that bear, in various ways, on the conflicted dynamics of postcolonial aspiration and future-seeking styles of life.

Michel-Rolph Trouillot's chapter steps back to question the larger assumptions about alterity that are both smuggled in and effaced in most conceptualizations of the modern. As he suggests, the ideological as well as the political and economic force of modernity is exposed by raw colonial exploitation that projected Others as backward and undeveloped. This is not a new phenomenon but is evident in the precapitalist mercantile exploitation of the Caribbean and Latin America by Spain and Portugal in the sixteenth century. As Trouillot also reminds us, non-Western alterity is close to the heart of modernity in the formulations of Baudelaire, whose mid-nineteenth-century conceptualization is often taken as the touchstone of this concept in Western thought. A relational notion of modernity that exposes the subaltern as Alter or Other is key to comprehending not just the polarization of the world into ostensibly central and peripheral regions but how this relational subordination is ideologically backgrounded and effaced. The projection of Otherness is both at the root of the modern and erased from the history of modern awareness. As Trouillot himself puts it, "modernity always required an Other and an Elsewhere."

If modernity is an ideology of value as well as a social condition, this very fact underscores its power and importance. Even as tropes of progress and being modern are in danger of being reified by us as academics, they are also and separately reified with great cultural, political, and economic power as ideologies of value in a multitude of alternative places and times. Ideologies of the modern are not simply our own; they are important propositions whose reality is symbolically and socially instituted in many parts of the contemporary world. The people described in the various chapters of this volume underscore the force of the modern as an ideology of aspiration and differential power. We find this among Ethiopian revolutionaries (per Donham's chapter); Zambian speakers of urbanity (per Spitulnik); rural New Guinea highlanders (per Wardlow and Foster); Caribbean slave women dedicated to fashionable clothing (per Trouillot); Christian fundamentalists from remote places (per my own chapter); and urbane subjects of the modern world system, who, as Rofel underscores, are more differentiated and less masculine than Hardt and Negri (2000) realize.

The critiques of modernity that conclude this volume highlight the need to rebraid our understanding of capitalist exploitation amid ideological constructions of "progress" and "development." John Kelly exposes the aesthetic tropes and sublime assumptions that are reproduced in our modernist thoughts and concepts. These include our general tendency to neglect the most power-laden and pernicious aspects of modern developments while being dazzled by glossy visions of a globalizing world. Donald Donham's contribution pulls us back to a more concrete understanding of capitalist economy and history. In particular, he critiques the Comaroffs' voluminous opus (1991, 1997) as well as parts of his own previous work to reach a more nuanced understanding of how capitalism and modernity have interacted in alternative parts of Africa—specifically, Ethiopia and South Africa. In the process, he illustrates how modernity emerges as the discursive space within which notions of what it means to be traditional or modern are contested and negotiated. In complementary fashion, Jonathan Friedman stresses the need for a wider historical purview and puts our understanding of modernity into a much larger civilizational and structuralist framework. This framework highlights the different strands that can inflect variously as traditionalist, primitivist, modern, or postmodern—all within the larger identity space of modernity.

Through their specifics, these critiques of modernity give us new perspectives for understanding the desires, motivations, and incitements to action that inform the lives of diverse people in a complex world. Certainly the ideologies of new value that impact these sensibilities may be sublime or grotesque, hardened by capital structures or softened by global flows. But sandwiched between a nagging continuation of cultural and subjective relativism on one hand, and capital superordination on the other, anthropologists can document and analyze exactly how and why people engage images of progress so forcefully, and how and why they associate these so consistently with manufactured commodities and special kinds of economic and institutional development. As I am repeatedly finding in my own ethnographic work among Gebusi, the motivations that attend these developments are often quite cultural and quite home grown—not just a reflex of an external modern, but an active crucible of local imagination amid contemporary incitement and subservience. The inflections of modernity are not just our own contestation, but that of others, in the rest of the world.

Alternative Problematics

As Gilles Deleuze suggested, a "concept" connects disparate ideas at infinite speed.[23] Accordingly, an important concept is really a theory writ small. In this sense, it can be useful to compare the alternatively modern with two of its conceptual complements in recent theorization. One of these is the long-standing importance of capitalism, which is undoubtedly crucial to understanding modernity. In the present book, the import of capitalism is foregrounded in Donham's and Friedman's chapters and is highly important in those of Trouillot and to some extent Kelly as well. A corollary concept of similar order is globalism or globalization. As reflected in current journal issues, conferences, and a host of new books, the idea of globalization is now taking its minutes of maximal attention in the academic sun.[24] In the present volume, the spread, threat, and refraction of global impact emerges in almost all the chapters.

Stepping back, it may be said that this triumvirate—modernity, capitalism, and globalization—inflects many new developments in cultural anthropology. More generally, cultural anthropology seems to be at a distinctive moment. Having shied away from theory building in a larger sense, our central concepts now assume the role of mini theories, tacit and often inexplicit, but quick and powerful in the breach.[25] Elaborate theories we seem to have given up, but pregnant and sweeping concepts we seem to like. Masterful tropes unmaster our narratives. In this sense, the assertions of capitalism on one hand, or globalism on the other, are perhaps equivalent to the conceptualization of modernity in scale, suggestiveness, and—one might add—lack of precision.

Within this general context, we can ask how an inflected notion of modernity stacks up against its main competitors in the current conceptual market—how it compares to a dominant emphasis on capitalism on one hand, or globalization on the other. My own view is that each of these megatropes evokes a distinct sensibility—a particular structure of feeling that has distinctive insights and oversights. Refractions of modernity usefully engage the discordant alternatives that galvanize culture and identity in a contemporary world. They articulate local features with global ones and dynamics that are cultural with those that are political and economic. Notions of progress provoke paradoxes and creative struggles that highlight the power of imagination in the face of violent interactions, deferments, and disillusionments.

Attending to these discordances puts large structural forces directly in play with subaltern subjectivities. Tropes and tensions of progress— what it means to be locally modern in a contemporary world—serve as a pivot between the entailments of global capitalism and national or local constructions of subjectivity, meaning, and agency. From this vantage point, it is a bit disingenuous to make of modernity something of an omnibus notion and then critique its conceptualization for being too encompassing or reified. Few would make the same requirement or impose the same limits on our notions of capitalism or globalism, or even, for that matter, on the concept of the sublime, the grotesque, the discourse of development, or the savage slot, to name a few concepts—all quite valuable and important—that are developed in this book's chapters.

Conceptual Slide

At present, our attempt to refine key concepts and articulate them with each other runs up against the sociology of our own knowledge. As Robert Foster mentions in his chapter, the key concept typically emerges in our intellectual discourse first as a singular noun—a reified entity that has capital pretensions even if it is not actually capitalized. Think of classic anthropological notions: Culture, Civilization, or Structure. All of these used to have the stature and weight of singular reference. Anthropologists used to seriously discuss how to draw firm boundaries between one culture, civilization, or structure and another. There were arguments about typologies and borders, categorical skirmishes and counterassertions. The ethnographic map seemed to be a terrain of limited good, fought over as turf for theoretical advance and control by alternative means of conceptual colonization.

During the late 1970s and 1980s, these older nouns were replaced with new ones in anthropology, including concepts of practice and hegemony, then reflexivity and postmodernism. By contrast, the older terms of favor were not so much dropped but weakened—first by making them more radically plural, and then by turning them into adjectives. The culture concept became a web of plural cultures and was then demoted to being "cultural." As least in anthropology, we rarely refer to "culture" as a bounded empirical referent with defined borders. But we are still perfectly comfortable talking and thinking about cultural this, cultural that, "cultural anthropology." This "adjectival softening" has been evident in other theoretical moves as well. "Structure" became "structures" and then "structural." "Hegemony" slid into "hegemonies" and then became "hegemonic." Bourdieu's *Outline of a Theory of Practice* (1977) became a flood of practices (see Knauft 1996, chap. 4).

In genealogical perspective, as Donald Donham's chapter clearly signals, "modernity" has now embarked down this same slippery slope—yesterday a singular noun, today a pluralized phenomenon, tomorrow perhaps a mere adjective: modern this, modern that. The modern thus becomes a modifier of other things; it has diminished analytic and theoretical heft.

Given general trends, however, the jump to nominate other singularities—be they capitalism, globalization, or even the sublime or the grotesque, per John Kelly's chapter—is to quickly beg for them the same fate. Capitalism and globalization are certainly ripe for pluralization if they have any pretense to avoid the same eurocentrism that has historically bedeviled the concept of modernity. We move quickly from capitalism writ large to regional or local or historically periodized capitalisms —Confucian capitalism; Latin capitalism; early, high, or late capitalism; electronic capitalism; virtual capitalism; and so on (cf. Blim 2000). In similar fashion, globalization in the singular is quickly dispensed with—especially by anthropologists—in favor of specific avenues or streams of global flow and transaction. This is also true of the ostensibly global dimensions of culture. We quickly devolve from global cultural to a horizontal series of global subject positions. There has been heightened interest in identity forms that are international in scope but segmented in applicability, including a range of recent work on cosmopolitanism, flexible citizenship, and other types of transnational identity (e.g., Cheah and Robbins 1998; Ong 1999; Appadurai 2000; Anderson 1998). As these subsidiary domains are themselves exposed as imprecise and unstable in reference, we can expect them to slide into adjectives: capital this, capital that, transnational this, cosmopolitan that, global whatever, and so on.

In short, the problem of pluralization and adjectival softening is common to our intellectual time. In the present case, this means that the ills of modernity as a concept cannot be easily cured by simply replacing it with another conceptual eminence, such as "capitalism" or "globalization." This tendency is nonetheless encouraged by the quickening speed at which new ideas are generated; they emerge for a few months of critical attention and then become debris at the feet of another new angel of backward-looking academic history. This problem is what I call the decreasing half-life of ideas in cultural anthropology. This is the tendency to efface our concepts in the very process of their formulation and presentation. Like physicists, we seem to work harder and harder to create newer and newer elements that disappear faster and faster—surviving only long enough to trace their names before vanishing. Ultimately, however, this disappearance is of our own choosing. So before we drive our concepts down the slide, it is worth considering how hard we want to push them and how fast we want them to fall.

Capitalism

Critical analysis of capitalism, for its part, is particularly good for considering the historical development and profound implications of wage labor, especially in the mechanized production of commodities and the implications of these for capital surplus and world historical inequality. For all its limitations, capitalism harkens us back to the inexhaustible insights of Marx. Expanding on this legacy, Trouillot's chapter in this volume (complemented by the work of Andre Gunder Frank) suggests how capitalism has been historically linked to forced labor and the expropriation of material resources in *non*-Western areas for several centuries. These implications can be productively pursued in the present— that is, to see how current flows of goods and information ensconce new forms of exploitation that are either hidden from view or smoothed over by modern ideologies of a global free market. In a late modern capitalist world, the global study of flexible *accumulation*, à la David Harvey, needs now to be complemented by local study of flexible *exploitation*. "Flexploitation," as such, is particularly ripe for ethnographic study in non-Western areas. So, too, conversely, we can consider the flexible and sometimes quite reactionary or violent means used to combat or oppose flexploitation.

What about politics? Though capitalism does not link in and of itself to dynamics of state and multistate power, it does beg for and articulate easily with such analysis—as Marx illustrated so brilliantly in "The Eighteenth Brumaire of Louis Bonaparte" (Marx 1977). In a contemporary world, capitalism and state politics go hand in hand.

Capitalist analysis is far weaker, however, when it comes to engaging the cultural meaning, motivations, and significations of action, both in the metropole and, even more, in the reticulated periphery. Without an understanding of cultural engagements with and resistances to domination—the focus of modernity's alternatives and alterities— capitalist analysis rings culturally flat. This criticism now applies to the latest Marxist work, including Hardt and Negri's *Empire* (2000), which, as Rofel demonstrates, provides an only ostensibly cutting-edge Marxism for the coming century. It seems woefully inadequate to emphasize the Euro-American foundation or global spread of capitalism as a way to circumvent this problem. This reemphasis on the global West merely siphons its Alters into residual categories; they become new varieties of the savage slot.

The Frankfurt School attempted to bridge the gap between capitalism and cultural possibility, of course. But the aestheticized results of these attempts—the legacy of Horkheimer, Adorno, and even Benjamin if one reads him critically—are not always useful for understanding what meanings, motivations, and actions are in fact informing the lives of common people in so many parts of the contemporary world. Lamentably, the same has become increasingly true, I think, of contemporary cultural studies, notwithstanding its scintillating earlier strains from Raymond Williams and E. P. Thompson. We sorely need but presently lack an understanding of what Lisa Rofel describes in her chapter as the cultural production of contemporary capitalism in alternative world areas.

Globalization

What about globality as a contemporary condition? Though of course evident in Marx, globalization has recently—until 11 September—swelled with academic interest. In this sense, it echoed the economic boom and Internet hopes of the 1990s. Globalism has given us lots of coverage, of course, and lots of flow—flows of commodities, flows of people, flows of imagination, flows of transnational discourse. In the process, it also foregrounds consumption. By contrast, capitalism as a trope centers on production. This production is ultimately grounded in labor and the expropriation of landed resources, as Coronil (2000) makes clear. Capitalism stresses differential appropriation of surplus by some people and places. If the profit of exploitation is almost always made elsewhere through movement (and increasingly so in the present), capitalism stresses how the fruits of profiteering are even more importantly brought back home to roost. The ultimate nail of exploitation under capitalism is the hard-rootedness of possession. Profits are *not* shared globally but are decidedly unequal in distribution and deployment.

Though intertwined, globalism as a trope runs in a different direction. Globalization supplies lateral axes of circulation and distribution. It proffers the prospect of equalization. And it sacrifices historical depth for what is distinctly and globally new in the present. Where images of capitalism stress economic possessiveness and territoriality, globalism stresses a newly deterritorialized space of possibilities. But because the global is so big and unwieldy by itself, its conceptualization quickly shifts, particularly in cultural terms, from globalism in general to a horizontal stratification of global subject positions—to cosmopolitanism, flexible citizenship, various types of transnationalism, or different kinds of flows. Among cultural anthropologists, the culturally transnational celebrates a Bakhtinian world in which capitalist enclaves of possession can be transgressed through hybrid creativities. This trend is appreciative and ultimately rosy. Where capitalist tropes tend toward pessimism, those of the global are optimistic. It may be more than a passing irony that optimism about the global has been shared not only by economists, political scientists, and positivist sociologists—ideological champions of a free market world—but also by critical theorists of globality. Even as it cultivates aesthetic irony and reversal, the critical theorization of global movement shades toward an elite and top-down orientation, as Arif Dirlik (1998) has stressed. Stepping back, then, we can see that concepts of globalization contrast with those of capitalism as much as they complement them.

Amid these competing images, it is important to keep our eye on the concrete accumulation of wealth and power in some areas and classes at the expense of others. This underscores rather than undercuts our appreciation of how exploitation is spatially flexible and symbolically fluid in a contemporary world. Globalism is not a wonderful new age but a new twist of subordination. We can here concur with Victor Li's (2000) trenchant critique of globalization and Dirlik's (1999) salutary reminder not to neglect the continuing hard structures of Western-style, political, and military domination.

From the perspective of cultural anthropology, however, neither globalism nor capitalism are very good at plumbing the subjective diversity and cultural practices of subaltern circumstance. As opposed to reflexive optimism or pessimism, inflections of alternative modernity—like Max Weber himself, if you read him closely—tend to be situational in assessment. By contrast, the long-standing problems of Marxism and of political economy—that they are robust in historic structure but weak in cultural sensitivity—persist and beg for reconceptualization. Notions of cultural globalization, for their part, still tend to be vague and upper class.

Alternatively Modern Redux

Viewed in larger context, the problematics of the alternatively modern are both distinctive and analytically productive. They focus our attention on the contemporary experience of alterity and how this is impacted by larger structures of exploitation and domination. These dynamics are open to capitalist analysis but ultimately cannot be understood by privileging economic or political determinism over subjective orientations. The latter keep our understanding in touch with local and regional specifics of cultural engagement, including the process of subject making and the collective imagination of communities, ethnic groups, and nations. Through their articulation with economic and political dynamics, these illuminate axes of difference and domination that emerge with respect to gender, sex, and generation, as well as those of class, ethnicity, and nationality.

The alternatively modern is concrete because ideologies and institutions of so-called progress and development are increasingly influential and increasingly differentiated across a contemporary world. These ideologies and institutions are deeply entwined with the momentous and continuing changes of capitalism even as they are not fully reducible to them. The same can be said of their articulation with development plans and programs associated with the nation-state and with international or multinational organizations. It is the connection and yet the local indeterminacy of these articulations—between ideologies of progress versus history on one hand, and between culture and political economy on the other—that gives the study of the alternatively modern both ethnographic purchase and theoretical value.

Modern alterity focuses our attention on a nexus of articulations rather than specifying a predetermined outcome or content. It suggests analytic and theoretical connections for an engaged anthropology but does not provide a recipe of outcomes or results. Its analytic does not restrict results or structure them in an empirical or categorical grid. Relatedly, an alternatively modern perspective does not ensure that the resulting analysis will be insightful; as in all ethnography and theory, this depends on the ethnographic rigor and intellectual skill with which the tools of analysis are applied. It is telling, however, that many of the most productive and insightful studies by cultural anthropologists in recent years—both ethnographic and theoretical—have resonated with if not been centrally concerned with the tensions of being or becoming alternatively modern. The present book attempts to draw on this critical trend, to critique and to clarify it, and to suggest how it may be extended and improved on in the future.

Beyond the Academic

If our conceptualizations of modernity have exploded during the last twenty years, the impact and ideology of becoming progressive or developed in different world areas has also burgeoned over this same period.

In the wake of two world wars, theories of modernization were accompanied by master plans to "lift up" and improve the lives of people in non-Western areas. Economic development projects, the green revolution, regimes of political intervention, and financial loans from wealthy nations were all designed to modernize social life and institutions in so-called developing countries. It is now widely agreed, of course, that many if not most of these plans went greatly awry, had unanticipated and unfortunate consequences, and often intensified the problems they were ostensibly designed to resolve (e.g., Escobar 1995; Scott 1998; Gupta 1998; Ferguson 1999; cf. Worsley 1984). Nevertheless, the peoples of the world become increasingly capitalized by the march of wage labor, the massively unequal profits of flexible exploitation and accumulation, and stratification based on unequal access to money in general and to goods, information, education, technology, and decent standards of living in particular.

If the decade of the 1990s was one of comparatively conspicuous growth and opulence among the Western and transnational elite—and if it spawned rosy theories of global connection in its wake—the problems bequeathed to the increasing proportion of the world who see themselves as marginal, disempowered, and peripheralized by these developments are intensified by the relentlessly increasing exposure to and internalization of ideologies of "progress" and "development." Becoming "modern" is all the more problematic as standards of progress intensify along with their impossibility of being satisfied. These drive each other reciprocally to yet greater extremes. We see that the gap between expectation and experience that Koselleck (1985) documented in Western notions of "progress" during the late eighteenth century is not just alive; it reinvents itself with ferocious and pernicious intensity in many if not most corners of the contemporary world. Ultimately enforced by military power, the increasing intensity of international development projects, of well-meaning human rights initiatives, of leveraged control of poorer nations by the International Monetary Fund and World Bank, and the NGO-ization of international influence—all of these fuel escalating ideologies of progress and "development" even as their well-intentioned agents strive in vain to close the reality gap. It is a hopeless battle. In outcome, the problems of cold war schemes for modernization have not subsided. Rather, they have expanded, intensified, and insinuated themselves into social lives and subjectivities in new and more fearful ways. If the academic conceptualization of modernity still borrows too much from its intellectual predecessors, the work of modern progress as ideology and as power cannot be ignored. It is important to remember this as we use our skills as ethnographers and theoreticians to expose the meanings and inequities of contemporary lives in newly critical ways.

Notes

1. E.g., see Gaonkar 1999; Mitchell 2000; Eisenstadt 2001; Lichtblau 1999; Chatterjee 1997; Prakash 1998.

2. See Rofel 1999; Piot 1999, 2001; Donham 1999; Knauft 2002; Larkin 1997; Schein 1999; Ferguson 1999; LiPuma 2000; cf. Comaroff and Comaroff 1993; Appadurai 1996; Nonini and Ong 1997.

3. Quoted by Dussel 1993:68.

4. Cf. more generally Foucault 1970, 1973, 1979, 1980, 1983.

5. See Greenblatt 1980; Horkheimer and Adorno 2000, chap. 3.

6. Of course, the development of modern*ism* as a Western artistic movement pervaded much of the twentieth century. And the use of "modern" as a casual descriptor has long been common in both popular and academic discourse.

7. See Lyotard 1984, 1988; Baudrillard 1988, 1990a, 1990b, 1996, 1997; Kroker et al. 1989; Haraway 1997. Among anthropologists, see Marcus and Fischer 1986; Tyler 1990; Clifford 1997.

8. See Baudrillard 1975, 1981, 1983; Jameson 1981, 1991; Lyotard 1989a, 1989b, 1993; Butler 1987, 1990; Spivak 1987; Kellner 1989; Bronner and Kellner 1989; Featherstone 1991.

9. For Habermas, an analytic and philosophical understanding of the modern lifeworld integrates with analysis of "external" structural systems to provide proper grounding for general social theory.

10. In a longer temporal perspective, the relationship between rationality and anti-rationality has been a key tension in Western thought at least since the growth of romanticism during the eighteenth century (see Berlin 1999).

11. E.g., Guha and Spivak 1988; Spivak 1987, 1996, 1999; Chakrabarty 2001; Bhabha 1994; see Williams and Chrisman 1994.

12. Outhwaite (1994:152, 154), who describes himself as an "unabashed enthusiast" of Habermas, writes, "He has clearly become a classic, often anachronistically set among the previous generation of the founders of the Frankfurt School." In terms of the debate concerning modernity specifically, Outhwaite (1994:136) suggests, "Habermas' own critique inevitably begins to look, even more than it did before, like the American and Soviet anti-guerrilla campaigns which unsuccessfully deployed what should have been devastating firepower against an army which refused to stand still and be shot at."

13. In this regard, Harvey's scholarship provides a salutary counterexample to

the excesses of slipshod impressionism that marked the high-water mark of postmodernism during the late 1980s.

14. E.g., Lash and Friedman 1992; Friedman 1994; Berman 1994; Touraine 1995; Miller 1994, 1995; Manganaro 1990.

15. Rostow (1952, 1960, 1963, 1971) was one of the strongest and most consistent advocates of growth through the global spread of Western-style modernization (see critique by Arndt 1987).

16. See, for instance, the theme issue of *Public Culture* on "Alter/Native Modernities" (1999, no. 27), and the special issue of *Daedalus* devoted to "Multiple Modernities" (winter 2000, vol. 129, no. 1). A similar emphasis can be found in books such as Timothy Mitchell's edited collection, *Questions of Modernity* (2000).

17. The size and speed of this trend was thrown into relief by the circumstances of my own research. During extended fieldwork in a remote rainforest area of interior Papua New Guinea in 1998 (Knauft 2002), I was struck by how peculiarly modern the Gebusi people I had previously lived with had since become. On my return to the United States, I started to organize a session for the ensuing annual anthropology meetings on "Alternative Modernities"—thinking that this was a relatively novel way to conceptualize such development. My plan was short-circuited by a request by my university to propose a program for the Ford Foundation's "Crossing Borders" funding initiative. My proposal for Emory was entitled "Vernacular Modernities." Only in the ensuing months did I realize how rampant the notion of plural modernities had become during my absence in the field. When the Emory project was funded (with me as its director—see <http://www.emory.edu/COLLEGE/ICIS/programs/vm/index.html>), one of the other initiatives simultaneously funded by Ford was a program on "Alternative Modernities" (my original title), submitted by the five-college consortium in Massachusetts. Later that semester, I was invited to the University of Chicago, where I presented a version of my chapter on the oxymodern (published as chapter 3 in the present volume). A scant fifteen minutes after my presentation, Marshall Sahlins announced that he had just pulled from his office mailbox the new special issue of *Daedalus*— entitled "Multiple Modernities."

18. See Comaroff and Comaroff 1991, 1997; cf. 1993.

19. For instance, the omnibus sociology textbook of contemporary societies by Stuart Hall et al. is titled *Modernity* and subtitled *An Introduction to Modern Societies* (1996)—but it has precious little analysis of the concept itself. Hall et al. suggest simply that modernity entails a decline of tradition and of associated religious practices amid the rise of a market economy and secular forms of political power (1996:8). Toward the end of the book, Giddens's notion of modernity is summarized as entailing capitalism, industrialism, administrative power, and military power (1996:452 ff.). These features are mixed in a vague manner rather than differentiated or analyzed

in relation to historical or cultural specifics. Such formulations do little to capture the subjective and cultural—much less the sociopolitical and economic—dimensions of alternative modernities, which are importantly different in different world areas. This problem also pervades influential works such as Held and colleagues' *Global Transformations* (1999).

20. Rofel is concerned with the implications of Chinese socialist and postsocialist ideologies for gendered subjectivity and labor. She states toward the end of her book that "the state has generated multiple imaginaries of modernities" (1999:279). Rofel focuses on the way these versions of modernity are differentially responded to, appropriated, or resisted by different groups of Chinese women—in generational terms, in discursive histories, and in micropractices of work.

21. In a Melanesian context, see also Akin and Robbins's important edited collection *Money and Modernity: State and Local Currencies in Melanesia* (1999), and Friedman and Carrier's collection *Melanesian Modernities* (1996).

22. The comments of Slavoj Žižek on the book jacket of *Empire* aver that "What Hardt and Negri offer is nothing less than a rewriting of *The Communist Manifesto* for our time."

23. As Gilles Deleuze and Félix Guattari put it in *What Is Philosophy?*, "The concept is defined by the inseparability of a finite number of heterogeneous components traversed by a point of survey at infinite speed" (1994:21).

24. Prominent recent works concerning globalization include John Tomlinson's *Globalization and Culture* (1999), Anthony Held and colleagues' *Global Transformations* (1999), Saskia Sassen's *Globalization and its Discontents* (1998), Martin Albrow's *The Global Age* (1997), and a host of other more popular works, such as Thomas Friedman's *The Lexus and the Olive Tree: Understanding Globalization* (2000). This emphasis has been presaged by works such as Jonathan Friedman's *Cultural Identity and Global Process* (1994) and analyses of global political economy and history by Immanuel Wallerstein, Andre Gunder Frank, Giovanni Arrighi, and, in anthropology, the late Eric Wolf (1982). Current interest also includes avant-garde formulations, as in Arjun Appadurai's special issue of *Public Culture* on "Globalization" (2000).

25. By contrast, there is little current interest in cultural anthropology to develop grand theories. The same is generally true of cultural studies, postcolonial or diasporic studies, queer theorizations, and post-Marxist studies.

References

Abu-Lughod, Janet
  1989   *Before European Hegemony: The World System A.D. 1250–1350.* New York: Oxford University Press.

Akin, David, and Joel Robbins
  1999   [Eds.] *Money and Modernity: State and Local Currencies in Melanesia*. Pittsburgh, Pa.: University of Pittsburgh Press.

Albrow, Martin
  1997   *The Global Age: State and Society Beyond Modernity*. Stanford, Calif.: Stanford University Press.

Alonso, Carlos J.
  1998   *The Burden of Modernity: The Rhetoric of Cultural Discourse in Spanish America*. New York: Oxford University Press.

Anderson, Benedict
  1991   *Imagined Communities: Reflections on the Origin and Spread of Nationalism*. Expanded edition. London: Verso.
  1998   Long-Distance Nationalism. In *The Spectre of Comparisons: Nationalism, Southeast Asia, and the World*, pp. 58–74. London: Verso.

Appadurai, Arjun
  1996   *Modernity at Large: Cultural Dimensions of Globalization*. Minneapolis: University of Minnesota Press.
  2000   Grassroots Globalization and the Research Imagination. *Public Culture* 12: 1–19.

Arndt, Heinz W.
  1987   *Economic Development: The History of an Idea*. Chicago: University of Chicago Press.

Baudelaire, Charles
  1964 [1863]   *The Painter of Modern Life and Other Essays*. London: Phaidon.

Baudrillard, Jean
  1975   *The Mirror of Production*. St. Louis, Mo.: Telos Press.
  1981   *For a Critique of the Political Economy of the Sign*. St. Louis, Mo.: Telos.
  1983   *In the Shadow of the Silent Majorities*. New York: Semiotext(e).
  1988   *The Ecstasy of Communication*. New York: Semiotext(e).
  1990a   *Cool Memories*. London: Verso.
  1990b   *The Revenge of the Crystal*. London: Pluto.
  1996   *Cool Memories II*. Durham, N.C.: Duke University Press.
  1997   *Fragments: Cool Memories III*. London: Verso.

Berlin, Isaiah
  1999   *The Roots of Romanticism*. Princeton, N.J.: Princeton University Press.

Berman, Art
  1994   *Preface to Modernism*. Urbana: University of Illinois Press.

Berman, Marshall
  1982   *All That Is Solid Melts into Air: The Experience of Modernity*. New York: Penguin.
  1992   Why Modernism Still Matters. In *Modernity and Identity*. Edited by Scott Lash and Jonathan Friedman, pp. 33–58. Oxford: Blackwell.

Bhabha, Homi K.
  1994   *The Location of Culture.* London: Routledge.

Birth, Kevin
  1999   *Any Time Is Trinidad Time: Social Meanings and Temporal Conscious-ness.* Gainesville: University Press of Florida.

Blim, Michael
  2000   Capitalisms in Late Modernity. *Annual Review of Anthropology* 29: 25–38.

Bourdieu, Pierre
  1977   *Outline of a Theory of Practice.* Cambridge: Cambridge University Press.

Breckenridge, Carol A.
  1995   [Ed.] *Consuming Modernity: Public Culture in a South Asian World.* Minneapolis: University of Minnesota Press.

Bronner, Stephen E., and Douglas M. Kellner
  1989   [Eds.] *Critical Theory and Society: A Reader.* New York: Routledge.

Butler, Judith
  1987   *Subjects of Desire: Hegelian Reflections in Twentieth-Century France.* New York: Columbia University Press.
  1990   *Gender Trouble: Feminism and the Subversion of Identity.* New York: Routledge.

Calhoun, Craig
  1992   [Ed.] *Habermas and the Public Sphere.* Cambridge, Mass.: MIT Press.

Canclini, Nestor Garcia
  1995   *Hybrid Cultures: Strategies for Entering and Leaving Modernity.* Minneapolis: University of Minnesota Press.

Chakrabarty, Dipesh
  1992   Postcoloniality and the Artifice of History: Who Speaks for "Indian" Pasts? *Representations* 37: 1–26.
  2001   *Provincializing Europe: Postcolonial Thought and Historical Difference.* Princeton, N.J.: Princeton University Press.

Chatterjee, Partha
  1993   *The Nation and its Fragments: Colonial and Post-Colonial Histories.* Princeton, N.J.: Princeton University Press.
  1997   *Our Modernity.* Lecture to the South-South Exchange Programme for Research on the History of Development and the Council for the Development of Social Science Research in Africa. Rotterdam: Vinlin Press.

Cheah, Pheng, and Bruce Robbins
  1998   [Eds.] *Cosmopolitics: Thinking and Feeling Beyond the Nation.* Minneapolis: University of Minnesota Press.

An Introduction

47

Clifford, James
  1997   *Routes: Travel and Translation in the Late Twentieth Century.* Cambridge, Mass.: Harvard University Press.

Comaroff, Jean, and John L. Comaroff
  1991   *Of Revelation and Revolution, Volume 1: Christianity, Colonialism, and Conscious in South Africa.* Chicago: University of Chicago Press.
  1993   [Eds.] *Modernity and Its Malcontents: Ritual and Power in Postcolonial Africa.* Chicago: University of Chicago Press.

Comaroff, John L., and Jean Comaroff
  1997   *Of Revelation and Revolution: Volume 2: The Dialectics of Modernity on a South African Frontier.* Chicago: University of Chicago Press.

Coronil, Fernando
  1997   *The Magical State: Nature, Money, and Modernity in Venezuela.* Chicago: University of Chicago Press.
  2000   Occidentalist and Subaltern Modernities: The Point is their Counterpoint. Paper presented in the session "Inflections of Modernity" at the Annual Meetings of the American Anthropological Association, San Francisco, November 16.

Deleuze, Gilles, and Félix Guattari
  1994   *What Is Philosophy?* London: Verso.

Dirlik, Arif
  1998   *The Postcolonial Aura: Third World Criticism in the Age of Global Capitalism.* Boulder, Colo.: Westview.
  1999   Is There History after Eurocentrism? Globalism, Postcolonialism, and the Disavowal of History. *Cultural Critique* 42: 1–34.

Donham, Donald L.
  1999   *Marxist Modern: An Ethnographic History of the Ethiopian Revolution.* Berkeley: University of California Press.
  2002   On Being Modern in a Capitalist World: Some Conceptual and Comparative Issues. In *Critically Modern: Alternatives, Alterities, Anthropologies* [this volume]. Edited by Bruce M. Knauft. Bloomington: Indiana University Press.

Dussel, Enrique
  1993   Eurocentrism and Modernity. *boundary 2,* 20: 65–74.

Eisenstadt, S. N.
  2001   Multiple Modernities. *Daedalus* 129(1): 1–31.

Englund, Harri, and James Leach
  2000   Ethnography and the Meta-Narratives of Modernity. *Current Anthropology* 41(2): 225–48.

Escobar, Arturo
  1995   *Encountering Development: The Making and Unmaking of the Third World.* Princeton, N.J.: Princeton University Press.

Featherstone, Mike
1991   *Consumer Culture and Postmodernism.* London: Sage.

Felski, Rita
1995   *The Gender of Modernity.* Cambridge, Mass.: Harvard University
        Press.

Ferguson, James
1999   *Expectations of Modernity: Myths and Meanings of Urban Life on the
        Zambian Copperbelt.* Berkeley: University of California Press.

Foucault, Michel
1970   *The Order of Things: An Archaeology of the Human Sciences.* New
        York: Vintage.
1973   *The Birth of the Clinic: An Archaeology of Medical Perception.* New
        York: Pantheon.
1979   *Discipline and Punish: The Birth of the Prison.* New York: Vintage.
1980   *Power/Knowledge: Selected Interviews and Other Writings, 1972–
        1977.* Edited by Colin Gordon. New York: Pantheon.
1983   The Subject and Power. In *Michel Foucault: Beyond Structuralism
        and Hermeneutics.* 2nd ed. Edited by Hubert L. Dreyfus and Paul
        Rabinow, pp. 208–26. Chicago: University of Chicago Press.
1984   *The Foucault Reader.* Edited by Paul Rabinow. New York: Pantheon.

Foster, Robert J.
2002   Bargains with Modernity in Papua New Guinea and Elsewhere. In
        Critically Modern: Alternatives, Alterities, Anthropologies [this vol-
        ume]. Edited by Bruce M. Knauft. Bloomington: Indiana Univer-
        sity Press.

Freeman, Carla S.
1999   *High Tech and High Heels in the Global Economy: Women, Work, and
        Pink-Collar Identities in the Caribbean.* Durham, N.C.: Duke Uni-
        versity Press.
2001   Is Local: Global as Feminine: Masculine? Rethinking the Gender of
        Globalization. *Signs* 26(4): 1007–37.

Friedman, Jonathan
1994   *Cultural Identity and Global Process.* Thousand Oaks, Calif.: Sage.
2002   Modernity and Other Traditions. In *Critically Modern: Alternatives,
        Alterities, Anthropologies* [this volume]. Edited by Bruce M. Knauft.
        Bloomington: Indiana University Press.

Friedman, Jonathan, and James G. Carrier
1996   [Eds.] *Melanesian Modernities.* Lund Monographs in Social Anthro-
        pology No. 3. Lund, Sweden: Lund University Press.

Friedman, Thomas
2000   *The Lexus and the Olive Tree: Understanding Globalization.* New
        York: Anchor.

Gaonkar, Dilip Parameshwar
1999   On Alternative Modernities. *Public Culture* 11: 1–18.

Giddens, Anthony
   1990   *The Consequences of Modernity.* Stanford, Calif.: Stanford University Press.
   1991   *Modernity and Self-Identity: Self and Society in the Late Modern Age.* Stanford, Calif.: Stanford University Press.

Greenblatt, Stephen
   1980   *Renaissance Self-Fashioning: From More to Shakespeare.* Chicago: University of Chicago Press.

Greenhouse, Carol J.
   1996   [Ed.] *A Moment's Notice: Time Politics across Cultures.* Ithaca, N.Y.: Cornell University Press.

Guha, Ranajit, and Gayatri Spivak
   1988   [Eds.] *Selected Subaltern Studies.* New York: Oxford University Press.

Gupta, Akhil
   1998   *Postcolonial Developments: Agriculture in the Making of Modern India.* Durham, N.C.: Duke University Press.

Habermas, Jürgen
   1984a [1981]   *The Theory of Communicative Action, Volume 1: Reason and the Rationalization of Society.* Boston: Beacon.
   1984b   *The Theory of Communicative Action, Volume 2: Lifeworld and System: A Critique of Functionalist Reason.* Boston: Beacon.
   1987 [1985]   *The Philosophical Discourse of Modernity: Twelve Lectures.* Cambridge, Mass.: MIT Press.

Hall, Stuart, David Held, Don Hubert, and Keith Thompson
   1996   [Eds.] *Modernity: An Introduction to Modern Societies.* Oxford: Blackwell.

Haraway, Donna J.
   1997   *Modest*Witness@Second*Millennium.FemaleMan*Meets*OncoMouse: Feminism and Technoscience.* New York: Routledge.

Hardt, Michael, and Antonio Negri
   2000   *Empire.* Cambridge, Mass.: Harvard University Press.

Harvey, David
   1982   *Limits to Capital.* Oxford: Blackwell.
   1989   *The Condition of Postmodernity: An Enquiry into the Origins of Cultural Change.* Cambridge: Blackwell.
   1996   *Justice, Nature, and the Geography of Difference.* Oxford: Oxford University Press.
   2000   *Spaces of Hope.* Berkeley: University of California Press.

Held, David, Anthony McGrew, David Goldblatt, and Jonathan Perraton
   1999   *Global Transformations: Politics, Economics, and Culture.* Stanford, Calif.: Stanford University Press.

Horkheimer, Max, and Theodor W. Adorno
   2000 [1944]   *Dialectic of Enlightenment.* New York: Continuum.

Jameson, Fredric
1981   *The Political Unconscious: Narrative as a Socially Symbolic Act.* Ithaca, N.Y.: Cornell University Press.
1991   *Postmodernism, or the Cultural Logic of Late Capitalism.* Durham, N.C.: Duke University Press.
n.d.   The Four Maxims of Modernity. Unpublished manuscript.

Karp, Ivan
2002   Development and Personhood: Tracing the Contours of a Moral Discourse. In *Critically Modern: Alternatives, Alterities, Anthropologies* [this volume]. Edited by Bruce M. Knauft. Bloomington: Indiana University Press.

Kellner, Douglas
1989   *Jean Baudrillard: From Marxism to Postmodernism and Beyond.* Stanford, Calif.: Stanford University Press.

Kelly, John D.
2002   Alternative Modernities or an Alternative to "Modernity": Getting Out of the Modernist Sublime. In *Critically Modern: Alternatives, Alterities, Anthropologies* [this volume]. Edited by Bruce M. Knauft. Bloomington: Indiana University Press.

Kelly, Michael
1994   [Ed.] *Critique and Power: Recasting the Foucault/Habermas Debate.* Cambridge, Mass.: MIT Press.

Knauft, Bruce M.
1996   *Genealogies for the Present in Cultural Anthropology.* New York: Routledge.
1997   Gender Identity, Political Economy, and Modernity in Melanesia and Amazonia. *Journal of the Royal Anthropological Institute* 3: 233–59.
2002   Trials of the Oxymodern: Public Practice at Nomad Station. In *Critically Modern: Alternatives, Alterities, Anthropologies* [this volume]. Edited by Bruce M. Knauft. Bloomington: Indiana University Press.
2002   *Exchanging the Past: A Rainforest World of Before and After.* Chicago: University of Chicago Press.

Koselleck, Reinhart
1985 [1979]   *Futures Past: On the Semantics of Historical Time.* Cambridge, Mass.: MIT Press.

Kroker, Arthur, Marilouise Kroker, and David Cook
1989   *Panic Encyclopedia: The Definitive Guide to the Postmodern Scene.* New York: St. Martin's Press.

Larkin, Brian
1997   Indian Films and Nigerian Lovers: Media and the Creation of Parallel Modernities. *Africa* 67: 406–40.

Lash, Scott, and Jonathan Friedman
1992   [Eds.] *Modernity and Identity.* Oxford: Blackwell.

Latour, Bruno
  1993   *We Have Never Been Modern*. Cambridge, Mass.: Harvard University Press.

Li, Victor
  2000   What's in a Name: Questioning "Globalization." *Cultural Critique* 45: 1–39.

Lichtblau, Klaus
  1999   Differentiations of Modernity. *Theory, Culture, and Society* 16: 1–30.

LiPuma, Edward
  2000   *Encompassing Others: The Magic of Modernity in Melanesia*. Ann Arbor: University of Michigan Press.

Lutz, Catherine
  1995   The Gender of Theory. In *Women Writing Culture*. Edited by Ruth Behar and Deborah A. Gordon, pp. 249–66. Berkeley: University of California Press.

Lyotard, Jean-François
  1984 [1979] *The Postmodern Condition: A Report on Knowledge*. Translated by Geoff Bennington and Brian Massumi. Minneapolis: University of Minnesota Press.
  1988   *The Differend: Phrases in Dispute*. Minneapolis: University of Minnesota Press.
  1989a   *The Lyotard Reader*. Edited by Andrew Benjamin. Oxford: Blackwell.
  1989b   *La guerre des Algériens: Écrits, 1956–1963*. Paris: Galilée.
  1993   *Political Writings*. Minneapolis: University of Minnesota Press.

Maggi, Wynne R.
  2001   *Our Women are Free: Gender among Kalasha of Northwestern Pakistan*. Ann Arbor: University of Michigan Press.

Manganaro, Mark
  1990   [Ed.] *Modernist Anthropology: From Field Work to Text*. Princeton, N.J.: Princeton University Press.

Mankekar, Purnima
  1999   *Screening Culture, Viewing Politics: An Ethnography of Television, Womanhood, and Nation in Postcolonial India*. Durham, N.C.: Duke University Press.

Marchand, H. Marianne, and Anne Sisson Runyan
  2000   *Gender and Global Restructuring: Sightings, Sites, and Resistances*. New York: Routledge.

Marcus, George E., and Michael M. J. Fischer
  1986   *Anthropology as Cultural Critique: An Experimental Moment in the Human Sciences*. Chicago: University of Chicago Press.

Marx, Karl
  1977   The Eighteenth Brumaire of Louis Bonaparte. In *Karl Marx: Se-*

lected Writings. Edited by David McLellan, pp. 300–325. New York: Oxford University Press.

Massey, Doreen
1994   *Space, Place, and Gender.* Minneapolis: University of Minnesota Press.

Miller, Daniel
1994   *Modernity, An Ethnographic Approach: Dualism and Mass Consumption in Trinidad.* Oxford: Berg.
1995   [Ed.] *Worlds Apart: Modernity through the Prism of the Local.* London: Routledge.

Mitchell, Timothy
2000   [Ed.] *Questions of Modernity.* Minneapolis: University of Minnesota Press.

Nonini, Donald M., and Aihwa Ong.
1997   Chinese Transnationalism as an Alternative Modernity. In *Ungrounded Empires: The Cultural Politics of Modern Chinese Transnationalism.* Edited by Aihwa Ong and Donald M. Nonini, pp. 3–33. New York: Routledge.

Ong, Aihwa
1999   *Flexible Citizenship: The Cultural Logics of Transnationality.* Durham, N.C.: Duke University Press.

Outhwaite, William
1994   *Habermas: A Critical Introduction.* Cambridge: Polity Press.

Piot, Charles
1999   *Remotely Global: Village Modernity in West Africa.* Chicago: University of Chicago Press.
2001   Of Hybridity, Modernity, and Their Malcontents. *Interventions* 3: 85–91.

Prakash, Gyan
1998   A Different Modernity. Unpublished manuscript.

Pred, Allan
1995   *Recognizing European Modernities: A Montage of the Present.* London: Routledge.

Pred, Allan, and Michael J. Watts
1992   *Reworking Modernity: Capitalisms and Symbolic Discontent.* New Brunswick, N.J.: Rutgers University Press.

Rofel, Lisa
1999   *Other Modernities: Gendered Yearnings in China after Socialism.* Berkeley: University of California Press.
2002   Modernity's Masculine Fantasies. In *Critically Modern: Alternatives, Alterities, Anthropologies* [this volume]. Edited by Bruce M. Knauft. Bloomington: Indiana University Press.

Rosenthal, Michael
1992   What *Was* Postmodernism? *Socialist Review* 22: 83–105.

Rostow, Walter W.
1952   *The Process of Economic Growth.* New York: Norton.
1960   *The Stages of Economic Growth: A Non-Communist Manifesto.* Cambridge: Cambridge University Press.
1963   *The Economics of Take-off into Sustained Growth.* New York: St. Martin's Press.
1971   *Politics and the Stages of Growth.* Cambridge: Cambridge University Press.

Sahlins, Marshall D.
2001   Six Are Honored at Commencement 'o1. [An interview with Marshall Sahlins by Britt Halvorson.] *Michigan Today* 33(2): 7.

Sassen, Saskia
1998   *Globalization and its Discontents: Essays on the New Mobility of People and Money.* New York: New Press.

Schein, Louisa
1999   Performing Modernity. *Cultural Anthropology* 14: 361–95.
2000   *Minority Rules: The Miao and the Feminine in China's Cultural Politics.* Durham, N.C.: Duke University Press.

Scott, James C.
1998   *Seeing Like a State: How Certain Schemes to Improve the Human Condition have Failed.* New Haven, Conn.: Yale University Press.

Smith, Carol A.
1995   Race–Class–Gender Ideology in Guatemala: Modern and Anti-Modern Forms. *Comparative Studies in Society and History* 37: 723–49.

Spitulnik, Debra A.
2002   Accessing "Local" Modernities: Reflections on the Place of Linguistic Evidence in Ethnography. In *Critically Modern: Alternatives, Alterities, Anthropologies* [this volume]. Edited by Bruce M. Knauft. Bloomington: Indiana University Press.
In press   *Media Connections and Disconnections: Radio Culture and the Public Sphere in Zambia.* Durham, N.C.: Duke University Press.

Spivak, Gayatri
1987   *In Other Worlds: Essays in Cultural Politics.* New York: Methuen.
1996   *The Spivak Reader: Selected Works of Gayatri Chakravorty Spivak.* Edited by Donna Landry and Gerald MacLean. New York: Routledge.
1999   *A Critique of Postcolonial Reason: Toward a History of the Vanishing Present.* Cambridge, Mass.: Harvard University Press.

Stoler, Ann L.
1995   *Race and the Education of Desire: Foucault's* History of Sexuality *and the Colonial Order of Things.* Durham, N.C.: Duke University Press.

Swingewood, Alan
1998   *Cultural Theory and the Problem of Modernity.* New York: St. Martin's Press.

Taylor, Charles
1989   *Sources of the Self: The Making of Modern Identity.* Cambridge, Mass.: Harvard University Press.
1992   *The Ethics of Authenticity.* Cambridge, Mass.: Harvard University Press.
1999   Two Theories of Modernity. *Public Culture* 11: 153–74.

Tomlinson, John
1999   *Globalization and Culture.* Chicago: University of Chicago Press.

Tönnies, Ferdinand
1957   *Community and Society (Gemeinshaft und Gesellschaft).* East Lansing: Michigan State University Press.

Touraine, Alan
1995   *Critique of Modernity.* Oxford: Blackwell.

Trouillot, Michel-Rolph
1991   Anthropology and the Savage Slot. In *Recapturing Anthropology: Working in the Present.* Edited by Richard G. Fox, pp. 17–44. Santa Fe, N.M.: School of American Research Press.
2002   The Otherwise Modern: Caribbean Lessons from the Savage Slot. In *Critically Modern: Alternatives, Alterities, Anthropologies* [this volume]. Edited by Bruce M. Knauft. Bloomington: Indiana University Press.

Tyler, Stephen
1990   *The Unspeakable: Discourse, Dialogue, and Rhetoric in the Postmodern World.* Madison: University of Wisconsin Press.

Wardlow, Holly
2002   "Hands-Up"–ing Buses and Harvesting Cheese-Pops: Gendered Mediation of Modern Disjuncture in Melanesia. In *Critically Modern: Alternatives, Alterities, Anthropologies* [this volume]. Edited by Bruce M. Knauft. Bloomington: Indiana University Press.

Weber, Max
1958   *The Protestant Ethic and the Spirit of Capitalism.* New York: Scribners.

Williams, Patrick, and Laura Chrisman
1994   [Eds.] *Colonial Discourse and Post-Colonial Theory: A Reader.* New York: Columbia University Press.

Wolf, Eric
1982   *Europe and the People without History.* Berkeley: University of California Press.

Worsley, Peter
1984   *The Three Worlds: Culture and World Development.* Chicago: University of Chicago Press.

Yack, Bernard
1997   *The Fetishism of Modernities: Epochal Self-Consciousness in Contemporary Social and Political Thought.* Notre Dame, Ind.: University of Notre Dame Press.

PART I

One

Bargains with Modernity in Papua New Guinea and Elsewhere

Robert J. Foster

The anthropological urge to pluralize applies a critical brake to the discipline's complementary tendency to singularize—to speak of Culture with a capital C, Human Nature with a capital H and a capital N. Pluralizing is a familiar in-house technique for provincializing metropolitan ideas, for identifying eurocentric conceits. Pluralizing Modernity thus rightly challenges the shared conceit of modernization theory and dependency theory—the unexamined assumption that modernity comes in one size only, whether for its victors or for its victims. That is, the notion of plural modernities calls attention to how various combinations of local, regional, and global forces have historically produced coeval but differently placed versions of modernity—including versions of its opposite, "tradition"—both beyond and within Europe (Mitchell 2000).[1]

Yet the strategy of pluralizing creates new problems even as it resolves old ones. For example, what Mitchell (2000:xii) dubs "the easy pluralism of alternative modernities" can lead directly to a politically and analytically disabling position. Politically, easy pluralism runs the risk of sustaining an illusion of symmetrical modernities reminiscent of the chimerical "new world order" of self-determining, formally equivalent nation-states discussed by John Kelly in this volume. By sidestepping questions of power—of structural inequalities and violent histories of colonization and decolonization—easy pluralism comfortably reproduces liberal visions of multiculturalism: trite relativism, mere plurality (Rofel, this volume).

Analytically, easy pluralism runs a different, though not unrelated, risk. Pluralization assumes that different modernities are specific versions of a universal form, particular inflections of a generic social condition. Unless this assumption is made explicit, its validity remains difficult to assess. More importantly, the failure to articulate such an assumption tacitly supports a position that regards the generic form of modernity (itself assumed to originate within the West) as archetypically modern and all other particular instances (usually non-Western) as lesser approximations of the generic form, and hence less modern (in other words, traditional or "more cultural" by comparison with the "universal" generic form; Mitchell 2000). This unhappy position reinstates the singular, eurocentric view of modernity—complete with its constitutive and invidious distinction from the nonmodern (Trouillot, this volume)—that notions of alternative or plural modernities putatively critique. (Construing and celebrating the nonmodern as resilient and resistant perhaps complicates this view but does not alter its basic premises.)

I want to argue that assumptions about the general and particular with regard to plural modernities must be made explicit in order not only to ensure whatever critical advantage pluralism might claim, but also to answer two prior questions: what do we mean by the term "modernity," and why ought anthropologists bother to retain the concept at all? Such explication perforce makes clear what the anthropological goals of pluralizing modernity might be other than that of announcing a keen sense of intellectual fashion or of evoking the sublime, as Kelly (this volume) might suspect. I suggest that one goal is comparison; that is, I propose to move away from a notion of alternative modernities to a notion of comparative modernities, retaining the relativist critique of the former while exploring ways offered by the latter to articulate commensurable contemporary social experiences. The promise of a comparative approach to modernity lies in its capacity to define the limits of theoretical pronouncements about universal or global social conditions at the same time as it identifies the shared and/or linked experiences of people that an earlier anthropology depicted as worlds apart. In this sense, perhaps, the promise of pluralizing modernity is a modest one, equivalent to that of more familiar concepts deployed by comparative anthropology, such as rites of passage and social structure.

While I am aware that the project of comparison was integral to a previous preoccupation in which Western Modernity functioned as a standard against which to measure non-Western efforts at modernization, I am not convinced that comparison is doomed to eurocentrism. I say so inasmuch as I propose that comparison should proceed ethnographically. As Miller (1994:58) asserts: "An ethnographic approach to modernity requires the direct juxtaposition of two elements: a theory of modernity and a descriptive ethnography." This juxtaposition, moreover, is neither the test of an hypothesis nor the presentation of a representative case, but, rather, an attempt to rub theoretical accounts of modernity against the lived experience of ordinary people, thereby exposing the extent to which theoretical accounts of global transformations with homogenizing consequences do and do not make sense of the diversity of specific social and historical contexts. I therefore suggest that in addition to comparison, ethnographically grounded theory is another important consequence of making explicit the assumptions of pluralization.

The goals I have thus far identified suggest that the stakes in pluralizing modernities include the capacity to inform assertions of world-historical import with descriptions of intimate and everyday aspects of life in diverse local settings—and vice versa. These goals, however, still beg the question of what we mean by modernity. Here I agree with Kelly (this volume) that a list of disparate traits or characteristics which point to something so awesome it can only be evoked has limited theoretical use as a definition of modernity. Indeed, any definition (as well as periodization) of modernity in terms of the presence or absence of institutions (capitalist markets, nation-states, etc.) and values or ideologies (individualism, secularism, etc.) inevitably leads to the problem of unevenness—that is, to the recognition that such institutions and ideologies are unevenly distributed both geographically and historically. By this definition, we—and I mean all of us—have indeed never been modern. Nor will we ever be. The term "modernity" can at best designate an ideal type.

I propose beginning with a different, more methodological recognition, namely, that what we take modernity to mean will have much to do with the ethnographic particulars we hope to understand. In other words, the juxtaposition of abstract theory and descriptive ethnography is deliberately selected; ethnographic particulars are deemed appropriate for problematizing aspects of social life deemed to be intrinsic to the modern condition. In this approach, I follow Miller (1994), whose study of Trinidad juxtaposes an ethnography of material culture and mass consumption with a theory of modernity derived from Hegel via Habermas. Miller's intention was to link a description of everyday social life in Trinidad to a model of modernity that foregrounds shifts in temporal consciousness—"a new consciousness about the present and its separation from the past" (1994:61). His attention was drawn to mass consumption—ethnographically, inasmuch as he found himself in the particular historical context of the end of Trinidad's oil boom; and theoretically, inasmuch as mass consumption heightens "the consumer's" consciousness of the fact that one lives through "objects and images not of one's own creation" (Miller 1995:1). These alien things represent a potential condition of rupture symptomatic of a more fundamental ontological shift: the self-knowledge that modern subjects of history must reconcile an expanding gap between themselves and the products of history and so must continually forge the criteria by which they live (for examples of a similar approach to modernity in Papua New Guinea, see Wardlow, this volume; Gewertz and Errington, 1996).

I share Miller's optimism about a project of comparative modernities that explicitly shuttles between theory and ethnography, and which puts European social theory in the telling light of non-European empirical realities. I look, however, not to Hegel but to Anthony Giddens (1990, 1991) for a pluralizable way of theorizing modernity (see Lien 1997 for another example). In this chapter, I will juxtapose some of Giddens's ideas about the dynamic character of modern social life with selected ethnographic materials from Papua New Guinea. My aim will be to demonstrate how Giddens's discussion of modernity defines clear and traceable connections between changes in the objective conditions of social life and changes in the contours of (inter)subjective experience. More specifically, I will demonstrate how an ethnographic focus on trust—on the practical means by which social relations of trust are generated and sustained—creates a perspective from which to understand the various encounters between Papua New Guineans on the one hand and ideas and institutions of exogenous origin on the other. Before doing so, however, I want to revisit some of the issues just outlined by looking at a critique of pluralization of modernities that clarifies some of my concerns about the relationship between theory and ethnography.

Multiple Modernities: Ethnography, Theory, and Comparison

In a good-to-think *Current Anthropology* article, "Ethnography and the Meta-Narratives of Modernity," Harri Englund and James Leach (2000) have raised both political and analytical concerns about pluralizing Modernity. Their first concern is one of specifically *academic* politics; Englund and Leach ask whether the current fascination with multiple modernities is nothing more than a pathetic attempt on the part of anthropologists to make themselves relevant to public debates within the humanities and social sciences—that is, to enter the arena of high-prestige social theory and thereby escape the trap of the notorious "savage slot" (Trouillot 1991). Their second concern is one of logic; after all, the notion of multiple, plural, or alternative modernities implies variation on a theme or different illustrations of the same phenomenon. In other words, the notion of multiple modernities logically implies a comparative project that requires analytical specification. What might this project look like?

I leave aside the issue of academic politics and address only the already posed question of comparison: of what do all these plural modernities purport to be so many versions? Much of the work done under the rubric of multiple modernities gives accounts, written from the perspective of different cultural or national sites, of the reception of Western Modernity (Gaonkar 1999; see also Comaroff and Comaroff 1993; Piot 1999; LiPuma 2000). Generally speaking, these accounts understand Western Modernity to mean certain institutional arrangements—popular government, bureaucratic states, market-driven economies—and certain cultural values—rationalist secularism, possessive individualism, pragmatic instrumentalism. Reception, of course, is never a matter of passive acceptance but always a process of creative adaptation and unintended consequences, often a story of conscious resistance to the project of powerful colonizers seeking to shape people in forms taken to be universal. Otherwise said, the encounter with Western Modernity is "relentlessly dialectical" (LiPuma 2000:5), altering "everyone and everything involved, if not all in the same manner or measure" (Comaroff and Comaroff 1997a:5). As LiPuma insists, "the changes induced were dialectical because the presence of Western practices reshaped indigenous ones and simultaneously the determinate appearance of Western practices (schooling, medicine, Christian rites, elections), which were inseparable from, because mutually determined by, their local counterparts" (2000:5). The encounter produces modernity in divergent and convergent forms—and in combinations that can't be known in advance. Because the encounter unfolds in a specific cultural and historical context, different starting points will ensure different outcomes in response to relatively similar changes. (Neither the nation-state nor capitalism in Fiji is the same as the nation-state or capitalism in Papua New Guinea.) Hence, as Dilip Parameshwar Gaonkar concluded in his introduction to a special issue of *Public Culture* on "alter-native modernities,"

This double relationship between convergence and divergence, with their counterintuitive dialectic between similarity and difference, makes the site of alternative modernities also the site of double negotiations—between societal modernization and cultural modernity and between hidden capacities for the production of similarity and difference. Thus, alternative modernities produce combinations and recombinations that are endlessly surprising. (1999:18)

This view of modernity as dialectical emphasizes, of course, plurality and particularism in the face of the singularizing and generalizing tendencies of eurocentric narratives of modernization. Thus Comaroff and Comaroff, considering the heyday of colonialism, observe that

> Macrocosmic modernities, in sum, were at once singular and plural, specific and general, parochial and global in their manifestations. Notwithstanding the homogenizing thrust of Market Capitalism, Protestantism, and other "isms" of the age, there grew up, all around the so-called peripheries of empire, multiple market systems and modes of production, differently domesticated churches and creeds and currencies, homegrown nationalisms and hybrid rationalisms. These call for understanding not as tokens of a generic type or as mere vernacular facsimiles of one another. They are to be accounted for in terms of what made them particular. (1997a:6)

Along with the twin emphases on plurality and particularity, then, this view of modernity equally stresses historical process. The trajectory of modernity everywhere is neither certain nor predetermined; it is openly indeterminate and nonlinear. Indeed, LiPuma likens the transformative process of modernity not to a synthesis of imported and domestic models of reality, but to an "improvisational dance, which is also a struggle, in which the participants, wittingly and unwittingly, continually respond and change over the course of a dance that does not, cannot, end" (2000:19). By this definition of modernity, too, then, we will not ever be "fully modern," for modernity describes an always unfolding, ever contingent process moving along pathways that are necessarily not the same for everybody.

From a dialectical point of view, not only is modernity an incomplete project, but so is the project of comparison implied in the notion of multiple modernities—endless, surprising, and, perhaps, somewhat unfocused. Englund and Leach (2000:228) make this point in their article as part of a more general critique of the dialectical approach to modernity. They claim that because the "institutional configuration" of modernity—Gaonkar's combinations and recombinations—cannot be defined in advance, the analyst is free to move about the ethnographic cabin, focusing on witchcraft in one setting (cultural site), Christianity in another, and political economy in a third. These particular illustrations of particular modernities bespeak a new rhetoric of ethnographic holism that "simultaneously celebrates cultural diversity and resists [eurocentric] parochialism" (Englund and Leach 2000:228) by placing emphasis on variation.

Englund and Leach push their argument further, claiming that the logical requirement of representing variation against something that is invariable compels dialectical analyses to invoke sociological abstractions familiar from Marx ("commodification") and Weber ("disenchantment"). Disparate ethnographic observations are thereby linked to debates about modernity not by explicit theorizing but instead by unenunciated metanarratives or organizing assumptions. These assumptions, according to Englund and Leach, inevitably highlight the ruptures and discontinuities thought to be brought about by modernity in its multiple refractions. Englund and Leach (2000:229) thus characterize Comaroff and Comaroff's (1999, 2000) more recent ideas about alienating "occult economies"—a global nightmare of pyramid schemes, zombie labor, and traffic in body parts—as stuck in the "ethnocentric legacy of social scientific discourse on modernity," a discourse long concerned with the specter of inexorable and total disenchantment. Occult economies *presume* "feelings of erasure and loss"—alienation and disenchantment— as the main matter, in South Africa today and the world historically (Comaroff and Comaroff 2000:316–17). Englund and Leach do not deny that people in Comaroff and Comaroff's South Africa and elsewhere are fearful and anxious, but they contend that understanding such fear and anxiety as a reenchanting reaction to "creeping commodification" presupposes prior knowledge about the context of people's concerns—knowledge supplied by a specific metanarrative of modernity. In effect, Englund and Leach accuse the proponents of "multiple modernities" of the same unselfconsciousness that these proponents impute to modernization theorists. So much for provincializing Europe; under the disguise of plurality and diversity lurk familiar theoretical premises about the Big Picture—the "wider context" of local particularities. (For a differently motivated but not unrelated critique of how Comaroff and Comaroff link "general context" with "local particularities," see Moore 1999.)

The merits and demerits of Englund and Leach's claims deserve sustained attention. Their claim, for example, that accounts of multiple modernities stress radical rupture should be balanced by the observation that such accounts often highlight, with approval, those elements of Western Modernity that have been subsumed in local projects of value, thus rendering multiple modernities as complex mixtures of continuity and discontinuity. Here, however, I will consider only Englund and Leach's call for greater reflexivity in using comparative ethnography for

making contributions to debates about modernity. They offer two suggestions. The first, which I have already intimated and which Englund
and Leach pass over quickly, is better theory, "better" meaning more
explicit propositions about how to shift analytical scales between situated ethnographic observations and generalizations of world-historical
import. The second, which Englund and Leach settle on, is better
ethnography, "better" meaning a recommitment to what they term
"ethnographic knowledge practices." Ethnographic knowledge practices require both long-term localized fieldwork (a question of academic
politics, in part) and intellectual partnership with interlocutors who
begin with different preconceptions about what matters but who are
also engaged in their own kind of social science (see Wagner 1976).
Ethnographers so engaged generate theory, or at least generalizations,
from a standpoint reflexively understood as such—that is, a standpoint
grounded in the historical, cultural, and biographical specificities of
the ethnographic encounter, including the limitations of language (conceptual and otherwise) within which the ethnographer communicates.
Comparison is thus built into all ethnography, even if only implicitly.
Just how we get from this sort of implicit comparison to general theoretical propositions remains, however, not fully clear from Englund and
Leach's essay (but see Strathern 1988).

Let me return, then, to Englund and Leach's first suggestion about
better theory. I want to try and make the metanarrative of modernity
more explicit so that—as with reflexive ethnography—theory building
and field research can occur together. I want, in other words, to meet
the challenge posed by Steven Sangren (2000:244) in his comments on
Englund and Leach's article, the challenge of "developing conceptualizations of social and cultural processes at a level of abstraction sufficiently general to make sense in comparable terms not only of vastly
differing societies but also of the complex local and global realities so
portentously proclaimed by anthropology's would-be pundits." Can
Leach and Englund's respect for ethnographic context be accommo-
dated by explicit theoretical abstraction—a way of thinking about modernity that recapitulates neither nineteenth-century narratives of goal-
directed history and radical rupture nor lengthy checklists of modern
institutions and ideologies, but that instead enables the comparative
analysis of historical change within and across different cultural and
national sites? I am reluctant to abandon metanarratives—or, if you will,
theory—even if I leave myself vulnerable to the charge of making the
abstractions associated with modernity the "natural" foundations for
comparison (Englund and Leach 2000:238). It is this reluctance that

accordingly motivates my turn toward some conceptualizations of high-level abstraction that derive from the work of Anthony Giddens.

Distanciation, Disembedding, Reembedding

"Accordingly" might seem the wrong word, since many scholars, including Englund and Leach, regard Giddens as a prophet of Modernity in the singular, exactly the sort of sociologist who emphasizes historical ruptures of global proportion. Knauft (in his introduction to this volume) similarly aligns Giddens with theorists "who champion a homogeneous view of modernity" and who fail to consider the articulation of features of global (i.e., Western) modernity with those of non-Western modernity. But if we can pluralize Modernity, then we can surely pluralize Giddens. Tomlinson's (1999) sympathetic interpretation of Giddens's treatment of modernity as time–space transformation is helpful in this task.

Giddens defines modernity in terms of four "institutional dimensions"—capitalism, industrialism, organized and extensive surveillance (especially the political control of the nation-state), and industrialized military power (see Giddens 1990:55–78). Each of these dimensions is interdependent, though not reducible to any one other dimension. The dimensions, moreover, are not all equivalent. For Giddens and Pierson (1998:97), capitalism "is the most significant driving force of change": "The emergence of modernity is first of all the creation of a modern economic order, that is, a capitalistic economic order" (1998:96). What matters most in Giddens's theory of modernity, however, is neither the relative weight of each institution nor when or where any one institution is or was present or absent—the tedious questions of periodization and provenance—but, rather, how this complex of institutions facilitates and presumes changes in routine social life. It is this dynamic process—primarily, a shift in the social organization of time–space—that Giddens attempts to grasp through the concepts of distanciation and disembedding.

Time–space distanciation refers to the "stretching" or coordination of social relations across time and space, such that, for example, persons distant in time–space can be controlled or supervised by a superordinate authority. That is, both time and space become abstracted from context and separated from each other; mechanical clocks and standardized time zones detach time from locality. This "emptying of time" allows and fosters an "emptying of space," a "separation of place from space" or relations between people who occupy different and distant physical set-

tings of interaction (Tomlinson 1999:52). Put more generally, distanciation refers to the way in which locally situated lifeworlds become saturated with distant social influences and events. As Tomlinson puts it,
modern locales express "the *disembedding* of social activity from contexts of presence" (1999:54).

Disembedding refers more specifically to "abstract systems," mechanisms that disembed or lift out social relations from localized contexts
of interaction and stretch them out or restructure them across indefinite
spans of time–space. Such mechanisms include "symbolic tokens," such
as money or written records, and "expert systems," the technical knowledge of anonymous others (experts) upon which people depend in going
about their day-to-day lives. Disembedding mechanisms enable the spatial and temporal expansion of state administrations (nation-states) and
commodity and labor markets (capitalism); they imbue a locale with
the "curious reality" of a chain store: "it is present in the physical sense
of course, but it subsists as an entity in a web of relations that are
not present; a substantive part of the store's being is absent" (Cassell
1993:28).

In principle, distanciation and disembedding—unlike, say, disenchantment and alienation—can be recognized as sociohistorical processes
without presuming anything about how they might register in the concerns of people in any given locale. Yet Giddens is sensitive to this question, as evidenced by his focus on the significance of "trust" in modernity, the way in which routine activities like eating and drinking today
require people's trust in abstract systems. In this sense, for Giddens,
distanciation and disembedding—and modernity—are above all a matter of faceless (not always conscious) commitments or distanciated social relations of trust. Distanciation and disembedding render locally
situated lifeworlds "phantasmagoric"—peopled with the absent, living
or dead.[2] Speaking of chain stores, consider the following newspaper
report from South Portland, Maine, where the local Best Buy has no
light switches: "The bright fluorescent lights in the sprawling store at
the Maine Mall are told by a computer in Minnesota when to turn
themselves on and off." Similarly, at the local Wal-Mart, everything
from the in-store televisions to the thermostat are controlled from the
home office in Bentonville, Arkansas. The reaction of one former store
manager in South Portland is entirely apposite: "It's creepy. If you
trust me with your product, you can trust me to turn off the light
switch. I would much rather have control in my own store" (*Democrat
and Chronicle*, 30 June 2001, p. 9D)

Distanciation and disembedding thus create potentially troubling
existential situations, crises of trust, which prompt people to make

a "bargain with modernity": "This 'bargain'—'governed by specific admixtures of deference and skepticism, comfort and fear' [Giddens 1990:90]—is a way of coping with forced reliance on abstract systems" (Tomlinson 1999:57). It is at this point that Giddens's theory of modernity links world-historical transformations to everyday lived experience. However, it is important not to misread Giddens as saying that modernity describes a unidirectional, inexorable process of disembedding, of abstraction-from-context, of "emptying out" the particular (local) contents of time and space. Nor does Giddens say that abstract systems are all bad or all good; they have both costs and benefits, neither of which can be known fully in advance. Not everyone, moreover, makes the same bargain with modernity, mainly because abstract systems are subject to the effects of "reembedding"—that is, the constant efforts of human beings, embodied and physically located, "to make themselves at home in the modern world" (Tomlinson 1999:62, quoting Berman 1983). In other words, modernity describes an uneven dialectical process—"an ongoing relation between distanciation and the chronic mutability of local circumstances and local engagements" (Giddens 1991:21–22). As Tomlinson (1999:61) notes, "There is therefore always a 'push-and-pull' between 'disembedding forces' of [globalizing modernity] and countervailing 're-embedding forces' coming from localities." Distanciation and disembedding do not, then, inevitably lead to an increase in real or perceived powerlessness, even if the dialectic of disembedding/reembedding frequently distributes its costs and benefits in highly unequal ways.

Tomlinson, like Giddens (Giddens and Pierson 1998; see Cassel 1993:23), clearly formulates a dialectically contingent rather than teleologically evolutionist approach to modernity. I readily grant, however, that both Giddens and Tomlinson do very little by way of empirically documenting how reembedding works; they prefer to focus more on the mechanisms of disembedding (or deterritorialization; Tomlinson 1999:106–149). The promise of their theory is hardly redeemed, ethnographically. Nevertheless, this recognition of dialectical contingency—reminiscent of Gaonkar's comments quoted above—brings Giddens's social theory into conversation with available approaches, such as that of Comaroff and Comaroff, to multiple modernities. I suggest that disembedding/reembedding counts as one instance of the dialectical notion that, Knauft claims (in his introduction to this volume), inheres in formulations of plural modernities. It is the conceptual means to ground Giddens's theory ethnographically, even if he himself rarely uses it. But it also defines a strategy for comparative research by focusing ethnographic attention on the ways in which people contest faceless commitments—that is, the ways in which people engage, form, and transform distanciated relations of trust. I will attempt to illustrate this strategy by turning briefly to a pair of related ethnographic examples from contemporary Papua New Guinea.

Reembedding the State in
Papua New Guinea

New Guinea—its imposing highlands and neighboring islands, divided today between the independent state of Papua New Guinea (PNG) and the Indonesian colony called Irian Jaya or Papua (West Papua)—held a privileged place in the development of twentieth-century anthropology. Long regarded as a "natural laboratory" because of both its absolute cultural diversity and relative historical distance from Euro-American (pre)occupations, the region challenges its current inhabitants and observers with the task of making sense of modernity. In recent years, then, anthropologists working in PNG have increasingly turned their attention to the ways in which, throughout the country, people—compelled by new desires and confronted by new inequalities—shaped and were shaped by their encounter with capitalism, the state (colonial and national), and imported categories of knowledge and personhood (LiPuma 2000; see Knauft 1999 for an overview).

The ethnographic examples I will discuss aptly illustrate Giddens's idea of disembedding abstract systems, for I seek to indicate how contests over trust crystallize around the expert system known as "the state" and the state-issued symbolic token known as "money." But these examples accomplish an additional purpose: namely, to demonstrate how a dialectical notion of multiple modernities provides an alternative to the conceptual dualisms that have characterized Melanesianist contributions to anthropological theory. These dichotomies, though often potent heuristic devices, run the risk of reproducing singular, evolutionary narratives of modernity by building typologies on a fundamental opposition between Modernity and Tradition.

On the evening of 23 June 1992, in a rural island setting (Tanga Islands, New Ireland Province), just before the close of the polling period of the national election, I sat in conversation with two friends, both local middle-aged men. We talked about government corruption. Anton Neof informed me that local supporters of an opposition party had challenged supporters of the party in government with the charge that the current government was corrupt. The government supporters replied that it was not the government that was corrupt, but rather certain individuals. Neof countered by asking: "What is the government if not these people?

If I went to see the government, what would I see but them?" The questions recall Max Weber's claim that "one of the most important aspects of the existence of a modern state, precisely as a complex of social interaction of individual persons, consists in the fact that the action of various individuals is oriented to the belief that it exists or should exist, thus that its acts and laws are valid in the legal sense" (Weber 1978:14). Neof's rhetoric raises the question: What happens when people refuse to treat an abstract system as abstract, and instead meet its disembedding effects with countervailing forces derived from local exigencies?

In PNG, many people not only distrust politicians, whom they vote out of office at an astounding rate, but they also refuse to accept the idea of the state, to grant it the status of an expert system, a transcendent abstraction which commands trust, however grudging. Instead, they imagine the state as the particular officials who actually compose it, officials (including bureaucrats) to whom they relate much as clients to patrons dispensing largesse and ensuring the people's well-being (see Foster 1996 for further discussion). Thus Jeffrey Clark (1997) argues that Pangia people in the Southern Highlands imagine the PNG state as a classic Melanesian "big man" whom they follow *if and only if* the big man remains bound by moral obligations of reciprocity and redistribution. By putting a face on "the state," Papua New Guineans resist the "lifting out" of political relations from the exigencies of localized social interactions; they register practical skepticism about the expert system called the state—the much-heralded and hope-laden independent nation-state—as the vehicle for delivering "development" (see Karp, this volume), desire for which and exclusion from which are increasingly felt in all quarters of the country (Knauft, "Trials," this volume; Foster, 2002).

While an earlier anthropology attempted to grasp the distinctive realities of Melanesian polities in terms of an opposition between "big men" and "chiefs" and between both of these traditional political figures and modern bureaucratic states, such dualisms obscure more than they illuminate contemporary politics in PNG. They fail to account, for example, for the way in which "big men" are not remnants of the past, but rather creatures of the political present. That is, reembedding has produced a vernacular version of liberal democracy in PNG, a specific conjunction of an imported political system with preexisting conventions about authority and leadership.[3] Dinnen (1998:348) refers to this conjunction as "a process of upward colonization, whereby social forces emanating from the most local levels have penetrated even the commanding heights of the modern state" (see also Jacobsen 1995 and especially Strathern 1993). From one point of view, this process has woven corruption and clientelism into the fabric of the state, as the state has become the primary instrument of accumulation for politicians (Ghai 1997:314). From another point of view, this process has woven into state politics indigenous expectations about the obligations of leaders to members of their community, so that, as Yash Ghai observes (1997:325), "state roles cannot—any more than state resources—be separated from communal exchanges." In other words, the dynamics of PNG politics spring from the politician's need to reciprocate the support of his (almost always his) local constituents with material resources—to act morally like a big man. Accountability to his local supporters overrides and undermines accountability to the Rule of (national) Law. While Ghai's lucid analysis of the establishment of liberal political order in PNG goes well beyond the scope of this chapter, his ironic conclusion is highly pertinent.[4] An unintended consequence of the Constitution's respect for "Papua New Guinea ways" has been the entrenchment of a liberal democracy which, oddly, works—elections have been held regularly and governments have changed peacefully—but in which almost all national goals have become subverted.[5] Reembedding the state has left most Papua New Guineans little grounds for trusting it twenty-five years after independence.

If political modernity in PNG escapes the dualism of "big man" and "bureaucratic state," then economic modernity likewise exceeds analysis framed in terms of the classic opposition between "gifts" and "commodities." The point can be made by looking at the various ways in which state-issued money circulates in PNG—that is, by asking not whether money circulates as a gift or a commodity, but instead how tokens that mediate one set of trust relations become entangled with another set. For Giddens, money is the prime means by which economic relations are "lifted out" from the time–space determinations of physical locales. In fact, colonial schooling sought to impart this very lesson in order to convince Papuans and New Guineans of the superior convenience and efficiency of money relative to more familiar exchange tokens, such as pearlshells (Foster 1998). But for people like the Anganen described by Michael Nihill (1989), money—specifically, crisp red twenty-kina notes—is the material instrument for making embodied social relations locally visible. Like ochre-coated pearlshells, red twenty-kina notes are displayed by men in prestations made in respect of bodies—undertaken to alleviate illness, compensate death, or combine a woman's "womb blood" with her husband's semen and thereby create children. Whatever trust Anganen men here invest in red twenty-kina notes to evince and effect the reproduction of healthy bodies, it is certainly not the same sort of trust involved in accepting money as the guaranteed means for balancing debt and credit over an indefinite chain of transactions. Indeed, *only* clean, red, crisp twenty-kina notes will do, not other denominations of paper currency or metal coins.

In any case, Papua New Guineans regularly question money's tacit guarantee precisely because they refuse to erase from consciousness the manifestly stateish iconography of coin and currency, reading these signifiers as expressions of shifting relations with powerful persons. Thus, according to Clark (1997:81), Pangia complain that "Australian money was made by the Queen, Papua New Guinea money made by [Sir Michael] Somare [PNG's first prime minister]." Here the invidious distinction between wealthy Australia and impoverished PNG posits Somare as the personification of the state and identifies him with PNG currency. The equations are not unpersuasive, especially given that the fifty-kina note—the highest denomination in circulation—bears the images of both Sir Michael himself and the National Parliament building, itself partly built in the unmistakable shape of a "spirit house" (*haus tambaran*) from the Sepik area, Somare's place of origin. In effect, Papua New Guineans reembed money by intensively scrutinizing money's irreducibly material forms—precisely what ought to be least relevant to money's capacity for disembedding economic relations (for further discussion, see Foster 1998, 1999).

The way Anganen reembed state-issued money suggests how processes of distanciation may be channeled into local projects of value. In fact, the distanciating qualities of money are perhaps precisely what the Anganen prize in media of exchange, for like their analogs, the once-scarce pearlshells, twenty-kina notes evince the capacity of people, especially "big men," to "draw in outside wealth for the reproduction of local society" (Robbins and Akin 1999:23), to "pull" wealth from distant sources. Money, in effect, enhances the project of social reproduction as Anganen define it: "Money, with its wide usage and state backing, is a potent conductant of power, conveying more of it over greater distances than shells ever could" (Robbins and Akin 1999:22). But it would be misleading only to celebrate the Anganen case as an instance of local "appropriation" or "domestication" of the state, for the cultural continuities involved in reembedding generate discontinuities. Reembedding here recalibrates Anganen time–space; as LiPuma (1999) has noted for the Maring, by comparison with money, pearlshells now come to symbolize "the local," relative immobility instead of border-crossing agency. Similarly, the trust that Anganen men invest in the efficacy of twenty-kina notes for reproducing local society has a corollary: anxiety about the destabilizing effects on social reproduction put in play by the wide circulation of money. For example, Anganen associate small denominations of paper currency (two-kina and five-kina notes) with mundane productive activities (wage labor, coffee selling) on the one hand, and acts of consumption (buying cigarettes and beer, paying taxes) in which money is "lost" on the other. This association also metaphorically links small denomination paper notes to women, who grow and sell coffee, and, in the eyes of men, "eat" cash by funneling it into wasteful consumption (Wardlow, this volume). New crises of legitimacy thus emerge, pitting men against women and generation against generation, and engendering a range of new responses (see Robbins and Akin 1999; Foster 1999).

These two examples point at the many ways in which people in PNG are engaging and transforming distanciated relations of trust integral to the dynamism of modernity as theorized by Giddens. They also make it plain that such engagements and transformations, however comparable to processes at work in, say, Togo (Piot 1999) or Trinidad (Miller 1994), assume distinctive local forms. These examples from PNG also function critically, like the notion of comparative modernities itself, to remind us of the "bargains with modernity" that people make without really noticing, about which a few words before concluding.

Coca-Cola, Consumerism, and Breakdowns of Routine Trust

Although Giddens conceptually ties the question of trust to time–space distanciation, he does not presume that distanciation implies let alone increases skepticism. On the contrary, most of the everyday social activity bound up with abstract systems that Giddens has in mind—his favorite example is driving a car—involves routine trust. Routine trust becomes exposed only in its breach, sometimes with significant financial consequences. Consider the well-publicized contamination scare in Belgium—perhaps a rare instance of mass sociogenic illness (Nemery et al. 1999)—in which hundreds of people (in a country recovering from a scandal over dioxins found in meat and dairy products) developed vague constitutional symptoms which they associated with drinking Coca-Cola beverages. The result was one of the largest consumer product recalls in history, a charge of $103 million to the second-quarter earnings of The Coca-Cola Company's bottling operation (Coca-Cola Enterprises Inc.). Millions more were spent on a "Coke's Back" public relations campaign—beach parties, rock concerts, and free handouts as well as the appearance of company representatives in grocery stores to speak directly with consumers—all to restore trust in the world's most famous brand. The Belgian crisis reminds us of how consumer products—especially ingestibles and comestibles—can define flashpoints for struggles over trust relations. Such struggles emerge most clearly in situations where people encounter goods not previously seen in the local marketplace. Timothy Burke thus describes the introduction of Stork margarine to southern Africa in the 1940s and 1950s. Originally marketed by Lever Brothers in a wrapper with a picture of a baby on it, the margarine quickly prompted rumors that it was in fact "rendered baby fat, proof of the ghoulish practices of the settlers" (Burke 1996:162).

Whether or not the Stork rumor counts as an early instance of the occult economy, it surely registers the way in which goods made in unknown places by unknown people harbor the capacity to disrupt the distanciated relations of trust intrinsic to modernity. Miller has argued that it is this capacity that makes "consumption" good to think about modernity, for goods can "highlight the sense that one is consuming in the more abstract sense of dealing with forces which have come from the outside and that one does not have the experience or knowledge to properly harness them to one's own historical project" (1995:7). His remark recalls not only the specific anxiety that shadows the Anganen use of money in ceremonial displays, but also the more general challenge posed by having to make sense of oneself and others through material culture produced elsewhere. Ethnographers of New Guinea have of course written extensively on this challenge under the rubric of cargo cults. I turn, then, to a last brief example from PNG, in order to illustrate how an ethnographic focus on the (routine) trust relations entailed by distanciation might be refined further by paying attention to how people regard consumer commodities.

I take this example from the film *Advertising Missionaries* (1996), which documents the activities of a traveling theater troupe in the employ of a local marketing firm. The troupe visits some of the most inaccessible areas of PNG, where, portraying a mildly dysfunctional family, it performs humorous skits that demonstrate the nature and uses of brand name products—Colgate toothpaste, Omo laundry powder—to audiences beyond the reach of other commercial media. In one such skit, "Child" introduces "Uncle" to Coca-Cola soft drinks. Uncle asks, "What is it?" He expresses wonder and confusion at both the bottle and can held before him. The audience of Southern Highlanders—men and boys—laugh at Uncle's shock and surprise at the popping sound made when the can is opened, and at Uncle's ignorant gesture of placing the bottle cap, "eye of the bottle" in Tok Pisin, over his own eye. Eventually, Uncle is persuaded to drink from the can. He rolls his eyes with obvious delight, and then follows Child's exhortation to "down" the entire can in a single gulp, a style of imbibing often associated with alcohol consumption. The audience responds with good humor, and the camera lingers on one young man, downing his own bottle of Coke in apparently playful imitation of Uncle.

While the narrative thrust of *Advertising Missionaries* romantically laments the incorporation of "remote" and "traditional" populations into the market for consumer commodities, the actual content of the Coca-Cola skit suggests that other concerns are at work. The skit offers up to an ostensibly out-of-the-way audience the image of a man—Uncle—who is indeed truly marginal, a *bus kanaka* ("country bumpkin" in Tok Pisin) who does not even know what Coke is. Here, I submit, is an anxiety dramatized and deflected, a fear that what ought to be taken for granted (something as banal as carbonated soft drinks) is not, and that in not taking it for granted, one's exposure as not modern is publicized. Like the commonly told ethnic joke about the *bus kanaka* who "cooks" his mackerel by tossing the unopened tin into the fire, the skit enacts discomfort about the relationship to an abstract system materialized as a mundane item of consumption.[6] That is, the skit enables its audience to distance itself from Uncle's uncomfortable and potentially discomforting relationship to images of progress and development. I say discomforting inasmuch as these images, which now measure and mark moral and material worth, present modernity as an ideology of continual improvement (Karp, this volume). Do I/we measure up? Am I/are we like Uncle after all? Live on stage for all to see, "the oxymodern" unfolds as "an acute and self-conscious semblance of progress" fashioned out of "the opposition between local constructions of tradition and those of modernity" (Knauft, "Trials," this volume).

Conclusion: Bargains with the Concept of Modernity

Giddens's notion of distanciation, as my final example shows, calls attention to the subjective dimensions and diversities of modernity—to lived experiences of fear, comfort, skepticism, and indifference. Knauft (in the introduction to this volume) argues that it is precisely these aspects of lived experience—bargains with modernity—that competing concepts of world-historical process such as globalization or capitalism occlude. Hence, we ought not to be too quick to jettison the concept of modernity, whatever bargains it compels us as analysts to make and make explicit. Perhaps this is even more so the case when the concept of modernity (not to mention globalization or even privatization) becomes a self-reflexive part of the discourse of the people whose lives anthropologists seek to understand (see Meyer 2000).[7] Thus the inquiring title of an opinion piece in one of PNG's daily newspapers: "How modern do we want to be?" (*The National*, 5 April 2001). Put differently, despite the reasonable concerns of Englund and Leach that metanarratives of modernity might erase the particular concerns of people in particular locales, I submit that an explicit theory of modernity will do otherwise. Continually tempered by the ethnography it underwrites, such a theory will connect lived experience in particular localities not only with world-historical social shifts, but also with lived experiences in other localities. This is the import and promise of "comparative modernities."

The question of comparative modernities, however, is ultimately a question of scale, the scale on which to do ethnography. It is a question of how to avoid dissolving local particularities in the uniform sameness of global conditions without treating the radical distinctiveness of the local as if it stood against or apart from the global (as opposed to, say, being an effect of it). As Tomlinson (1999:33) asks, "How useful [is] the cluster of ideas that constitute 'modernity' . . . for making sense of cultural experience in a globalizing world"? My answer, given here by way of Giddens's theory, is that it is especially useful in undertaking the comparative project that an increasingly globalizing world requires of local ethnography—multisited or not (Marcus 1995). I advocate a pluralizable theory of modernity—flexible enough to preserve our freedom to move about the ethnographic cabin and unambiguous enough to specify why we are doing so. So, for example, if we pay attention to money in one setting and consumer goods in another, this is because the situations in which distanciated relations of trust are contested—the access points to abstract systems—vary across historical and cultural contexts. These variations, still in the making, are no doubt endless and no doubt surprising. But at least by focusing our ethnographic attention on the construction and destruction of trust relations, we entertain the possibility of interpreting locally lived experiences within an explicit theoretical framework for the comparative study of modernities.

Acknowledgments

I thank Bruce Knauft for inviting me to participate in the conference session from which this volume originated and for his helpful comments on my chapter. I also thank Richard Wilson for his comments. I am grateful to the National Endowment for the Humanities and the University of Rochester for their material support of my research and writing.

Notes

1. Attempts at pluralizing Capitalism with a capital C aim at similar effects (see, e.g., Kelly 1992; Yang 2000; Blim 2000).

2. The word resonates well with Comaroff and Comaroff's vision of a South African occult economy in which new forms of wealth appear "to be a consequence of the capacity to siphon goods, people, and images across space in no time at all" (1999:291).

3. Comaroff and Comaroff's (1997b) discussion of "political modernity" in Botwsana is a relevant example of how the conjuncture of homegrown political theory and the workings of the postcolonial nation-state could produce a popular desire for one-party rule in a so-called model democracy.

4. It is important to note that not only the particularities of indigenous conventions about leadership affected the "structure of the conjuncture," but also (1) specific features of the Westminster model adopted by the Constitutional Planning Committee (such as plurality or "first past the post" voting and provisions to call for motions of confidence without having to dissolve Parliament) and (2) specific political and economic circumstances at the time of independence (such as the almost complete lack of political parties and the relative lack of coincidence between political and economic power) (Ghai 1997).

5. Paying narrow attention to the "stability" and "success" of *procedural* democracy in PNG can make for misleading political analysis. See, for example, Reilly's (2000/2001:177; *passim*) argument that "PNG's highly fragmented ethnic structure" actually promotes "democratic persistence."

6. The skit is one instance of a genre of auto-orientalizing performances of the transition from savagery to civilization reported widely in PNG (Kulick and Wilson 1992; Errington and Gewertz 1995; Young 1997; Knauft, "Trials," this volume).

7. The emphasis in Giddens's theory on the reflexivity of modern life, which I have not highlighted in this chapter, would anticipate this outcome.

References

Advertising Missionaries
  1996 Aspire Films. Bondi, NSW: Australia. Directed by Chris Hilton and Gauthier Flauder.

Berman, Marshall
  1983 *All That Is Solid Melts into Air: The Experience of Modernity.* London: Verso.

Blim, Michael
  2000   Capitalisms in Late Modernity. *Annual Review of Anthropology* 29:
          25–38.
Burke, Timothy
  1996   *Lifebuoy Men, Lux Women: Commodification, Consumption and Clean-
          liness in Modern Zimbabwe.* Durham, N.C.: Duke University Press.
Cassell, Philip
  1993   Introduction. In *The Giddens Reader.* Edited by P. Cassell, pp. 1–37.
          Stanford, Calif.: Stanford University Press.
Clark, Jeffrey
  1997   Imagining the State, or Tribalism and the Arts of Memory in the
          Highlands of Papua New Guinea. In *Narratives of Nation in the
          South Pacific.* Edited by T. Otto and N. Thomas, pp. 65–90. Amster-
          dam: Harwood Academic Press.
Comaroff, Jean, and John L. Comaroff
  1993   [Eds.] *Modernity and Its Malcontents: Ritual and Power in Postcolo-
          nial Africa.* Chicago: University of Chicago Press.
  1999   Occult Economies and the Violence of Abstraction: Notes from the
          South African Postcolony. *American Ethnologist* 26: 279–303.
  2000   Millennial Capitalism: First Thoughts on a Second Coming. In
          Millennial Capitalism and the Culture of Neolibralism, volume 3 of
          Millennial Quartet. *Public Culture* 12(2): 291–343.
Comaroff, John L., and Jean Comaroff
  1997a   *Of Revelation and Revolution: Volume 2: The Dialectics of Modernity
          on a South African Frontier.* Chicago: University of Chicago Press.
  1997b   Postcolonial Politics and Discourses of Democracy in Southern Af-
          rica: An Anthropological Reflection on African Political Moderni-
          ties. *Journal of Anthropological Research* 53: 123–46.
Dinnen, Sinclair
  1998   Law, Order and State. In *Modern Papua New Guinea.* Edited by
          Laura Zimmer-Tamakoshi, pp. 333–50. Kirksville, Mo.: Thomas
          Jefferson University Press.
Englund, Harri, and James Leach
  2000   Ethnography and the Meta-Narratives of Modernity. *Current An-
          thropology* 41: 225–48.
Errington, Frederick, and Deborah Gewertz
  1995   From Darkness to Light in the George Brown Jubilee. In *Articulat-
          ing Change in the "Last Unknown."* By F. Errington and D. Gewertz,
          pp. 77–106. Boulder, Colo.: Westview Press.
Foster, Robert J.
  1996   State Ritual: Ethnographic News on Voting in the Tanga Islands,
          Namatanai Electorate, New Ireland Province, June, 1992. In *The
          1992 Papua New Guinea Election: Change and Continuity in Electoral
          Politics.* Edited by Y. Saffu, pp. 144–67. Canberra: Department of

Political and Social Change, Research School of Pacific and Asian Studies, Australian National University.

1998   Your Money, Our Money, the Government's Money: Finance and Fetishism in Melanesia. In *Border Fetishisms: Material Objects in Unstable Places*. Edited by Patricia Spyer, pp. 60–90. New York: Routledge.

1999   In God We Trust? The Legitimacy of Melanesian Currencies. In *Money and Modernity: State and Local Currencies in Melanesia*. Edited by Joel Robbins and David Akin, pp. 213–31. Pittsburgh, Penn.: University of Pittsburgh Press.

2002   News of the World: Millenarian Christianity and the Olympic Torch Relay in Papua New Guinea. In *Materializing the Nation: Commodities, Consumption and Commercial Media in Papua New Guinea*. Bloomington: Indiana University Press.

Gaonkar, Dilip Parameshwar
1999   On Alternative Modernities. *Alter/Native Modernities*, volume 1 of Millennial Quartet. *Public Culture* 11(1): 1–18.

Gewertz, Deborah, and Frederick Errington
1996   On PepsiCo and Piety in a Papua New Guinean "Modernity." *American Ethnologist* 23(3): 476–93.

Ghai, Yash
1997   Establishing a Liberal Political Order through a Constitution: The Papua New Guinea Experience. *Development and Change* 28: 303–30.

Giddens, Anthony
1990   *The Consequences of Modernity*. Stanford, Calif.: Stanford University Press.
1991   *Modernity and Self-Identity: Self and Society in the Late Modern Age*. Stanford, Calif.: Stanford University Press.

Giddens, Anthony, and Christopher Pierson
1998   *Conversations with Anthony Giddens: Making Sense of Modernity*. Stanford, Calif.: Stanford University Press.

Jacobsen, Michael
1995   Vanishing Nations and the Infiltration of Nationalism: The Case of Papua New Guinea. In *Nation Making: Emergent Identities in Postcolonial Melanesia*. Edited by Robert Foster, pp. 227–49. Ann Arbor: University of Michigan Press.

Karp, Ivan
2002   Development and Personhood: Tracing the Contours of a Moral Discourse. In *Critically Modern: Alternatives, Alterities, Anthropologies* [this volume]. Edited by Bruce M. Knauft. Bloomington: Indiana University Press.

Kelly, John D.
1992   Fiji Indians and "Commoditization of labor." *American Ethnologist* 19(1): 97–120.

2002   Alternative Modernities or an Alternative to "Modernity": Getting
        Out of the Modernist Sublime. In *Critically Modern: Alternatives,
        Alterities, Anthropologies* [this volume]. Edited by Bruce M. Knauft.
        Bloomington: Indiana University Press.

Knauft, Bruce M.
1999   *From Primitive to Postcolonial in Melanesia and Anthropology*. Ann
        Arbor: University of Michigan Press.
2002a   Critically Modern: An Introduction. In *Critically Modern: Alterna-
        tives, Alterities, Anthropologies* [this volume]. Edited by Bruce M.
        Knauft. Bloomington: Indiana University Press.
2002b   Trials of the Oxymodern: Public Practice at Nomad Station. In
        Critically Modern: Alternatives, Alterities, Anthropologies [this vol-
        ume]. Edited by Bruce M. Knauft. Bloomington: Indiana Univer-
        sity Press.

Kulick, Don, and Margaret Willson
1992   Echoing Images: The Construction of Savagery among Papua New
        Guinean Villagers. *Visual Anthropology* 5: 143–52.

Lien, Marianne E.
1997   *Marketing and Modernity*. Oxford: Berg Publishers.

LiPuma, Edward
1999   The Meaning of Money in the Age of Modernity. In *Money and
        Modernity: State and Local Currencies in Melanesia*. Edited by Joel
        Robbins and David Akin, pp. 192–213. Pittsburgh, Penn.: Univer-
        sity of Pittsburgh Press.
2000   *Encompassing Others: The Magic of Modernity in Melanesia*. Ann Ar-
        bor: University of Michigan Press.

Marcus, George
1995   Ethnography in/of the World System: The Emergence of Multi-
        Sited Ethnography. *Annual Review of Anthropology* 24: 95–117.

Meyer, Birgit
2000   Comments. *Current Anthropology* 41(2): 241–42.

Miller, Daniel
1994   Modernity: An Ethnographic Approach. Oxford: Berg Publishers.
1995   Introduction: Anthropology, Modernity and Consumption. In *Worlds
        Apart: Modernity through the Prism of the Local*. Edited by Daniel
        Miller, pp. 1–22. New York: Routledge.

Mitchell, Timothy
2000   Introduction. In *Questions of Modernity*. Edited by Timothy Mitchell,
        pp. xi–xxvii. Minneapolis: University of Minnesota Press.

Moore, Sally Falk
1999   Reflections on the Comaroff Lecture. *American Ethnologist* 26(2):
        304–6.

Nemery, Benoit et al.
1999   Dioxins, Coca-Cola, and Mass Sociogenic Illness in Belgium. *Lancet* 354(9172), p. 77.

Nihill, Michael
1989   The New Pearlshells: Aspects of Money and Meaning in Anganen Exchange. *Canberra Anthropology* 12: 144–60.

Piot, Charles
1999   *Remotely Global: Village Modernity in West Africa.* Chicago: University of Chicago Press.

Reilly, Benjamin
2000/2001   Democracy, Ethnic Fragmentation, and Internal Conflict: Confused Theories, Faulty Data, and the "Crucial Case" of Papua New Guinea. *International Security* 25(3): 162–85.

Robbins, Joel, and David Akin
1999   Introduction to Melanesian Currencies: Agency, Identity and Social Reproduction. In *Money and Modernity: State and Local Currencies in Melanesia.* Edited by David Akin and Joel Robbins, pp. 1–40. Pittsburgh, Penn.: University of Pittsburgh Press.

Rofel, Lisa
2002   Modernity's Masculine Fantasies. In *Critically Modern: Alternatives, Alterities, Anthropologies* [this volume]. Edited by Bruce M. Knauft. Bloomington: Indiana University Press.

Sangren, P. Steven
2000   Comments. *Current Anthropology* 41(2): 243–44.

Strathern, Andrew
1993   Violence and Political Change in Papua New Guinea. *Pacific Studies* 16(4): 41–60.

Strathern, Marilyn
1988   *The Gender of the Gift: Problems with Women and Problems with Society in Melanesia.* Berkeley: University of California Press.

Tomlinson, John
1999   *Globalization and Culture.* Chicago: University of Chicago Press.

Trouillot, Michel-Rolph
1991   Anthropology and the Savage Slot: The Poetics and Politics of Otherness. In *Recapturing Anthropology: Working in the Present.* Edited by Richard Fox, pp. 17–44. Santa Fe: School of American Research Press.
2002   The Otherwise Modern: Caribbean Lessons from the Savage Slot. In *Critically Modern: Alternatives, Alterities, Anthropologies* [this volume]. Edited by Bruce M. Knauft. Bloomington: Indiana University Press.

Wagner, Roy
  1976   *The Invention of Culture.* Chicago: University of Chicago Press.
Wardlow, Holly
  2002   "Hands-Up"–ing Buses and Harvesting Cheese-Pops: Gendered
           Mediation of Modern Disjuncture in Melanesia. In *Critically Mod-
           ern: Alternatives, Alterities, Anthropologies* [this volume]. Edited by
           Bruce M. Knauft. Bloomington: Indiana University Press.
Weber, Max
  1978 [1922]   *Economy and Society: An Outline of Interpretive Sociology.* Ed-
           ited by G. Roth and C. Wittich. Berkeley: University of California
           Press.
Yang, Mayfair
  2000   Putting Global Capitalism in its Place. *Current Anthropology* 41(4):
           477–509.
Young, Michael
  1997   Commemorating Missionary Heroes: Local Christianity and Narra-
           tives of Nationalism. In *Narratives of Nation in the South Pacific.* Ed-
           ited by Ton Otto and Nicholas Thomas, pp. 91–132. Amsterdam:
           Harwood Academic.

Two

Development and Personhood
Tracing the Contours of a
Moral Discourse

Ivan Karp

In an interview he gave towards the end of his life, Jomo Kenyatta was asked why he wrote so much about his "people," the Kikuyu of Kenya:

> One of my deliberate interests. . . . was to produce a book on some aspects of African tradition and culture which would make a real impact on those who had no real knowledge of how Africans lived and thought and organized their own societies. It has often seemed frustrating to represent or negotiate on behalf of people only barely visualized under headings of character or personality. (*Daily Nation*, 24 August 1974)

This remark seems to me to produce the predicament of development written, as it were, from the standpoint of the subjects of development policy and practice. These subjects are called to account in a discourse that defines them as failing to exhibit in their cultures or persons the qualities of developed persons. I argue that this is a discourse with strong continuities derived from the colonial period, but with roots that are far deeper and earlier than colonialism itself. Imperial expansion and colonial rule were the historical mechanisms through which development discourse was transmitted and interpellated; it provided the word system through which imperialism and colonialism were embedded. For the purposes of this chapter, however, I am not going to engage in systematic historical research. Rather, I will present an analysis derived from the materials of my experience in Kenya by considering how Kenyans were presented in administrative discourse during the colonial period in development documents, in media representations of Africa and Africans, and in contemporary Kenyan discourse about personhood and Nation—as in Kenyan president Daniel Arap Moi's assertion a few years ago that Kenya was two hundred years behind the West.

Both modernity and development were present in President Moi's declaration. Development was surely seen as what Kenya presently lacks, but the time frame suggests a specific time lag that placed Kenya in a premodern temporal relationship to the contemporary West. President Moi's public assertions illustrate the connection between development as an ideology and concepts of modernity, as does much of development discourse.

"Development" and "modernity" are key words that are intimately related to one another. They often share a relationship of foreground and background to one another. The invocation of one side of the term customarily depends on implicit understandings of the other. In postcolonial societies, development can be the more pressing and visible term, and the extensive literature on development discourse indicates this. Yet modernity is not something that is left undiscussed; the connection between the two is frequently drawn, even if neither is capable of precise definition. We can note here that precise definition is not a feature of key words. As Williams (1976) shows us, key words are sites of contest and change, where shifts over time express and reflect changing social circumstances while also formulating responses to them. Development and modernity act this way: they take on different meanings depending on the register in which they are used and the circumstances in which they are invoked.

This relationship is manifested both conceptually and in practice. In theories of development, such as modernization theory, modernity is seen as the motor of development. Modern forms of organization related to bureaucracy and industrialization become the cause of development, while development becomes the measurable index of modernity. This is still the case for much of the macroscholarship and policy work on development, where large-scale surveys, such as the World Bank Development Report, are used to measure and rate the state of development —typically in terms of indexes derived from "modern" economies and societies.

Development discourse at the local level in so-called underdeveloped societies may use terms that are translated as "development" but which easily invert the relationship between development and modernity. In East Africa, for example, "development" is the translation term for *maendelo*. *Maendelo* translates literally from the Swahili as "going forward"; it connotes rapid movement toward the some future goal (compare Spitulnik, this volume). Surely this is not completely different from the sense in which "progress" is used in English. It may be noted that progress, including rapid change, can be a defining feature of modernity (e.g., Berman 1982). In Melanesian Tok Pisin, similar connotations are found in the word *kam-ap*, literally to "take off" or "come up" (Dahl and Rabo 1992). Yet as Angelique Haugerud (1995) has shown in her excellent study of development discourse in Kenya, while *maendelo* can be defined as progress, it is measured primarily in terms of goods derived from the outside, such as roads, schools, clinics, and consumer goods. The Kenyan government is judged, in fact, by how successful it has been in providing those goods, even when the government, through its representatives, seeks to allocate responsibility for lack of development to the local people themselves. Thus the local-level discourse and formal government meetings that Haugerud examines display a contest between competing definitions of development that are masked by a shared formal meaning attributed to the term.

This combination of apparent agreement and actual contest is a fundamental aspect of how key words operate in discourse. This operation is given a further twist by the association of some key words with others. In the case of *maendelo*, aspects of both development and modernity are inextricably mixed; the choice to translate the term as one or the other can seem arbitrary from a lexical point of view. Thus, Don Kulick (1992) argues that in the New Guinea society where he did research, Gapun, *kam-ap*, which has real formal similarities to *maendelo* as a concept, is translated as "development" but associated with numerous locally defined attributes of modernity, such as Christianity and command of nonlocal language. Depending on who uses concepts such as *kam-ap* or *maendelo*, and for what purposes, one aspect of these concepts may be foregrounded or backgrounded. Readily available in debate and other forms of discourse is the potential to shift perspective—to engage in what Rodney Needham (1983) refers to as a "change of aspect." The meaning of a concept can shift the terms of discourse itself and create a very different picture of person and society than that implied in an earlier usage. This is certainly true of the concept we easily gloss as "development."

Hence it is not easy or even profitable to define either development or modernity as mutually exclusive concepts that can be contained in any of the many aspects that are used to define them. Modernity is a notoriously slippery concept, the meaning of which ranges from rapid change to abstraction, depending on context. As a concept, "development" may not be as elusive in use, but it is not easy to pin down despite strenuous efforts on the part of development agencies themselves. In practice, development can be measured and defined in both material and nonmaterial terms. But in use, it is highly heteroglossic and contested, as I have shown above.

Clearly what we have here is a complex of ideas and images that is used in manifold ways. But these ways are not unpatterned or lacking in history. This relates to the fact that the association of development and modernity has its origins in the emergence of industrial capitalism and with its accompanying forms of metropolitan life. In the many examples of development discourse and their association with ideas about modernity, substantial contrasts are often drawn between the qualities of urban life and those of rural life and culture. In Kenyan colonial discourse, for example, the Country and the City—to use Raymond Williams' (1973) phrase—defined a contrast between space that was static (lacking in capacity and will to change), as opposed to being dynamic and progressive. As Williams (1973) shows, this association was historically pronounced in England. In further parallel with William's analysis, the Kenyan countryside was seen as a space of stability and morality where "natives" were attached to tribal authorities. By contrast, the city was seen as a space of disorganization and anomie, at least for Africans —more Hobbesian than anything else.

Two government policy papers, published five years apart, show these contrasting images in stark form. In 1947, Norman Humphrey, the senior agricultural officer of the Kenya Colony, argued in an excellent study, *The Liguru and the Land,* that farming practices could be reformed and the countryside made productive if the colonial administration used "traditional land authorities" for whom natives felt a natural attachment. By 1952, the newly installed governor of Kenya Colony, Sir Phillip Mitchell, one of the key figures in the development of indirect rule, argued that these same African countrymen had to be introduced to more rational means of understanding and managing their land if they were to deal with problems of population growth and underdevelopment of productive resources. Mitchell draws a stark contrast between the cultural achievements of Europeans and the absence of technological advancement found among rural Africans. For Mitchell, the problem had nothing to do with "traditional authorities" (notwithstanding his advocacy of indirect rule) but with agricultural education. Yet within a decade, after the Mau Mau rebellion, the cultural discourse in Kenyan official and settler society was concerned with turning the Kikuyu people (and other Africans) from detribalized urban dwellers into an organized tribe once again.

These striking and rapid shifts in discourse about development and other matters seem to me to draw on the imagery of early industrial capitalism described by both Williams and E. P. Thompson. Both argue that these discursive formations are carried forward in association with capitalist and imperial expansion. Their suggestions are, in my judgment, more than borne out by the Kenyan experience. More than agricultural policy in a settler colony is at stake in the post–World War II Kenyan official documents cited above. A key problem that officials have grappled with in their official discourse is how to transform one kind of society—primarily rural and focused on reproduction of personnel—to one designed to provide rural resources to the industrial or (in the case of Kenya) export sector of society. This problem—the production of a labor force that could also feed itself—was a key economic concern of colonial Kenya, focused as it was on a plantation-based settler economy and agricultural export.

The transformation of labor is just what Thompson points to in his many studies of early industrialization in England. From a cultural point of view, Thompson shows that what is at stake is the nature of the laborer and the means required to turn a rural subject into an urban, industrial worker. This has obvious parallels in the colonial experience, even when the transformation is supposed to happen primarily in the countryside. This was not lost on E. P. Thompson (1991:396), who observes, "For what was said by the mercantilist moralists as to the failures of the eighteenth century English poor to respond to incentives and disciplines if often repeated, by observers and by theorists of economic growth, of the people of developing countries today." Those failures, as Thompson shows, were attributed to Human Nature itself. "the transition to industrial society entailed a severe restructuring or working habits—new disciplines, new incentives, and a new human nature on which these incentives could bite effectively" (1991:354). For Thompson, the inevitably and always unfinished transition opened up a debate and contest over economic growth that was also a debate about human nature itself. And it is precisely in the intersection between assertions about the conditions under which growth will happen and the nature of the subjects that should be the motor of growth that ideas about modernity (as a phenomenon that is opposed to what comes before) and development once again intersect. How they intersect will be the subject of the remainder of this chapter, where I seek to examine the nature of human nature, as exhibited in ideas about the person, and the concept of development as ambivalently elaborated in different contexts and debated in practice.

Development Discourse

Development discourse predicates two kinds of human nature in conflict and describes the result in terms of agency—the raw material on which development is worked, and the agents of development. This discourse, derived from the aftermath of Western imperial and colonial expansion, reproduces startlingly similar ideas about the person in a wide range of settings. These include popular presentations that seek to interpret and explain difference of all sorts, academic contexts that make development the object of inquiry, professional events held within the development community and for its clients, and official and political discourses ranging from policy documents and reports to political speeches and parliamentary debates. Not all of these forums reproduce these ideas in the same fashion. The majority of technical reports tend to assert ideas about human agents more by asides than through explicit texts. By contrast, popular presentations are more explicit about how human agents are classified than is the case in the technical reports they draw on.

From a narrow point of view, development discourse refers primarily to materials produced during technical assessment, policy making, and implementation. This definition has the merit of limiting development policy, plans, and reports to those produced by a correspondingly narrow range of individuals: professionals who write for one another and who are generally aware of their shared identity, however geographically dispersed. This restricted view of development discourse makes some sense for the residents of the metropolitan countries that once possessed colonies—that is, for what is now thought of as the first, developed world, but which is better conceived of as the dominant pole of the world capitalist system. But this definition of development discourse makes no sense whatsoever for the other pole: the people acted upon in the ex-colonies themselves, where "development" (or the lack of it) is a fundamental feature of national and personal discourse.

Understanding development discourse as only the product of a narrowly defined professional cadre greatly limits our understanding of its discursive field and social consequences in at least three ways. First, development professionals produce knowledge not only for their own professions but for the communities whose interests they claim to serve; they seek to mobilize communities for development and to legitimize their activities to make them more effective. Second, because they are culturally formative, professionals actively share notions of development with their clients and sponsors, and with the broader publics to which they relate. These communications interact in recursive fashion with the clients' and sponsors' own responses concerning what it means to be developed or to lack development. Third, development is no more a purely technical concept than is "civilization" or "primitive." Much of the recent work that unpacks these terms in popular discourses, such as travel writing, applies equally well to development discourse.[1] Popular presentations of development mobilize support for or against activities ranging from projects to foreign policy itself.

All the parties engaged in development institutions and encounters have ideas about development. Often the parties assume that these ideas are commensurate and do not inquire about how local terms share or do not share meaning with discourse produced out of other settings. Anthropology, more than any other discipline, has shown that development projects cannot be portrayed as consensual affairs. The goals and practices associated with "development" are not necessarily shared by all the participants. Misunderstanding is produced as well as communication, and local participants can subvert development goals at the same time as they produce the semblance of assent (Crehan and Von Oppen 1988).

Neither professional concepts nor popular ideas about development— nor the judgments and ideas about cultures and persons that these imply—are exclusively made and produced inside the "developed" world for export to the "undeveloped" remainder. Like colonialism, development is not for export only. The media in the United States and Kenya participate in a global system, often sharing the same ideas and imagery. But surely there are significant differences in circulation and reception within these spaces. In the developed world, ideas and images of the undeveloped, and the contrasts drawn between the undeveloped world and the developed countries, often appear as a contemporary parallel to the turn-of-the-century World Fairs described by Tony Bennett (1988): settings where a disparate Western audience can imagine itself as a homogenous same juxtaposed to an exotic Other.

Nor is this connection between colonialism and imperial expansion on the one hand and development on the other only a parallel. Ideas about development and the persons who possess or lack developed qualities are a central feature of colonial ideology carried over to and flourishing in the postcolonial period. Development ideology is one of the constituting features of a global system that is heir to colonial and imperial domination. The central place that ideas about development and personhood play in the world system make them *dominant*, in Raymond Williams' (1977) terminology. From this point of view, postcoloniality is barely emergent, more a hope than a reality.

Discourse in and about Kenya

Development discourse in and about Kenya illustrates many of the above points. Some years ago, National Public Radio's (NPR's) *Weekend Edition* aired an extraordinary fifteen-minute report featuring a labor cooperative founded by residents of Mathare Valley in Nairobi, Kenya. This women's cooperative had been contracted to make roof tiles for a large local housing development, providing its members with substantial incomes for the first time in their lives. "To understand how far these women have come in the past year," said Daniel Zwerdling, the program's producer, "you need to know where they began—in the slums of Mathare Valley. Some say Mathare is one of the worst slums in Africa. One of the co-op members who lives there . . . took me on a tour down twisting alleyways of mud and sewage past unemployed men sitting on rocks for stools, past babies crawling through goat excrement. Hundreds of thousands of people live here in tiny shacks squeezed together like cells of a honeycomb and the shacks, as [she] showed me in her home, are made of garbage" (1991). Violence, theft, and wife-beating are endemic.

Many of these observations are accurate—but severely limited in what they admit. Houses in Mathare Valley are made of materials that American consumers would either discard as refuse or save for recycling. In some areas of urban Kenya (as in rural America and many other parts of the world where incomes are limited and government housing codes are erratically enforced), bricolage housing is not unusual. In Mathare Valley, houses are also built with found materials by use of techniques adapted from "traditional" wattle-and-daub rural housing. But cardboard and tin constructions are not necessarily watertight, as the women interviewed by Zwerdling tell us, and Mathare Valley, after all, is a slum.

Visitors to Kenya are often taken to Mathare Valley to see poverty in its extreme form, as well as for the ironic contrast that its geography provides. Mathare is situated across a river valley from Muthaiga—a Nairobi suburb whose luxurious homes are occupied by wealthy Kenyans, diplomats, and well-paid expatriate development officials. It is also the home of the famous colonial country club that provided a major set for the popular American film *Out of Africa*. The visual contrast between Muthaiga and Mathare is sharp.

All the same, Mathare Valley is not a scene of total disorganization. The community is a setting for intense informal sector economic activity. Jewelry-making and weaving cooperatives are common. Mathare is also a primary Nairobi setting where *Jua Kali* ("hot sun") artisans work and live. Jewelry making, weaving, auto repair, tin smithing, and brewing are all thriving industries in Mathare. In fact, a line of expensive Mercedes and Peugeots can often be found outside a mud and tin Mathare house and garage, awaiting repair.[2]

Although the 240 members of the women's roof-tile cooperative had clearly acquired new technical skills and found an economic niche (first-year earnings: 1 million Kenyan shillings), Zwerdling nonetheless argues that their success was due to an additional factor:

> Development specialists say one reason a lot of projects fail in Africa is because the organizers spend all their time training people how to do specific tasks such as how to make a tile that doesn't crack, and they neglect another kind of training that's even more important in the long run. The Humama Co-op is trying to avoid that by giving the women hours of what [the Norwegian development specialist who started the self-help group] calls "social training."

[The specialist tells us:]

> How to interact in a group, how you cope with the fact that one is a manager, one is a foreman, several people are workers, some are on machines producing fancy things, others are just carrying. When they were all neighbors in a slum and equally poor, how do you cope with that? That is a skill you have to develop. (1991:5)

These assertions were followed by a member of the cooperative describing how she had learned to "listen" and adjudicate disputes, unlike her usual experience of life in Mathare Valley.

The laudable goal of this well-meaning presentation was to prove to its audience that development projects can be effective in Africa and that it is worthwhile to spend resources, if done properly. Yet the subtext of the report subverts that goal. This is the picture of the life and culture of Mathare Valley residents drawn by NPR: these are a people living in substandard, crowded conditions, brutalized by violence, lacking basic "social skills" (like cooperation) that would enable them to ameliorate their dire condition. They are the victimized poor, utterly lacking in both material and cultural means of improving themselves.

Weekend Edition's audience learns that successful development demands more than a transformation in technical knowledge and material existence, since the women of Mathare Valley must also learn how to become new kinds of persons. Lacking "social skills," they must be shown the values of cooperation. Totally ignored in this picture is

Mathere Valley's thriving informal sector economy and the complex, ingenious ways the slum's residents have already managed to "develop" themselves through the extensive use of cooperatives.

Zwerdling may have learned about the tile-making cooperative from an article in the magazine section of the *Kenya Times*, the generally celebratory national party newspaper, which described the successes of this group as "a shining example of poor women's determination" (*Kenya Times*, 4 April 1990, Focus 7).[3] It described Mathere as a slum and the achievement of the women of one cooperative as an escape from the poverty of their residential environment and the degraded life they led as prostitutes and liquor brewers:

> Humama is a success and should inspire other poor women. Their advice to their sisters: "Unity is strength and we would be happy to be emulated by other poor people in the world."

Both accounts of the labor cooperative are confident that Mathare Valley is a scene of economic and spiritual poverty, and both are equally confident that its economic success is the product of alterations of internal states. NPR predicates an internal change in moral attitudes derived from without, while the *Kenya Times* celebrates the innate personal qualities that enabled the women to transcend the conditions of their existence, which make them different from their sisters.

Zwerdling's well-intentioned account of Mathare Valley echoes an assertion made in Kenya at an earlier time, but spoken with a less indulgent attitude. Writing about his African medical assistants in 1926, the head of the colonial medical service in Kenya declared that their "technical knowledge is easily acquired . . . but a sense of responsibility, pertinacity, honesty and general trustworthiness are woefully lacking" (Arnold 1988:7). Then as now, African subjects were defined as possessing two aspects to their person—a practical side associated with mastery over nature, and a social side associated with the skills and moral attributes derived from the dominant patterns in their social relations.

Although I suspect that the chief medical officer did not think that fundamental alterations in the social-skills or moral attribute side of African personhood would be as easy to accomplish as Daniel Zwerdling does, both define the human material on which development works (and out of which it emerges) in the same fashion: as inert material to be transformed from outside—by means of new social forms called "discipline" in the colonial period and "social training" in the NPR report.

The "social training" provided to the Humama cooperative presumably teaches its members to rely on one another and to perform their duties in a responsible, honest, and trustworthy fashion. The moral coloration of Zwerdling's judgments, while less overt and more charitable than those of Kenya Colony's chief medical officer's opinions about African morality, nonetheless bears a strong resemblance to them. By virtue of an external agency, the woman who comprise this cooperative become exceptions to the Mathare (and by extension, African) rule. Even the *Kenya Times* treats the subjects of its story as exceptions. They are "shining examples" only because they had unusual internal qualities that enabled them to rise above Mathare. While the NPR report makes the women of the Humana cooperative like the mass of undeveloped Africans, except for their training, the *Kenya Times* makes them the exception to the masses by virtue of their personal qualities. Neither report questions the assumption that internal states such as moral qualities are the effective cause of underdevelopment. As a result, the only means through which underdevelopment can be opposed is through some form of personal transformation or conversion.

NPR's account of a successful development project in Kenya explicitly derives its authority from no less a source than the 1989 World Bank report, *Sub-Saharan Africa: From Crisis to Sustainable Growth,* which advocates a populist "bottom-up" development agenda combined with stringent structural adjustment policies. According to this report, a major source of Africa's failure to implement successful development programs has been a "misconceived" government-sponsored "dash for 'modernization,' copying, but not adapting Western models" (World Bank 1989:3). It is not difficult to see that the outcome of this influential policy statement, along with its predecessors, has been structural adjustment rather than the populist goal of shifting development away from the government and to the people.

What concerns me in this chapter is not policy as such, but the grounds out of which development discourse and, ipso facto, policy statements are generated. The NPR example is public discourse and not policy statement, but the grounds remain the same. Development discourse moves easily among media and through the different spheres of public and popular life, governmental and policy forums, and into academic life itself. An American story *about* Kenya is (in all likelihood) derived from a Kenyan newspaper story *about* Kenya, and these in turn are derived from development activities themselves which legitimate the stories and are, in turn, legitimated by the stories. What all of these share in common are the grounding assumptions about cultures and persons that authorize them. At the same time, the challenges to these stories that are articulated at the local level or in movements that pose alternatives to development orthodoxies also share their same grounding assumptions, even if and when they share them primarily to contest them.

Grounds of Development Discourse

What, then, are some of the grounding assumptions of development discourse? Development discourse consists of hierarchical images of self and other based on shared personal qualities and the cultural and social institutions that produce the "developed" or "undeveloped" person. The fragments of this discourse echo and quote one another, often unknowingly; their signs and images become systemic through repetition and reproduction across time, space, and social setting. Sometimes sincerely produced, sometimes ironically quoted, used to defend or oppose, this discourse nurtures a cultural environment in which humans are classified, interpreted, and ultimately explained. These fragments are used in the production of stories, such as Daniel Zwerdling's attempt to explain why Africa should not be abandoned by American foreign aid and development agencies, or the *Kenya Times*' attempt to demonstrate that development works in Kenya for some *kinds* of people. By implication, these stories assert that only a personal transformation will make development work.

The history of development theory, its Enlightenment roots, its colonial associations, and the positions of its various proponents and scholarly critics all suggest that development discourse, in the narrow sense, is sustained by a classificatory scheme that establishes differences among cultures and in types of personhood.[4] Arturo Escobar (1988), for example, has examined a series of development documents pertaining to Latin America and concludes that development projects invariably identify the subject's culture and society as the cause of backwardness or resistance to change. Perhaps the most elegant version of this discourse cited by Escobar is the World Bank report on a project in Colombia that begins, "Culture always lags behind economic change." Other scholars provide accounts of the semantics of development, and a long-standing literature relates assumptions of development discourse to modernization theory (Binder 1986; Sachs 1992). What is missing in this history, however, are accounts of development theory's *assumptions* about personhood and the moral judgments they imply.

The nature of persons on whom development processes were presumed to work was clearly set out in David McClelland's orthodox but still popular model for teaching people to desire economic achievement (McClelland 1961; McClelland and Winter 1969). McClelland's liberal and relativist model of economic action argued that under the right conditions, members of other societies could be taught to strive for economic achievement. For McClelland, economic achievement does not raise problems of translation between cultures. People placed in the right situations will recognize the rational basis of achievement desires, and in principle, there are no cultural obstacles to appreciating the rationality of forms of maximization. Hence, successful development depended on producing persons who have learned and internalized the appropriate set of values and desires.

Generations of development specialists were trained in McClelland's theory and techniques of inducing motivational change. Although the new conservative development orthodoxy no longer favors McClelland's notions, much of the current popular and economic discourse, perhaps most recently in Eastern Europe, seems to have adopted McClelland's position without attribution. Media discussions accordingly feature "experts" who argue the contradictory but fruitful propositions that (1) the lasting effect of communist rule is that Eastern Europeans must be taught to value profit making, and that (2) the entrepreneurial spirit is stifling economic change by being refractory to larger-scale orchestration and direction.

Even the new conservative orthodoxy in development planning and research, which is antistatist and market oriented, articulates a theory of culture and personhood not fundamentally different from McClelland's. It still sees the person either as material to be developed or as trapped in a system that prevents development. One of the major statements of the conservative orthodoxy, the 1984 World Bank report, is unswerving both in its devotion to an antistatist position and in its faith that the public sector prevents development. But the manner in which it identifies local impediments to development echoes approaches from older theories of development that aspire to use the state as an instrument of change.

In one of the most important precursors to the 1984 report, the so-called Berg report on Africa, a policy statement which also favors the free play of markets and condemns government intervention, the World Bank announces that "physical investment is only one determinant of the spread of development. Human development is at least as important, and sound government action remains at its core" (1982:1). This relatively opaque statement might be construed as a common-sense appeal for training in new techniques of production and management skills. When John Toye (1987) examined this specific literature and the studies underlying the World Bank position, he found that when the role of physical capital formation is discounted, it is usually accompanied by unelaborated statements about problems inherent in existing forms of human capital. Toye tells us that for P. T. Bauer (one of the leading theorists of the new development economics), "the explanatory weight [of why economies grow] is borne by [what Bauer called] personal qualities, social institutions, and mores and political arguments that make for endeavor and achievement . . . or people's capacities, attitudes, values and beliefs" (Toye 1987:62). Bauer's writings assert that different cultures affect the distribution of these capacities, attitudes, values, and beliefs, but in common with virtually all studies in development economics, they contain no empirical demonstration of these assertions. Toye (1987:62) observes:

> It is ironical that, as a young economist, Bauer began by criticizing the stereotypes which colonial administrators applied to colonial populations. Not all peasants [in Bauer's view] were lazy, of limited ambition, and risk adverse, he saw, although his elders believed otherwise. But having rejected one stereotype, he quickly settled for another. Whether they have these qualities or not depends on which cultural group they belong to.

World War II marks the transition from colonial discourse to development discourse. The end of the colonial period manifested a concern with social welfare and infrastructure development (concerning Africa, see Cooper 1996). These became major concerns of the post–World War II period, which was also distinguished by remarkable swings from state-oriented to market-oriented development policies, articulated by such major government and international organizations as the World Bank, African nations, and donor country agencies such as USAID. As Michael Watts (1995) argues, this literature and the programs it authorizes have oscillated between two poles: top-down, state-oriented programs and bottom-up, populist development agendas. These policy debates divide the development community over points of entry, means of development, and factors that retard economic development. As disputatious and labile as development debates and projects appear to be over time, changes in critical assumptions are nonetheless restricted by limits. Although their mechanics, strategies, and rationalizations may exhibit drastic changes, assumptions about the people involved in development enterprises change far less. Development discourse retains and reproduces notions about how cultures and persons are ranked, and these notions preserve the boundaries of theoretical discourse by providing reasons for the success or failure of development projects. Both the 1950 World Bank plan for Colombia and the Berg report contain these notions, despite the fact that they are otherwise opposed about the possibility of producing change with government collaboration. Yet neither the World Bank nor any other development entity has ever undertaken a major, systematic research program to test whether such factors as culture, religion, gender, class, or community of origin affect willingness and ability to engage in economic development projects.[5]

Ideas about differences in culture, capacity, morality, and personhood in development discourse are guided by an ostensibly "anthropological paradigm" that is mostly apparent more by asides and assumptions than in writing and planning. This is rarely the object of comment except by a few dissenting scholars such as John Toye, as mentioned above. The larger paradigm is familiar because it reproduces major features of colonial and orientalist thinking about exotic cultures.

This discourse is anthropological because it is based on a scheme for classifying cultures. I would hope that it is superfluous to add that it is not a discourse made *by* anthropologists or characteristic of professional anthropologists' thinking about cultures. This conflation is often made by the less alert readers of accounts of anthropological discourses. For instance, most who read V. Y. Mudimbe's *The Invention of Africa* (1988) fail to read the last chapter of the book, in which Mudimbe pleads for an empirically engaged anthropology as a solution to the dilemmas of operating within the limits of the dominant discursive formation. In a more historical vein, Henricka Kuklick (1991) has shown how Africanist anthropologists of the functionalist sort were regarded as a hindrance by colonial officials interested in research that would confirm *their* anthropological discourse. Kuklick's report of Lord Hailey's "exasperation" with functionalist anthropologists is telling. "Anthropological expertise was so vital to colonial development," said Hailey in 1946, "that if the anthropologist would not supply colonial regimes with necessary information, we must find someone calling himself by a different name who will do so" (quoted in Kuklick 1991:14). Perhaps this is a privileged insight into the birth of the development expert? Kuklick describes how anthropologists were viewed as both useless and resistant. If anthropologists were in the pay of colonial regimes, they had a very poor employment record, one which has been confirmed in the notorious reluctance of development agencies to employ anthropologists.

What is anthropological about development discourse is hence not that it draws on anthropological theory, but that it is a set of assumptions about how cultural differences are constituted and manifested in action. What links development discourse to these other discourses are the similarities in the ways they define "same" and "other," and the ways in which these are constructed as exotic and quotidian. The primary element in development thinking that concerns me here, however, is less the orientalist trope of defining the other as lacking features of the Western self than the more oblique discursive strategy of thinking about subjects of development as exceptions to the universal rules that govern the evolution of human societies. This is the special, but not unique, twist that development discourse gives to the construction of the Other. What are involved here are not simply exoticizing strategies of representation, for the semiotic movements are more complex. All peoples are initially made equivalent only to set up a hierarchy in which some peoples are shown to be exceptions to historical processes. At one and the same time, all people are admitted to a universal category, even as some are denied full membership on the grounds that they are excep-tions to the rule.[6]

Writing as the subject of this type of universalizing discourse, Carlos Fuentes (1974:85) describes this discursive strategy as follows:

A writer born in Poland or Mexico, so far from the gods and so near to the devils, realizes before he is out of knee pants that it is one thing to write from within a culture that deems itself central and another to write from the boundaries of eccentricity—an ec-centricity defined by the central culture's claim to universality. The central culture tends to believe that it speaks with the words of God, or, at least, that it has a direct and open line to the ear of divinity. Behind [these] unselfconscious attitudes . . . stood the weighty conviction, elaborated by the philosophy of the Enlighten-ment, that human nature is always one and the same for all men, although imperfectly developed, as Locke put it, in children, mad-men and savages; and that this true human nature is to be found, permanently fixed, in Europe and in European elites.

Carlos Fuentes writes to a different audience than development special-ists. Addressing a literary audience, his concern is to explore differences in the experience of acknowledged heirs to a literary tradition and of those who are granted grudging admission to it. Fuentes describes the marginalization that excludes some cultural formations from admission to a canon. Development discourse shares some of these features but operates in a slightly different fashion. It cannot explicitly exclude or marginalize the very agents whom it addresses and strives to transform. Instead, it defines the subjects of development as exceptions whose very exceptional nature is the problem that development theory seeks to un-derstand and that development practices seek to transform. Develop-ment discourse creates both the material to be transformed and defines the process of transformation.[7]

The very act of creating exceptions to the processes deemed to be universal, such as development itself, generates a puzzle about human nature. In particular, it raises questions about differences in personhood and agency answered by the assumptions enshrined in the anthropological paradigm of development theory. If all people are equal, are there exceptions to this generalization? What causes can be adduced to account for these exceptions? Most importantly, what actions are needed to move people from being exceptions to serving as examples of universal rules?

At this point, we seem to have moved a long way from the Industrial Revolution as it is described by E. P. Thompson, where a new form of human nature is the apparent goal of practices such as time keeping in factories and the discourse of human nature that is associated with them. The problem of human nature specified here is exceptionalism, the anthropological puzzle of why people seemingly possessed with the same capacities as the dominant fraction of a colonial or postcolonial society appear and act differently—especially when this difference manifests itself as a "lack of development." But the differences are not so great as they might appear, especially if one considers differences between early and late capitalist development itself. The puzzle of how to produce a different human nature is prospective. It envisions a future in which all are the same. Seen from the perspective of that future, which has actually been characterized by patterns of uneven development and acts of passive and active resistance, the puzzle takes the form of triumphalism disappointed. It is not how to make new human beings, but given that all human beings are alike, why are "they" so different?

Whichever historical juncture one uses to situate the problem of human nature, the solutions posed assume that there are categories of people—members of different cultures, men and women, young and old—whose critical differences in personhood and agency have consequences for development. Personhood and agency are concepts that mutually implicate one another (Jackson and Karp 1990). Agency refers to the effects of actions on the world, while concepts of personhood entail notions about the different capacities people have to produce these effects. Any scheme for classifying cultures and persons will carry with it ideas about personhood and agency.

In the long anthropological and philosophical tradition of writing about personhood, a major distinction stands out. Meyer Fortes (1989) formulated this as a distinction between two aspects of personhood: the person and the individual. The person is the "objective side," the roles, capacities, rights, and duties that a society endows upon its members. By contrast, the individual is the "subjective side," related to how the person knows or experiences what is socially endowed. Fortes's extensive work on personhood explores the space between social endowment and subjective experience.[8] In encounters organized by the discourse of development, a space is set up in which different concepts of personhood and agency are put forward, and some actors, at least, experience considerable discrepancies between who they think themselves to be and how they find themselves defined.

This is the space that Fuentes describes in his essay, a space which also emerges in colonial or orientalist discourse. The anthropological paradigm of development theory constructs categories of persons and grants greater capacities and authority to some categories on the basis of differences in the presumed effects they have on the world. Development theory and its anthropological paradigm pose solutions to development problems in emotionally flat and neutral terms associated with most professional communities. There are moral overtones and discriminatory attitudes manifested in development theory, but they remain implicit and understated. It is difficult to imagine, however, that they have no consequences. They inform more general notions of what it means to be modern—both ours and theirs. Not that these notions are entirely accepted. The ways that ideas about development, such as the Swahili concept of *maendeleo,* take on different meanings according to who expresses them—how they become redefined in unpredictable ways—show that personhood is more than simply a matter of being assigned a status and identity. It is a field in which the discrepancies between the definition of the person and the experience of the individual are played out in complex discourses of development and in ideas about hierarchies of cultures and persons that are encoded in them.

Fundamental questions are encoded in professional and popular uses of the concept of development. I have already argued that development invokes ideas about modernity, who possesses them, and how they are possessed. But we should not forget that development is the discourse of nation-states and the global political structures that cut across them. International agencies and governmental and nongovernmental organizations alike are engaged in the task of development. In many postcolonial societies, the development agency is the form through which the international order connects the local to the global. Hence it is vitally important to keep in mind that the discourse of development is at one and the same time a global discourse, an ambivalent discourse that cannot fully make up its mind about the nature of the subjects who act and are acted on, and a hierarchical discourse that sets up distinctions among cultures and persons. In the end, I believe that discourses of development are a key means through which the world system defines itself. Development and the questions raised by various forms of international inequality are "the hidden text of the discourse between North and South" (Thompson 1991).

Acknowledgments

Earlier versions of this chapter were delivered before the Program of African Studies at Northwestern University and the Committee on African and African American Studies at the University of Chicago at their Red Lion seminar series, and to the Anthropology Department of Emory University. I would like to thank Chris Udry, William Monroe, Micaela di Leonardo, Tim Burke, Luise White, Randall Packard, and, most of all, Corinne Kratz for comments and suggestions. The final version of this paper owes a great deal to Bruce Knauft's suggestions and criticisms.

Notes

1. An excellent account of travelers' narratives that show the relationship between ideas about human nature and labor is J. M. Coetzee's "Idleness in South Africa" (1988).

2. In *The African Artisan: Education and the Informal Sector in Kenya*, Kenneth King makes the ironic point that the success of this thriving artisanal sector is due largely to Kenya's heavy reliance on imported machinery that can be cannibalized, such as automobiles (1977:57).

3. The *Kenyan Times'* shining light at the end of the tunnel language in fact recurs in the imagery through which Zwerdling contrasts the horrifying lives of the drinking, drug-abusing, spouse-abusing slum dwellers (before) and the warm glow that emanates from the happy, productive cooperative members (after): "When I visited the factory one morning, I found thousands of roof tiles drying in the sun like pink slippers on giant shoe racks. The women stopped the machines and put down their shovels for a few minutes and formed a circle to give a traditional visitor's welcome."

4. See H. W. Arndt's *Economic Development: The History of an Idea* (1987) for an excellent historical account of the origins of ideas about economic development, primarily in the post–World War II era.

5. See John Peel's (1977) excellent article on how cultural and religious factors have been used as isolated elements in explaining responses to development. Peel rightly points out that a major conceptual flaw in the academic research on development is that culture is conceived of in isolation from spheres of human activity such as politics and economy. He writes, "The serious task for sociology, and especially the sociology of development, is to

set about the analysis of cultural traditions, not as disembodied emanations of original ideals, but as definitions that shape and are modified by each new context. Development does not occur apart from men's interpretations of their situation and ideas for the future" (1977:303).

6. The semiotic structure of asserting a universal category of human being and setting up exceptions depends on establishing a dialectic of sameness and difference, in which the other is made different after being assimilated to the same. This process has been described primarily in the contexts of exhibits of other cultures (Karp 1991; Karp and Kratz 2000; cf. Barthes 1972).

7. See a similar argument about the ways in which multiple discursive spaces are constructed around Okiek notions of "tradition" in Kratz's "We've Always Done it this Way, Except for a Few Details: 'Tradition' and 'Innovation' in Okiek Ceremonies" (1993).

8. Most of Fortes' essays on personhood and the individual have been collected in *Religion, Morality and the Person* (1989).

References

Arndt, Heinz W.
  1987   *Economic Development: The History of an Idea.* Chicago: University of Chicago Press.

Arnold, David
  1988   *Imperial Medicine and Indigenous Societies.* Manchester: Manchester University Press.

Barthes, Roland
  1972   The Great Family of Man. In *Mythologies*, pp. 100–103. New York: Hill and Wang.

Bennett, Tony
  1988   The Exhibitionary Complex. *New Formations* 4 (spring): 73–102.

Berman, Marshall
  1982   *All That Is Solid Melts into Air.* New York: Simon and Schuster.

Binder, Leonard
  1986   The Natural History of Development Theory. *Comparative Studies in Society and History* 28: 3–33.

Coetzee, J. M.
  1988   Idleness in South Africa. In *White Writing: On the Culture of Letters in South Africa*, 12–36. New Haven, Conn.: Yale University Press.

Cooper, Fred
  1996   *Decolonization and African Society.* Cambridge: Cambridge University Press.

Crehan, Kate, and Achim Von Oppen
1988 Understandings of "Development": An Arena of Struggle. *Sociologia Ruralis* 28 (2/3): 113–45.

Dahl, Gudrun, and A. Rabo
1992 [Eds.] *Kam-Ap or Take-Off: Local Notions of Development.* Stockholm: Almquist and Wiksell for Stockholm Studies in Social Anthropology.

Escobar, Arturo
1988 Power and Visibility: Development and the Invention and Management of the Third World. *Cultural Anthropology* 3(4): 428–43.

Fortes, Meyer
1989 *Religion, Morality and the Person.* Cambridge: Cambridge University Press.

Fuentes, Carlos
1974 Central and Eccentric Writing. *American Review* 21: 84–102.

Haugerud, Angelique
1995 *The Culture of Politics in Modern Kenya.* Cambridge: Cambridge University Press.

Humphrey, Norman
1947 *The Liguru and the Land.* Nairobi: Government Printer of the Colony and Protectorate of Kenya.

Jackson, Michael, and Ivan Karp
1990 Personhood and Agency. In *Personhood and Agency: The Experience of Self and Other in African Societies.* Edited by Michael Jackson and Ivan Karp, pp. 15–30. Washington, D.C.: Smithsonian Institution Press.

Karp, Ivan
1991 Culture and Representation. In *Exhibiting Cultures: The Poetics and Politics of Museum Display.* Edited by Ivan Karp and Steven D. Lavine, pp. 11–25. Washington, D.C.: Smithsonian Institution Press.

Karp, Ivan, and Corinne Kratz
2000 Reflections in the Fate of Tippoo's Tiger: Defining Cultures through Public Display. In *Cultural Encounters: Communicating Otherness.* Edited by E. Hallam and B. Street, pp. 194–229. London: Routledge.

King, Kenneth
1977 *The African Artisan: Education and the Informal Sector in Kenya.* London: Heinemann Educational.

Kratz, Corinne
1993 We've Always Done it this Way, Except for a Few Details; "Tradition" and "Innovation" in Okiek Ceremonies. *Comparative Studies in Society and History,* 35(1): 30–65.

Kuklick, Henricka
  1991 *The Savage Within: The Social History of British Anthropology, 1885–1945.* Cambridge: Cambridge University Press.

Kulick, Don
  1992 "Coming Up" in Gapun: Conceptions of Development and Their Effect on Language in a Papua New Guinea Village. In *Kam-Ap or Take-Off: Local Notions of Development.* Edited by Gudrun Dahl and A. Rabo, pp. 10–35. Stockholm: Almquist and Wiksell for Stockholm Studies in Social Anthropology.

McClelland, David C.
  1961 *The Achieving Society.* Princeton: Van Nostrand.

McClelland, David C., and David G. Winter
  1969 *Motivating Economic Achievement.* New York: Free Press.

Mitchell, Sir Phillip
  1952 *The Agrarian Problem in Kenya.* Nairobi: Government Printer, Colony and Protectorate of Kenya.

Mudimbe, V. Y.
  1988 *The Invention of Africa.* Bloomington: Indiana University Press.

Needham, Rodney
  1983 *Against the Tranquility of Axioms.* Berkeley: University of California Press.

Peel, J. D. Y.
  1977 Cultural Factors in the Contemporary Theory of Development. *Archives Européennes de Sociologie* 14(2): 283–303.

Sachs, Wolfgang
  1992 *The Development Dictionary.* New York: St. Martin's Press.

Spitulnik, Debra A.
  2002 Accessing "Local" Modernities: Reflections on the Place of Linguistic Evidence in Ethnography. In *Critically Modern: Alternatives, Alterities, Anthropologies* [this volume]. Edited by Bruce M. Knauft. Bloomington: Indiana University Press.

Toye, John
  1987 *Dilemmas of Development: Reflections on the Counter-Revolution in Development Theory and Practice.* Oxford: Basil Blackwell.

Thompson, E. P.
  1991 *Customs in Common: Studies in Traditional Popular Culture.* New York: New Press.

Watts, Michael
  1995 "A New Deal in Emotions": Theory and Practice in the Crisis of Development. In *Power of Development.* Edited by Jonathan Crush, pp. 44–62. London: Routledge.

Williams, Raymond
  1973 *The Country and the City.* London: Oxford University Press.

1976   *Keywords: A Vocabulary of Culture and Society.* New York: Oxford.

1977   *Marxism and Literature.* London: Oxford University Press.

World Bank

1982   *Accelerated Development in Sub-Saharan Africa: An Agenda for Action.* Washington, D.C.: World Bank.

1984   *Toward Sustainable Development in Sub-Saharan Africa: A Joint Program of Action.* Washington, D.C.: World Bank.

1989   *Sub-Saharan Africa: From Crisis to Sustainable Growth.* Washington, D.C.: World Bank.

Zwerdling, Daniel

1991   Transcript of National Public Radio's *Weekend Edition on Sunday* report on a development project in Mathare Valley, Nairobi, Kenya (19 May 1991).

Three

Trials of the Oxymodern
Public Practice at Nomad Station

Bruce M. Knauft

The impetus to be or become modern refracts differently in alternative world areas, and anthropologists have considered this process through a range of related terms and concepts. In recent years, multiples of modernity have been referred to as "alternative modernities," "parallel modernities," "vernacular modernities," "subaltern modernities," "other modernities," "multiple modernities," or simply "our modernity."[1] Most of these formulations have several features in common. First, they focus our attention on the articulation between features that are international or global and those that are national or local in scale. Second, they force us to consider the relation between structures of market economy or political power and those of cultural orientation and subjective experience. The conceptualization of an alternative modernity attempts to capture the discordance that actors face as they grapple with a desire to be progressive or modern while attempting to do so on their own terms and in ways that are meaningful to them. As Marshall Sahlins (2001:7) put it, "people all around the world. . . . recycle elements of their traditional existence in the construction of their own indigenous versions of modernity."

A relativized notion of modernity is designed to make our understanding of contemporary circumstance acute by fusing into a single concept the paradox of contemporary experience: people are subject to increasing influences in common at the same time that they maintain, if not increase, their cultural and subjectivity diversity. The alternatively modern captures and internalizes this contradiction. In a sense, the notion of a plural modern is an oxymoron: it combines discordant or contradictory elements—the global and the local, the cultural and the politicoeconomic—to focus our attention and spur our thought and investigation. Focusing on the relative nature of modernity connects our understanding of global forces to our understanding of local responses; it brings the hegemonic and subaltern directly together and prompts us to view each in the context of the other's so-called development.

The tensions inherent to the alternatively modern raise larger questions. In what ways does the experience of actors echo the literal meaning of an oxymoron—not just a contradiction in terms, but a meaningfully acerbic discontinuity? Does this conceptualization resonate importantly with how people in various parts of the world experience contemporary life?

These questions pose what might be called the trials of the oxymodern. The "oxymodern" here is the notion that modernity proliferates and becomes acerbic through the disjunction or contradiction between globalizing forces and localizing ones. It suggests that actors live significant dimensions of their lives as a schism, an embraced contradiction, between practices and beliefs seen as historical, conventional, or more traditional, and those viewed as newly progressive. It suggests that this schism proliferates outcomes that are increasingly diverse while nonetheless promoting desires for success associated with wider standards of progress—for instance, through wage employment, education, or business activity associated with cash and commodities. The trials of the oxymodern are a process of constructing an acute semblance of progress through the opposition between local constructions of history or tradition and those of being or becoming modern. The oxymodern directs us to the process whereby people accommodate increasingly common standards of value at the same time that they become culturally diverse and typically more unequal than they were before. In the process, the reinvention of tradition becomes directly related to the complementary process of becoming locally modern (cf. Hobsbawm and Ranger 1983; Keesing and Tonkinson 1982).

The way that modernity becomes intensively local is thrown into relief by the relatively impersonal, distanced, and yet insinuating way that modern standards of value and success impact local subjectivities and identifications. Social and cultural change is nothing new; a tension between older practices and newer ones has been common if not intrinsic to human experience for many millennia. Increasingly, however, this tension is intensified by growing expectations of this-worldly improvement in the near future. In many world areas, desires for betterment create tension between customary or historical beliefs and practices, and those perceived to ride the wave of the future. Relational ties with a larger kin group or community easily compete with growing desires for individual reward and success. The social disembedding and individualization that are so often associated with modern identity accentuate this process while threatening the depersonalization and alienation of a market economy. Though social and cultural change has often juxtaposed competing alternatives, this process intensifies and is made more acerbic by the subjective and politicoeconomic features that attend the process of becoming alternatively modern.

Modern Is as Modern Does

My ethnographic engagement with alternative ways of becoming modern stems from my fieldwork among the Gebusi of Papua New Guinea in 1998, where I returned after an absence of sixteen years. Tucked away in a remote rainforest area of Papua New Guinea,[2] Gebusi social life in 1980–1982 was a virtual treasure trove of customary beliefs and practices. These included all-night dances replete with ornate ritual costumes; spirit séances held by entranced spirit mediums; elaborate initiations accompanied by homosexual insemination of male novices; and a dramatic array of sorcery inquests and divinations that, in preceding decades, had resulted in the execution and common cannibalism of up to one-third of adult Gebusi.[3]

By 1998, however, so many of these practices had ceased or grown moribund that if I had been a first-time fieldworker, I doubt I could have uncovered more than a small fraction of their previous significance. Reciprocally, the social and cultural changes that had occurred among Gebusi far exceeded expectations. During the intervening years, the community I lived with had moved to the edge of the government post and had traded in much of their previous life for the social and cultural centrality of the Nomad subdistrict station. Gebusi themselves say they have exchanged their old practices for new ones (*sesum degra*). Social life is now pervaded by three varieties of fundamentalist Christianity, daily schooling for children, the sale of local garden produce at the Nomad market, the playing of rugby and soccer in sports leagues on Saturday and Sunday, and the holding of discos and "parties" that have transformed the structure of ritual feasts (Knauft 2002). Indigenous dances and initiations are now mostly limited to remote villages; spirit mediumship is defunct; and sorcery inquests are moribund. In many ways, Gebusi have undergone a remarkable degree of social and cultural change in a short period of time.

For present purposes, two features of this change are noteworthy.

First, the alterations in Gebusi life have occurred largely as a function of their own desires. Gebusi have never been subject to significant land alienation, resource extraction, colonial depredation, taxation, or out-migration. The area is entirely dependent on air transport for outside supplies; it has no roads to other parts of the country. Most Gebusi communities, including those that I worked with most closely, have never been subject to Western missionization; their conversion to Christianity has been of their own volition—as spurred by Papua New Guinean pastors from other parts of the country. Gebusi could easily live deep in the rainforest rather on the edge of the government station. Their association with the Nomad churches, school, market, sport league, and aid post—the institutions of their local modernity—was initiated and continues through their own action.

Second and relatedly, the Gebusi process of becoming locally modern has occurred largely through cultural and subjective means in the relative absence of economic and political development. The Nomad area has no marketable resources for an outside world; its cash economy is minuscule, and the possibilities of developing it are virtually nil.[4] Except for a few government officials, schoolteachers, aid post workers, and pastors—whose positions were for the most part similarly staffed in 1980–1982—there is little outside encroachment or coercion. The Gebusi process of becoming locally modern stems to a great extent from their own desire for change despite the relative absence of capitalist penetration or political compulsion (see similarly Dwyer and Minnegal 1998).[5]

To a significant extent, Gebusi social life now revolves around institutions led by outsiders—the Nomad churches, school, market, sports leagues, and government projects (figure 3.1).[6] These developments are thrown into contrastive relief by Gebusi attempts to redefine and historicize their indigenous customs and traditions. One of the biggest changes in Gebusi ceremonial performance has been the development of cultural shows and historical enactments. These accompany local celebrations at the Nomad Station for the Papua New Guinean Independence Day on 16 September. For several days during the week of Independence Day, communities from the various groups of the Nomad Subdistrict—which covers 4200 km² and includes some 9000 people—gather for organized rugby and soccer tournaments, disco dances, and county fair-type contests such as archery, foot races, greased-pole climbing, holding one's breath under water, drinking hot tea, and so on. A major component of these modern festivities—and one of their greatest attractions—is the staging of traditional dances in indigenous costuming on the parade field adjacent to the central government station house

Figure 3.1. A teacher addresses an assembly of pupils at the Nomad Community School.

Figure 3.2. A Gebusi man and woman dance in traditional dress before an interethnic crowd on Independence Day.

All photographs were taken by the author in 1998 except figure 3.7, which was taken in 1981 by Eileen M. Cantrell. Permission to use this photograph is gratefully acknowledged.

Figure 3.3. Gebusi performers in mock traditional costume present themselves to
the evening crowd before
performing a drama skit of
old-time customs.

(figure 3.2). Attended by a thousand or more people, these performances
are judged by government officials, and at the conclusion of the festivities, participants are awarded nominal prize money.

Dance performances at Nomad are complemented during the evenings
of the Independence Day celebration by costumed skits or "dramas."
Like the dance performances, these are dominated by men and enacted
in front of a large and appreciative local audience—for rating and judg-
ing by government officials. The great majority of these staged portray-
als are parodies or spoofs of traditional practices (figure 3.3). Indigenous customs such as sorcery divinations, the use of magical spells, or
belief in mythic spirits are pantomimed and made fun of with slapstick
humor—to the great enjoyment of the assembled audience. By contrast,
other skits appreciatively convey a contemporary world of modern practices and beliefs associated with Christian teaching, wage labor, and
classroom schooling.

In several respects, the performances at Nomad on Independence
Day are oxymodern in character: they enact a poignant sense of becoming locally modern through the opposition between practices deemed to
be progressive, on the one hand, and those now seen as historical and

traditional, on the other. In the process, traditional practices that were undertaken quite genuinely when I conducted my first fieldwork are now historical and only performed in slapstick fashion at the Nomad Station for a large multiethnic audience. This modern framing is accentuated by procedures of so-called etiquette that accompany these reenactments. Before beginning their performances, actors in traditional costume line up and bow solemnly in unison to all four sides of the encircling audience—to the front, back, left, and right. After the skit is over, they bow again and describe the "meaning" of the skit to the audience over a battery-operated bullhorn. This performative distancing of the past renders it safe for enactment and underscores the fact that its reference is historical rather than contemporary. Indigenous culture is increasingly seen as a kind of reenacted folklore. Reciprocally, distance from this history becomes an indication of being modern (see Dirks 1990). In contrast to traditional dances performed in a village longhouse (which I observed in abundance in 1980–1982), those enacted at Nomad for Independence Day were staged for officially sanctioned cultural competition. Indeed, the Nomad officials in 1998 missed only narrowly in their efforts to get a TV crew flown in to videotape the daytime dance performances for airing on Papua New Guinea national television.[7]

In the context of this modern framing, even good Christians can don traditional costumes and enact their customs in hopes of getting prize money and recognition. Indicative here was the display considered to be the most alluring and successful, performed by a group of men and women from a remote Kabasi village, several days' walk from the Nomad station. The Kabasi group performed in a haunting manner—reminiscent of a Kaluli *gisaro*—for over a half hour (figure 3.4; cf. Schieffelin 1976; Feld 1982). The next day, the lead dancer was wearing his clean white shirt while standing with his son watching a rugby game (figure 3.5). The following Sunday, he was in the evangelical church wearing his glasses so he could better read his Bible.

The contexts embraced by this Kabasi man are contradictory—it is widely accepted that church is the spiritual path to the future and that traditional dancing is a sign of the receding past. The moral divide between these realms is clearly evident in church indoctrination posters. The heart of the heathen is depicted as dark and closed to God; the book of the Bible is shut and the fire of the Lord is almost out. This darkness is caused by traditional cultural elements, held by the devil, that intrude on the heart and make it unenlightened and resistant to God (figure 3.6). Similar themes are stressed by the Christian pastors: customary ways of life preclude Christian goodness. The features

Figure 3.4. Independence Day dancing and singing by a Kabasi man from a remote village, dressed in traditional costume.

Figure 3.5. The same man shown in figure 3.4, dressed in a white shirt, accompanied by his son. They are watching a rugby game at Nomad Station the day after the dance performances.

Figure 3.6. Church poster of a pagan heart closed to God due to Satanic traditions associated with indigenous spirits.

of tradition that are rejected in the poster—the bird of paradise, the cassowary, the cuscus, and others—were central spirits and species in Gebusi cosmology and were important in spirit séances. Gebusi dramatically symbolized these spirits by literally embodying their plumage, skin, and fur on the male dancer at ritual feasts (figure 3.7). As such, the traditional dancer iconized the social and aesthetic harmony of the spirits. In Christian cosmology, however, these elements are antithetical to the "good news" of the Bible and to the enlightenment of Christian teaching that parishioners are admonished to embrace—lest they be cast into hell and damnation.

The complement to heathen darkness is the promise of ascending to heaven at the end of a good Christian life—attended by a conspicuously white angel (figure 3.8). Though it may be asked how deeply such images internalized by Gebusi and others at Nomad, the answer for many is "quite a bit." Eighty-four percent of Gebusi are now baptized Christians—meaning they have attended church regularly for several years—and church attendance is generally high.[8] Gebusi spiritual beliefs and their practices of sorcery attribution, divination, and violent retribution have been dramatically impacted over the past fifteen years by Christian beliefs and injunctions (Knauft 2002, chaps. 5 and 6). As

Figure 3.7. Traditional costumed dancer performing in a village longhouse, 1981. Costuming combines elements of the bird of paradise, cassowary, cuscus, egret, crocodile, and other spirits of the forest. Photograph courtesy of Eileen M. Cantrell.

part of these changes, the rate of violent retribution against Gebusi sorcery suspects has declined greatly and is now close to zero. Gebusi explain this by saying that God has taken over the task of punishing sorcerers and taking retribution against them—that is, when they get sick, die, and are condemned to hell.

A graphic indication of Christian impact came to light when I sponsored a contest for children at the Nomad Community School to draw a picture of what they wanted to be in the future. To my surprise, some of these drawings recapitulated quite closely the church poster of everlasting life: children foresaw their future as being in heaven (figure 3.9). (The drawings were made more than a month after the preceding posters had been shown in the evangelical church.)

For a few Gebusi, however, the current enactment of tradition also remains important. Some young men, including two in my village of residence, have decided to devote their lives to hunting in the forest and to dancing traditionally at outlying settlements rather than gravitating to the government station or learning English (figure 3.10).[9] Their cos-

Figure 3.8. Church poster of the death of a good Christian man. He lies contented with a Bible open on his chest. His spirit ascends to heaven, directed by a white angel, as his wife cries.

Figure 3.9. Drawing by a Nomad schoolgirl who pictures her spirit ascending to heaven in the future.

Figure 3.10. Two young Gebusi men in traditional costume prior to entering an initiation feast.

tuming at dances in remote villages was identical to that which Eileen
Cantrell and I saw and documented in 1980–1982 (see figure 3.7). For
two of the forty-nine schoolboys, the lure of this image informed their
drawings of what they wanted to be in their future—that is, a traditional dancer (figure 3.11). For many if not most Gebusi, however, the
dances in question—even at the most remote villages—were occasions
of hybrid costuming (figures 3.12 and 3.13). Even these traditional
events reflected an increasing emphasis on modern forms of decora-
tive self-presentation and entertainment, including cassette music from
national rock groups played from battery-operated boom boxes. This
is consistent with the drawings of the vast majority of Nomad school-
children, who depicted themselves in modern occupations: policemen,
soldiers, airplane and helicopter pilots, heavy equipment operators,
teachers, nurses, and doctors (figures 3.14 and 3.15). In all, 99 of the
104 children who made drawings portrayed themselves in a decidedly
modern or Christian future; only five children depicted themselves in
village or traditional contexts.

What you like to be in futere when you leave school

Topiai

Figure 3.11. Drawing by a Nomad schoolboy who pictures himself as a traditional dancer.

Figure 3.12. Men in hybrid traditional and modern costumes at a Gebusi initiation feast.

Figure 3.13. Man in jersey
and nontraditional flowered
headdress at a Gebusi initiation feast.

At places like Nomad, a sense of becoming modern does not exclude
the construction of neotradition. Rather, each of these depends on the
other; they develop as reciprocals through complementary definition. At
a male initiation in a remote village, for instance, one of the leaders of
the Seventh Day Adventist church—the most rigid in its taboos against
traditional practices—dressed up and visited the festivities by presenting himself in the traditional role of a ritual transvestite (figure 3.16).
This erotic persona evokes ritual homosexuality and the insemination of
initiands (which was highly developed in 1980–1982).[10] Shortly thereafter, however, this same man was once again at the front of the congre-
gation and helping to lead the Seventh Day Adventist church service
(figure 3.17). Such alternatives provide complementary identities that
individuals may embrace contextually in different situations. This recalls Stuart Hall's suggestion that a given form of modern identity
"does *not* signal that stable core of the self, unfolding from beginning
to end through all the vicissitudes of history without change." Rather,
as he suggests, contemporary identities are points of temporary attachment that "suture" an actor contextually to a subject position—they ar-

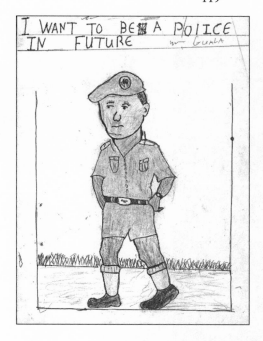

Figure 3.14. Nomad schoolboy draws himself as a policeman in the future.

Figure 3.15. Nomad schoolboy pictures himself as a pilot in the future.

Figure 3.16. Gebusi man
dressed as a ritual transvestite at a male initiation feast
in an outlying village.

ticulate ego investments situationally and strategically among a range of
possibilities (1996:6).[11]

The evolving relationship between modern and traditional identities
does not reflect a lack of comprehension or dissimulation by Gebusi
about either contemporary or indigenous practices; each can be contextually appropriate. Nor do these developments suggest a performance
theory of cultural hybridity, as if either tradition or modernity were
each other in drag. Alternatives are clearly opposed and clearly recognized. Through their contextual enactments, indeed, they codefine each
other. In the process, traditional culture is labeled as "custom" (*kastom*)
and becomes the generic complement to practices that are taken to
be more progressive and contemporary (see Errington and Gewertz
2001).[12]

This spiraling antinomy is a pivotal means by which Gebusi become
alternatively modern. This process is galvanized as Gebusi juxtapose
practices that are locally assessed as traditional against those seen as

Figure 3.17. The same man as in figure 3.16, serving as a lay leader at the Seventh Day Adventist Church.

contemporary and progressive. Oxymodern sensibilities are in this sense both modern and antimodern at the same time. As Foucault (1980, 1983, 1984) suggests, the question of how to make of oneself a modern subject is incited and made problematic. But among Gebusi and many other non-Western peoples, the sharpening stone against which local modernity becomes acute is formed by the practices of a richly remembered past. For many Melanesians, the negotiation of progress and custom is a contemporary form of deep play that, over time, reflects a process of becoming alternatively modern.[13]

Oxymodern II

A second aspect of oxymodern sensibility is a sense of inadequacy or backwardness associated with life in rural areas. Here we find a perception and self-perception of marginality—including in places much less remote than Nomad. At issue here is the creation of cultural as well as economic and political deficiency—a self-admitted lack of accomplishment that resonates as if naturally with hesitancy and lack of confidence in matters of modern lifestyle, language, and manners (cf. Elias 1978). This is the alternatively modern dimension of subordination and disempowerment through cultural distinction (Bourdieu 1984). In locally modern contexts, class distinction operates as a judgment of taste and lifestyle that easily accords low symbolic capital to customary ways of life while affording elevated prestige to more modern ones. Against ever-increasing standards of contemporary wealth and power, the tensions inherent to the alternatively modern often stigmatize a range of traditional practices as clumsy or oafish. This dimension of the oxy-modern is literally oxy, like an ox, bovine, seen as stupid.

I am reminded here of my friend Imbo in the town of Kiunga for the first time, courtesy of my plane ticket. After carefully picking out his very first pair of shoes at the local store—from a jumbled pile of singles—he laboriously made his way to the head of the cash register line. There he was told, to his great embarrassment, that he was about to walk out of the store, quite literally, with two left feet. I remember as well the young married woman who chose, with proper decorum, to hide her pregnancy by covering up her stomach and waist in the traditional manner. But she did so with her one wraparound, which happened to be a fluorescent chartreuse. Her pregnant bulge was not hidden but turned into an embarrassing beacon that riveted public attention.

Likewise, the Nomad dramas sometimes enact failed attempts to be modern. In one skit, local boys skip school to explore the workings of the local power generator. However, they don't know how the powerful machinery works, and they end up being electrocuted one after another in turn—to the great laughter of the audience. If modern developments are remarkable, they can also be seriously shocking.

Against the threat of being locally deficient, the majority of dramatic skits at Nomad on Independence Day entail buffoonish renditions by villagers of what they used to do. These include farcical renditions of old-time sorcery inquests, spirit medium séances, corpse divinations, and men in traditional costume trying with great clumsiness to chop down the smallest of trees with a traditional stone ax. By contrast are proud and assertive enactments of the first white patrol officers. In the skits, these officers brandish their guns and bring order and peace to villagers who are portrayed as scared, uncoordinated, and prone to fighting. The winning skit at the 1998 Independence Day ceremony portrayed the ignorant responses of a traditional man during the early days of colonial contact when he is given a bag of rice and a tin of fish by a benevolent patrol officer. The audience erupts in laughter as the villager first tries to bite open the tin of fish and then smashes it against a rock—but the pulverized can refuses to yield. He then builds a large bonfire to cook this important food. Not knowing how to cook it, the man puts the still-unopened tin and the sealed bag of rice into a bucket —which happens to be plastic—and puts it directly on the roaring fire. The entire assemblage promptly erupts into a ball of fire. The audience convulses in mirth as the man races off in fear, ending the skit.

Such enactments mock attempts to be modern that are oafish and oxy. But they also render these actions safe by making them humorous and historical vis-à-vis the progress of the present.[14] The celebration of national independence at the government station provides a modern setting in which the "primitive" parts of the past can be reenacted from a safe cultural and temporal distance. Modern temporality is important in this respect: a belief in progress disconnects the present from the past (see Koselleck 1985). Among Gebusi, the emergent notion of time as an arrow of progress contrasts diametrically with indigenous temporal sensibilities, in which the passage of time was cyclical and repeating rather than unidirectional in nature (see Knauft 2002, chap. 1).

Despite the recent emergence of a self-conscious sense of history among Gebusi, the local modern that is oxy rarely disappears. Though it may be slain or gored through criticism or in farce, the awkward past inexorably reappears in new guises. This is expectable because what is modern and what is traditional are intrinsically relational; they define each other reciprocally as figure and ground. At Nomad, this process is evident on a daily basis. Villagers act cautiously to avoid exposing the habitus of their backwardness—of being seen as bumpkins at church, school, or market. Even on the ballfield, the plays of greatest commentary and enjoyment are not the goals scored but the foibles of the player who awkwardly misses a kick, slips, or falls. This awkwardness defines itself against the symbolic capital of an imagined modernity that can never be completely obtained no matter how locally modern Gebusi become. This is the oxymodern equivalent of Homi Bhabha's postcolonial quip: almost white, but not quite."[15]

At Nomad, the oxyness of being traditional is also evident in common patterns of speech. The multilinguistic environment of the Nomad Subdistrict includes seven local languages and dialects as well as Motu, Tok Pisin, and smatterings of English. At the center of this diversity, the Nomad Station is a polyglot nexus in which many people, if not most, are bi- or trilingual. But even for villagers who have had years of English instruction at the Nomad Community School, there is a clear divide between villagers, who can *hear* modern language—the national language of English or the lingua franca of Melanesian pidgin (Tok Pisin)—and workers from the Nomad Station, who authoritatively *speak*

Figure 3.18. A policeman interrogates a villager at the Nomad Police
Detachment.

these languages to direct the actions of others. Across this divide is a
world of difference in modern agency (figure 3.18). The longtime government worker, professional pastor, or policeman speaks in English or
Tok Pisin, and his words are more or less understood. But even when
the official knows the local tongue, he doesn't use it; he speaks in pidgin
and hears back the local vernacular. As such, even conversations with
officials who have some vernacular knowledge reciprocate through an
asymmetry of modernity and tradition; both forms of discourse may be
understood, but neither side speaks the language of the other. This is
not a linguistic mix and match (though this can also take place), nor is
it linguistic code switching. Rather, its discursive dynamic accentu-
ates an overall modernizing process of asymmetrical Enlightenment in
which the vernacular and the modern are intimately brought together
while being kept resolutely apart. Maintaining this division is central to
differences of power. Outsiders dominate modern institutional contexts
with their assertive and directive agency, while villagers remain subordinate in settings such as church, school, the market, sports leagues, the
police station, and in the general features of life in and around the Nomad Station.

Songs of Modern Sadness

For many rural peoples, a sense of second-classness in town or city is complemented by a greater sense of assurance in homegrown space. Though they are loath to speak Tok Pisin or English in public, Gebusi play ingeniously with foreign languages and employ new linguistic forms in their own community. This occurs especially in "string-band singing." Accompanied by ukulele and guitar, string-band songs in Tok Pisin and other foreign languages have supplanted the singing by entranced spirit mediums that provided the focus of traditional Gebusi spirit séances. (The only séance singing that can now be heard in the Nomad vicinity is performed as a traditional enactment on Independence Day.) As was also the case with traditional séance singing, string-band songs are sung in haunting harmonies and employ sparse and evocative lyrics that are like haiku in style. The song images of string-band singing draw upon indigenous aesthetics of sexual longing and nostalgia but articulate these with decidedly contemporary notions of romantic love in modern contexts (contrast Knauft 1986, 1989). For instance:

> I go to school
> I look at my friend from before
> She looks at me and I look at her, her eyes fill with tears
> Why did you come to play with me?

Or the following:

> Woman, companion
> Your thoughts you planted in me, you can't plant them in another man.
> You write a letter to me at Elabea [a place said to be in the New Guinea highlands]

String-band singing draws selectively on older performative genres. The songs of the traditional spirit medium employed arcane and exotic speech forms that were associated with the spirit world and hence opaque to some Gebusi listeners—just like the foreign words and idioms of new songs (Knauft 1989). Similarly to spirit séance songs, the haunting melodies and vague meanings of string-band singing evoke longing and sadness among the men in the audience. Audience members may be moved to displays of emotion, such as yelling or stamping their feet. On rare occasions, string-band singers may be doused with water or singed with torches by audience members who vent their emotions onto the performers. Such displays indicate that the performance was particularly moving and successful. Similar acts of aggressive melancholy were occasionally directed at traditional Gebusi dancers or singers in 1980–1982—as they were in the traditional *gisaro* performances of the related Mount Bosavi peoples to the southeast of the Gebusi (Schieffelin 1976; Feld 1982).[16]

Unlike traditional séance songs, however, string-band singing has no divinatory or revelatory function: it does not provide a conduit for dialogue and communication with a world of unseen spirits. In the indigenous spiritual world of 1980–1982, these communications were the linchpin for an elaborate cosmology that is now defunct, including extensive divination and inquest practices (contrast Knauft 1985a, chap. 11, 1989). By contrast, the songs of the string band are associated with radio and cassette recordings by national rock bands, local versions of which are also played at Independence Day (figure 3.19). The desire to create music that resonates with a wider world has been an important reason why young men have shunned traditional séance singing.[17] As part of this replacement, the fantasy of becoming a modern singer or rock star has supplanted the desire to be a spirit medium.

The reproduction and playing of cassette-recorded music through boom boxes impacts the memory and transmission of music in the Nomad area (cf. Benjamin 1969). The boom box and its owner easily travel to play music at modern feasts or "parties" (*fati*), which have increasingly replaced traditional dance rituals. The boom box provides the young man who owns it the modern pizzazz of being a dandy; he becomes a man-about-town who can go at will to other settlements near Nomad and host disco dances where teenage boys and girls can dance directly together.[18] This modern practice contrasts markedly with the stately and somber dances of traditional performers, who wore ornate costumes and danced slowly with long drums (see figure 3.7). At the same time, however, cassettes, boom boxes, and batteries to run them are all expensive and difficult to obtain in the cash-poor economy of Nomad.

Oxymodern III: Mod-earn as Illusion

Gebusi are highly aware that much of their modern awkwardness stems from not having enough money. They attribute this quite accurately to a painful absence of wage labor and a paucity of cash in the remote rainforest of the Nomad area—where there is virtually nothing to sell

Figure 3.19. Men in neotra-
ditional costume play string-
band music on electric gui-
tars for a large audience on
Independence Day.

to the outside world, little to earn, and yet everything to imagine to buy.
Modern aspiration for Gebusi is most basically the desire for cash and
commodities in their absence. It is not the ill effects of commodity fetishism that bother Gebusi (contrast Taussig 1980), but their inability to
earn money—the literal absence of the mod-earn. This frustration—the
desire for money in the absence of paid work—is a central dynamic of
oxymodern tension among Gebusi. The thwarted desire to earn money
is of course common among peripheralized peoples from many world
areas, including in Melanesia (e.g., Smith 1994; LiPuma 2000). But
many critical theorists and anthropologists, being properly skeptical
of modernization theories, have hence been slow to appreciate the intensity of local desires to obtain wage labor where there is little or none
in fact.

Gebusi are keenly aware that government employees and other outsiders who come to Nomad are paid wages while villagers are not. This
awareness provides Gebusi some counterbalance against guilty inade-

quacy—that is, against Immanuel Kant's notion that Enlightenment occurs through "the exodus of humanity by its own effort from a state of guilty immaturity."[19] Here we are reminded of Sahlins's (1992) prescient discussion of the Melanesian develop-man—the man defined into shame by the never-ending quest for economic development.

Levering against shame and guilt, Gebusi at Nomad seem perceptively aware of who in their world gets more than their share, and why. They see what it takes to lead a modern existence: to have a wage-earning government job, a Western-style house, and a range of clothes and commodities; to speak English or Tok Pisin; to consume store-bought foods; and to travel by air to other parts of the country. Against their aspirations for such things, Gebusi awkwardness is crosscut by sarcasm and irony. Some of them are quick to criticize *wantokism*—the solidarity that develops among those who speak the same language—as the reason why the children of government officers attend high school in the district capital of Kiunga while their own children do not. They know that villagers like themselves are awkward with the Bible, and they say that this hampers their spiritual progress. But they also attribute their inability to read to poor schooling, for which they fault the government. Government officials, by contrast, fault local people and say that residents don't work hard enough to create conditions that attract and keep good teachers (Knauft 2002, chap. 7).

Gebusi attitudes sometimes verge on bolder sentiments—that there is little shame in circumventing the mod-earn however one can. Hence, for instance, was the Independence Day skit of the teenage boy in town. Walking with cool and carefree gait despite his rags and urban poverty, the young man in the skit pounds the streets and finally finds work from a miserly, well-dressed, and overweight bureaucrat (figure 3.20). The youth toils laboriously picking up trash and is told to cut grass on the lawn with a small pair of scissors. His patron eventually reaches into his briefcase and pays him a few measly coins. Finally the boss gets bored in his inert luxury and takes a walk, leaving his case full of cash in the care of his bodyguards. While the boss is gone, the nimble youth sees his chance and rushes in; he grabs the satchel and runs off before the security men can react. The patron returns shortly thereafter and discovers his loss, but the boy is nowhere to be found. In frustration and anger, the boss then pulls out a gun and shoots his own security guards until they are dead—for not protecting his money. The boss stands alone with his gun by the bodies of these men as the skit ends.

The mod-earn in this presentation becomes the arbitrary fruit of whoever has the chance to exploit or take it. Reciprocally, it is the boss

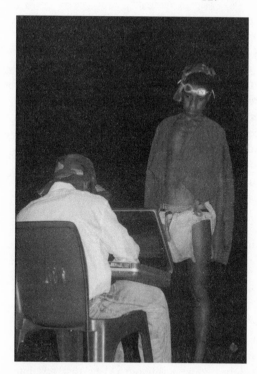

Figure 3.20. A skit of modernity on Independence Day: A displaced village boy, dressed in rags, is paid a miserly wage by an urban employer who reaches into a suitcase full of money to pay him.

in the skit rather than the slovenly teenager who becomes an evil murderer, due to his financial loss. But the boy has also been tainted, becoming a criminal or "rascal" (*raskol*). Gangs of violent and disaffected young *raskols* are widely acknowledged to be a major social problem in contemporary Papua New Guinea—and one of the country's major impediments to so-called modern progress.[20] In the skit, as in Papua New Guinea as a whole, modernity easily becomes acute through irony: a boy cuts grass with scissors but happens to wealth, while his boss becomes a murderer and seems slated for jail. This latter result parallels the real-life actions of the premier of the Gebusi's Western Province, who in 1998 was indicted for embezzlement and attempted murder. Improprieties also reach higher levels. These were openly acknowledged by the then–prime minister of Papua New Guinea, Bill Skate, who drunkenly announced in front of a video camera that he himself was "the biggest *raskol* of them all."[21]

This brings us to the political inequality that absorbs economic royalties of mining and mineral projects, which give Papua New Guinea its relative wealth as a developing country. The Western Province is home to the Ok Tedi gold and copper mine, which supplied a greater percentage of Papua New Guinea's gross domestic product than any other development project from the mid-1980s to the mid-1990s. The royalties from this venture continue to furnish the small provincial government of the Western Province with a whopping 9.7 million kina per year—for a population of slightly over 100,000.[22] To these funds are added large government royalties filtered through tax credit schemes and national and international grants and subventions, including quite sizable ones from Australia for education and health. (Australia is desperate to forestall the possibility that Papua New Guinea will become a "West Africa on its doorstep.") Gebusi are well aware of this continuing windfall. But they see almost none of it themselves except for the well-intentioned ineffectiveness of local officials, who continually plan development projects that seldom come to fruition and rarely benefit local people.

Here, then, is a third dimension of oxymodern circumstance—its political and economic aspect. This is the acute *exposure* to the possibilities of becoming modern while being *blocked* from them in material terms. At issue here is the modern waste that flourishes amid the largesse that remains beyond the purview of local people.

The political economy of the Nomad Station underscores this paradox of modern presence through material absence. An isolate, the Nomad Subdistrict is serviced only by air at inflated prices that few but government employees can afford. Nomad has no roads to anywhere, and its tiny cash economy depends largely on the paltry wages of government officials and pastors. The tenuousness of Nomad is epitomized by the history of its one motor vehicle. Back in 1980–1982, the station boasted a bright yellow truck. The officer in charge proudly drove this chariot around the station and coaxed it up the one bouncing road that the Australians had managed to construct (with local labor) from Nomad to the Bedamini station at Mougulu, some twelve miles away. By 1998, however, the Nomad truck had long since broken down and had not been replaced. There was little reason for a new one to be air-lifted to Nomad in any event, since the one road had been washed out by rainforest floods and erosion. As a monument to backwardness, the rusting yellow hulk of this vehicle was buried—upside down, tail in the air—in the front lawn of the main government office. At the very center of the Nomad Station, it provides a fitting monument to the lack of the modearn at Nomad.

The material plight at Nomad, as in many fourth world contexts, includes the deterioration, crumbling, or simple disappearance of modern infrastructure. Reciprocally, it includes the herculean difficulty of maintaining roads or airstrips, schools, stores, health posts, and civil administration. At places like Nomad, exportable resources that could bolster the local economy are nonexistent. Problems of poor transportation and communication are compounded by national and provincial graft, inefficiency, and complicated paperwork that begs completion by officials who may themselves be barely literate. Both as cause and result of this situation, the Nomad government accommodates a dozen or so government workers who are ever busy with regulations, budgets, and protocols. All of these conditions spell financial impediment. Here is a bureaucracy Max Weber could hardly have imagined, a white-collar agency that rationalizes its activity in a plethora of regulations designed to prevent the wasting of government money but which promote its loss in fact (cf. Weber 1958, chap. 8).

The political economy of marginality—begging for what Ferguson (1999) calls the ethnographic study of decline—had little impact on Gebusi in 1980–1982. Gebusi were poor by modern standards but rich in their own world. In the interim, however, things have dramatically changed. For subjects newly rife with modern aspirations, subjectivity has everything to do with an economy that stays peripheral to a wider world. The third aspect of oxymodernity is hence the semblance and possibility of progress that is subjectively present despite its material paucity and economic absence.

Given these circumstances, it is little wonder that Gebusi have had strong recourse to progress in spiritual and moral terms, including through fundamentalist Christianity (see Knauft 2002, chaps. 5–6). Christian teaching promises enlightenment in an afterworld of plenty that compensates for and supersedes a lack of material and political accomplishment. Christian proselytization galvanizes the desire for moral and material progress and assesses this progress against a divine scale of nontraditional judgment. Conversely, Christian teaching condemns the shortcomings and lack of accomplishment associated with a backward-looking past. More generally, the trials of the oxymodern become increasingly acute as outside standards of progress highlight the perception of local inadequacy.

Nomads of the Oxymodern

Gebusi experience reflects an acutely local modernity that is forged through compromise and contradiction. Oxymodern tensions are evident in at least three ways: first, as an antinomy between the past and the present; second, as the awkward second-classness of local people in regimes of modern symbolic distinction; and third, as exposure to the possibility of progress in the face of its economic impossibility and political disempowerment. As such, the tensions of becoming locally modern have a temporal dimension, which highlights and makes problematic the relation between the past and the present; a moral dimension, which stigmatizes rural beliefs and customary practices as "backward"; and a political and economic dimension, which exposes people to images of modern commodities amid a frustrating lack of material possession.

Despite academic worries that local modernity may only be a scholarly projection, one stubs one's toe on places like Nomad. In the early 1960s, the outpost was named for nomads of the colonial imagination: nomadism was projected onto sparse local peoples, who in fact were sedentary but difficult for colonial officers to find in the rainforest. Now, however, the Nomad area cultivates a different kind of nomadism—one associated with the trials of becoming a locally modern subject. Gebusi confront a newfangled array of personal choices, decisions, and activities that lead them in different directions. They may aspire to be a successful student, member of a sports team, prayer leader at church, disco dancer, or a dandy with a boom box who hangs out at the Nomad Station. These choices rebound discordantly between the continuing construction of neotraditions and the powerful influence of modern institutions such as the church, school, market, and aid post. None of these institutions exerted much influence on Gebusi in 1980–1982. Amid the growing desire to be modern, however, these institutions have become all the more central—and disempowering—to Gebusi, who gain little material benefit from these arenas of modernity. Their participation is based on subordination to the outsiders who direct them.

Places like Nomad are not rare. In a world of aspiring imaginations, fantasies of wealth and power easily fuel a sense of being left behind and out of the way. In this respect, the process of becoming alternatively modern is as cultural and subjective as it is material and economic. To extrapolate from Marx, we can say that people make their own modernity, but not under conditions of their own choosing. From an economic perspective, places like Nomad reveal an alternative modernity replete with all the counterintuitiveness that a Max Weber would appreciate. New desires thrive despite and even because there is little way they can be instrumentally satisfied. From a local perspective, however, this persistence is not at all irrational. The cultural and spiritual pursuit of modernity is perfectly reasonable when aspirations repeatedly confront a dearth of wage labor, a lack of money, and a scarcity of commodities.

The subaltern modern is uninstrumental only from the perspective of modernization theorists who assert a global world of progress through the rational pursuit of economic opportunity. Places like Nomad expose such ideologies as platitudes. They reveal the material inequity and emergent forms of cultural subordination that attend the construction of local modernities. These constructions are reinforced rather than undercut by the material absence that the imagination of modernity itself makes palpable.

The making of modern subjects has often been said to entail individuation, social disembedding, and the disjunction of identity across discordant contexts.[23] But in postcolonial contexts, this process has a pronounced double aspect. On one hand, it is invariably contextualized by the specifics of local and national cultural history. On the other, it engages as if naturally with the values and disempowerments of modern inequality. "Development" is central to the goals and ideologies of postcolonial nation-states as well as to international organizations.[24] As occurs at Nomad, the agents and institutions of state influence easily fuel the desire to be locally modern. But these desires and expectations serve in fact to create subordinates within a highly unequal structure of wealth and power.[25]

Though there is no fixed relation between modern modes of subjectivity and politicoeconomic specifics, it does seem evident, as Foucault (1983) suggested, that regimes of modernity develop hand in hand with new modes of subject making. What it means to "make of oneself a subject" becomes increasingly problematic in a world of increasing individuation, moral differentiation, and social decontextualization. In many marginalized and disempowered areas, the local making of modern subjects entails the incitement, categorization, and denigration of what it means to be "backward," "uncivilized," and "unenlightened." These stigma provide the local background against which "progress" and "development" are configured.

Grounded in cultural desire and material frustration, the trails of the oxymodern do not produce a march of economic and political progress —as mythologized for the West and hoped for the Rest. Rather, they reflect the experienced contradictions of local modernity. Contrary to what many economists, political scientists, and policy makers may suggest, culture is not a shackle of the past upon a line of modernizing progress. What we have academically glossed as modernity and as tradition define each other reciprocally, not through our theoretical projections, but through the tension between cultural history and ideologies of progressive change.

Even as they are highly diverse, the outcomes of this process cannot be accounted for on the basis of cultural relativism. Patterns and structures of modern engagement are increasingly shared at the same time that these engagements produce a panoply of culturally specific responses. Culture acts like water on a grease fire of modernity: the fire spreads and becomes diverse through the very attempt to negotiate its heat. Reciprocally, however, modern desires do not determine how new hopes and frustrations will be responded to by individuals and groups in different parts of the world; modern influence is yoked to local contingency. The result is not cultural convergence but ethnomodern diversity.

The conflicted terms of the alternatively modern shed a contemporary light on issues that have long been of concern to anthropologists. These include the respective importance of the contemporary versus the traditional, the hot versus the cold, the global versus the local, and urban versus the rural. The experienced disjunction between modernity and alterity provides a concrete ethnographic way to illuminate these issues in contemporary circumstances while capturing important dimensions of lived experience. In the mix, an underlying tension proliferates: how to make of oneself a modern subject amid demands for progress, the absence of its means, and the predisposing orientations of local culture. The result is both globally influenced and locally spun. Its seeming antinomy or self-contradiction is not an anomaly but an engine of larger change and subordination. The trials of the oxymodern easily make subaltern circumstance at once more modern and yet more self-consciously local and unequal than it was before.

Acknowledgments

This essay is based on fieldwork undertaken from June to December 1998. Support for this research and the ensuing write-up is gratefully acknowledged from the National Science Foundation, the Wenner-Gren Foundation, the Fulbright-Hays Faculty Research Abroad Program of the U.S. Department of Education, the Harry Frank Guggenheim Foundation, and the Emory University Research Committee. An earlier version of this chapter was presented for the Department of Anthropology at the University of Chicago in the spring of 2000. Thanks are extended to many colleagues and students who offered helpful thoughts and suggestions; shortcomings remain my own. Permission to reproduce figure 3.7 is gratefully acknowledged from Eileen Cantrell, who took this photograph in 1981.

Notes

1. E.g., Rofel 1999; Gaonkar 1999; Larkin 1997; Chatterjee 1997; Prakash 1998; Lichtblau 1999; Donham 1999; Coronil 1997; Eisenstadt 2001; cf. Dussel 1993.

2. Presently numbering about 615 people, Gebusi live toward the northern edge of the extensive south lowland rainforest in Papua New Guinea's Western Province. They were first effectively contacted by patrol officers in 1962 and were under nominal colonial influence until the departure of the Australians and the independence of Papua New Guinea in 1975.

3. See Knauft 1985a,b, 1986, 1987a–c, 1989; cf. 1998, 1999, 2002.

4. The threat of logging exists further to the south and across the Strickland River to the west, but logging is unlikely to approach the areas of secondary forest that have been expanding in the vicinity of Nomad Station, where most Gebusi now live.

5. During the period of colonial presence from 1962 to 1975, Gebusi received, on average, one census patrol per year. Though the colonial administration spent significant time and energy pacifying the militaristic Bedamini people, to the east of Gebusi, they considered the Gebusi to be "quiet and tractable people" and so left them largely alone (see Knauft in press, chap. 4).

6. Through particularities of history, Gebusi have long viewed themselves as subject to the influence of powerful outsiders. In the precolonial era, Gebusi were raided with impunity by their more populous and warlike neighbors, the Bedamini. Late in the colonial era, Australian patrol officers "pacified" Bedamini, supplanted their influence, and established themselves as benevolent if ignorant authorities at the Nomad Patrol Post during the late 1960s. More recently, Gebusi have welcomed the influence of Papua New Guineans from other parts of the country who have administered the Nomad Station during the postcolonial era.

7. Concerning the role of mass media in Papua New Guinea, see Sullivan 1993; Foster 1996–1997, 1999, cf. 1995; Errington and Gewertz 1996; Gewertz and Errington 1996.

8. Gebusi affiliate variously with Catholic, Evangelical, or Seventh Day Adventist Churches. Though in some Melanesian societies baptism has been a relatively superficial act, Gebusi tend to take their Christianity fairly seriously (see Knauft in press, chaps. 5–6; cf. Robbins 1995, 1997, 1998a,b).

9. One of these young men had previously worked for a geopetrol exploration team, became fluent in Tok Pisin (the neo-Melanesian lingua franca), and had been temporarily rich.

10. The man in figure 3.16 was not a participant in homosexual practices,

which are now vestigial for Gebusi. However, the man's costuming as a transvestite is highly symbolic of traditional male homosexuality. Concerning Gebusi sexual changes and homosexuality, see Knauft 2001; cf. Knauft 1986, 1987b. Concerning indigenous sexual practices among the neighboring Bedamini people, see Sørum 1982, 1984; see more generally for south New Guinea, Knauft 1993, chap. 3, and for Melanesia, Herdt 1992, cf. 1999.

11. People in decentralized societies such as Gebusi have often embraced different kinship, political, or ritual roles in different contexts—for instance, acting in one setting as a spouse, in another as a parent, sibling, ritual leader, dancer, and so on. However, alternative choices among a greatly increased number of roles and contexts—each with its own entailments—become intense in contemporary conditions.

12. Cf. Keesing and Tonkinson 1982; Jolly and Thomas 1992; White and Lindstrom 1993.

13. Similarly, see Wardlow (this volume) and Foster (this volume); Errington and Gewertz 2001; cf. LiPuma 2000; Akin and Robbins 1999; contrast Geertz 1973.

14. See also Errington and Gewertz 1995.

15. See Bhabha 1994:89–92.

16. In contrast to the Kaluli and other Mount Bosavi peoples, however, Gebusi performers were not burned repeatedly or severely. Most indigenous Gebusi dancers were not burned.

17. Spirit séance performances also became problematic because of their association with the worship of pagan spirits (see Knauft 2002, chaps. 5–6).

18. The dandyism of young men at Nomad provides an interesting and alternatively modern parallel to Baudelaire's (1964:9) early depiction of modernity as the roaming excursions of the mannered man-about-town or "*flaneur.*"

19. Quoted by Dussel 1993:68.

20. See Wardlow (this volume); Goddard 1992, 1995; Hart Nibbrig 1992; Roscoe 1999; Sykes 1999.

21. Cited in Sykes 1999.

22. See Temu 1997, pt. 2, p. 3; cf. Banks and Ballard 1997. The exchange rate of the kina vacillates; during 1998, one kina was worth approximately U.S. $0.50.

23. See Giddens 1991; Harvey 1989; Appadurai 1996; Taylor 1989; cf. Tönnies 1957; Durkheim 1964.

24. E.g., Escobar 1995; Gupta 1998; Scott 1998; Anderson 1983; Hobsbawm 1990; see Karp (this volume).

25. See more generally Hardt and Negri 2000; Worsley 1984; cf. Held et al. 1999; see more historically Wolf 1982; Wallerstein 1979; Arrighi 1994.

References

Akin, David, and Joel L. Robbins
  1999   [Eds.] *Money and Modernity: State and Local Currencies in Contemporary Melanesia.* Pittsburgh: University of Pittsburgh Press.
Anderson, Benedict
  1983   *Imagined Communities: Reflections on the Origin and Spread of Nationalism.* London: Verso.
Appadurai, Arjun
  1996   *Modernity at Large: Cultural Dimensions of Globalization.* Minneapolis: University of Minnesota Press.
Arrighi, Giovanni
  1994   *The Long Twentieth Century: Money, Power, and the Origins of Our Times.* London: Verso.
Benjamin, Walter
  1969   The Work of Art in the Age of Mechanical Reproduction. In *Illuminations.* Edited by Hannah Arendt, pp. 217–52. New York: Schocken.
Banks, Glenn, and Chris Ballard
  1997   [Eds.] *The Ok Tedi Settlement: Issues, Outcomes, Implications.* Canberra: Australian National University Press.
Baudelaire, Charles
  1964 [1863]   *The Painter of Modern Life and Other Essays.* London: Phaidon.
Bhabha, Homi
  1994   *The Location of Culture.* New York: Routledge.
Bourdieu, Pierre
  1984   *Distinction: A Social Critique of the Judgement of Taste.* Cambridge, Mass.: Harvard University Press.
Chatterjee, Partha
  1997   *Our Modernity.* Lecture to the South-South Exchange Programme for Research on the History of Development and the Council for the Development of Social Science Research in Africa. Rotterdam: Vinlin Press.
Coronil, Fernando
  1997   *The Magical State: Nature, Money, and Modernity in Venezuela.* Chicago: University of Chicago Press.
Dirks, Nicholas B.
  1990   History as a Sign of the Modern. *Public Culture* 2: 25–32.
Donham, Donald L.
  1999   *Marxist Modern: An Ethnographic History of the Ethiopian Revolution.* Berkeley: University of California Press.
Durkheim, Émile
  1964   *The Division of Labor in Society.* New York: Free Press.

Dussel, Enrique
1993   Eurocentrism and Modernity. *boundary 2* 20: 65–74.

Dwyer, Peter D., and Monica Minnegal
1998   Waiting for Company: Ethos and Environment among Kubo of Papua New Guinea. *Journal of the Royal Anthropological Institute* 4: 23–42.

Eisenstadt, S. N.
2001   Multiple Modernities. *Daedalus* 129(1): 1–31.

Elias, Norbert
1978   *The History of Manners: The Civilizing Process.* Volume 1. New York: Pantheon.

Errington, Frederick K., and Deborah Gewertz
1995   From Darkness to Light in the George Brown Jubilee. In *Articulating Change in the "Last Unknown,"* pp. 77–106. Boulder, Colo.: Westview Press.
1996   The Individuation of Tradition in a Papua New Guinea Modernity. *American Anthropologist* 98: 114–26.
2001   On the Generification of Culture: From Blow Fish to Melanesian. *Journal of the Royal Anthropological Institute* 7: 509–525.

Escobar, Arturo
1995   *Encountering Development: The Making and Unmaking of the Third World.* Princeton, N.J.: Princeton University Press.

Feld, Steven
1982   *Sound and Sentiment: Birds, Weeping, Poetics, and Song in Kaluli Expression.* Philadelphia: University of Pennsylvania Press.

Ferguson, James
1999   *Expectations of Modernity: Myths and Meanings of Urban Life on the Zambian Copperbelt.* Berkeley: University of California Press.

Foster, Robert J.
1995   [Ed.] *Nation Making: Emergent Identities in Postcolonial Melanesia.* Ann Arbor: University of Michigan Press.
1996–1997   Commercial Mass Media in Papua New Guinea: Notes on Agency, Bodies, and Commodity Consumption. *Visual Anthropology Review* 12(2): 1–17.
1999   The Commercial Construction of "New Nations." *Journal of Material Culture* 4: 263–82.
2002   Bargains with Modernity in Papua New Guinea and Elsewhere. In *Critically Modern: Alternatives, Alterities, Anthropologies* [this volume]. Edited by Bruce M. Knauft. Bloomington: Indiana University Press.

Foucault, Michel
1980   *Power/Knowledge: Selected Interviews and Other Writings, 1972–1977.* Edited by Colin Gordon. New York: Pantheon.

1983   The Subject and Power. In *Michel Foucault: Beyond Structuralism and Hermeneutics*. 2nd ed. Edited by Hubert L. Dreyfus and Paul Rabinow, pp. 208-26. Chicago: University of Chicago Press.

1984   *The Foucault Reader*. Edited by Paul Rabinow. New York: Pantheon.

Gaonkar, Dilip Parameshwar
1999   On Alternative Modernities. *Public Culture* 11: 1-18.

Geertz, Clifford
1973   Deep Play: Notes on the Balinese Cockfight. In *The Interpretation of Cultures: Selected Essays*, pp. 412-53. New York: Basic Books.

Gewertz, Deborah, and Frederick Errington
1996   On PepsiCo and Piety in a Papua New Guinea "Modernity." *American Ethnologist* 23: 476-93.

Giddens, Anthony
1991   *Modernity and Self-Identity: Self and Society in the Late Modern Age*. Stanford, Calif.: Stanford University Press.

Goddard, Michael
1992   Big-Men, Thief: The Social Organization of Gangs in Port Moresby. *Canberra Anthropology* 154: 20-34.

1995   The Rascal Road: Crime, Prestige, and Development in Papua New Guinea. *The Contemporary Pacific* 7: 55-80.

Gupta, Akhil
1998   *Postcolonial Developments: Agriculture in the Making of Modern India*. Durham, N.C.: Duke University Press.

Hall, Stuart
1996   Introduction: Who Needs Identity? In *Questions of Cultural Identity*. Edited by Stuart Hall and Paul Du Gay, pp. 1-17. London: Sage.

Hardt, Michael, and Antonio Negri
2000   *Empire*. Cambridge, Mass.: Harvard University Press.

Hart Nibbrig, Nand E.
1992   Rascals in Paradise: Urban Gangs in Papua New Guinea. *Pacific Studies* 15(3): 115-34.

Harvey, David
1989   *The Condition of Postmodernity: An Enquiry into the Origins of Culture Change*. Cambridge: Blackwell.

Held, David, Anthony McGrew, David Goldblatt, and Jonathan Perraton
1999   *Global Transformations: Politics, Economics, and Culture*. Stanford, Calif.: Stanford University Press.

Herdt, Gilbert H.
1992   [Ed.] *Ritualized Homosexuality in Melanesia*. Rev. ed. Berkeley: University of California Press.

1999   *Sambia Sexual Culture: Essays from the Field*. Chicago: University of Chicago Press.

Hobsbawm, E. J.
1990   *Nations and Nationalism since 1780: Programme, Myth, Reality.* Cambridge: Cambridge University Press.

Hobsbawm, E. J., and Terence Ranger
1983   [Eds.] *The Invention of Tradition.* Cambridge: Cambridge University Press.

Jolly, Margaret, and Nicholas Thomas
1992   [Eds.] *The Politics of Tradition. Oceania* 62(4): 241–54.

Karp, Ivan
2002   Development and Personhood: Tracing the Contours of a Moral Discourse. In *Critically Modern: Alternatives, Alterities, Anthropologies* [this volume]. Edited by Bruce M. Knauft. Bloomington: Indiana University Press.

Keesing, Robert M., and Robert Tonkinson
1982   [Eds.] *Reinventing Traditional Culture: The Politics of Kastom in Island Melanesia.* Special issue, *Mankind* 13: 297–399.

Knauft, Bruce M.
1985a   *Good Company and Violence: Sorcery and Social Action in a Lowland New Guinea Society.* Berkeley: University of California Press.
1985b   Ritual Form and Permutation in New Guinea: Implications of Symbolic Process for Socio-political Evolution. *American Ethnologist* 21: 321–40.
1986   Text and Social Practice: Narrative 'Longing' and Bisexuality among the Gebusi of New Guinea. *Ethos* 14: 252–81.
1987a   Managing Sex and Anger: Tobacco and Kava Use among the Gebusi of Papua New Guinea. In *Drugs in Western Pacific Societies: Relations of Substance.* Edited by Lamont Lindstrom, pp. 73–98. Lanham, Md.: University Press of America.
1987b   Homosexuality in Melanesia. *Journal of Psychoanalytic Anthropology* 10: 155–91.
1987c   Reconsidering Violence in Simple Human Societies: Homicide among the Gebusi of New Guinea. *Current Anthropology* 28: 457–500.
1989   Imagery, Pronouncement, and the Aesthetics of Reception in Gebusi Spirit Mediumship. In *The Religious Imagination in New Guinea.* Edited by Gilbert H. Herdt and Michele Stephen, pp. 67–98. New Brunswick, N.J.: Rutgers University Press.
1993   *South Coast New Guinea Cultures: History, Comparison, Dialectic.* Cambridge: Cambridge University Press.
1998   How the World Turns Upside Down: Changing Geographies of Power and Spiritual Influence among the Gebusi. In *Fluid Ontologies: Myth, Ritual, and Philosophy in the Highlands of Papua New Guinea.* Edited by Laurence R. Goldman and Chris Ballard, pp. 143–61. Westport, Conn.: Bergin and Garvey.

1999   *From Primitive to Post-colonial in Melanesia and Anthropology.* Ann Arbor: University of Michigan Press.

2001   What Ever Happened to Ritual Homosexuality?: The Incitement of Modern Sexual Subjects in Melanesia and Elsewhere. Keynote address presented at the third annual conference of the International Study of Sex, Culture, and Society (Melbourne, Australia).

2002   *Exchanging the Past: A Rainforest World of Before and After.* Chicago: University of Chicago Press.

Koselleck, Reinhart
1985 [1979]   *Futures Past: On the Semantics of Historical Time.* Cambridge, Mass.: MIT Press.

Larkin, Brian
1997   Indian Films and Nigerian Lovers: Media and the Creation of Parallel Modernities. *Africa* 67: 406–40.

Lichtblau, Klaus
1999   Differentiations of Modernity. *Theory, Culture, and Society* 16: 1–30.

LiPuma, Edward
2000   *Encompassing Others: The Magic of Modernity in Melanesia.* Ann Arbor: University of Michigan Press.

Prakash, Gyan
1998   A Different Modernity. Unpublished manuscript.

Robbins, Joel
1995   Dispossessing the Spirits: Christian Transformations of Desire and Ecology among the Urapmin of Papua New Guinea. *Ethnology* 34: 211–24.

1997   666, or Why is the Millennium on the Skin?: Morality, the State and the Epistemology of Apocalypticism among the Urapmin of Papua New Guinea. In *Millennial Markers.* Edited by Pamela J. Stewart and Andrew J. Strathern, pp. 35–58. Townsville: Centre for Pacific Studies, James Cook University.

1998a   Becoming Sinners: Christian Transformations of Morality and Culture in a Papua New Guinea Society. Ph.D. dissertation. University of Virginia.

1998b   Becoming Sinners: Christianity and Desire among the Urapmin of Papua New Guinea. *Ethnology* 37: 299–316.

Rofel, Lisa
1999   *Other Modernities: Gendered Yearnings in China after Socialism.* Berkeley: University of California Press.

Roscoe, Paul
1999   The Return of the Ambush: *"Raskolism"* in Rural Yangoru, East Sepik Province. *Oceania* 69: 171–83.

Sahlins, Marshall D.
1992   Economics of Develop-Man in the Pacific. *RES* 21: 12–25.

2001   Six are Honored at Commencement 'o1. [An interview with Marshall
        Sahlins by Britt Halvorson.] *Michigan Today* 33(2): 7.

Schieffelin, Edward L.
1976   *The Sorrow of the Lonely and the Burning of the Dancers.* New York:
        St. Martin's Press.

Smith, Michael French
1994   *Hard Times on Kairu Island: Poverty, Development, and Morality in
        a Papua New Guinea Village.* Honolulu: University of Hawaii Press.

Sørum, Arve
1982   The Seeds of Power: Patterns of Bedamini Male Initiation. *Social
        Analysis* 10: 42–62.
1984   Growth and Decay: Bedamini Notions of Sexuality. In *Ritualized
        Homosexuality in Melanesia.* Edited by Gilbert H. Herdt, pp. 318–
        36. Berkeley: University of California Press.

Sullivan, Nancy
1993   Film and Television Production in Papua New Guinea: How Media
        becomes the Message. *Public Culture* 5: 533–55.

Sykes, Karen
1999   After the "Raskol" Feast: Youth's Alienation in New Ireland, Papua
        New Guinea. *Critique of Anthropology* 19: 157–74.

Taussig, Michael T.
1980   *The Devil and Commodity Fetishism in South America.* Chapel Hill:
        University of North Carolina Press.

Taylor, Charles
1989   *Sources of the Self: The Making of Modern Identity.* Cambridge,
        Mass.: Harvard University Press.

Temu, Andrew I.
1997   *Administrative and Financial Brief for the New [Western Province Pro-
        vincial] Government.* Daru, Western Province, Papua New Guinea.
        Government document.

Tönnies, Ferdinand
1957   *Community and Society (Gemeinshaft und Gesellschaft).* East Lansing:
        Michigan State University Press.

Wallerstein, Immanuel
1979   *The Capitalist World-Economy.* Cambridge: Cambridge University
        Press.

Wardlow, Holly
2002   "Hands-Up"–ing Buses and Harvesting Cheese-Pops: Gendered
        Mediation of Modern Disjuncture in Melanesia. In *Critically Mod-
        ern: Alternatives, Alterities, Anthropologies* [this volume]. Edited by
        Bruce M. Knauft. Bloomington: Indiana University Press.

Weber, Max
   1958   *From Max Weber: Essays in Sociology*. Edited by H. H. Gerth and C. Wright Mills. New York: Oxford University Press.

White, Geoffrey M., and Lamont Lindstrom
   1993   [Eds.] *Custom Today. Anthropological Forum,* 6(4).

Wolf, Eric R.
   1982   *Europe and the People without History*. Berkeley: University of California Press.

Worsley, Peter
   1984   *The Three Worlds: Culture and World Development*. Chicago: University of Chicago Press.

Four

"Hands-Up"-ing Buses and Harvesting Cheese-Pops

Gendered Mediation of Modern Disjuncture in Melanesia

Holly Wardlow

Many theorists and ethnographers of modernity have suggested that gender influences how people engage changing patterns of commodity production, acquisition, and consumption. But in what ways are the meaning and experience of modernity intrinsically gendered? I begin this chapter with a brief anecdote about one quite gendered means of modern acquisition among the Huli of Papua New Guinea.

During my first visit to Tari—an airstrip in the highlands of Papua New Guinea surrounded by a few stores, a hospital, a community school, a police station, and a courthouse—I and my companions, some British volunteers who had lived there for more than a year, were accosted while out walking by a small band of prepubescent Huli boys with machetes. We were probably only twenty minutes from the volunteers' house, but we had lost our way in the tangle of paths and deep ditches around people's gardens. "*Mipela ensapim yupela,*" the boys shouted ("we are hands-up-ing you"). Having previously lived in Papua New Guinea, but in a village close to the coast, I used what might be considered a stereotypical "coastal" approach to dealing with the boys. I yelled back that they "*nogat sem*" (they didn't have any shame) and that I was going to inform their parents about their *rabis pasin* (rubbish/ despicable behavior). My tirade gave pause to about half the boys; the other half were not intimidated or embarrassed in the way that I had anticipated, but they ceased waving their machetes and instead threw handfuls of mud at us. Finally one of the boys in the former group apologized and led us back home. When I returned to the Tari area two

144

years later to conduct my fieldwork, I learned very quickly that armed hold-ups (by adult men)—of public buses, of people traveling by foot from the nearby Mt. Kare gold mine into Huli territory, of stores in town, and even of whole flights of passengers arriving at the airstrip—were regular occurrences. While it was rare for people to be injured during these thefts, the assailants (known as "rascals" in Papua New Guinea) were usually armed with guns. Most of the adults I knew had one or more stories to tell of the times they had fallen victim to, or managed to outwit, rascal banditry.

While there are certainly other practices and social dynamics that have been analyzed as iconic of the "modern" in Papua New Guinea—consumption of imported media (Wardlow 1996; Kulick and Wilson 1994); the self-conscious performance of "tradition" (Knauft, this volume; Errington and Gewertz 1996); the ambivalent embrace of Christianity (Robbins 1998a; Tuzin 1997; LiPuma 2000); tensions between nationalism and other identifications (Foster 1995; Robbins 1998b)—many people, Huli and non-Huli, would quickly name rascal-ism as one of the important ways in which Papua New Guinea is quite different from the way it was during the precolonial period. As a number of Huli men noted, "Before, we used to covet just with our eyes, but now, where the eyes go first, the hand quickly follows." Less common but equally "modern," I think, was the practice of one of my Huli friends of surreptitiously burying store-bought food in her garden for her four-year-old daughter to dig up.

In this chapter, I compare these two practices—theft and the "planting" of commodities—as "ideal-typical" gendered responses to a Melanesian modernity. While these two specific practices may appear to overly delimit the field of possible modern markers and practices, both importantly address a larger dynamic that characterizes what it means to be modern in Papua New Guinea: disjunctures in the meanings and values of production and consumption. On the surface, these two practices might also seem to be incomparable phenomena: one is widespread, one is not; one is culturally elaborated (Kulick 1993; Sykes 1999; Roscoe 1999; Leavitt 1998), one is idiosyncratic. Nevertheless, I argue that these behaviors are actually quite similar in that they are both responses to the devaluation of embodied and socially embedded labor in the context of increasingly commoditized social relations. At the same time, these behaviors are obviously quite different, and I argue that they reflect the ways in which these disjunctures differently position men and women, and therefore, how men and women experience and respond to quite different "modernities."

Analytics of the Modern

In discussing "alternative" or "vernacular" modernities, it is important to bear in mind that there is no easy or seamless consensus on what so-called Western modernity is or was. Our exegeses of "other" modernities are sometimes done with the implicit assumption of a somewhat monolithic and unproblematic, if unspecified, idea of the grand narrative for white, Euro-American modernity, when, in fact, this narrative has been multiple and contradictory. As Gaonkar has pointed out, "Western discourse on modernity is a shifting and hybrid configuration consisting of different, often conflicting, theories, norms, historical experiences, utopic fantasies, and ideological commitments" (1999:14). Such narratives may have had white Western European men as their subjects and narrators, and they may have put forward universalizing claims about history and human experience, but this does not mean that the narrators have been in agreement. Narratives about progress through reason, for example, can be contrasted with those of the Weberian "iron cage"—"a disenchanted world of shrinking freedom bereft of meaning," as Gaonkar puts it (1999:7). Other narratives of Western modernity have emphasized the celebration of artifice and aestheticization, or the dystopic fall from prealienated grace (Felski 1989, 1995). Gaonkar himself distinguishes (somewhat in the way Trouillot does in this volume) between "societal modernization"—characterized by "the growth of scientific consciousness, the development of a secular outlook, the doctrine of progress, the primacy of instrumental rationality" (1999:2)—and a contemporaneous but oppositional "cultural modernity" —characterized by an "aesthetics of self" which embraced anything that "would spur the imagination, quicken sensibilities, and deepen feelings" (1999:3). In this case, Gaonkar suggests that Western "cultural modernity" was an explicit reaction to, and resistance against, Western "societal modernization." In sum, to the extent that the process of exploring "alternative modernities" is one of writing through and against Western representations of history, it is important to keep in mind that these representations are not unitary.

Admitting this caveat, I will draw on two recent theorizations of modernity "elsewhere" and examine the ways in which gender is used to define and mediate the contradictions inherent to the modern moment among the Huli of Papua New Guinea. I discuss modernity as the complex of values, beliefs, and practices surrounding the acquisition of cash and commodities made both possible and impossible by capitalism. Taking my cue from Rita Felski's (1989, 1995) analysis of the multiple and contradictory deployments of gender in discourses about "Western" modernity, my aim is to show that gender is a central axis of difference through which the disjunctures of modernity are engaged, performed, and instantiated. One question implied through this analysis is this: if men and women perform, consume, appropriate, and inhabit very different facets and locations of modernity—as is true in the case of the Huli—can we talk about "vernacular" modernities without discussing "male" and "female" as yet another kind of vernacular? In other words, is "modernity" so internally differentiated by gender that even at the most "local" level we cannot talk about homogenous modernities? Further, is this internal differentiation by gender necessary for local modernities to be instantiated?

Ethnographic Background

Before discussing how modernity is parsed along gendered lines among Huli, I should provide some ethnographic background. The Huli number approximately 80,000, and they are often described in the literature as "fringe highlanders"—that ambiguous label used to describe those societies that have some characteristics in common with the highlands groups that were first colonized by Australia and first studied by anthropologists, and yet also different from them (Glasse 1968; Biersack 1995; Hays 1993). In common with other highlands societies, Huli subsistence is based on the cultivation of sweet potato, and they raise large numbers of pigs, which are used for homicide compensation and bridewealth, and at present are often sold to pay for school fees, transportation, clothing, and medical care.

The Huli are also known in the ethnographic literature for their warlike ethos. At present, both men and women are quite proud of their now national reputation for physical aggression and emotional volatility. Although "pacified" during the colonial period, there has been a resurgence of violence among Huli during the last decade, as is also true of other highland areas (Strathern 1993). (Indeed, one high-school teacher liked to tell the story of a "home economics" class in which the students were told to compare "traditional" housing with "modern" housing. One student ingenuously replied to a question about durability by saying that both types only last a couple of years since tribal fights, during which houses are burned down, occur so often.) Moreover, Huli are also known for their expansionist and appropriative ethic, and they have a long intellectual tradition of discursively incorporating the religious and economic practices of smaller neighboring cultural groups into their own cosmology (Frankel 1986; Ballard 1994). For example, according to their own eschatological constructions of local geography and ethnic history, five cultural groups in the area—the Huli and four of their smaller, contiguous neighbors—are all descended from the same ancestor, Hela.[1] Hela placed the Huli at the center for a reason: if any of the surrounding groups come into direct economic or ritual contact with each other, then the world will very quickly come to an end. This ideology has been used by the Huli to justify their mediating role in trade relations between these groups. It has also been used to justify the simultaneous appropriation, fetishization, and trivialization of the other groups' religious rituals; that is, Huli insist that their neighbors' rituals are critical to cosmological continuity, but only as components of larger, encompassing Huli rituals. In sum, the Huli are no strangers to creating metanarratives about culture and history, narratives which place them at the center and which assert that Huli dominance and mediation is critical to cultural continuity for the region as a whole. As might be expected, these neighboring groups do not share Huli versions of culture and history.[2]

Huli notions of modernity have been heavily influenced by a massive gold rush at the northern periphery of Huli territory during the late 1980s (Wardlow 2001; Ryan 1991; Vail 1995; Clark 1993; Biersack 1999). The multinational mining company CRA had exploration rights to the desolate Mt. Kare area, but when Australian employees returned to the site after a Christmas break, they found that thousands of people from local groups—including the Huli who claim Mt. Kare as a traditional religious site—had preemptively begun gathering surface gold. "Gathering" is the correct word in this case, since people claim that during the early part of the rush, gold nuggets could be plucked right off the ground. During this period, thousands of dollars passed through Huli people's hands "like water," as many people say; that is, the alluvial gold was quite accessible, so the wealth derived was easy to come by, but also fleeting; it was quickly spent on alcohol, goods helicoptered into the mine site and sold at highly inflated prices, and trips to the capital city (Vail 1995). This experience has strongly shaped Huli imaginings of modernity as a cosmologically ordained time of extreme wealth and exuberant consumption. According to most Huli, the gold rush and subsequent development of a mine were promised long ago by primordial ancestors, and myths concerning Mt. Kare are now reinterpreted as ancient "prophecies" foretelling the gold to come (Wardlow 2001; Clark 1993; Stürzenhofecker 1994). This vision of modernity as cosmologically ordained wealth is tempered by an equally strong belief that what makes the Huli distinctive, and makes for their continuity as a cultural group, is a moral superiority based on adherence to taboos, injunctions, and prohibitions (Goldman 1983; Frankel 1986). Thus, the process of forging a Huli modernity is a continual process of weighing the competing desires to become rampant consumers and to remain morally disciplined and ascetic.

Much of this moral discipline takes the form of rigid codes of heterosexual avoidance (Glasse 1968, 1974; Goldman 1983; Frankel 1986). In the past, and to some extent today, men and women lived in separate houses, men maintained separate gardens and cooked for themselves, and in some areas, there were separate walking paths for men and women. Iconic of the intense importance of gendered spatial boundaries was the injunction that the sweet potato runners from a woman's garden should not touch those from a man's garden; and it was—and still is for some married couples—women's duty to discipline the "female" vines that constantly threaten to encroach on male space. While many of the more strenuous injunctions are no longer adhered to, the idea that maleness is innately more pure, beautiful, compelling, and vulnerable is still strong. Young men and women are still taught that men in particular need to be protected from premature and unprotected exposure to women's sexual substances, behaviors, and talk.

"Consuming" Modernity: "Gifts," "Commodities," and Gender

With this background, I now turn to two recent conceptualizations of modernity that are concerned with changing patterns, meanings, and valuations of consumption and production. While it would certainly be possible to discuss modernity among the Huli in more "psychological" or "cultural" terms as a fundamental change in subjectivity (Wardlow n.d.) or as a reconfiguration of the national mediascape (Wardlow 1996), in the current context of resource extraction, increasing participation in wage labor, and the attenuation of local circuits of exchange, it is important to be wary of dematerialized theorizations of modernity (Lazarus 1998). Moreover, many Huli people themselves are preoccupied with, and worry over, the inundation of commodities from elsewhere, the decreasing prestige and moral value of physical labor, and the willingness of people to sell or consume objects—such as pigs—which in the past would have been saved, nurtured, and contributed to larger social projects. Thus, I have chosen two discussions of modernity that emphasize the material domain and people's anxieties about this domain.

According to Daniel Miller, modernity can be usefully understood as consumption, or more specifically, the self-conscious awareness that one is forging identity through the consumption of objects "not of one's own creation," as he puts it—through things produced elsewhere (Miller 1995a,b; see also Appadurai and Breckenridge 1995). Miller is, for the most part, sanguine about the ways in which people use alien objects for their own creative and heterogenous purposes (see also Sahlins 1999), but he does suggest that since "authenticity" is often associated with one's own labor and creative efforts, the subject position of the modern consumer can easily be unstable, volatile, and fraught with the possibility of "inauthenticity." As he writes,

> This sense of consumption as a secondary relationship takes on particular importance within an ideology which espouses . . . the aesthetic ideal of authenticity through creation . . . Within such a dominant *ideology the condition of consumption is always a potential state of rupture.* Consumption, then, may not be about choice, but rather the sense that we have no choice but to attempt to overcome the experience of rupture using those very same goods and images which create for many the sense of modernity as rupture. (1995a:2; my emphasis)

This potential experience of rupture and inauthenticity may be especially poignant in the Melanesian context, given long-standing emphasis on the construction of subjectivity and social relations through the objectification and exchange of embodied productive and reproductive effort in "gift economies" (Gregory 1982; Strathern 1988). Contrasting Melanesian economies with capitalist ones, Gregory (1982:29) asserts that the former are characterized by a process of "consumptive production" through which things are converted into persons, while the latter convert persons into things through the abstraction and commoditization of labor. The dichotomy between what have been called "commodity economies" and "gift economies" has been critiqued on a number of fronts (Thomas 1991; Gell 1992). Nevertheless, this distinction remains heuristically useful, and ethnographers of contemporary Melanesia continue to struggle with the idea that Melanesian societies might have (or have had) phenomenologically different relationships to the objects in their environment; that the production and circulation of these objects composes an idiom through which persons are transactionally made and unmade; and that objects and persons travel along social pathways that are constrained by antecedent exchanges and by local constructions of value (Lattas 1993; LiPuma 1999, 2000). As Lattas puts it,

> phenomenological approaches to the gift are not denying the existence of "self-interest" or treating the gift as an antieconomic

principle. Instead, I see them as seeking to expand our notion of
economies so as to encompass alternative forms of circulation,
where self-interest is invested with a whole heap of other desires. . . .
There are other forms of power, self-interest and self-aggrandize-
ment which go beyond . . . the pursuit of capital [and] . . . which
are inscribed and emergent from economies built on the continual
movement of wealth objects and the dispersion and "colonization"
of one's self which this often may involve. (1993:106)

Thus, while many highlands groups were quite used to incorporating
objects from elsewhere into networks of exchange, the inundation in the
contemporary context of objects "not of one's own creation" that can
only be obtained through money and that escape the constrained paths
of traditional exchange is, in fact, recent.

The consumption of objects produced elsewhere poses a dilemma:
either one takes the antimodern stance and rejects these goods (Watts
1992), or one appropriates them, tames them, and makes them indigenous and "authentic." Among the Huli, I suggest, this dilemma is
strongly mediated through gender. In other words, women are expected
to enact the former solution while men undertake the latter. Thus, for
example, when Huli men take up the prestigious symbols of modernity
—sunglasses, blue jeans, Australian boots, cowboy hats—these objects
are not seen as foreign, but rather are already appropriated as the modern equivalents of traditional male display items. For example, Australian cowboy hats have for many young men unproblematically replaced
the traditional Huli wigs of human hair. Moreover, wearing a wig and
wearing a cowboy hat are not seen as mutually exclusive choices and do
not necessarily imply the embrace or rejection of "tradition" or "modernity." A man can wear one one day, and wear the other the next.

In contrast, women's consumption and display of counterpart feminine markers of modernity—makeup, purses, or even shoes, for example
—are perceived as a permanent repudiation of "*rot bilong tumbuna*" (the
ancestors' way). I knew a number of women who had been physically
punished by brothers or husbands for wearing shoes, and all of the
women I knew who had bought or been given radios had these stolen or
broken by disapproving male kin. The Huli have very high rates of mari-
tal violence; in my sample of fifty life-history interviews with women of
varying ages and educational levels, fifty-eight of their seventy-three
marriages involved physical fighting (also see Toft 1985; Counts 1993).
Many of these altercations were triggered by men's suspicions that
women had spent money on modern consumption items such as cigarettes or soda, or had publicly engaged in "modern" practices—gam-

bling, going to town, or riding on public transportation—without their husband's permission. Women who actually did such things were gossiped about as being *bighed*, a Tok Pisin term often translated as stubborn or willful that, when applied to Huli women, implies impertinence, effrontery, and being overly self-assured. Since the explanation given for why a woman has been beaten or raped is often that "she was *bighed*," this label, along with physical violence itself, works effectively to limit women's consumption of modern things.

Moreover, women's consumption of modern items is often interpreted, and punished, as the attempt to be "*olsem misses*," that is, like a white woman—an epithet which implies vanity, sloth, parasitism, bossiness, self-importance, and inappropriate sexual display (Wardlow 2002). Diane Fuss—discussing Fanon's essay, "Algeria Unveiled" (1970)—deliberately opposes imitation (dressing like white women) and identification (wanting to be white women), arguing that women's agency, vitiated by colonialism, is recuperated by "locating politics in the space where imitation exceeds identification" (1994:29; see also Bergner 1994). In other words, "identification" represents an embrace of colonial domination, while "imitation" offers possibilities for subversive parody or appropriation. Female intentionality—in the Algerian case, what a woman has in mind when choosing whether or not to wear a veil, or in the Huli case, what she has in mind when choosing whether or not to wear shoes—becomes central to the politics of colonialism and postcolonialism. Importantly, when Huli women consume the commodities or engage in the practices associated with white women, their behavior is largely perceived as "identification," not "imitation," and their behavior is stigmatized. Here, then, I would suggest that gender is used to mediate the potential disjuncture of modernity: inauthenticity is located in women's practices and controlled by limiting their access to exogenous goods, while men embody a seamless continuity between past and present.

This "division of consumption labor" may be particularly compelling in places where the attempt to forge an "alternative" modernity is inflected by, and defined against, a history of colonialism. In other words, to become "modern," one must consume modern objects, but to be "authentic," one must avoid consumption practices that are identified with colonization. Gender is thus exploited as a difference that enables groups to do both, as it were (see Chatterjee 1993). Of course, one could argue that this differential access by gender to exogenous commodities is simply the continuation of more "traditional" practices of female restriction rather than a response to a sense of rupture or inauthenticity (cf. Englund and Leach 2000). Certainly, Huli men have long been the ones associated with prestigious display items (Goldman 1983). However, Huli women are explicitly forbidden to consume commodities precisely because for them to do so is to abandon that which is now construed as "traditional" and authentic (see also Knauft 1997). In other words, while women's consumption of prestigious goods has long been circumscribed, the reasons for this have changed. As Comaroff and Comaroff (citing Max Gluckman, who cites Evans-Pritchard) assert about the apparent resurgence of South African interest in the occult, "new situations demand new magic" (1999b:283). In the Huli case, one could say that new situations demand new taboos. What may look like "traditional" practice—gender-based injunctions about consumption and display—imposed on a new situation "does not imply an iteration of, a retreat into, 'tradition.' On the contrary, it is often a mode of producing new forms of consciousness; of expressing discontent with modernity and dealing with its deformities" (1999b:284). One outcome of the attempt to mediate this disjuncture between modernity and authenticity is that the entire process by which modern goods are engaged by the Huli becomes deeply gendered.

"Producing" Modernity: The Abstraction and Devaluation of Labor

Comaroff and Comaroff also note the importance of exogenous commodities to people's experience of modernity, but they draw more attention than does Miller (1995a,b) to increasing disparities in wealth in the modern context. They argue that "as consumption has become the moving spirit of the late twentieth century, so there has been a concomitant eclipse of production; an eclipse, at least, of its perceived salience" (1999a:3). "People all over the world—not least those in places where there have been sudden infusions of commodities . . . have been quick to give voice, albeit in different registers, to their perplexity at the enigma of this wealth. Of its origin and the capriciousness of its distribution" (1999a:5). In other words, as commodities from elsewhere inundate people's life worlds and are distributed in apparently haphazard and inequitable ways, the visible and palpable connection between work and value becomes effaced, throwing into question what counts as work, what counts as value or wealth, and the moral relationship between these two categories.[3]

This increasing intangibility of the tie between productive work and modern wealth may be particularly poignant in the Melanesian context. According to more traditional conceptualizations, work is embodied as physical labor that generates wealth and reproduces sociality. Gardening, reproductive sexuality, building fences, caring for pigs, digging trenches that demarcate property, and hunting are all work. The corporeality of work—the sweat produced, the sexual fluids exuded, the energy expended, indeed the physical life force invested in creating the next generation—is critical to this conceptualization (Biersack 1995; Knauft 1999; cf. Povinelli 1993). As Biersack describes it for the neighboring Paiela,

> Among Paielas, life is work, a mobilization of the body by the mind in the pursuit of certain ends . . . The life cycle is actually a cycle of work in which a person takes up or retires from a succession of projects as he or she first matures, then ages. . . . Everyone is given the gift of life through the life and work of his or her mother. . . . As a child matures, he or she is expected to eradicate this birth debt by making payments that compensate the mother. . . . The pigs that compensate the mother have been produced through the labor of the children. . . . Gift exchange is one manifestation of the more global principle that work, in the sense of life-work, is the ultimate prestation. In Paiela society, work-as-transaction is the primary mode of sociality . . . One does not eat one's own pigs, marry one's own sibling, or deploy one's labor in the pursuit of one's own interests. Rather, one lives in service to others, as an expenditure, a sacrifice, of life—but under a condition of reciprocity. (1995:241–43)

Here Biersack deliberately shifts the analytical focus away from those moments when "gifts" are transacted in order to demonstrate that objects to be given are temporary precipitates of perpetually deployed life energy. "Gifts," then, through "consumptive production," become substances and persons who work to create the next generation. In such a system, it is difficult to demarcate "production" from "reproduction"— or even "production" from "consumption"—since the pigs that are "produced" through work are given to obtain the woman who will "reproduce" the next generation, and the sweet potatoes that are "consumed" are explicitly seen as "producing" the bodily substances that are necessary for the "reproduction" of bodies. Indeed the inextricability of reproduction and the production of wealth is key in this kind of economy. As Dalton points out, "For the Rawa, money can be multiplied in their indigenous economy only through the intermediation of human reproduction. Bridewealth is paid to those who paid a bride's mother's bridewealth, and bridewealth yields profits as a woman's daughters are married" (1996:121).

While the debate about "gift economies" and "commodity economies" has been framed largely as one about the nature of, and relationship between, subjects and objects, one can, as Biersack does, choose to focus more processually on labor, on those moments of making, rather than on those transactional moments of persons and objects which have already been made. One consequence of this shift in perspective is greater clarity about the radical difference between the notion of "production" described above and "production" in the context of capitalist wage labor (Postone 1993). In other words, the encompassment of indigenous "labor relations" by capitalism entails a profound loss of meaning—or at least perplexity—about what "work" is, what it means, what it does, and what it is worth. As LiPuma puts it, "There was no abstract labor or value in precontact Melanesia. So the commodity as the West knows it cannot exist. . . . Shells and money are exemplars of that qualitative difference between societies in which kinship mediates social relations and those societies in which labor itself mediates social relations" (1999:195).

Not surprisingly, in the contemporary monetized context, "work" (as described above by Biersack) and wealth (defined now as money and the things to be obtained through money) often seem only tenuously and unpredictably connected. In the Huli context, this apparent ellipsis between work and wealth is perhaps most dramatically incarnated in the person of the tourist, who never appears to do any physical labor and yet has hundreds of dollars to spend at the local tourist resort. People sometimes spoke of tourists as if they were another kind of being, something quite other that embodied a new, not quite figured out relationship between corporeality, agency, and wealth.

The surfeit of wealth some Huli obtained by gathering surface gold at Mt. Kare, or the wealth acquired by trade store owners simply through raising prices, epitomizes this disjuncture. Many in the Huli ethnoscape—including many Huli themselves—appear to gain wealth without investing any apparent effort, to the consternation of those around them. This consternation is demonstrated in Huli women's inability to answer my question of whether they or their husbands "worked." On the one hand, work to many people means corporeal, socially embedded labor. On the other, to some people, work now means anything—or almost anything—that results in money. And to many others, this very question is the subject of interesting and troubling debate. Thus, some women would answer "yes" to my question only if their husband had engaged in wage labor; others would count gambling as a form of work, as long as one won. Similarly, whether the practices of *pasinja meri* (literally, "passenger women," women who engage in multiple-partner, sometimes-paid sex) counted as "work" was also a fruitful topic of discussion (Wardlow 2002). For some, since the actions and substances of these women were not deployed in the production of wealth or persons, what they did was not work. Indeed, quite in contrast to "work," *pasinja meri* activities were sometimes labeled "theft"—that is, the theft by a woman of her own sexual and reproductive resources, resources that rightfully belonged to those kin who had "made her." For others, since *pasinja meri* were given money in exchange for sex, what they did counted as work. (*Pasinja meri* themselves often did not share this latter view, and in fact tended to identify with the former interpretation.) Thus, while increasing disparities in wealth are perhaps the most problematic dimension of "modernity" for Huli people, the baffling relationship—or apparent lack of relationship—between work and wealth also contributes to a crisis in meaning and value.

Comaroff and Comaroff assert that this predicament motivates a desire, as they put it, "to restore some transparency to the relation between production and value, work and wealth. Also to multiply modes of accumulation, both fair and foul" (1999a:12). Comaroff and Comaroff focus primarily on the latter impulse, and they analyze the intensification of witchcraft and zombie beliefs as stemming from the logic of "casino capitalism"—that is, "the impetus to acquire vast fortunes without ordinary labor costs" (1999a:12)—much like pyramid saving schemes, the sale of body parts, and the futures market. As will be seen below, in the Huli context, the restoration of "transparency" occurs in less "occult," more literal, and quite gendered ways. We can now return to the two seemingly disparate scenarios described at the outset of this chapter that typify men's and women's different approaches to "restoring some transparency to" the relationship between work and wealth.

To "Plant" or to "Steal" Modernity?
Restoring Some Transparency

One female friend of mine would regularly bury small packets of Cheese-Pops (cheese–puff–like snack food) in her garden and then have her four-year-old daughter dig for them while she herself was digging up sweet potatoes. This practice is reminiscent of studies from a range of world areas about the transformation of money and commodities through ritual burying, "cooking," or other conversion processes (Toren 1989; Lan 1989). In many cases, the goal is either to transform the nature of money or commodities, or to make it increase (May 1982; Shipton 1989). In contrast, this woman was not attempting to transform or multiply commodities through magical or "occult" means. Rather, she worried that her daughter would come to believe that packaged foods

and other desirable goods just appeared and had no relationship to productive activity. She wanted her daughter to learn that human desire
must always be connected to wealth through purposeful physical labor.
In other words, her actions were deliberately anti-occult and intended
to forestall any tendency to believe in the possibility of magical commodity acquisition. In this case, then, where the relationship between
work and wealth has been effaced, this woman tried to restore it by
reinserting productive labor back into the equation—forcing a mass-
produced commodity to take the form of garden produce which can be
harvested.

Armed theft, a stereotypically male modern activity, would appear to
be quite incommensurate with "planting" store-bought food; yet, I argue, this too is a response to the tenuous relationship between work and
wealth in the modern context, and the consequent ambiguity about what
exactly constitutes "work."[4] Because "rascalism" is now so prevalent in
Papua New Guinea, there is an emerging ethnographic literature on
what this practice means (Goddard 1995; Kulick 1993; Sykes 1999;
Reay 1982; Roscoe 1999; Leavitt 1998). Leavitt (1998) focuses on how
rascals have become important symbols of a willful and obstreperous
masculinity, particularly important in a context where both state and
church authorities encourage docility and obedience. Goddard (1995),
pointing out that most victims are poor and most of the attacks oppor-
tunistic, takes issue with the idea that armed theft by rascal gangs is
motivated by perceived social inequalities. Instead, he analytically situ-
ates rascal activities in the context of exchange, arguing that the distribution of the booty rascals obtain is a means for them to gain prestige
in a still robust gift economy. Thus, rascalism helps to sustain competitive gift exchange, and gift exchange fuels rascalism. Further,

> In the Papua New Guinea idiom, finding a "road to development"
> is a common expression, and communities and individuals try vari-
> ous strategies, including *rot bilong bisnis* (the business way), *rot
> bilong lotu* (the religious way) . . . and *rot bilong raskol* (the criminal
> way). . . . In the absence of adherence to the ideology of capital-
> ism, these different strategies are regarded as having equal legiti-
> macy . . . The term *wok* in Tok Pisin [from the English, "work"] . . .
> means any goal-oriented activity and does not recognize distinc-
> tion in this regard between, for instance, crime, manipulation of
> kin ties, business entrepreneurship, or manual labor. (1995:70–71)

Thus, crime is a form of work according to Goddard. As should be
clear from my discussion above, I think Goddard's analysis of what
"work" means—"any goal-oriented activity"—is somewhat simplified;

indeed, what is perhaps most important about work in the contemporary context is that what it is, means, and does is a lively topic of debate. Most Huli would agree that although theft does result in the acquisition of money, it does not count as work since it involves the victimization of its targets. However, rascals themselves are not so sure, and they suspend judgment by glibly labeling their activities as "shortcut fortnight." This phrase refers to the fact that government workers are paid once every two weeks, and rascals thus imply that they collect their fortnightly "wage" the "shortcut" way. On the one hand, the term "shortcut fortnight" captures exactly what Goddard is saying about theft being synonymous with wage labor; on the other, this quip is said with tongue in cheek and should not be taken as a literal statement of equivalency. The witticism is as much a sardonic commentary on the nature of wage labor as it is a discourse on theft. Huli exhibit a strong ironic sensibility, but in their less wry and more earnest moments, they claim that "*Mipela free. Ol waitskin save stop long muni, tasol mipela save stap long graun. Olsem, mipela stop free*" ("We are free. Whites depend on money, but we depend on land. Therefore, we are free"). In other words, because they do not have to make money but can survive from subsistence horticulture, they are not subject to the disciplining routines of wage labor, including when to get up, when to work, when to sleep, when to eat, and so on. Thus, according to some men, the shortcut method of obtaining a fortnightly paycheck is far preferable to the conventional one since it doesn't require subjection (in the dual senses of becoming a certain kind of subject and of being submissive).

While I agree with Goddard's move to contextualize rascalism in the interstices between "gift" and "commodity" economies, I think his analysis focuses unduly on the act of redistribution and insufficiently on the actual act of taking. Unfortunately, the theoretical meaning of theft is not well developed for either "gift" or "commodity" economies. Oddly, while we have elaborate theorizations of gifts, money, commodities, exchange, consumption, labor, and even barter, there is not much theorization of theft. Even current interests in transnationalism and "the global flows of people and things" assume that these flows are generated primarily through capitalism and for the most part do not consider or theorize the ways that objects circulate through theft.

In his discussion of the identification between the thing given and the donor, Mauss (1990) suggests that the theft of property is therefore the theft of the person to whom it belonged. Thus, theft is the opposite of, though analogous to, the violence intended by the gift that cannot be reciprocated. The former reduces personhood directly, while the latter reduces it by inflicting an unanswerable debt. This explanation of theft certainly seems appropriate for understanding theft (and rape) that occurred during tribal warfare in the past but is not particularly helpful in explaining the contemporary armed hold-up of public buses.

While ethnographers often make casual mention of theft as one of the features of the modern moment, there is a tendency to treat the meaning of theft as "naturally" transparent and not in need of explication.[5] However, the theft of commodities, while perhaps universal, is as socially constructed as any other practice and does not necessarily mean the same thing everywhere. For example, one problem for Huli men working in towns outside Huli territory is the difficulty of sending remittances home to kin since other kin, intended as messengers, sometimes "steal" that which they were supposed to deliver. Men lament that such thefts are not really thefts since "we belong to one clan. He is related to me just as my own family is, so how can he steal from me if he is me?"[6]

Simmel, one of the few theorists of theft, draws parallels between gift giving and theft, arguing that both are examples of a relationship of "pure subjectivity" between persons and objects:

> This state of affairs serves to explain numerous phenomena, including, first of all, the naturalness and honorableness of robbery, of the subjective and normatively unregulated seizure of what is immediately desired. . . . Indeed, among many primitive peoples, armed robbery is held to be superior to honest payment. This latter point of view is thoroughly understandable: in exchange and payment one is subordinated to an objective norm, which the strong, autonomous personality must defer to. (1971:63–64)

It would be easy to dismiss Simmel's comparison as the assertion that "primitive" peoples are so compelled by their intimate and immediate relationship to desired objects that they cannot help but steal. However, his larger point is that money—and by extension capitalist relations—erodes the human capacity for phenomenologically "subjective" relationships with both things and people:

> Now an object is not a value so long as it remains a mere emotional stimulus enmeshed in the subjective process—a natural part of our sensibility, as it were. It must first be separated from this subjective sensibility for it to attain the peculiar significance which we call value . . . exchange is what sustains or produces the distance be-

tween subject and object which transmutes the subjective state of
feeling into objective valuation. (1971:55–56)

For Simmel, the distance between a desired object and the desiring person is overcome through economic exchange, what we might call barter.
As Appadurai puts it, "one's desire for an object is fulfilled by the sacrifice of some other object, which is the focus of the desire of another.
Such exchange of sacrifices is what economic life is all about. . . . Economic value, for Simmel, is generated by this sort of exchange of sacrifices" (1986:3). Further, Simmel asserts that when exchange becomes
monetized, objects, nature, and even persons all become potentially
commensurate.

Huli men's rascalism, then, can be read as the refusal to engage in
mutual sacrifice, the refusal to give up something of one's own in exchange for another more desired thing belonging to someone else. In the
contemporary context—in which exchange happens not through the
barter of objects, but through the commoditization of labor—their refusal translates as an unwillingness to "sacrifice"—or make commensurate—embodied labor.[7] Yes, commodities are desired, but if the only
possible "reciprocal" sacrifice is the abstraction of labor from socially
meaningful projects, then one choice is to reject the sacrifice altogether.
In other words, men's rascal practices can be read as a refusal of the
equation that to obtain a desired commodity, one must sell one's labor.
Thus, when rascals refer to their actions as "shortcut fortnight," this is
a sly means of implying that in the present historical regime, there is
little difference between wage labor and criminal labor: neither is integral to local projects of value; neither embodies a connection between
production, reproduction, and wealth, as "traditional" labor does; both
are capriciously distributed; and if you cannot get one, you resort to the
other.[8]

In contrast to the practice of "planting" commodities, then, rascalism, and the discourse about it, is not about reinserting physical productive labor back into the relationship between work and wealth. Instead,
rascalism acknowledges that the relationship between wealth and embodied, socially embedded labor is no longer tenable, but it simultaneously asserts that wage labor is not a meaningful substitute. Both of
these practices—burying store-bought food in the ground and referring
to theft as a kind of wage—attempt to "restore transparency" to the
tenuous relationship between production and wealth, but it is women
who are holding onto the innate value and constitutive power of physical
subsistence labor, while men ironically suggest that since socially em-

bedded labor is no longer crucial to the acquisition of wealth, and since wage labor does not succeed in producing social meaning or value, any kind of activity potentially counts as work, as long as it succeeds in procuring cash.

Conclusions

Both Miller and Comaroff and Comaroff suggest that potential disjunctures are inherent to modernity—disjunctures having to do with the moral relationship between production, consumption, and value. I suggest that gender is an important means through which people attempt to make sense of and suture these disjunctures. In terms of consumption, Huli women are expected to embody what are now thought of as "authentic" and "traditional" practices and are often punished for the acquisition of modern commodities, while men display and domesticate these new kinds of goods. In terms of production, it is women who maintain the meaning of embodied, socially embedded labor by doing most gardening and pig raising. My friend's attempt to force an exogenous commodity to act as a locally produced object is iconic of this more general pattern. In contrast, men—or at least those who resort to rascalism—seem to adopt a more cynical and subversive attitude, implying that neither socially embedded nor wage labor are reliable sources of meaning and value. Moreover, these gendered trends are being transmitted from one generation to the next: my friend was trying to teach her daughter about the value of productive labor, and it was boys who were "trying on" the possibility of rascalism in the story that opened this chapter. What I am suggesting, then, is that if modernity is inherently disjunctive, and if people must find the means to make sense of such ruptures, then perhaps vernacular modernities cannot be forged without gender—or perhaps some other creation of essential difference. This axis of difference is crucial to how people experiment with creative hybridities and appropriations on the one hand, and simultaneously embody and enact the nonmodern on the other.

In this volume, Trouillot asserts that "modernity implies first and foremost a fundamental shift in regimes of historicity, most notably the perception of a past radically different from the present"; thus, "modernity as a structure requires an other, an alter, a native . . . for as soon as one draws a single line that ties past, present, and future, and yet insists on their distinctiveness, one must inevitably place actors along that line. In other words, not everyone can be at the same point along that line . . . others are somewhere else, ahead or behind." What I suggest is that this may be an internal process as much as an external one. In other words, the logic of "modernity" requires a double distancing: not only the ability to look out and see external "others" behind one on the teleological line between tradition and modernity, but also the ability to look within and see internal "others" always in the past, enacting the "traditional," demonstrating how far one has come, and enabling one to be both "authentic" and "modern."

Partha Chatterjee and others have made similar points in their discussions of the postcolonial nation-state. Chatterjee argues that while the nationalist elite in newly independent India deliberately imitated the material and technical accomplishments of the West, they insisted that the "modern" woman would "have to display the signs of national tradition and therefore would be essentially different from the 'Western' woman" (1993:9). Schein likewise notes for China that "certain cultural conservatives of the May Fourth period . . . held fast to otherwise widely rejected gender practices precisely because they were seen as emblematic of Chinese tradition" (1996:80). Abu-Lughod likewise asserts that the "remaking" of women was critical in attempts to forge an "alternative" Islamist modernity that could mirror the achievements of the West but retain a cultural and moral vision that was distinctively Middle Eastern (1998; see also Smith 1996; Maggi 2001). All in all, then, as Rofel puts it, "rather than being one factor to be considered in or added to discourses of modernity, [gender] is formative of relations of power in visions of what constitutes modernity" (1998:4).[9] All these analyses discuss the relationship between gender and modernity primarily in terms of the specific compulsions of nationalism. However, I suggest that the "traditionalization" of women is also a function of modernity as a "geography of imagination" (Trouillot, this volume). Along the "single line that ties past, present, and future, and yet insists on their distinctiveness," women come to serve as placeholders of "the past" which others can look at to either proudly assess how far they have come or to lament about how much they have lost.

Trouillot suggests that one can read through historical data on production and consumption to observe the agentive creation of modern selves even within the most constraining and brutal of circumstances. Thus, in the Caribbean context, the small plots in which slaves could grow their own crops "can also be read as symbolic fields for the production of individual selves by way of the production of material goods" (this volume). Likewise, the creative and individualizing dress of mulatto and slave women demonstrate "the production of individual selves through patterns of production and consumption." In the Huli context, however, we see that men and women inhabit different niches in relation to both consumption and production, as well as elaborate different meanings out of these different niches. In Trouillot's terms, one could say that Huli men and women occupy different places both in the "geography of management" and in the "geography of imagination." In other words, if subjectivity changes through labor and the possibilities for consumption, then Huli men and women are becoming very differently modern subjects.

This differential positioning calls into question the use of modernity as a periodizing term. Challenging masculinist narratives about modernity in the West, Rita Felski has pointed out that "the feminist reconstruction of women's past has refuted eloquently evolutionist narratives of universal progress, *revealing often radical disjunctures between the periodization of men's and women's history*; periods of supposedly progressive change have frequently coincided with a loss of power and status for women and have in fact occurred at their expense" (1989:47, my emphasis; see also 1995). An examination of Huli men's and women's different locations in their "local modernity" similarly reveals radical disjunctures and raises questions about the meaningfulness of periodizing their experiences in the same way. Huli modernity can be read as the embrace of a teleological narrative of progress, with women cast into the role of performing nostalgic antimodernism. Thus, I end with some questions: if Huli men and women are forming very different relationships to shifting practices of production, consumption, and value, can they be said to live in and through the same "vernacular" modernity? Is it the case that the structure of modernity—perhaps postcolonial modernities in particular—requires "internal others," and therefore a "vernacular modernity" always already encompasses yet more vernaculars? Perhaps it is better to conclude as Lazarus (1998:12) does, that

> to conceptualize capitalism as a world system is to situate modernity as its action-horizon, such that, "even if before there were histories—many of them, and unrelated—now there is tendentially only one" (Jameson 1992). . . . This is a modern but not a Western history. Nor does it suppose that the "development" that has marked the history of the West within modernity corresponds to the telos of modernity. On the contrary, capitalist modernity is characterized by unevenness. . . . There are not comparative modernities, but rather different ways of living in and through modernity.

Acknowledgments

Research for this chapter was made possible by grants from Fulbright Hays (grant PO22A40008), Wenner-Gren (grant 5848), the National Science Foundation (grant 9412381), the Harry Frank Guggenheim Foundation, the Association for Women in Science, and the National Women's Studies Association. Comments are gratefully acknowledged from Bruce Knauft, Rudolf Colloredo-Mansfeld, Robert Foster, and Gayatri Reddy.

Notes

1. According to Huli terminology—which does not accord to how these groups organize and label themselves—the groups are the Duna to the west, the Obena to the north, the Dugube to the south, and the Hewa to the east.

2. Thomas Ernst once commented following a talk I gave on contemporary Huli myths concerning a recent gold rush that "the Onabasulu think that's just more hegemonic Huli bullshit" (cf. Wardlow 2001).

3. Comaroff and Comaroff can be critiqued for privileging their mission to tie translocal processes to local events over the possibility of more local continuity and causation (Englund and Leach 2000; Moore 1999). Nevertheless, in the midst of a heady celebration of research on consumption, they are to be commended for drawing attention to disparities in wealth, changing constructions of production, and what Carrier and Heyman call "dis-consumption" (1998).

4. While I refer to these engagements with modernity as "female" and "male," I do not imply that all men are rascals or endorse rascal behavior, or that all men have given up agricultural labor or the possibility that value is produced through such labor. Women also steal; for example, it is often women who are caught shoplifting soap and other small items. And men do garden, although this activity is increasingly feminized. One Huli man— infamous for his irascibility—confided to me that, in fact, he loved gardening; however, in public he professed to make his living through gambling and scoffed at the suggestion that he might spend his time gardening. Thus, the attempt to reaffirm embodied labor as a source of value can be seen as a female tendency, and a cynical and more pessimistic attitude toward both embodied and wage labor as a male tendency. Such tendencies probably derive from more traditional gendered modes of producing value and acquiring prestige. According to now classic depictions of gender in Melanesia, women have always been much closer to the labor process, while

men derive prestige through attempting to transcend and transform the realm of productive labor through exchange transactions.

5. Thus, for example, Comaroff and Comaroff (1999a) and Weiss (1998:176) mention more "mundane" kinds of stealing—e.g., gangsters who prey on third-class passengers on trains—but choose only to analyze more lurid kinds of theft, such as that of human blood or organs. I would suggest that both kinds of theft are quite similar in that both may be commentaries on, or refusals of, the commoditization of the labor and the body.

6. Another example in a very different context (and yet also a case in which modernity is associated with both commercial and thieving activity), is Pinch's discussion of the gray area between shopping and shoplifting among the upper classes in nineteenth-century England: "the Times asserted in 1855 that 'everyone who is acquainted with London society could at once furnish a dozen names of ladies who have been notorious for abstracting articles of trifling value from the shops where they habitually dealt' " (1998:124). This ambiguity between buying and stealing was facilitated by a credit system in which "the wealthier or more prestigious the customer, the longer the leash of his or her credit." Thus, "cash rarely changed hands [between customer and shopkeeper, and] . . . walking out of stores with merchandise one hadn't actually paid for was the norm, rather than the exception" (1998:127–28). Pinch suggests that in an era when England had been derided by Napoleon as "a nation of shop-keepers," shoplifting on the part of the upper classes was a way of expressing contempt for commercial activity and its message that "the external markers of distinction were truly available to anyone who could pay" (1998:129). As she puts it, theft raises "questions about how a thing comes to be legitimately one's own" (1998:122).

   In another example, Geary argues that theft was a valorized means of "translation" (the transferral from one community to another of sacred medieval relics—saints' bones, to be precise): "the account of the relics' translation . . . was itself part of the explanation of who they were and what their power was. In this context, accounts of thefts, as opposed to gifts or purchases, was particularly appropriate and satisfactory . . . The Saints were clearly too precious to their communities to be parted with willingly. Thus, they had to be stolen, or rather kidnapped" (1986:186).

   In sum, theft may not be as transparent a practice as we often assume.

7. Foster, analyzing educational pamphlets distributed by the Royal Bank of Australia and targeted toward Papua New Guineans, demonstrates that one of the goals of the colonial administration was exactly to instill the commensurability of money and work (quotes of pamphlets in italics): " '*In this country, metal coins and paper notes are replacing things such as shells, clay pots, feathers and pigs*' . . . This strategy begins by identifying 'money' with specific wealth items . . . but having done so, it then discounts these wealth items as inferior . . . due to their irreducible materiality . . . In other words, the challenge of colonial education lay in teaching a mode of symbolization

in which money could be apprehended as a signifier referring beyond itself. To what? Work . . . '*When people buy things with money they have earned, they are really paying with their work or their goods or services which are stored up in the money they have earned . . . money can be either metal or paper, but it still represents the value of the work or goods which people bring into existence by their efforts*' " (1998:64–66). Foster's analysis focuses on colonial efforts to prevent a feared "(non-commodity) fetishization of money" (1998:85), but his analysis serves equally well to reveal colonial efforts to naturalize the abstraction and commoditization of labor.

8. Douglas Dalton similarly analyzes gambling as a Melanesian commentary on the commoditization of labor: "[card] games harbor no illusions that money can multiply by itself. Instead, they make clear . . . that money is always gained at someone else's expense . . . card game 'work' constitutes a parodic, comic demystification of Western privilege and the humanist, colonial bourgeois culture that rationalizes it" (1996:132).

9. Rofel (1998), Schein (1999), Abu-Lughod (1998), and Yang (1999) all complicate their analyses of nationalist discourses with nuanced analyses of how women embrace, undermine, or ambivalently perform a range of responses to the attempts of others to "traditionalize" them. As Schein says, "that feminized Miao emblematize tradition and backwardness within China does not mean that they routinely perform only that" (1999:372).

References

Abu-Lughod, Lila
    1998   Introduction: Feminist Longings and Postcolonial Conditions. In *Remaking Women: Feminism and Modernity in the Middle East*. Edited by Lila Abu-Lughod, pp. 3–32. Princeton: Princeton University Press.

Appadurai, Arjun
    1986   Introduction: Commodities and the Politics of Value. In *The Social Life of Things: Commodities in Cultural Perspective*. Edited by Arjun Appadurai, pp. 3–63. Cambridge: Cambridge University Press.

Appadurai, Arjun, and Carol Breckenridge
    1995   Public Modernity in India. In *Consuming Modernity: Public Culture in a South Asian World*. Edited by Carol Breckenridge, pp 1–20. Minneapolis: University of Minnesota Press.

Ballard, Chris
    1994   The Centre Cannot Hold: Trade Networks and Sacred Geography in the Papua New Guinea Highlands. *Archeology Oceania* 29: 130–48.

Bergner, Gwen
    1994   Who is that Masked Woman? Or, the Role of Gender in Fanon's Black Skin, White Masks. *PMLA* 110(1): 75–88.

Biersack, Aletta
  1995   Heterosexual Meanings: Society, Economy, and Gender among Ipilis. In *Papuan Borderlands: Huli, Duna, and Ipili Perspectives on the Papua New Guinea Highlands*. Edited by Aletta Biersack, pp. 231–63. Ann Arbor: University of Michigan Press.
  1999   The Mount Kare Python and His Gold: Totemism and Ecology in the Papua New Guinea Highlands. *American Anthropologist* 101(1): 68–87.

Carrier, James G., and Josiah McC. Heyman
  1998   Consumption and Political Economy. *Journal of the Royal Anthropological Society* 3: 355–73.

Chatterjee, Partha
  1993   *The Nation and its Fragments: Colonial and Postcolonial Histories*. Princeton: Princeton University Press.

Clark, Jeffrey
  1993   Gold, Sex, and Pollution: Male Illness and Myth at Mt. Kare, Papua New Guinea. *American Ethnologist* 20(4): 742–57.

Comaroff, Jean, and John Comaroff
  1999a Alien-Nation: Zombies, Immigrants, and Millennial Capitalism. Paper presented at the Emory University Historical Anthropology Workshop, Atlanta, Ga.
  1999b Occult Economies and the Violence of Abstraction: Notes from the South African Postcolony. *American Ethnologist* 26(2): 279–303.

Counts, Dorothy
  1993   The Fist, the Stick, and the Bottle of Bleach: Wife Bashing and Female Suicide in a Papua New Guinea Society. In *Contemporary Pacific Societies: Studies in Development and Change*. Edited by V. S. Lockwood, T. Harding, and B. Wallace, pp. 249–55. Englewood Cliffs, N.J.: Prentice-Hall.

Dalton, Douglas
  1996   Cargo, Cards, and Excess: The Articulation of Economies in Papua New Guinea. *Research in Economic Anthropology* 17: 83–147.

Englund, Harri, and James Leach
  2000   Ethnography and the Meta-Narratives of Modernity. *Current Anthropology* 41(2): 225–39.

Errington, Frederick, and Deborah Gewertz
  1996   The Individuation of Tradition in a Papua New Guinea Modernity. *American Anthropologist* 98(1): 114–26.

Fanon, Frantz
  1970   Algeria Unveiled. *A Dying Colonialism*, pp. 21–52. Harmondsworth: Penguin.

Felski, Rita
  1989   Feminism, Postmodernism, and the Critique of Modernity. *Cultural Critique* (fall): 33–56.
  1995   *The Gender of Modernity*. Cambridge: Harvard University Press.

Holly Wardlow

168

Foster, Robert
1995   [Ed.] *Nation Making: Emergent Identities in Postcolonial Melanesia.* Ann Arbor: University of Michigan Press.
1998   Your Money, Our Money, the Government's Money: Finance and Fetishism in Melanesia. In *Border Fetishisms: Material Objects in Unstable Places.* Edited by P. Spyer, pp. 60–90. New York: Routledge.

Frankel, Stephen
1986   *The Huli Response to Illness.* Cambridge: Cambridge University Press.

Fuss, Diane
1994   Interior Colonies: Frantz Fanon and the Politics of Identification. *Diacritics* 24(2–3): 20–42.

Gaonkar, Dilip Parameshwar
1999   On Alternative Modernities. *Public Culture* 11(1): 1–18.

Geary, Patrick
1986   Sacred Commodities: the Circulation of Medieval Relics. In *The Social Life of Things: Commodities in Cultural Perspective.* Edited by Arjun Appadurai, pp. 169–94. Cambridge: Cambridge University Press.

Gell, Alfred
1992   Inter-tribal Commodity Barter and Reproductive Gift-Exchange in Old Melanesia. In *Barter, Exchange, and Value.* Edited by C. Humphrey and S. Hugh-Jones, pp. 142–68. Cambridge: Cambridge University Press.

Glasse, Robert M.
1968   *Huli of Papua: A Cognatic Descent System.* Paris: Mouton.
1974   Le Masque de la Volupte: Symbolisme et antagonisme Sexuels sur les hauts plateaux de Nouvelle-Guinee. *L'Homme* 14(2): 79–86.

Goddard, Michael
1995   The Rascal Road: Crime, Prestige, and Development in Papua New Guinea. *Contemporary Pacific* 7(1): 55–80.

Goldman, Laurence
1983   *Talk Never Dies: the Language of Huli Disputes.* London: Tavistock.

Gregory, Chris
1982   *Gifts and Commodities.* London: Academic Press.

Hays, Terence
1993   The New Guinea Highlands: Region, Culture Area, or Fuzzy Set? *Current Anthropology* 34(2): 141–48.

Jameson, Fredric
1992   *Postmodernism, or the Cultural Logic of Late Capitalism.* Durham, N.C.: Duke University Press.

Knauft, Bruce M.
  1997   Gender Identity, Political Economy, and Modernity in Melanesia and Amazonia. *Journal of the Royal Anthropological Institute* 3: 233–59.
  1999   *From Primitive to Postcolonial in Melanesia and Anthropology.* Ann Arbor: University of Michigan Press.
  2002   Trials of the Oxymodern: Public Practice at Nomad Station. In *Critically Modern: Alternatives, Alterities, Anthropologies* [this volume]. Edited by Bruce M. Knauft. Bloomington: Indiana University Press.

Kulick, Don
  1993   Heroes from Hell: Representations of "Rascals" in a Papua New Guinea Village. *Anthropology Today* 9(3): 9–14.

Kulick, Don, and Margaret Wilson
  1994   Rambo's Wife Saves the Day: Subjugating the Gaze and Subverting the Narrative in a Papua New Guinea Swamp. *Visual Anthropology Review* 10(2): 1–13.

Lan, David
  1989   Resistance to the Present by the Past: Mediums and Money in Zimbabwe. In *Money and the Morality of Exchange.* Edited by Jonathan Parry and Maurice Bloch, pp. 191–208. Cambridge: Cambridge University Press.

Lattas, Andrew
  1993   Gifts, Commodities and the Problem of Alienation. *Social Analysis* 34: 102–18.

Lazarus, Neil
  1998   Comparative Modernities? Marxism and the Critique of Eurocentrism in Postcolonial Studies. Paper presented at Emory University as part of the Crossing Borders workshop.

Leavitt, Stephen
  1998   The *Bikhet* Mystique: Masculine Identity and Patterns of Rebellion among Bumbita Adolescent Males. In *Adolescence in Pacific Island Societies.* Edited by Gilbert Herdt and Steven Leavitt, pp. 173–94. Pittsburgh: University of Pittsburgh Press.

LiPuma, Edward
  1999   The Meaning of Money in the Age of Modernity. In *Money and Modernity: State and Local Currencies in Melanesia.* Edited by David Akin and Joel Robbins, pp. 192–213. Pittsburgh: University of Pittsburgh Press.
  2000   *Encompassing Others: the Magic of Modernity in Melanesia.* Ann Arbor: University of Michigan Press.

Maggi, Wynne
  2001   *Our Women Are Free: Gender and Ethnicity in the Hindukush.* Ann Arbor: University of Michigan Press.

Mauss, Marcel
  1990   *The Gift: The Form and Reason for Exchange in Archaic Societies.*
          New York: W. W. Norton.

May, R. J.
  1982   The View from Hurin; the Peli Association. In *Micronationalist
          Movements in Papua New Guinea.* Edited by R. J. May, pp. 31–62.
          Canberra: Australian National University.

Miller, Daniel
  1995a   Introduction. In *Worlds Apart: Modernity through the Prism of the Lo-
          cal.* Edited by Daniel Miller, pp. 1–22. New York: Routledge Press.
  1995b   Consumption and Commodities. *Annual Review of Anthropology* 24:
          141–61.

Moore, Sally Falk
  1999   Reflections on the Comaroff Lecture. *American Ethnologist* 26(2):
          304–6.

Pinch, Adela
  1998   Stealing Happiness: Shoplifting in Early Nineteenth-Century En-
          gland. In *Border Fetishisms: Material Objects in Unstable Places.* Ed-
          ited by P. Spyer, pp. 122–49. New York: Routledge.

Postone, Moishe
  1993   *Time, Labor, and Social Domination.* Cambridge: Cambridge Univer-
          sity Press.

Povinelli, Elizabeth
  1993   *Labor's Lot: The Power, History, and Culture of Aboriginal Action.*
          Chicago: University of Chicago Press.

Reay, Marie
  1982   Lawlessness in the Papua New Guinea Highlands. In *Melanesia: Be-
          yond Diversity.* Edited by R. May and H. Nelson, pp. 623–37. Can-
          berra: Australian National University Press.

Robbins, Joel
  1998a   Becoming Sinners: Christianity and Desire among the Urapmin of
          Papua New Guinea. *Ethnology* 37(4): 299–316.
  1998b   On Reading "World News": Apocalyptic Narrative, Negative Na-
          tionalism and Transnational Christianity in a Papua New Guinea
          Society. *Social Analysis* 42(2): 103–30.

Rofel, Lisa
  1998   *Other Modernities: Gendered Yearnings in China after Socialism.* Berke-
          ley: University of California Press.

Roscoe, Paul
  1999   The Return of the Ambush: Raskolism in Rural Yangoru, East Sepik
          Province. *Oceania* 69(3): 171–83.

Ryan, Peter
  1991   *Black Bonanza: A Landslide of Gold.* South Yara, Australia: Hyland
          House Press.

Sahlins, Marshall D.
1999   What is Anthropological Enlightenment? Some Lessons of the Twentieth Century. *Annual Review of Anthropology* 28:1–23.

Schein, Louisa
1996   Multiple Alterities: The Contouring of Gender in Miao and Chinese Nationalisms. In *Women out of Place: The Gender of Agency and the Race of Nationality*. Edited by Brackette Williams, pp. 79–102. New York: Routledge.
1999   Performing Modernity. *Cultural Anthropology* 14(3): 361–95.

Shipton, Parker
1989   *Bitter Money: Cultural Economy and Some African Meanings of Forbidden Commodities*. Monograph Series, no. 1. Washington, D.C.: American Ethnological Society.

Simmel, Georg
1971   *On Individuality and Social Forms*. Chicago: University of Chicago Press.

Smith, Carol
1996   Race/Class/Gender Ideology in Guatemala: Modern and Anti-Modern Forms. In *Women out of Place: The Gender of Agency and the Race of Nationality*. Edited by Brackette Williams, pp. 50–78. New York: Routledge.

Strathern, Andrew J.
1993   Violence and Political Change in Papua New Guinea. *Pacific Studies* 16(4): 41–60.

Strathern, Marilyn
1988   *The Gender of the Gift: Problems with Women and Problems with Society in Melanesia*. Cambridge: Cambridge University Press.

Stürzenhofecker, Gabriele
1994   Visions of a landscape: Duna Pre-meditations on Ecological Change. *Canberra Anthropology* 17(2): 27–47.

Sykes, Karen
1999   After the "Raskol" Feast: Youths' Alienation in New Ireland, Papua New Guinea. *Critique of Anthropology* 19(2): 157–74.

Thomas, Nicholas
1991   *Entangled Objects: Exchange, Material Culture and Colonialism in the Pacific*. Cambridge, Mass.: Harvard University Press.

Toft, Susan
1985   [Ed.] *Domestic Violence in Papua New Guinea*. Port Moresby: Law Reform Commission of Papua New Guinea.

Toren, C.
1989   Drinking Cash: The Purification of Money through Ceremonial Exchange in Fiji. In *Money and the Morality of Exchange*. Edited by Jonathan Parry and Maurice Bloch, pp. 142–64. Cambridge: Cambridge University Press.

Trouillot, Michel-Rolph
    2002   The Otherwise Modern: Caribbean Lessons from the Savage Slot. In *Critically Modern: Alternatives, Alterities, Anthropologies* [this volume]. Edited by Bruce M. Knauft. Bloomington: Indiana University Press.

Tuzin, Donald F.
    1997   *The Cassowary's Revenge: The Life and Death of Masculinity in a New Guinea Society.* Chicago: University of Chicago Press.

Vail, John
    1995   All that Glitters: The Mt. Kare Gold Rush and Its Aftermath. In *Papuan Borderlands: Huli, Duna, and Ipili Perspectives on the Papua New Guinea Highlands.* Edited by Aletta Biersack, pp. 343–74. Ann Arbor: University of Michigan Press.

Wardlow, Holly
    1996   Bobby Teardrops: A Turkish Video in Papua New Guinea. Reflections on Cultural Studies, Feminism, and the Anthropology of Mass Media. *Visual Anthropology Review* 12(1): 30–46.
    2001   The Mt. Kare Python: Huli Myths and Gendered Fantasies of Agency. In *Mining and Indigenous Life Worlds in Australia and Papua New Guinea.* Edited by Alan Rumsey and James F. Weiner. Adelaide, Australia: Crawford House Press.
    2002   Headless Ghosts and Roving Women: Spectres of Modernity in Papua New Guinea. *American Ethnologist* 29(1): 5–32.
    n.d.   Transformations of Desire: Envy and Resentment among the Huli of Papua New Guinea. Unpublished manuscript.

Watts, Michael J.
    1992   The Shock of Modernity: Petroleum, Protest, and Fast Capitalism in an Industrializing Society. In *Reworking Modernity: Capitalisms and Symbolic Discontent.* Edited by Alan Pred and Michael Watts, pp. 21–63. New Brunswick, N.J.: Rutgers University Press.

Weiss, Brad
    1998   Electric Vampires: Haya Rumors of the Commodified Body. In *Bodies and Persons: Comparative Perspectives from Africa and Melanesia.* Edited by Michael Lambek and Andrew Strathern, pp. 172–94. Cambridge: Cambridge University Press.

Yang, Mayfair
    1999   From Gender Erasure to Gender Difference: State Feminism, Consumer Sexuality, and Women's Public Sphere in China. In *Spaces of Their Own: Women's Public Sphere in Transnational China.* Edited by Mayfair Yang, pp. 35–67. Minneapolis: University of Minnesota Press.

PART II

Five

Modernity's Masculine Fantasies

Lisa Rofel

Perhaps the most important question to ask of modernity is the following: What is it that critics, scholars, and activists want to challenge when we address the category "modernity"? Discussions of modernity, in my work and others, were never meant to devolve into abstract niceties. The stakes in confronting modernity are about politics, in all the fullness of that term. The implications of its ubiquity as a means to make political sense of the world have been profound and immediate. What is it, then, that not just scholars, but various citizens of the world find worth struggling over when they invoke modernity and all its attendant permutations? Which sorts of desires do they invest in the category? What material effects does engagement with the category produce? Rather than treat modernity as a reified certainty, or worse, a singular certainty—an era arrived at teleologically, a set of practices uniformly discerned, a universal state of being—I have argued (1999) that instead we need to trace how rhetorics, claims, and commitments to modernity get put into play. Only in this way do we have a chance of finally moving beyond the forms of domination and exclusions enacted in the name of modernity. For such discursive struggles are fully imbricated in their materiality as transnational policies, labor migration, gendered divisions of labor, and the articulations of race, sex, and gender with nationalism.

Let there be no misunderstanding. Modernity may well have some kind of universalizing power, though I do not think all people are equally invested in the category or the condition. If so, it is only in the sense that, like the category "human rights," it represents a terrain that signals an interconnected world simultaneously built on momentous exclusions. We should not, however, be seduced by its universalist pretensions. On the other hand, it will not suffice to reduce the discrepancies of modernities to cultural pluralism. By "discrepant modernities," I mean a world of forced and violent interactions, in which emerges an imaginary space that produces deferred relationships to modernity (Rofel 1999). Modernity is something people struggle over because it has life-affirming as well as life-threatening effects. This struggle is what people share, rather like the floor of a boxing match (including fixed bets and outcomes), rather than a universal form with its local particulars. The latter view is the ideology of structural adjustment programs.

Politics of Modernity

My argument joins a larger debate over modernity's political investments. I begin by rehearsing three arguments. Bruno Latour (1993), for example, engages with the problematic of modernity in order to trouble the purported purity of categories and to embrace a more democratic method of conducting science in relation to the nonhuman world. Supplementing the line of criticism in anthropology linking Franz Boas (1940), Mary Douglas (1966), and Brackette Williams (1991)—which has taught us that the danger in the purity of categories (e.g., race, ethnicity, nation) lies in the hierarchies, exclusions, and the murderous rage that such purifications can produce—Latour examines the line drawn between the nonhuman realm of nature and the human realm of society, culture, and language. The purification of these realms—the heart of modernity, for Latour—in turn obscures the translations that occur between nature and culture. Paradoxically, the proliferation of hybrids relies on the pretense that these purified realms exist. Latour believes that the Euro-American West needs to acknowledge that it has never been modern so that it can embrace these hybridities of nature and culture. Such an embrace signals a more democratic world.

Paul Gilroy (1987, 1993, 2000) offers yet another critique of modernity, even as he also stresses hybridity. Gilroy places the Black Atlantic world at the heart of modernity by arguing that modernity has been generated within the "fatal junction" of slavery, racial domination, and racialized reason underlying the imperial world. Gilroy's political aim is to displace the characteristically modern phenomena of nationalism, ethnicity, and authenticity by challenging notions of immutable ethnic difference. We can undo modernity's legacies of racism, Gilroy argues, only by exposing these ideologies of absolute difference.

Foucault's (1979, 1980) attention to modernity, to take a final example, grew from his desire to expose modernity's practices of subjectification that inhere in disciplinary regimes of biopower. Foucault forcefully tore open the self-congratulatory paeans to greater individual freedom and progress in the pursuit of modernity. For him, modernity signaled an ever more thorough form of domination. The subtle technologies of modern power produce sovereign subjects who assume responsibility for self-discipline through the discursive practices of various institutions as well as the disciplines of the human sciences. Modern power, for Foucault, exists not merely "out there" in macroinstitutions but in the very formation of bodies and desires. It operates most effectively when subjects transformed into individuals believe they are most free.

My own goal in exposing the terrain of modernity (1999) was to emphasize the power of the imagination that modernity unleashes to create geopolitical exclusions and markings of difference. Viewing modernity in this manner, I argued, reveals the politics of colonial and postcolonial orderings. I proposed that modernity persists as an imaginary and continuously shifting site of global–local claims, commitments, and knowledges, forged within uneven dialogues about the place of those who move in and out of categories of otherness. At the heart of this imaginary (and, needless to say, very real and material) space, I highlighted the central politics of gender in shaping both the experiences of modernity in non-Western locations and narratives about modernity. By "gender," I mean contingent, nonfoundational differentiations of femininity and masculinity that are mapped onto social relations and bodies, defining the nexus of power/knowledge that permeates social life. Attention to gender defamiliarizes the common-sense understanding that often accompanies the invocation of modernity. It has been very difficult for my position not to be taken as a reification of the local and a culturally relativist celebration of plural modernities. I was rather arguing for a critical perspective on projects carried out in the name of an imagined space called modernity.

Given that each of these positions is political, it should not be surprising that they have been taken to task in one form or another by those worried about other effects of power. These interlocutors emphasize the fact that creative paradoxes exist in engaging with the terrain of modernity. Thus, Marilyn Strathern (1994) astutely points out that Latour's hybrid networks of artifacts, ideas, and persons, notably his celebration of the inventiveness of "us" moderns to construct such networks, uncannily echoes recent extensions of intellectual property laws. Rather than bring us more democracy and freedom, as Latour implies, such a view might instead lend itself to more proprietorship. Jacqueline Nassy Brown (1998) engages with Gilroy and argues that it is crucial to trace the politics not only of a shared Black Atlantic sensibility, but also the hierarchies of imagination within that Black Atlantic which engender diasporic movement as masculine (e.g., seafaring) and strategically erase or marginalize other movements (e.g., women who marry across the Black Atlantic). We should not, she tells us, take movement for granted but must ask about its meaningful construction. Ann Stoler (1995) argues that we need not so much reject Foucault as extend him into a colonial sphere. And finally, I have been thoughtfully criticized for invoking a postcolonial perspective on modernity in China. As one interlocutor pointed out (Kipnis 2000), since the Chinese state has colonized the postcolonial perspective, perhaps we need to find another angle from which to capture the dynamics I was describing in China.

Those of us intent on resisting and reworking the onslaught of imaginations and programs in the name of modernity have had to grapple with a number of paradoxes. One means of handling these paradoxes, through the method of "critical interruption," recognizes the necessary multiplicity of political interpretations, using one position to critically interrupt, or find the limits, of the other.[1] The method of critical interruption allows us to address two paradoxes in writings about modernity: one is that between treating modernity as an overarching, universalizing force—a *sui generis* actor not simply *in* the world but as a maker *of* "the world"—versus attending to the politics of representing modernity in that manner. The second paradox is that of assuming modernity to be an a priori unity versus analyzing it as the outcome of diverse conjunctures. Pheng Cheah (2000) has argued that to resolve the hoary dichotomy of universality versus particularity, we should move beyond Hegel's version of universality as the transcendence of finitude and specificity. Instead, we might conceive of universality as precisely the "radical openness to contamination by alterity," thus confronting a universality that claims it is not located anywhere (2000:17).

Paradoxes of Modernity

These paradoxes of modernity and their critical interruptions continue to haunt scholarly works that purport to move us far beyond modernity. Take the much touted book *Empire,* by Michael Hardt and Antonio Negri (2000). I engage with this book at length because of the worrisome praise it has received as the new bible for those who want to comprehend and challenge the new world order. Hardt and Negri paint a grandiose and oracular vision of a global order of postmodern Empire in which, they claim, the modernist imaginaries of the old world order are no longer relevant. Thus, the modern institutions of Foucault's disciplinary regimes, capitalist Fordist production, center-periphery divisions of labor and wealth, and the nation-state, along with fixed boundaries and territories and the immobility of labor, have been transcended by new technologies of capitalism and political sovereignty. Imperialism, too, is over. Taking their inspiration from Deleuze and Guattari's theories of power and subjectivity, Hardt and Negri imagine Empire as the sovereign power that unites the globe under a singular logic of rule through networks of power that are flexible, rhizomatic rather than vertical, and move, in nomadic fashion, across decentered, deterritorialized space. This Empire, according to Hardt and Negri, is irreversible and irresistible. It is the latest stage within the capitalist mode of production. Empire arises neither spontaneously out of heterogeneous global forces, "as if this order were a harmonious concert orchestrated by the natural and neutral hidden hand of the world market" (2000:3), nor is it dictated by a single power, as if it were a conspiracy of globalization. Rather, its juridical basis has been conceptually pieced together out of disparate origins, from its genealogy in Christian universal ethics; elements of the United States constitution, including federalism ("a democratic interaction of powers linked together in networks" [2000:161]); and a concept of sovereignty that refers to a power entirely within society —the juridical positivism of the United Nations that inscribes a notion of supranational authority and the communications networks laid down by transnational corporations. According to Hardt and Negri, Empire has four major characteristics: (1) its rule has no spatial limits, encompassing the social totality within its open, expanding frontiers; (2) it presents itself as a regime with no temporal boundaries, suspending history and fixing the existing state of affairs for eternity; (3) it regulates not just territory but social life in its entirety; thus, its major mode of rule is biopower; and (4) though bathed in blood, Empire always presents itself, in the guise of the concept of a "just war," as dedicated to peace. In the rhetorical tradition of prophecy, Hardt and Negri unveil Empire as both already in existence and just over the horizon of our future.

One of Hardt and Negri's goals in describing the new world order is to imagine a counter-Empire, an "alternative political organization of global flows and exchanges" (2000:xv). Indeed, they make the bold, optimistic claim that Empire has come into existence in response to workers' struggles around the world. They view the tactics of imperial rule as having developed out of a need to crush the impending success of international workers' uprisings. The political subject of their counter-Empire is "the multitude"—a new, more global version of the proletariat whose previous internationalism of the 1960s is once again "united by a common desire for liberation" (2000:42). Empire, they conclude, is better "in the same way that Marx insists that capitalism is better" (2000:43)—that is, because it provides the necessary conditions for potential liberation. They explicitly reject "leftist nationalism"—the desire to resurrect the nation-state to battle global capital—as well as various forms of what they label "localism." By contrast, several of the last decade's social movements they pinpoint may appear to be local—from Beijing's Tiananmen to the Los Angeles rebellion to the strikes in Paris and Seoul—but according to Hardt and Negri, these presage the coming into existence of the multitude because each struggle leaps immediately to the global level and destroys conventional distinctions between the economic, the political, and the cultural. To reach the unity of the multitude, however, these struggles will have to agree on a common enemy ("Clarifying the nature of the common enemy is thus an essential political task" [2000:57]) and develop a common language ("Struggles in other parts of the world and even our own struggles seem to be written in an incomprehensible foreign language. This too points toward an important political task: to construct a new common language that facilitates communication, as the languages of anti-imperialism and proletarian internationalism did for the struggles of a previous era" [2000:57]). In their view, only a "universal, catholic community" will bring together all peoples "in a common journey" (2000:207). "Cosmo-political liberation" (2000:64) is within our sight if we admit, along with Spinoza, that "prophetic desire" is irresistible (2000:65).

There is much that is suggestive in this account. Thus we can glimpse intimations of their vision of the new imperial sovereignty in the operation of power in certain countries (though not all countries) increasingly through deterritorialized institutions like the World Trade Organization, International Monetary Fund, and World Bank, as well as the horizontally networked nongovernmental organizations (NGOs). Achille Mbembe's (2001) and Charles Piot's (1999) descriptions of the disarray of postcolonial power in certain African countries certainly resonate here. Echoing other critiques, Hardt and Negri pinpoint the "moral instruments" of power in the "just wars" that NGOs conduct without arms or violence but rather, in an eerie echo of Christian missionaries, via definitions of human needs and rights. These "charitable campaigns and the mendicant orders of Empire," as Hardt and Negri call them, embrace an ethics resonant of Christian moral theology where "evil is first posed as privation of the good and then sin is defined as culpable negation of the good . . . In this way, moral intervention has become a frontline force of imperial intervention" (2000:36). According to Hardt and Negri, then, the problem with NGOs is that they, wittingly or unwittingly, provide moral justification for the spread of Empire. Tellingly, Hardt and Negri oppose the instrumental effects of NGO morality but do not seem troubled by the problem of universality, specifically the imposition of universal definitions of human needs and desires.

Their analysis of international military interventions is also prescient, especially in cases such as the Persian Gulf War. These military interventions, they argue, are increasingly based on portraying force as existing in the service of right and peace (as opposed, for example, to democracy) and on the juridical capacity to define every case as an exception. The result is a new "science of the police that is founded on a practice of just war to address continually arising emergencies" (2000:18). Finally, while their description of transformations in capitalist modes of accumulation echoes numerous others, Hardt and Negri admirably bring back a dialectic of human struggle to the development of global capitalism, in contrast to other scholarly work that describes capitalism as developing globally from within its own internal financial or accumulation logic. Moreover, Hardt and Negri want to emphasize the political sovereignty that "fits" with this stage of capitalism, though it cannot be reduced to it.

Imperial Prophecies

Empire speaks in prophetic tongue. Indeed, it is written in the manner of a progressive, monotheistic bible; part Star Wars–inspired apocalypse for these dark times and part genealogy of European philosophy read as world social and cultural history, *Empire* is filled with palpable desires to arouse the masses. In an echo of Christian biblical rhetoric, Hardt and Negri portray a singular world order characterized, they claim, by its totality, irresistibility, and irreversibility.

Exactly at this point, I begin to worry about the sort of prophesying that goes on in a book like *Empire,* for its claims resonate too closely with those representational politics of modernity that I and others have found most troubling. Take their approach to capitalism. Hardt and Negri are not alone in casting capitalism as a uniform or monolithic force, pursuing the same outcomes everywhere around the world. Such a view assumes capitalism's influence is overpowering and, as a result, that its effects are homogenizing. As a corollary, capitalism is then treated in contrast to the local as if it were a deterritorialized force, without reference to the specific and uneven spatial grounding of the different elements and processes involved. It is ironic that such totalizing images have rushed in to fill the space pried open by the critique of the totalizing narrative of modernity. They have returned us once again to pretensions that modernity (or postmodernity) has a universal form with local particulars. The perspective on world order reflected in an enterprise like *Empire* can only sustain itself if it retains tropes of pure categories, evolutionary stages, unilinear development, and a singular world history which, I have argued, reproduce the very problems of co-lonialist modernity that we need to interrogate.

To develop a critique of capitalism at the new millennium, we need to find more critical distance. Analyses of capitalism should not merely sound like the underside of paeans to capitalism. Marx dedicated him-self to exposing not just the dark side of capitalism but the partiality of the political economists' ideology of his day. The critiques of modernity could lead us in other directions: focusing on the cultural production of capitalism and the transformations currently taking place in this pro-duction; emphasizing the culturally, geographically, and historically specific and uneven manifestations of these processes; treating dis-courses of global capitalism and globalization as, themselves, elements within this cultural production that require critical scrutiny not only regarding their accuracy but also, and more importantly, regarding the kinds of work to which they are being put.

But Hardt and Negri refuse these analytical directions because they have a particular political project in mind: the rising up of a singular mass political subject, "the multitude." Here, too, we find modernist predilections surfacing through the Sturm und Drang drama of their prophecies. For Hardt and Negri, the multitude's ability to liberate themselves lies in their liberation from the dualism that Hardt and Negri see as defining modernity: immanence versus transcendence. On the one hand exist

> the immanent forces of desire and association, the love of the com-munity, and on the other, the strong hand of an overarching au-thority that imposes and enforces an order on the social field. This tension was to be resolved, or at least mediated, by the sovereignty of the state, and yet it continually resurfaces as a question of either/or: freedom or servitude, the liberation of desire or its sub-jugation. (2000:69)

They proceed to trace this modern dualism through European philoso-phy: first, the discovery of the plane of immanence, or the singularity of being, in Duns Scotus, Dante, Pico della Mirandola, Sir Francis Ba-con, and Galileo. These thinkers reappropriated what medieval notions of an overarching, transcendent authority took away: the foundation of authority in the immanence of universal humanity. Hardt and Negri interpret this singular universal as the multitude. It embodies the progressive force they would like to draw from. Then follows the philosophical struggles of the Renaissance, which continue the battle of immanent forces versus transcendent authority. Above all, Spinoza is the person who continues to speak in the name of revolutionary humanism. Finally, beginning with Descartes, we get the reestablishment of a transcendent order to repress and control the multitude. Throughout European philosophy, the forces of light battle the forces of darkness.

Is this the history of modernity as a European philosophical concept, or are we meant to understand this discussion as a description of world history? For Hardt and Negri, they are one and the same. They reveal this modernist Hegelian approach to History—where the universal Idea is the driving force of social life—in two contradictory assertions: that they plan to pursue "Empire" not as a "metaphor" which would require an historical discussion, but rather as a "concept" which calls for a philosophical approach; and that they plan to focus on Europe and "Euro-America" because the dominant path along which the concepts developed which animate Empire reside in these places. For Hardt and Negri, these are not hyperreal figures of a geopolitical imaginary; they are merely "real." They feel no need, then, to explicate the making of Europe and the continuous work required to maintain Euro-America as a stable subject. Thus, they try to have it both ways—while ignoring the rest of the world and telling a eurocentric tale of everyone else's histories.

It is ironic that Hardt and Negri, in a later section, dismiss postcolonial theory, for they reproduce the colonial modernist mode of producing knowledge as we have come to distinguish it, with its assumptions about the unfolding of a master imperial logic, the singularity of being, and the teleologies of history. Their central assumption is that only the concepts of European philosophy—and Christianity—contain within them the possibility for universalization. They do not even venture as far as Charles Taylor, who hopes to encapsulate non-European histories and philosophies as the particulars of a universal history whose theoretical subject remains Europe (see Chatterjee 1990). Only Europe, it appears, is *theoretically* knowable; all other histories are matters of empirically fleshing out the European theoretical subject.

In a chapter entitled "The Dialectics of Colonial Sovereignty," Hardt and Negri acknowledge the grievous nature of European supremacy. But their modernist logic does nothing to decenter that rule—which, as postcolonial theory has taught us, resides not just in political governance narrowly defined but in governmentality that includes philosophy (i.e., the production of eurocentric knowledge that justifies that rule). Rather than continue the modernist assumption, though with a sympathetic gesture, that Europe gave birth to itself, a critique of modernity requires that we decenter or provincialize Europe (Chakrabarty 1992, 2001). This alternative view is that Europe can only be known as such through the sets of oppositions between "Europe" and the colonized world that particular colonizers constructed. European philosophy is rife with presumptions about colonized subjects that inform their universalist theories of human reason; such theories used these subjects to sustain their exclusionary views of race and difference. Hardt and Negri might at least have noted, for example, the long centuries of interaction between the Christian and Islamic worlds that ultimately constructed Europe, ranging from aesthetics to mathematics to philosophy.

The political unconscious of *Empire* is the European subject looking out. Viewing the new world order from other perspectives might offer a method for taking seriously the experiences and world views of those "Others" who exist not merely to construct a European subject but have multiple relationships with multiple non-European others (e.g., China with Southeast Asia). Postcolonial theory argues that modernity operates by way of exclusions and by the constitution of difference that together generate the Euro-American sense of a unified subjectivity. Rather than assume that all non-European subjects merely rehearse Europe's history of modernity, we must instead delineate the articulations configured in modernities that do not simply replicate eurocentric teleologies even as non-Western nationalists struggled to make their country's modernity stand on its own as a metanarrative of non-Western history. Postcolonial scholarship, then, points in the direction of a critique of modernity that explores the existence of power through "agencies whose contingent patterns always admit the possibility of otherwise" (Johnson and Chiu 2000:2).

Engendering Modernity

If endeavors imagined under the sign of modernity are racialized projects of difference, they are also gendered. Gender differentiation and subordination have been explicit projects by which various states have crafted their modernities, both liberal and authoritarian capitalist states as well as radical and authoritarian socialist ones. Gender differentiation and subordination are found in divisions cast between family, civil society, and the state; in the attention, or lack thereof, to the politics of family; in divisions of labor that naturalize a realm called "reproductive work"; and in the politics of bodies that debate such matters as reproductive technologies, abortion, pornography, and licit and illicit sex. These differentiate violable women from unviolable ones and create scares over "trafficking" that signal the fact that women's and children's bodies are the most sensitive barometers of struggles over labor migration. Among other things, these scares lead to paternalistic legislation that further harasses women who wish to cross borders without documentation. Tracing these politics of gender offers remarkable clarity on modernity as an imagined project of historical contingency, gaps, and disjunctures. Viewing modernity through these gendered perspectives, then, opens up modernity as a singular project.

The politics of gender devised in the imagined reaches of modernity continue to underlie visions of postmodern empire and rhizomatic capitalism—and most tellingly when they are ostensibly ignored. The silences about gender in these versions of the new world order paradoxically highlight the masculinity that implicitly defines them. The masculinist fantasies that infuse such visions become evident once we know how, following Wendy Brown, to "find the man in the state" (1992, 1995). *Empire* reflects these masculinist fantasies in four ways that overlap with one another: the description of sovereignty, the discussion of body politics, the portrait of the international division of labor, and the new political hero of empire. Postmodern sovereignty, for Hardt and Negri, is a relationship between imperial rule and individual bodies. On the one side is a saturation of bodies with power, and on the other, bodies that evade or stand up and fight all the way to the top. Nowhere in this picture can we discern relationality, especially relationality of kinship and family.[2]

This view of state power in fact reflects the classic liberal account, which divides the polity into ostensibly autonomous spheres of family, civil society (economy), and state. The family is cast as "natural," and thus so also is woman and women's work within it; personhood inside households is not recognized. Gendered limitations in exercising political rights and power are obscured. Men, on the other hand, exist as rights-bearing individuals who, by definition, hold the prerogative to procure rights and power for themselves in society. Even for those women who manage to act like men in obtaining rights and power, they hold substantively different meanings in their lives, given the constraints of household labor. Finally, the masculine political subject, in the classic account of sovereignty, is oriented toward autonomy and individual power. This political subject has no need for the kinds of body politics that feminism has placed on the public agenda, such as reproductive rights, freedom from domestic violence, and control over one's sexuality. Indeed, though Hardt and Negri argue that bodies are saturated with power in the new empire, these bodies seem rather abstract and undefined—precisely the masculine bodies of liberalism.[3]

If *Empire*'s version of postmodern sovereignty is masculinist, so too is its vision of the new political hero—the multitude. Hardt and Negri argue that the multitude is developing out of the novel modes of production in which the information economy predominates. But here one finds a striking paradox at the heart of their argument. They insist that "the central role previously occupied by the labor power of mass factory workers in the production of surplus value is today increasingly filled by intellectual, immaterial, and communicative labor power" (2000:29). By "immaterial," they mean symbolic, affective, and informationalized labor. Much later in the book, they acknowledge the obvious: that much industrial labor has been moved to non-Western countries and is performed by women. So what exactly is the "role" of factory labor that has been reduced? Not, I believe, its importance to a world economy but rather its place in an economy of heroic politics. Whereas the working-class hero of the nineteenth and early twentieth centuries was a masculine hero based in industrial labor, it is absolutely clear that this figure cannot function as such any longer. Where we can look for this hero today, they suggest, is in information labor. The role of allegorical heroes, rather than contributions to the economy, is at issue here. It is striking, then, that their notable inclusion of service and affective work in the information sector elides gender as well: they locate service and affective work in the financial and media entertainment sectors. In the "old world" of modernity, one of the main locations of affective labor was the raising of children and the labors of sex and love. Hardt and Negri do not discuss these labors either in their version of modernity or of postmodernity; they have once again made them invisible.[4]

The Melancholic Subject

The modernist desire to have a masculine hero of politics leads Hardt and Negri to argue that the politics of difference—by which they explicitly target postcolonial politics but also, by implication, politics that highlight race, gender, and sexuality—are part of the problem, not the solution. At best, they argue in their chapter "Symptoms of Passage," these politics have already been coopted by capitalist machinations that celebrate difference in order to extend the reach of markets. Here they engage in the modernist conceit that a sign has one, stable meaning. It is odd that Hardt, a literary theorist, would reduce "difference" to a fixed meaning rather than a discursive, unstable, contested field. "Difference," in fact, is a rhetorical terrain with a wide variety of meanings, including those produced by postcolonial scholars like Said (1978), who aspires to overcome the colonial production of difference in the hope of reaching a common humanity; Spivak (1987), Chatterjee (1993), and Chakrabarty (2001), who deconstruct and reverse the hierarchies of co-lonial difference in order to engage with Other worlds; scholars of color in the United States, like Patricia Williams (1991, 1995), who argues that differences are often effaced and need to be brought to the fore; transnational scholars such as Paul Gilroy (1993) who celebrate trans-national Black Atlantic culture even as they criticize essentialist no-tions of racial difference; and Derrida's (1976) notion of différance as a problem within Western metaphysics—as well as the diversity rhetoric of specifically American businesses interested in investment in Asia. (Companies in China, for example, do not invoke "diversity" or "multi-culturalism" as their business strategy.) If Judith Butler (1997) is cor-rect that melancholia (the inability to mourn loss) is instrumental in forming subjectivity, that it represents an otherwise unrepresentable ambivalence about that loss, and that the violence of social regulation emerges in the power to regulate which losses will and will not be grieved, then we might well argue that the dismissal or silencing of these diverse politics by Hardt and Negri betrays an underlying melan-cholia for the imagined ideal of the modern Western subject.[5]

Why must we be forced into a dream of unity? Why can we not dream of flexible alliances and articulations? On one level, they would certainly agree. Their Deleuze and Guattari–inspired vision of rhi-zomatic politics leaves room for a wide variety of alliances. Yet I find their dream of a common language frightening. Who will establish the proper grammar of this language? Set the communicative import of its terms? What of those who wish to speak in multiple tongues? They traipse over the issue of translation as if it were merely a pragmatic di-lemma, rather than, as many scholars (Liu 1995; Rafael 1988) have shown, a question of power. For those who live on the sexual margins, for example, the dream of the multitude brings not hope but fear. What reassurances do Hardt and Negri offer that the recent history of de-graded existence for those forced out of the multitude in the name of sexual respectability will not be repeated in their version of unity?[6] The specificities of heteronormativity will not merely wither away in the unity of the multitude against capitalism. Can we not dream of fighting capitalism through articulations and alliances of variously identified subjects? Can we not dream of fighting capitalism in the manner, for example, of those who have fought AIDS? AIDS activism has addressed the mutual imbrication of power in the endless relays between expert discourse and institutional authority, between medical truth and social regulation, and between popular knowledge practices and struggles for survival. AIDS activism has thus multiplied the sites of political contestation to include immigration policy, public health policy, the practice of epidemiology and clinical medicine, the conduct of scientific research, the operation of the insurance and pharmaceutical industries, the role of the media, the decisions of rent-control boards, the legal definition of "family," and ultimately the public and private administration of the body (Halperin 1995). It is unsettling that Hardt and Negri do not discuss these politics. Why must they dismiss them as having been incorporated into capitalism? Hardt and Negri have missed the enormous body of work that has shown that we do not have to pit class against other identities, but rather that we can conceive of class in a manner that does not implicitly make the class subject a white, masculine, Euro-American subject. If bodies do matter, then Hardt and Negri still have a long way to go.

Star Wars as Allegory of Modernity

The gender and sexual politics of *Empire*, cast as they are in a narrative structure resembling biblical allegory, turn us irresistibly toward other popular cultural productions with which it eerily resonates. One prime example is the Star Wars series. Here, we find the modernist desires that animate one story of empire resonating in another story of empire.

You may recall the story of the George Lucas prequel, *Star Wars, Episode 1: The Phantom Menace*: the Galactic Republic has been disrupted by turmoil over the taxation of trade routes to outlying star systems. The powerful Trade Federation tries to resolve the matter by intimidation, putting a stranglehold on the peaceful planet of Naboo. Two Jedi come to the aid of its ruler, Queen Amidala, against the darker forces at work in the Trade Federation. The dark Siths try to assassinate the Jedi ship on its way to argue Naboo's case before the Senate, forcing it to land on Tatooine, an area resembling North Africa. There, they meet the young slave boy Anakin Skywalker, discern that the Force is unusually strong within him, win his freedom, and convince his mother to allow them to take him for training as a Jedi. They return to Naboo and fight the Trade Federation army, which is defeated only when Anakin Skywalker enters the nerve center of a Trade Federation battleship and manages to turn off their army droids.

The resonance of allegories in both Hardt and Negri's and George Lucas's productions of Empire is striking. Both stress the duality of empire. In the book, the duality is between the multitude and the new imperial sovereignty. In the film, the duality is similarly a dialectic between the forces of good and evil. The trick is to embody the Force—or, in the book, the masculine desire of the multitude for oneness. The film also agrees with the book that there is a new homogeneous world capitalism, based in free trade, though its evaluation of that capitalism is obviously distinct. *Star Wars*, like *Empire*, subsumes a diverse world into a rhizomatic oneness—all peoples must unite against the Dark Forces. Of course, the fact that the leaders are white men and the others are various markers of difference is both the point of the film and made to seem irrelevant.

Christian monogenetic paternity further animates these allegories. Our young Jesus figure, Anakin Skywalker, was conceived by midichlorians —living organisms found in cells—through which people are able to communicate with the Force. Anthropologist Carol Delaney (1991) has argued that Christianity gives a monogenetic meaning to paternity. Paternity means begetting, while maternity means nurturing and bearing. Paternity in this view is the primary, essential, and creative role. This meaning of paternity is exemplified by the virgin birth and is consistent with the theological concept of monotheism. In the film, the microorganisms give birth to Anakin, but the human men make him what he will become. His mother, the virgin-birth mother, is the vessel for holding him and nourishing him until the men come to take him away and make him a man. In this view, men have creative power within them, which gives them a core of identity, self-motivation, and autonomy. Women lack the power to create and therefore to project themselves. Likewise, in the book *Empire*, affective labor gets subsumed under the new masculine labor of information technology, while the multitude—a universality that subsumes particularity—births itself.

We do not need to end up in a Star Wars world. One gets there by treating modernity as a reified and universal state of being. Modernity persists as a powerful narrative, but there are Other stories to be told.

Hardt and Negri's account of Empire reproduces the very master narrative they ostensibly wish to undermine. By trafficking in singularities, becoming seduced by dualities, and remaining attached to a concept of a unified subject, Hardt and Negri perpetuate a narrative of modernity—and postmodernity—built on the very exclusions and differentiations they claim are magically irrelevant in the new world order. An anthropology of modernity must move in a different direction. It must maneuver between the twin dangers of universalizing and creating separate, holistic cultures (such as an undifferentiated Europe). Instead, we must develop an anthropology of intersecting global imaginations. Attention to the cultural negotiations in which power relations, racial, gender and sexual identities, and subaltern politics are formulated will provide a truly rhizomatic alternative. The masculine singularity of voice in the narrative of Empire must give way to the specific narratives and stories of variously positioned actors. This approach is not a paean to "diversity" but a commitment to the contingency of politics. It is, to mangle Geertz, politics all the way down. And stories of modernity continue to enframe the globalization of these politics. Thus, the urgency with which we must attend to the way imaginings of modernity, purported to lie in the past, continue to haunt narratives of the future.

Notes

1. Gayatri Spivak (1987) has most fully explored the potential fruitfulness of the method of critical interruption. Critical interruption rejects the coherence of narratives while retaining what makes political sense in those narratives.

2. See Aihwa Ong (1997, 1999) and Sylvia Yanagisako (2002), for example, for distinct discussions of the central role of kinship in the development of capitalism.

3. For an extended discussion of these issues, see Wendy Brown (1992, 1995).

4. Hardt and Negri have one sentence on this topic: "Feminist movements that made clear the political content of 'personal' relationships and refused patriarchal discipline raised the social value of what has traditionally been considered women's work, which involves a high content of affective or caring labor and centers on services necessary for social reproduction" (2000:274). This statement segues into their argument that "communication, cooperation, the affective—would define the transformation of capitalist production in the subsequent decades" (2000:275). This transition allows them to proceed by ignoring gendered divisions of labor under Empire.

5. I read most of the outpouring of literature on melancholia as implicitly addressing the inability to mourn the loss of the modern Western subject.

6. See the memoir of Reinaldo Arenas (1993) for one experience of this marginalization.

References

Arenas, Reinaldo
    1993   *Before Night Falls: A Memoir.* Translated by Dolores M. Koch. New York: Penguin Books.

Boas, Franz
  1940   *Race, Language and Culture.* Chicago: University of Chicago Press.

Brown, Jacqueline Nassy
  1998   Black Liverpool, Black America, and the Gendering of Diasporic
          Space. *Cultural Anthropology* 13(3): 291–325.

Brown, Wendy
  1992   Finding the Man in the State. *Feminist Studies* 18(1): 7–34.
  1995   *States of Injury: Power and Freedom in Late Modernity.* Princeton,
          N.J.: Princeton University Press.

Butler, Judith
  1997   *The Psychic Life of Power.* Stanford, Calif.: Stanford University
          Press.

Chakrabarty, Dipesh
  1992   Postcoloniality and the Artifice of History: Who Speaks for "In-
          dian" Pasts? *Representations* 37: 1–26.
  2001   *Provincializing Europe: Postcolonial Thought and Historical Difference.*
          Princeton, N.J.: Princeton University Press.

Chatterjee, Partha
  1990   A Response to Taylor's "Modes of Civil Society." *Public Culture*
          3(1): 119–132.
  1993   *The Nation and Its Fragments: Colonial and Postcolonial Histories.*
          Princeton: Princeton University Press.

Cheah, Pheng
  2000   Universal Areas: Asian Studies in a World in Motion. Paper pre-
          sented at Place, Locality and Globalization Conference, University
          of California, Santa Cruz.

Delaney, Carol
  1991   *The Seed and the Soil: Gender and Cosmology in Turkish Village So-
          ciety.* Berkeley: University of California Press.

Derrida, Jacques
  1976   *Of Grammatology.* Translated by Gayatri Chakravorty Spivak. Balti-
          more, Md.: Johns Hopkins University Press.

Douglas, Mary
  1966   *Purity and Danger: An Analysis of Concepts of Pollution and Taboo.*
          London: Routledge and Kegan Paul.

Foucault, Michel
  1979   *Discipline and Punish: The Birth of a Prison.* Translated by Alan
          Sheridan. New York: Vintage.
  1980   *The History of Sexuality, Volume 1: An Introduction.* Translated by
          Robert Hurley. New York: Vintage.

Gilroy, Paul
  1987   *"There Ain't No Black in the Union Jack": The Cultural Politics of
          Race and Nation.* London: Hutchinson.

1993   *The Black Atlantic: Modernity and Double Consciousness.* Cambridge, Mass.: Harvard University Press.

2000   *Against Race: Imagining Political Culture beyond the Color Line.* Cambridge, Mass.: Harvard University Press.

Halperin, David M.
1995   *Saint Foucault: Towards a Gay Hagiography.* New York: Oxford University Press.

Hardt, Michael, and Antonio Negri
2000   *Empire.* Cambridge, Mass.: Harvard University Press.

Johnson, Marshall, and Fred Yen Liang Chiu
2000   Introduction to special issue on subimperialism. *Positions: East Asia Cultures Critique* 8(1): 1–7.

Kipnis, Andrew B.
2000   Review of *Other Modernities: Gendered Yearnings in China after Socialism* by Lisa Rofel. *Bulletin of Concerned Asian Scholars* 32(3): 61–64.

Latour, Bruno
1993   *We Have Never Been Modern.* Translated by Catherine Porter. Cambridge, Mass.: Harvard University Press.

Liu, Lydia H.
1995   *Translingual Practice: Literature, National Culture, and Translated Modernity China, 1900–1937.* Stanford, Calif.: Stanford University Press.

Mbembe, Achille
2001   *On the Postcolony.* Berkeley: University of California Press.

Ong, Aihwa
1997   The Gender and Labor Politics of Postmodernity. In *The Politics of Culture in the Shadow of Capital.* Edited by Lisa Lowe and David Lloyd, pp. 61–97. Durham, N.C.: Duke University Press.

1999   *Flexible Citizenship: The Cultural Logics of Transnationality.* Durham, N.C.: Duke University Press.

Piot, Charles
1999   *Remotely Global: Village Modernity in West Africa.* Chicago: University of Chicago Press.

Rafael, Vicente L.
1988   *Contracting Colonialism: Translation and Christian Conversion in Tagalog Society under Early Spanish Rule.* Ithaca, N.Y.: Cornell University Press.

Rofel, Lisa
1999   *Other Modernities: Gendered Yearnings in China after Socialism.* Berkeley: University of California Press.

Said, Edward
1978   *Orientalism.* New York: Pantheon.

Spivak, Gayatri Chakravorty
  1987   *In Other Worlds: Essays in Cultural Politics.* New York: Routledge.
Star Wars
  1977   *Star Wars* [film], directed by George Lucas. Lucasfilm Ltd.
Star Wars, Episode 1: The Phantom Menace
  1999   *Star Wars, Episode 1: The Phantom Menace* [film], directed by George
          Lucas. Lucasfilm Ltd.
Stoler, Ann
  1995   *Race and the Education of Desire: Foucault's* History of Sexuality *and
          the Colonial Order of Things.* Durham, N.C.: Duke University Press.
Strathern, Marilyn
  1994   The New Modernities. Paper presented at Conference of the Euro-
          pean Society for Oceanists.
Williams, Brackette
  1991   *Stains on My Name, War in My Veins: Guyana and the Politics of
          Cultural Struggle.* Durham, N.C.: Duke University Press.
Williams, Patricia J.
  1991   *The Alchemy of Race and Rights.* Cambridge, Mass.: Harvard Uni-
          versity Press.
  1995   *The Rooster's Egg: On the Persistence of Prejudice.* Cambridge, Mass.:
          Harvard University Press.
Yanagisako, Sylvia
  2002   *The Culture of Capital: Producing Italian Family Firms.* Princeton,
          N.J.: Princeton University Press.

Six

Accessing "Local" Modernities
Reflections on the Place of Linguistic Evidence in Ethnography

Debra A. Spitulnik

In this chapter, I raise several epistemological and methodological challenges inherent in trying to access "local" modernities by looking at language use. I draw on research into the colonial history and contemporary context of radio broadcasting in Zambia and on a longitudinal project on Bemba language change in Zambia's multilingual environment.[1]

Two basic issues concern me. First, what does it mean to access a local concept of modernity? What form does this take in language? Second and related to this, I am interested in teasing out the differences in types of linguistic meaning as they relate to what we identify as a "local" modernity. Specifically, I am concerned with the differences between (a) the linguistic forms and modes of language use that have a denotational function of *referring to a local concept of the modern or modernity,* and (b) the linguistic forms and modes of language use that have the pragmatic function of *performing or signifying a social identity of "being modern."* Examples of type (a) include what typically function as key words in referring to the modern, such as the English phrases "cutting edge" or "up to the minute." Examples from the Bemba language of Zambia, about which more will be said below, include the word *ubulaya,* "modern," "trendy," and the phrase *shino nshiku,* "nowadays," "these days." Expressions of type (b) tend to be much more numerous, more context bound, and more subjective in terms of their potential value as signifiers of modernity and related social meanings. For example, in many corners of the Atlanta, Georgia, corporate world, the expression "I'm all over that," said enthusiastically as a claim to worker

194

competence, indexes speaker identity as modern and progressive. To take just one example from urban Zambia, the Bemba expression "*Ee, ninjikata boyi*," "Yes, I understand my friend" (literally, "Yes, I grab [it/you], boy"), indexes a modern, trendy, urban, informal stance in the context of a conversation among peers.[2] This expression uses an urban variety of Bemba known as Town Bemba (Spitulnik 1998), here exemplified by the slang use of *-ikata*, "grab," for "understand" and the word *boyi*, "boy," an assimilated word from English. The essential difference is that the items in type (a) are used to denote elements of modernity, while the items in type (b) are used by speakers to signal or perform their own modernity.

Since modes of referring also often have performative functions with respect to social identity (Silverstein 1976), some of the same linguistic forms that fall under area (a) also fall under area (b). And both areas can contain types of linguistic evidence that reveal culturally specific *evaluations of modernity*. These are not necessarily worries, just realities that add more complexity to the issue of how linguistic evidence is useful for understanding local modernities, since linguistic evidence itself has different kinds of statuses both in ethnographic context and at different removes from ethnographic context.[3] Here, I wish to focus on what it means to draw on linguistic evidence of either the referring or performative type as we make analytic conclusions and select representational devices in our ethnographic work on modernity. For example, how do we look to area (a) or to area (b) to find translation equivalents of a "modernity" concept, for a source of authentic native terms that can be proposed as emic concepts, and for a form of data that is useful for understanding locally produced semantic and discursive fields relating to concepts of modernity?

By raising such issues, I raise some basic questions about the conduct of ethnography—as research and re-presentation—and the role of linguistic work in this. My general programmatic stance is one that is shared by the majority of linguistic anthropologists, one that is summed up quite aptly in the words of the late Charles Hockett: "linguistics without anthropology is sterile; anthropology without linguistics is blind" (1980:100). In terms of primary research, one small fraction of what is implied by Hockett's pronouncement is that language use—and communicative practice more generally—is an integral part of the human condition, lived realities, and the manufacture of the social. Elaborating on his vision metaphor, the point is that attending to language is a way of *seeing* and *seeing into* these phenomena. It is important to note, however, that language is not always a transparent window for seeing cultural content. Human language is a set of symbolic resources (as well as modes of practice), but as many linguistic anthropologists caution, it is not automatically or even frequently the case that one can read *directly* from linguistic data to cultural categories—despite the continued popularity of such an approach among many cultural anthropologists (Duranti 1997:2 ff.; Silverstein 1993). This is because language is not just a classification system, a way of representing independently established meanings, or a nonmediating tool of thought; it has dynamic creative functions as well. In Duranti's words, it is important to understand language "not only as a mode of thinking but, above all, as a cultural practice, that is, as form of action that both presupposes and at the same time brings about ways of being in the world" (1997:1; also see Mannheim and Tedlock 1995 for a concise synopsis of this type of approach).

In terms of ethnographic re-presentation, one small fraction of what is implied by Hockett's pronouncement is that we use language to render people's worlds intelligible to our readership. What linguistic choices are we making? What is revealed or concealed by the use of one or another word or phrase as a stand-in for "what the natives think" or "what is meaningful in this particular local world"? How do we avoid reification of local terms as key concepts when they may actually be quite multifunctional in real use? These questions are crucial to reflect on and attend to as we write ethnographies of any kind. To date, they have been relatively unasked, or unaddressed. My own work is certainly not immune, and even the discussion in this chapter only scratches the surface. Given the quagmires presented by issues of translation, incommensurability, intersubjectivity, and ethnographic authority, it may be much easier to raise such questions about the status of linguistic data for ethnographic re-representation and deduction than to satisfactorily solve them. That does not, however, defer engagement with them. And I would suggest that, in fact, to borrow a phrase from a colleague, this kind of engagement is required as part of "the reclaiming of ethnographic authority."[4]

For the subject at hand, it is noteworthy that many treatments of local or "vernacular" modernities or "discourses" of modernity pay little sustained attention to local terms or linguistic usage. This is part of a more general trend in the division of labor among the subfields of anthropology. For example, as Schieffelin (1993) so cogently observes, amid the increased attention to some analytical entity called "discourse" in recent cultural anthropology and cultural studies, it is paradoxical that one sees relatively little examination in this work of real, naturally occurring language in use, what most linguists and linguistic anthropologists term "discourse." Of course, snippets of discourse appear in ethnographic excerpts and the like, but this is not the same as asking about the epistemological or cultural status of language-based data. In the near decade that has passed since Schieffelin's observation, the situation is much the same. From a sociocultural perspective, the term "discourse" can be used either in a strict Foucauldian sense—to denote a culturally specific and historically contingent domain of knowledge and practice which establishes relations of power and truth—or, as a more general incarnation of this, for instance, as loosely equivalent to "ideology" or "way of understanding." Either way, this kind of "discourse" —what I call "Discourse" writ large—is organized, legitimated, stabilized, experienced, and even contested in large part through concrete events and patterns of speaking—that is, discourse writ small.[5] So how do we use all these small instances of speaking to distill ethnographic and analytical insights? How do we integrate an ac-knowledgment that participant-observation in/of "discourse" is often a very important—yet unspoken—part of what grounds our claims about Discourse? And how do we make this deductive process more transpar-ent in matters such as the study of alternative modernities?

These are key epistemological and methodological issues at the inter-section of linguistic anthropology and cultural anthropology, beyond the specific project on Zambian versions of modernity. They are proposed here more as directives for future research than as fully demonstrated or completed lines of inquiry. In the spirit of this volume, the following discussion serves as a brief meditation on how to comb through lan-guage and discourse to understand better the shape that modernity takes in a particular place. Before doing that, I will turn more directly to the modernity concept in general, some background on the Zambian context, and some further epistemological questions.

Modernity, the Moving Target

From an historical perspective, the introduction of electronic media in colonial Zambia in the late 1930s went hand in hand with the introduc-tion of a nexus of technologies, cultural practices, orientations, and evaluations related to ideas of progress, sophistication, consumption, in-novation, individual subjectivity, scientific rationality, and Westernization —a nexus that could be captured by the cover term "modernity." Dur-ing the colonial period, when Zambia was the British colony of North-ern Rhodesia, radio programs with the "world wide news" and "best songs" (Franklin 1950:11, 13) aired alongside "development" programs intended to drive "home to Africans the need for hard work, improved agriculture and stock-keeping, the protection of forests and grasslands, better hygiene and the need for education of African girls" (Franklin 1950:3). Programs such as *News from Cape to Cairo, Taxation, African Citizenship, Rabies, Music while You Work,* and *Land and Native Development* joined the sounds of the underground explosions of mining operations on the Zambian Copperbelt; the inscription of young men to fight on World War II battlefields; the noisy traffic of cars, trains, and airplanes in new urban centers; and the competitive dance songs of migrant laborers. This period of colonial radio's extensive development, particularly from the late 1940s and early 1950s through Zambian independence in 1964, was a time of rapid urban industrialization based on the mining of copper, intense Christian missionary influence, and a growing colonial state apparatus. Similar types of programming continue up through the present on state-run national radio in shows such as *News Flash, Party Time, Super Hit Parade, The Breakfast Show, Our Government, Health Education News,* and *Parliament in National Development.* There is a promotion of certain musical tastes, consumption patterns, scientific sensibilities, concepts of the self and the person, and preferences for particular modalities of newness, novelty, and progress —all of which seem to speak to Zambian radio's role in helping to introduce or amplify new forms of thinking, understanding, talking about, and living modernity.

In my work on Zambian media, however, I have increasingly come to the conclusion that using the cover term "modernity" in this way signifies both too much and too little. To turn to this point directly below, I bracket the longer story of the incomplete hegemony of both colonial radio and contemporary radio, and the complicated radio landscape which includes numerous programs with formats, contents, communication styles, languages, and ideologies that do not fit so well with the Western-derived modernities itemized above (Spitulnik 2003). Whether the concept of modernity is useful at all, analytically, is an open question, and one which is currently under great debate (Gaonkar 1999; Knauft, this volume; Piot 2001). There are "many modernities" (Comaroff and Comaroff 1993a:xi) and many ways of both consciously and unconsciously "playing with modernity" (Appadurai 1995). Given this multiplicity, a serious question arises concerning the analytical power of the very term "modernity" in anthropological work. If there are such wide-ranging cultural and historical particulars that fall under the umbrella of modernity, what warrants the use of the word as a single cover term in the first place? What is held constant? What is obscured in the cluster of conceptual distinctions and/or ethnographic realities that are grouped together under the shade of the modernity umbrella?

At base, the challenge involves using modernity as a metaoperator—a concept that transcends place, at least in part—while at the same time deconstructing and localizing it. For example, though writers now speak of "parallel," "alter-native," and "other" modernities—thus localizing and pluralizing the concept—the fact that the term "modernity" is used at all and then modified signals some interpreted commonality in the conceptualization of what "it" is. Comaroff and Comaroff expose this analytical conundrum when they explain that, when put under scrutiny, the concept of "modernity itself all too rapidly melts into air. As an analytic term, it becomes especially vague when dislodged from the ideal-typical, neo-evolutionary theoretical frame that classically encased it, defining it less in reference to the 'real' world than by contrast to that other chimera, 'tradition' " (1993a:xii). They propose that if the term is to have any utility at all within anthropology and cultural studies, it needs to be taken as "a (more-or-less) pliable sign" (1993a:xiii).

But even allowing modernity a certain pliability and plurality, from a critical standpoint, modernity as an analytical concept is constantly in danger of imploding as a victim of its own circumstances. As Latour (1993) and other scholars have argued since the early 1990s, the very idea of modernity is predicated on a mistaken eurocentric notion that precolonial societies were timeless, that they lacked innovation, and that they only valued tradition. For many contexts, however, the jury is still out over whether practices of consumption and the high value placed on "newness" and innovation actually came with colonialism or whether they predate it. Is the experience of modernity—understood as a complex of such dichotomies between old/new, traditional/modern, and so on—only confined to the modern period?

While such questions are receiving closer scrutiny,[6] I believe that the relatively unaddressed issues of translation and translatability push the critical envelope even further. How precisely does the English-language cover term "modernity" relate to culturally specific notions of the modern (or its translated equivalents)? From an anthropological perspective, approaching this problem "on the ground," we would want to ask first about how change, newness, progress, scientific rationality, and so on are named, located, and experienced in particular contexts. A very profound challenge to this emic/etic divide arises, however, when the language of the ethnographic context is the same as the language of analysis. This is indeed true in the case of Zambia, and so, too, in many other postcolonial societies. The very discourse of discussing and expressing "the modern" is often cast in the former colonial language (in this case, English) and derives, to a large extent, from the structures and ideologies of colonial rule. As I explain elsewhere (1998-1999, 2003), many of these English-language expressions for talking about modernity are in circulation in Zambia because of the operations of electronic media. For example, evidence from the early 1950s reveals the popular adoption of phrases such as "wake up," "modern world," "general knowledge," "become aware," "the best songs," "the latest world news," "progress," "development," "be civilized," "have a good chance of new life," and "make home a happy home" at the same time that these phrases are being used by colonial media to signal the elements of a new modern way of life. Similarly in the contemporary period, a whole host of English-language phrases, many of which derive directly from radio and popular imported music, are used to denote elements of modernity. Examples include "up to the minute," "up to date," "nonstop," "on the hour, every hour," "live," "the very best," "super," "hot," "switched on," and "jazzed up."

Even when data are in "indigenous" languages, however, there is no guarantee that one may make a direct read from "native terms" to "native consciousness." My general remarks above are pertinent here as well. Combined with this dilemma, there are cases where European-language formulations about modernity have been directly translated into indigenous languages and are part of everyday use. Do we take this direct transfer of expressions as an example of the "colonization of consciousness" (Comaroff and Comaroff 1991:26) or as an inhabitable discourse which one steps into, or as both? Or are there other techniques to understand the ways that expressions travel, permutate, and take root in the encounter between peoples, cultures, and languages?

Being Modern in Zambia

Despite all of these problems, I am compelled to use a collection of "M" terms in my work on Zambia because "being modern" and "the modern" are important cultural constructs—and phrases—in Zambia. They surface explicitly in state discourse and in everyday talk about culture and social change. They also exist more implicitly as cultural themes in the kinds of social distinctions and cultural values that inform people's words and actions. In my work, I use the term "modernity" to denote culturally specific ways of understanding and enacting what it means to "be modern." Fundamentally, this means taking modernity as an ethnographic problem and not as an overarching analytical category. In Zambia, this cultural construct takes shape in different ways across different sections of the population—an issue that admittedly merits more elaboration than I can offer at this time.

My usage differs from Ferguson's (1999), another scholar of contemporary Zambia, who uses the term "modernity" to denote a concept with direct linkage to the Western metanarrative of modernization. In his usage, modernity is a condition brought about by—or believed to result from—modernization (i.e., a form of economic, social, and cultural "advancement" linked to industrialization and Westernization). As Ferguson emphasizes, in the 1960s and early 1970s, Zambians expected this kind of modernity (i.e., advancement) to occur as a result of the country's booming copper export economy. By the late 1980s, however, this myth of modernization was shattered by more than a decade of dramatic economic decline. During this period, Zambians—or more specifically, most of the retiring miners that Ferguson interviewed—had rejected the colonial-derived and instilled metanarrative of progress along with its central idea: that through participation in an industrialized economy, Zambians could progress as a nation, as a people, and as individuals. While Ferguson makes a compelling argument about this historical shift and its contemporary ethnographic realizations, I believe it is crucial to stress that everyday life in Zambia is still very much structured by *an embrace* of this concept of *progress-oriented modernity,* even as people are rearticulating their relationship to its likely attainment. People still have what could be called "progressivist desires" and they still evaluate their lives, the national economy, and the nation-state itself in these terms.[7]

But most fundamentally, my analysis differs from Ferguson's in that I recognize a more polyvalent concept of modernity in Zambia. Some meanings of modernity—or senses of what it means to be modern—do stem from an idea of modernity grounded in the modernization myth. But others do not. From an ethnographic perspective, it is impossible to reduce the Zambian meanings of "modernity" or "being modern" to a unitary concept. What it means to "be modern" varies across individuals and intersects with numerous other culturally specific phenomena, such as class, status, generation, gender, desire, and pleasure. In the broadest sense, "Zambian modernities" encompass culturally specific practices, orientations, ideas, and evaluations related to ideas of progress, productivity, sophistication, consumption, innovation, and/or Westernization. Most relevant for the study of Zambian radio culture is the way in which "modernity," "being modern," and "the modern" operate as a set of interrelated cultural constructs about what it means to have a "better life" (e.g., in terms of money, goods, health, pleasure, and personal opportunity) and what it means to be "up to date" (e.g., living a lifestyle that displays knowledge of contemporary trends or acquiring new goods and practices that signify difference from "the local" and "the traditional"). There are many modernities within Zambia: a progress-oriented modernity, a consumption-oriented modernity, a stylistically oriented modernity, and a temporally clocked modernity. All have all been deeply shaped by radio. Many (but not all) of them could be clustered under an umbrella of what people understand to be the social, cultural, and technological transformations brought about by contact with the West. Moreover, many of these modernities *do* appear to be like "old orientalist binaries" (Piot 2001:89). Thus, as Ferguson (1999:82 ff.) argues, Zambians' discourse about social change and lifestyle choices reveals a very deeply rooted logic of cultural dualism that goes back to colonial times, one which aligns a modern versus traditional dichotomy with an urban versus rural dichotomy. To a great degree, these are also aligned with a foreign (or foreign-derived) versus indigenous dichotomy. Significantly, a rigid dualist logic is pervasive, despite the much more blurred and syncretic coexistence of "the modern," "the traditional," "the foreign," and "the local" in both urban and rural areas.

Some of these dynamics can be seen, for example, in the following remarks of Joseph Kabwe, a young office worker in the small provincial capital of Kasama. For Joseph, the national capital of Lusaka—four hundred miles away—is the place where one can be truly modern—that is, live the good life. In his words: "*Baleeliila saana ku Lusaka. Baleeumfwa bwino ku rhumba, disco. Kuli* beat twenty-three hours up to zero-six hours. Beat *ubushiku,* throughout." This translates as: "They are really enjoying life in Lusaka. They are listening wonderfully to rhumba, disco. There's a beat from 11 P.M. to 6 A.M. A beat all night, throughout."

The "good life" of Lusaka is exemplified in his emphasis on the twenty-four-hour radio channel, which plays dance music all night long and helps urban listeners enjoy their evenings. The modernity concept in this sense is also spatialized, with the "bright lights" and lively music of the big city contrasted with the slower and quieter small town of Kasama. This contrast allows people like Joseph, who live outside of Zambia's major urban centers, to still position themselves as modern vis-à-vis yet more traditional places. It is important to stress here that "being modern" from an ethnographic viewpoint encompasses a range of things—from the full attainment of the promises of modernity to the embrace of its value, from conversancy with the signs of modernity to its performance in a given moment of interaction.

Joseph's remarks, in both form and content, are a performance of modernity.[8] They are a form of data that falls under type (b) discussed above. He valorizes the idea of an active nightlife and emphasizes the thrill of consuming popular foreign music (Western disco and Congo/ Zairian rhumba). In doing so, Joseph uses a distinctive variety of the Bemba language, known as Town Bemba, which is a hybrid language featuring numerous borrowed words from English and various African languages in the region, Bemba–English codeswitching, and creative forms of linguistic innovation within Bemba (Spitulnik 1998). Because there are so many different registers of Town Bemba, and because varieties of it have been around for well over sixty years, speaking Town Bemba does not automatically signal an alignment with "being modern." But Joseph's usage *does* as it displays his conversancy with certain English language idioms—"beat" and "twenty-three hours up to zero-six hours"—which operate as commoditized linguistic forms. Radio broadcasting is itself a key agent in the commoditization and circulation of popular phrases such as these, which amplify the "structure of feeling" associated with being modern (Spitulnik 1996, 2003; cf. Williams 1961). This forms an important aspect of radio culture in an everyday sense.

Combing through Language

In this section,[9] I turn directly to a discussion of data in the Bemba language, Zambia's most widely spoken tongue. Of Zambia's population of approximately ten million, nearly four million people speak Bemba or very closely related varieties as their first language. Because of its prevalence across the country as a major urban lingua franca, Bemba is spoken as a second or third language by many Zambians, bringing the total number of Bemba speakers to well over six million.

In Bemba, there is no single word or phrase that is precisely equivalent to the English word "modern." There are, however, a range of words and phrases that capture many characteristics and states that fall under the rubric of being modern as it is understood in Zambia. These are listed in table 6.1: *icipya*, "new"; *shino nshiku*, "nowadays" ("the present"); *nshita sha nomba*, "modern times"; *ukucampuka*, "being alert or quick"; *ukuca*, "being enlightened"; *ubusungu*, "being European"; and *ubulaya*, "being in style or being affluent." All of these components are positively valued in the embrace of modernity, with the exception of *ubusungu*, "being European," which in its extreme form is negatively valued as "being un-Zambian." Most of the lexical items in table 6.1 resonate with a kind of modernity that is equated with novelty or newness, the present, urbanity, action, style, consumption, and progress.

Table 6.1. Toward Mapping a Semantic Field of "Modernity" in
Bemba: A Lexical Attempt at Bemba Equivalents for "Modern,"
"Modernity," and "Being Modern"

1. Realm of temporality

icipya	new; modern
shino nshiku	these days, nowadays
nshita sha nomba	nowadays, modern times
abandakai	the ones at this moment; the modern ones
ubuyantanshi	progress [lit., moving forward]
versus *icikote*	old
versus *sha kale*	of the past

2. Realm of speed and action

ukucampuka	to be alert, smart, quick
ukuca	to be enlightened, awake, sharp, modern
ifintu na bwangu	[having] things to do quickly, [being] busy

3. Realm of style and personal qualities

ubulaya	modern, in style; affluent, comfortable
ukuca	to be enlightened, awake, sharp, modern
ubusungu	being European; white (also see realm 2 above)

4. Realm of consumption

ubulaya	modern, in style; affluent, comfortable

5. Realm of nonindigenous culture

ubusungu	being European; white
versus *umubele; imisango; intambi*	custom; customs; tradition
versus *fya mushi*	of the village

6. Realm of space

ubulaya	from overseas
fya tauni	of the town
versus *fya mushi*	of the village

They resonate less with the kinds of modernities that are associated with science, rationality, individualism, state governance, or a market-driven economy.

While these words and phrases are revealing of diverse cultural readings of modernity, one must be wary of objectifying them as key words that stand in for cultural concepts (Silverstein 1993). What is a more useful approach, I believe, is to make the kinds of linguistic distinctions introduced at the beginning of this chapter—that is, distinctions between (a) linguistic forms that function to refer to elements of modernity and (b) linguistic forms and modes of language use that function in a pragmatic sense to signal a social identity of "being modern." What we have in table 6.1 is a collection of linguistic evidence that fits under type (a). It is a preliminary map of the universe of reference to modernity from a *lexical semantic* point of view. As lexical, it is word-based, instead of, say, grammatically based. As semantic, it involves mainly definitional meanings that are relatively decontextualized—that is, they are not represented as part of language-in-use. My distillations of these items are based on naturally occurring discourse, but that is elided in the presentation of the data.

A higher order of semantic organization to this lexical field is indicated by the six headings, a proposed scheme that involves a greater amount of researcher intervention and interpretation, and an even further remove from naturally occurring discourse. The six headers are distilled via a collection of rationales. Primarily they come from what I see as clusters of lexical meanings based on semantic similarities in my own language—this is the work I do as translator. They also are filtered by what I understand from my own research and that of others such as Ferguson (1999) and Hansen (2000) as the areas of greatest emphasis in Zambian understandings of modernity—this is the work I do as ethnographer. A secondary influence for choice of headers is the motive to articulate with a larger field of modernity studies, where the use of common superordinate descriptors can facilitate comparative research.

The data presented in table 6.1 would comprise a better map if it graphically displayed the many overlaps and cross-linkages among the lexical items. Again, this would be another kind of intervention that would illustrate a higher order of semantic organization in the lexical field surrounding modernity in Zambia. Table 6.1 includes some examples of antonyms, in the service of showing what is "*not* modern," but this is not exhaustive. They do, however, reveal how the cultural dualisms discussed above take shape in the Bemba language.

To some degree, the items in table 6.1 are key words that stand in for cultural concepts. They seem to both reflect and anchor a way of thinking about modernity, or at least a way of talking, in the sense that they are recurrent, pervasive, and taken for granted in everyday usage. Indeed, they might be termed part of *the everyday lexical taken-for-granted of modernity*. What is significant, however, is that these items are extremely prevalent within the discursive tropes of powerful speakers and institutions that make pronouncements on the nature of social reality, such as leading politicians, educators, clergy, government pamphlets, radio broadcasts, and educational curriculum material. They also have a deep history in colonial institutions. There is thus the possibility that the everyday recurrence, pervasiveness, and taken-for-grantedness of the items in table 6.1 is more a function of their prominent usage as key tropes in various forms of dominant discourse than it is of their ability to render the realities of cognition and experience into language. As already suggested above, the dominant discourse of cultural dualisms fixes the lexical semantic field regarding modernity in a way that is not completely congruent with experience.

Other dimensions of modernity in Zambia are hidden or just simply absent in table 6.1. For example, the realm of consumption has less lexical elaboration in terms of general nouns, verbs, and adjectives, but it is of no less importance ethnographically. Furthermore, the actuality of hybridity is one of the most unlexified. For example, as far as I know, there is no single term or phrase that captures the reality of being modern while not being un-African. Relatedly, there is a realm of un-labeled phenomena that lie somewhere between "the indigenous as traditional" and "the foreign as modern." It might be termed "the local as nontraditional," or "the foreign as indigenized." So there are important kinds of lexical gaps here, ones that would argue against a narrow reliance of table 6.1 as a lexical-based map of a cultural reality.

I wish to turn now to a closer look at language in use, and particularly at the types of linguistic evidence that I labeled above as type (b), where language in use functions in a pragmatic sense to signal a social identity of "being modern." I distinguish this from the type of linguistic evidence that is represented in table 6.1—that is, items that function to refer to elements of modernity (type a). Table 6.2 provides some examples of these two types of linguistic evidence and includes a few cases where items belong to both type (a) and type (b).

The key difference is that unlike the forms of type (a), those in type (b) involve an indexical meaning with respect to social identity. Indexicality is a process through which part of the meaning of a form either presupposes or creates its contextual relation to something else (Silverstein 1976). Examples of indexical forms include the words "you" and "this," phenomena such as regional accents, and forms of verbal politeness such as "sir" and "would it be possible . . . ?" For present purposes, I am interested in indexical forms that presuppose and/or create contextual meanings with respect to notions of modernity. Most of these contextual meanings are about speaker identity as "being modern."

Items 1 through 5 in table 6.2 are linguistic forms that are used to

Table 6.2. Examples of Types of Linguistic Evidence in the
Distillation of "Modernity" in Zambia

	Form	Meaning	Evidence of type (a); refers to "modern" and "modernity"	Evidence of type (b); indexes (performs/ signifies) "modernity"
1	-pya (adj.)	new; modern	X	—
2	-ca (verb)	up-to-date, alert, modern	X	—
3	shino nshiku	nowadays, these days	X	—
4	ubulaya	modern, in style, affluent	X	—
5	abandakai	the ones at this moment; the modern ones	X	—
6	Certain forms of linguistic innovation Unassimilated loan words from English, Bemba–English codeswitching and codemixing		—	X
7	spakajez, spaka, jez	switched on, exciting [< spark, jazz]	X	X
8	beat	dance music	X	X

Note: Type (a), linguistic forms and modes that refer to a local concept of the modern or modernity; type (b), linguistic forms and modes that have the pragmatic function of performing or signifying a social identity of "being modern."

name components of modernity or the modern; all appear in table 6.1, where more nuances of lexical meaning are indicated. These forms are used in a referential sense (i.e., to talk about or to refer to modern times, people, and things). Examples of items 1 through 5 in naturally occurring discourse are provided below. Due to constraints of space, I must skip much of the contextual information about speaker identity and performative occurrence. Clearly, however, more involved forms of commentary are occurring in these utterances with respect to evaluating modernity—as a problem, as an asset, as linked to consumption, as antithetical to cultural values of respect, and so on. Some of the difficulties of translation are hinted at in my parenthetical notes.

1a. *Kwena, ilya ing'anda iipya.*
"That's a really modern (new) house."

1b. *Ifipya fyaleta fye icifulunganya.*
"Modernity (new things) has only brought problems."

2. *Ulya umulumendo alica.*
"That guy is with it (sharp, up to date, modern)."

3a. *Nomba pali shino nshiku tuleeumfwa . . .*
"But in these times (nowadays), we are feeling . . . "

3b. *Umukashi obe, asebela mu fyuma. Ne ifyo fine cili, mu-muno nshiku.*
"Your wife, she simply goes after wealth. And that is the way it is in, in these days."

4. *Ukukwata* <u>Air Jordan 97</u> *bulaya.*
"Having Air Jordan 97 is the in thing." [in 1997]

5. *Nomba balya aba abandakai iyoo bena tabaleefwaya ukuti bacindike ifyo babapela.* "But those modern ones (the ones at this moment), no they themselves don't want to respect what they are given."

Consistently in my linguistic research, items 1 through 3 of table 6.2 were used by Bemba speakers as the closest translation equivalents to the English versions of the "M" words: "modernity," "modern," and "being modern." Item 1 (*-pya*) is used only for inanimate objects and general concepts, while item 2 (*-ca*) only applies to animate beings, primarily people. While there are strong reasons to select the adjective *-pya* as the closest single Bemba language translation equivalent to the English word "modern," it is rather empty semantically. It simply means "new." The word alone is not semantically nuanced with any particular social connotations or moral evaluations, as for example the English word "modern" is. The verb -ca, on the other hand, is incredibly rich with such meanings. In its infinitival form, ukuca means "to be enlightened, awake, sharp, up to date, alert." All of these states apply to someone who is considered modern. Collectively, this set of lexical meanings is a vivid commentary on what it means to be modern in Zambia. Significantly, the primary meaning of the verb ukuca is "to dawn," as in "The day is dawning." Historical evidence suggests that this narrow meaning of the verb was its *only* meaning until the colonial period and that during the colonial period, the verb meaning was extended to describe human qualities. Specifically when, how, where, and why this happened would be a spectacular story to tell, if only one could turn back the hands of time and witness the actual moments when this verb began to take on a heavier semantic load. We can, however, make inferences from what is well known about the ideological and discursive field of colonialism in Northern Rhodesia. The semantic extension of -ca from "dawn" to "be enlightened" has roots in the nexus of cultural dualisms that structured the colonial project: Africans were construed as being "in the dark" and "asleep" while Europeans were construed as bringing technologies, practices, and beliefs to "wake them out of their slumber" and "enlighten them." And more broadly, the coming of the Europeans was heralded as "the dawn of a new era in Africa." The Bemba word selected to capture all of this was -ca. What was once a way of describing modernity from the dominant European colonial perspective is now one of the most pervasive ways of describing modernity among Zambians.

Turning now to the items in table 6.2 which are of type b, item 6 indicates the existence of a kind of catchall category for a variety of linguistic phenomena that function in an indexical sense within Bemba language use to signify a "modern" social identity. Several illustrative examples are provided as text below. These include certain forms of Bemba linguistic innovation (6a), the use of unassimilated loan words from English in the context of Bemba speech (6b–d, 6f), and Bemba–English codeswitching/codemixing (6d–f). These phenomena are part of an urban variety of Bemba known as Town Bemba (Spitulnik 1998). When speakers use expressions of these types, they indicate an alignment with a particular social identity that can be described as "modern" or "progressive" or "urban." With the exception of 6d and 6f, alternate choices in standard Bemba are indicated in brackets alongside the Town Bemba examples. The use of such standard Bemba equivalents in place of the Town Bemba elements would eliminate any kind of performative function of indexing speaker's modernity.

6a. *Ee, ninjikata boyi* [versus *-umfwa*, "understand"; *mune*, "friend"]
"Yes, I understand my friend (boy)."

6b. *Cinjasuke apopene first.* [versus *pantanshi*, "first"]
"Let me answer on that point first."

6c. But *Lesa umo wine tupepa.* [versus *nomba*, "but"] "But to the
same one God we pray."

6d. *So ifi manje nalumfwile umwenso sana. Teti tulebomfya indalama ishi
tatwishibe uku cilefuma.* So that *calendetesha sana umwe—? Umwenso. Nomba apo namwebele ifyo umunandi kukalipa. Nomba ala-
cita* organize *ku banankwe bambi ati ulya tababwi—? Tababwino.*

"So like that now I felt a lot of fear. We should not use the
money if we don't know where it is coming from. So that it
brought much fe—? Fear. Now, when I told my friend that, he
became upset. So he organizes his other friends and tells them
that that guy [me] is not ni—? Nice."

6e. *Awe natufilwa ukucita* adopt the western culture. [versus *-belesha
imisango yabasungu*]
"No, we have failed to adopt the Western culture."

6f. *Icibemba telulimi ulyaba* permanent *iyoo.*
"Bemba is not a language that is permanent, no."

Utterance 6a, for example, illustrates the use of semantic innovations
which build on both standard Bemba words and on English-derived
words. Said typically to a friend, this expression uses the Bemba verb
-ikata, "grab," in a slang sense to mean "understand" and the English-
derived noun *boyi*, which is a contemporary reversal of the derogatory
colonial term "boy." The use of this expression has a performative function of indicating that one is not just modern, but cosmopolitan and
fashionable in a youthful sense. By contrast, the types of innovations
illustrated in utterances 6b and 6c are fairly commonplace among many
Zambians of all ages who are partial or full English-language bilin-
guals. Speakers who use such smatterings of unassimilated English loan
words within the context of Bemba discourse signal a degree of "urbanity" and "modernity" (or "nonruralness"), but this is not as heightened as the kind of modernity or trendiness signaled by an utterance
such as 6a.
These points can be further exemplified by a consideration of dis-

course excerpt 6d, which is part of a story told by a young man (KL) to a group of people, myself included. During his days in high school, KL had a friend who was clearly stealing money. The friend would regularly come to school with a lot of unexplained cash and want to spend it with his classmates. In the excerpt above, KL describes his feelings of fear and what happened when he expressed disapproval of the friend's behavior. KL's narrative exhibits the same kinds of English loans as 6c in the form of word initial discourse connectives _so_ and _so that_, but it also includes the Town Bemba adverb _manje_, "now," derived from another Zambian language, Nyanja. This Nyanja word, coupled with the unconventional -_cita_ organize construction a bit later marks KL's discourse as part of a more stylish modern or urban register than that of examples 6b and 6c.

A very pronounced form of codeswitching is illustrated in 6e, _Awe natufilwa ukucita_ adopt the western culture ("No, we have failed to adopt the Western culture"), which also contains a seemingly self-conscious ironic twist. The utterance is part of a longer stretch of discourse in which the speaker explains his views on how Zambians have failed to adopt Western values and practices of democratic governance. But while indicting his fellow Zambians for not embracing Western culture, the speaker simultaneously demonstrates this embrace by using a fully formed English-language phrase in his accusation. This ironic play with L1 (speaker's first language) and L2 (speaker's second language) contrasts in the service of producing metalinguistic commentary is pervasive among many Bemba speakers (Spitulnik 1998). An additional example can be found in 6f, a statement by the Bemba Paramount Chief Chitimukulu in response to my interview questions about how the Bemba language is different now from that of the past: "_Icibemba telulimi ulyaba_ permanent _iyoo_" ("Bemba is not a language that is permanent, no").

Lurking behind any interpretation of this type of data is the larger question of the social significance of codeswitching, codemixing, and lexical borrowing.[10] This is a very complex issue in the Zambian case, as it probably is for most multilingual contexts. The use of codeswitching and codemixing is one of the most commonly recognized (and often most subject to conscious reflection, and thus strategic manipulation) examples of how speakers signal in language different social identities and social orientations. Yet, contrary to the received wisdom about this within cultural anthropology, it is not always the case that a switch from L1 to L2 always means the same thing or that the relationship between L1 and L2 is the same in all instances. Particularly for the subject at hand—"modernity"—one cannot assume that use of a foreign L2, especially a European L2, automatically means an alignment with a foreign or Western or modern order of values and social identities. This kind of inference is too easy, and too common. Thus, incorporating English into Bemba does not automatically signal a desire to be modern, or an embrace of things European. And when it does, it is not always of the same degree. Some discursive ways of "being modern" are more stylish or trendy and some are more conservative. Increasingly, using a smattering of English in Bemba discourse is the norm for Bemba speakers of all walks of life. Therefore the use of L2 in the context of L1 does not necessarily indicate a difference from L1 and all of its social connotations per se—for example, as a way of indicating "otherness"; rather, it indicates a normal way of speaking as a Zambian (Spitulnik 1998).

Similarly, not all English loan words in Bemba are examples of modes of signifying modernity. Bemba has numerous phonologically and morphologically assimilated words from English which carry minimal or no social significance as "foreign."[11] Examples include the words for sugar, box, pot, table, chair, shirt, telephone, doctor, copy, lamp, pencil, glasses, company, receipt, bread, and hospital. As assimilated, most of these are ordinary loan words which are considered to be more or less part of the Bemba language by now, and their use in context has no indexical association with social identities of urbanity or modernity. They are simply examples of an instrumental type of word borrowing where a word that does not exist in a native language is borrowed from elsewhere. Such borrowed words fill a lexical gap and are typically used to name imported objects, technologies, institutions, ideas, and activities (see also Kashoki 1978). Sometimes, however, they push out existing equivalents (or near-equivalents) in L1 and over time become the preferred everyday terms. Thus, for example, at the present moment, the English words "first," "organize," "but," and "that" (6b–d) are marked loans, but over time they may go the way of "fail," -filwa (6e); "one," wanu; "copy," -kopa; "change," -cinja; and "sure," shuwa, which are now fully assimilated into everyday Bemba.

The last set of examples that I wish to consider are items 7 and 8, which fall under both columns a and b. They also exhibit the types codeswitching/mixing/borrowing as described in set 6. But because of their referential content, they provide, in addition, a window into some specific dimensions of modernity as it is understood in Zambia. Examples of their use in context are below:

7. *Ndi fye* <u>*spakajez*</u>.
   Ndi fye <u>*spaka*</u>.
   Ndi fye <u>*jez*</u>.
   "I'm just great (switched on, with it, excited)." ["spark," "jazz"]

8. Beat *ubushiku*, throughout.
   "There's a beat (dance music) throughout the night."

In these cases, the expressions carry a kind of double load of modernity (referring and indexing), in ways that the items in 1 through 5 do not. One can refer to oneself as being energized in a modern sense and also index this by using a trendy phrase from the world of the electronic or popular music, as in 7. Or one can refer to an exciting world of music and use English-language words that carry an indexical sense of this as well, as in 8. In this regard, the lexical items *spakajez*, *spaka*, *jez*, and beat can be entered into table 6.1 as part of the larger lexical semantic constellation of modernity.

Conclusion

So where does this discussion leave us? In sketching out how one could begin to map a semantic and discursive field of what "being modern" and "modernity" mean in Zambia (or more specifically, in Bemba language use), I have argued that one cannot do a word-based or phrase-based kind of localization of the modernity concept and just leave it at that. This kind of linguistic work needs to be guided by a sensitivity to discursive practices and language values, as well as by more general participant-observation research on everyday practices and values. It also needs to be guided by an understanding that language is not always a transparent window into culture, that important dimensions of cultural concepts may never surface in the lexicon, that there are rarely simple one-to-one correspondences in the act of translation, and that language has a kind of historical depth and institutional backing to it that informs both semantic fields and in-play values.

Using these guideposts, I have, by demonstration, proposed some modes of inquiry and ways of looking at language and communicative practice that help us access culturally specific (or "local") concepts, ways of understanding, and Discourses. One need not be "a real linguist" to do this kind of work. Nor does one need to apply this approach just to the unearthing of a "local" modernity concept. It can be applied to just about any other kind of anthropological inquiry, including culturally specific meanings of "the person," "respect," "humility," "family," or "being female."

In ethnographic terms, the idea of "being modern" is incredibly polyvalent in Zambia. It is discussed and performed primarily in terms of six interrelated themes: continuous or quick action (*bwangu*; *ukucampuka*; *spaka*; "nonstop"; "live"); newness or novelty (*icipya*); an idea of progress (*ubuyantanshi*); consumption; prosperity and affluence (*ubu-*

laya); and conversancy with outside forms of knowledge and goods ("being up to date"). Some of these are captured fairly well by common Bemba and English lexical items (indicated in parentheses above) and some are not. Some are captured better by longer kinds of narratives like the one that example utterance 5 derives from, a narrative by an elderly rural woman about how people should praise the Paramount Chief and how they've now forgotten how to do this. Such narratives provide the kinds of discourse-based evidence that is typically used (if any is used) in current ethnographic analyses of local modernities.[12]

Do we care whether specific local words or phrases can be used as translation equivalents for the words "modern" and "modernity"? Does it matter whether any are proposed as emic concepts? An anthropology that bypasses such local terms in an ethnographic account runs the risk of analytical override at best. Sticking strictly to single words and phrases runs the risk of a kind of lexical reductionism and a frequently false assumption about the transparency of language. It also neglects the indexical functions of some words to signal "being modern" without necessarily referring to it. I have suggested here that numerous types of language-based data and modes of linguistic analysis can be used to map out what might be viewed as an entire semantic/discursive field related to local concepts of modernity. One way to prevent the modernity concept from melting into air is to dissolve it—or better yet, to clarify it—into a richer array of points within a constellation of practices, with linguistic practices being one dimension of this.

Acknowledgments

For research support during 2000–2001 that relates to this chapter, I am indebted to the Wenner-Gren Foundation, the National Endowment for the Humanities, and Emory University's Institute for Comparative and International Studies. I am particularly grateful to the following people for their input at various stages of this work: Arthur Kabwatha, Mubanga Kashoki, Makasa Kasonde, Bruce Knauft, Maidstone Mulenga, Fenson Mwape, Anderson Mwembeshi, Rodney Siwale, and Indiana University Press reviewer Edward LiPuma.

Notes

1. Research data derived from ethnographic and linguistic field research in Zambia (1986, 1988–1990), ethnographic and linguistic research with

Zambians resident in the United States and particularly in Atlanta, Georgia (1997–present), discourse analysis of recorded radio programs (1986–2000), earlier published scholarship on Bemba language change, and archival research on colonial radio broadcasting.

2. This expression contrasts with the more standard Bemba expression *Ee, ninjishiba* (or *ninjumfwa*) *mune*, "Yes, I understand my friend." My conventions for linguistic representation in examples are as follows: *Italic text* indicates Bemba (unless otherwise noted), <u>*underscored italic text*</u> indicates Town Bemba elements, <u>underscored text, no italics</u> indicates English in the context of Bemba.

3. See Silverstein (1992), Silverstein and Urban (1996), and Urban (1996) for treatments of how different degrees of contextualization and decontextualization differentially affect the status of linguistic data in ethnographic argumentation.

4. This phrase has been proposed by my colleague Donald Donham at Emory University to articulate a vision of a cultural anthropology graduate training initiative.

5. See Fairclough (1989) for further discussion on conceptualizing the links between "discourse" as language in use and "discourse" in the sense of "orders of discourse" or "discursive formations."

6. See Guyer (1996) for an excellent discussion and review of these issues in African studies. For a specific case study, see Comaroff and Comaroff's (1991, 1997) discussion of how Tswana culture involved forms of commoditization, syncretic innovation, individualism, and pragmatic rationality long before encounters with European versions of these. See also Piot's (2001) cogent elaboration of how these ethnographic facts highlight the analytical shortcomings of confining a concept of "modernity" to the period after European contact.

7. This point is vividly demonstrated in the ethnographic material that pervades Ferguson's (1999) book. His primary focus, however, is less on the manifestation of progressivist desires and idioms of modernity than it is on the ways in which the metanarrative of modernization has been called into question.

8. To borrow from Ferguson's terms, Joseph is able to perform a certain kind of Zambian "cosmopolitan style" (1999:91 ff.). Many of the practices that Ferguson calls ways of "being cosmopolitan" I consider ways of "being modern." My usage is closer to the Zambian usage. The term "cosmopolitan" is rarely used in Zambian discourse. Ferguson uses "cosmopolitanism" in a very specific sense: to denote an urban cultural style that signals distance from or rejection of the expectations of rurally based allies. It is contrasted with "localism," which is an urban style of "signaling (and enacting) compliance" with these expectations, which usually concern financial demands (1999:211). This distinction works for Ferguson's analysis since it captures the key differences in and consequences of the choices that

are made by urban wage earners. But it is difficult to apply his usage more generally to describe Zambian ways of "being modern," since these are not defined primarily by compliance or noncompliance with the demands of rural kin. Cosmopolitan styles described by Ferguson include: "listening to Western or 'international' music, speaking English and mixing languages with ease, [and] dressing smartly (and even ostentatiously)," as well as "forms of playing at international sophistication" (1999:92, 226). All of these would be called ways of "being modern" in Zambia. They do, in part, signify "affinity with an 'outside,' a world beyond the 'local,' " to use Ferguson's definition (1999:212), but they also involve very specific "local" Zambian features.

9. The title of this section is inspired by Cohen's (1994) phrase "the combing of history," which signals a methodological approach of sifting through multiple orders of evidence for the accretion of clues and data on which a cultural interpretation can be made.

10. See Spitulnik (1998) for an extended discussion of how terms such as "loan," "codeswitching," and "codemixing" are often not refined enough to capture what is frequently a very complicated nexus of relations between systemic linguistic boundaries, social boundaries, cognitive systems, speaker intent, indexical effects, and language history (see also Wei 2000). In terms of basic definitions, codemixing refers to the co-occurrence of elements from two distinct languages *within a single phrase*, and codeswitching refers to this kind of co-occurrence at the level *above the phrase* (e.g., changes in code across clause or sentence boundaries). For examples of these complex phenomena in other multilingual African contexts, see Fabian (1982) and Swigart (2000).

11. For further discussion of the sources of loan words in Bemba and the phonological and morphological processes of assimilation, see Spitulnik (1998) and the references therein.

12. For some examples of studies which integrate analysis of people's explicit talk about the modern/modernity/modernization in a broader ethnographic analysis, see Comaroff and Comaroff (1993b), Schein (1999), and other contributions to the present volume.

References

Appadurai, Arjun
    1995   Playing with Modernity: The Decolonization of Indian Cricket. In *Consuming Modernity: Public Culture in a South Asian World*. Edited by Carol A. Breckenridge, pp. 23–48. Minneapolis: University of Minnesota Press.

Cohen, David William
    1994   *The Combing of History*. Chicago: University of Chicago Press.

Comaroff, Jean, and John L. Comaroff
1991 *Of Revelation and Revolution, Volume 1: Christianity, Colonialism, and Conscious in South Africa.* Chicago: University of Chicago Press.
1993a Introduction. In *Modernity and Its Malcontents: Ritual and Power in Postcolonial Africa.* Edited by Jean Comaroff and John Comaroff, pp. xi–xxxvii. Chicago: University of Chicago Press.
1993b [Eds.] *Modernity and Its Malcontents. Ritual and Power in Postcolonial Africa.* Chicago: University of Chicago Press.

Comaroff, John L., and Jean Comaroff
1997 *Of Revelation and Revolution: Volume 2: The Dialectics of Modernity on a South African Frontier.* Chicago: University of Chicago Press.

Duranti, Alessandro
1997 *Linguistic Anthropology.* Cambridge: Cambridge University Press.

Fabian, Johannes
1982 Scratching the Surface: Observations on the Poetics of Lexical Borrowing in Shaba Swahili. *Anthropological Linguistics* 24: 14–50.

Fairclough, Norman
1989 *Language and Power.* London: Longman.

Ferguson, James
1999 *Expectations of Modernity: Myths and Meanings of Urban Life on the Zambian Copperbelt.* Berkeley: University of California Press.

Franklin, Harry
1950 *Report on The Saucepan Special: The Poor Man's Radio for Rural Populations.* Lusaka, Northern Rhodesia (Zambia): Government Printer.

Gaonkar, Dilip Parameshwar
1999 On Alternative Modernities. *Public Culture* 11(1): 1–18.

Guyer, Jane I.
1996 Traditions of Invention in Equatorial Africa. *African Studies Review* 39(3): 1–28.

Hansen, Karen Tranberg
2000 *Salaula: The World of Secondhand Clothing and Zambia.* Chicago: University of Chicago Press.

Hockett, Charles F.
1980 Preserving the Heritage. In *First Person Singular: Papers from the Conference on an Oral Archive for the History of American Linguistics.* Edited by Boyd H. Davis and Raymond K. O'Cain, pp. 98–107. Amsterdam: John Benjamins.

Kashoki, Mubanga E.
1978 Lexical Innovation in Four Zambian Languages. *African Languages/ Langues Africaines* 4: 80–95.

Knauft, Bruce M.
2002 Critically Modern: An Introduction. In *Critically Modern: Alterna-*

tives, Alterities, Anthropologies [this volume]. Edited by Bruce M. Knauft. Bloomington: Indiana University Press.

Latour, Bruno
1993   *We Have Never Been Modern.* Translated by Catherine Porter. New York: Harvester Wheatsheaf.

Mannheim, Bruce, and Dennis Tedlock
1995   Introduction. In *The Dialogic Emergence of Culture.* Edited by Dennis Tedlock and Bruce Mannheim, pp. 1–32. Urbana: University of Illinois Press.

Piot, Charles
2001   Of Hybridity, Modernity, and Their Malcontents. *Interventions* 3(1): 85–91.

Schein, Louisa
1999   Performing Modernity. *Cultural Anthropology* 14(3): 361–395.

Schieffelin, Bambi
1993   The Current State and Fate of Linguistic Anthropology. *Anthropology Newsletter* 34(4): 1, 19–21.

Silverstein, Michael
1976   Shifters, Linguistic Categories and Cultural Description. In *Meaning in Anthropology.* Edited by Keith H. Basso and Henry A. Selby, pp. 11–55. Albuquerque: University of New Mexico Press.
1992   The Indeterminacy of Contextualization: When is Enough Enough? In *The Contextualization of Language.* Edited by Peter Auer and Aldo di Luzio, pp. 55–76. Amsterdam: John Benjamins.
1993   Of Dynamos and Doorbells: Semioitic Modularity and (Over) Determination of Cognitive Representation. *Chicago Linguistic Society* 29(2): 319–345.

Silverstein, Michael, and Greg Urban
1996   [Eds.] *Natural Histories of Discourse.* Chicago: University of Chicago Press.

Spitulnik, Debra
1996   The Social Circulation of Media Discourse and the Mediation of Communities. *Journal of Linguistic Anthropology* 6(2): 161–187.
1998   The Language of the City: Town Bemba as Urban Hybridity. *Journal of Linguistic Anthropology* 8(2): 30–59.
1998–1999   Mediated Modernities: Encounters with the Electronic in Zambia. *Visual Anthropology Review* 14(2): 63–84.
2003   *Media Connections and Disconnections: Radio Culture and the Public Sphere in Zambia.* Durham, N.C.: Duke University Press.

Swigart, Leigh
2000   The Limits of Legitimacy: Language Ideology and Shift in Contemporary Senegal. *Journal of Linguistic Anthropology* 10(1): 90–130.

Urban, Greg
    1996   *Metaphysical Community: The Interplay of the Senses and the Intellect.* Austin: University of Texas Press.
Wei, Li
    2000   [Ed.] *The Bilingualism Reader.* London: Routledge.
Williams, Raymond
    1961   *The Long Revolution.* London: Chatto and Windus.

Seven

The Otherwise Modern
Caribbean Lessons from the Savage Slot

Michel-Rolph Trouillot

"Modernity" is a murky term that belongs to a family of words we may label "North Atlantic universals." By that, I mean words inherited from what we now call the West—which I prefer to call the North Atlantic, not only for the sake of geographical precision—that project the North Atlantic experience on a universal scale that they have helped to create. North Atlantic universals are particulars that have gained a degree of universality, chunks of human history that have become historical standards. Words such as "development," "progress," "democracy," and indeed the "West" itself are exemplary members of that family which contracts or expands according to contexts and interlocutors.[1]

North Atlantic universals so defined are not merely descriptive or referential. They do not describe the world; they offer visions of the world. While they appear to refer to things as they exist, rooted in a particular history, they are evocative of multiple layers of sensibilities, persuasions, cultural assumptions, and ideological choices tied to that localized history. They come to us loaded with aesthetic and stylistic sensibilities, religious and philosophical persuasions; cultural assumptions that range from what it means to be a human being to the proper relationship between humans and the natural world; and ideological choices that range from the nature of the political to its possibilities of transformation. To be sure, there is no unanimity within the North Atlantic itself on any of these issues, but there is a shared history of how these issues have been and should be debated, and these words carry that history. Yet since they are projected as universals, they deny their localization, the sensibilities, and the history from which they spring.

220

Thus, North Atlantic universals are always prescriptive inasmuch as they always suggest, even if implicitly, a correct state of affairs—what is good, what is just, what is desirable—not only what is, but what should be. Indeed, that prescription is inherent in the very projection of a historically limited experience—that of the North Atlantic—on the world stage. Thus also, North Atlantic universals are always seductive, at times even irresistible, exactly because they manage, in that projection, to hide their specific—localized, North Atlantic, and thus parochial—historical location.

The ability to project universal relevance while hiding the particularities of their marks and origins makes North Atlantic universals as hard to conceptualize as they are seductive to use. Indeed, the more seductive these words become, the harder it is to specify what they actually stand for, since part of the seduction resides in that capacity to project clarity while remaining ambiguous. Even if we believe that concepts are merely words—a questionable assumption (Trouillot 2002), a quick perusal of the popular press in any European language demonstrates that North Atlantic universals are murky references: they evoke rather than define. More seriously, attempts to conceptualize them in the scholarly literature reveal little unanimity about their scope, let alone denotation (Knauft, this volume; Gaonkar 1999; Dussel 1993).

This chapter therefore is quite ambivalent about the extent to which modernity can be fully conceptualized. Yet at the same time, it would be disingenuous not to acknowledge that the word "modernity" evokes sensibilities, perceptions, choices, and indeed states of affairs that are not captured as easily by other words. Thus, my aim here is less to provide a conceptualization of modernity—or an illustration based on a shared conceptualization—than to bring to the table some issues we should discuss on our way to such conceptual attempts, and to evaluate both their terms and feasibility. If the seduction of North Atlantic universals has to do with their power to silence their own history, then our most immediate task is the unearthing of such silences. Only after bringing such silences to the fore will we know if and when claims to universal relevance and descriptive objectivity vanish into thin air.

This chapter thus argues that in its most common deployments as a North Atlantic universal, modernity disguises and misconstrues the many Others that it creates. A critical assessment of modernity must start with the revelation of its hidden faces. I set the ground by contrasting modernity and modernization as distinct and yet necessarily entangled. The global expansion of the North Atlantic juxtaposes a geography of imagination and a geography of management that are both distinctive and intertwined. Modernity and modernization overlap and contradict one another as epitomes of these two geographies. Then, I suggest that as a moment of a geography of imagination, modernity is necessarily plural. It is structurally plural: it requires an alterity, a referent outside of itself—a pre- or nonmodern in relation to which the modern takes its full meaning. It is historically plural: it did produce that alterity through both the management and the imaginary projection of various populations within—and especially outside—the North Atlantic. Yet the case of the Caribbean at the time of slavery shows that many of the features associated with North Atlantic modernity could actually be found in areas thought to be pre- or nonmodern. The point is not to insist that the Antilles or other regions of the world were as modern as Europe in the eighteenth and nineteenth centuries—though a legitimate argument can be made along those lines (Mintz 1971a, 1998). Rather, if my sketchy narrative about the Caribbean holds true, it suggests much less the need to rewrite Caribbean history than the necessity to question the story that the North Atlantic tells about itself.

Management of Imagination

From their joint beginnings in the late Renaissance to the recent dislocations attributed to globalization, the development of world capitalism and the cultural, ideological, and political expansion of the North Atlantic can be read through two different sets of lenses, two related mappings, two intertwined yet distinct geographies: a geography of imagination and a geography of management. Modernity and modernization each call to mind one of these two geographies and their necessary coexistence.

Commenting on the cultural domination of the North Atlantic, Martinican writer Edouard Glissant writes: "The West is not in the West. It is a project, not a place" (1992:2). Indeed, the geography of imagination inherent in that project did not need the concreteness of *place*. Rather, it emphasized *space*. More precisely, it required from the beginning two complementary spaces, the Here and the Elsewhere, which premised one another and were conceived as inseparable (Trouillot 1991). Yet inasmuch as Renaissance imagination entailed a universal hierarchy, control and order were also premised in the enterprise. So was colonization. That is to say, the geography of imagination went hand in hand with a geography of management, the elaboration and implementation of procedures and institutions of control both at home and abroad. That the two maps so produced do not fully overlap should not surprise us. Indeed, it is in the very disjuncture between these two geographies that we are likely to identify processes most relevant to the joint production of sameness and difference that characterizes the dual expansion of the North Atlantic and of world capitalism.

As moments and aspects within the development of world capitalism, yet figures within two distinctive geographies, modernity and modernization are thus both discrete and intertwined. Thus, a rigid distinction between societal modernization and cultural modernity can be misleading (Gaonkar 1999:1), especially when it couches them as separate historical developments that can be each judged on its own terms. The distinction remains useful only if we keep in mind that the bundle of facts and processes we can package under one label was at any moment of world history, *as a package*, a condition of possibility of the processes and phenomena that we cover with the second label. Better, the distinction becomes necessary inasmuch as it illuminates specific historical moments and processes.

To speak of modernization is to put the accent on the material and organizational features of world capitalism in specific locales. It is to speak of that geography of management, of these aspects of the development of world capitalism that reorganize space for explicitly political or economic purposes. We may note among the continuities and markers along that line the French Revolution as a moment in the modernization of the state—that is, a reorganization of space for political management. We may read the English Industrial Revolution as a moment in the reorganization of labor relations—here again a reorganization of space, primarily for economic purposes. Similarly, the wave of decolonization after World War II can be read as a moment in the modernization of the interstate system—one more moment of reorganization of space on a world scale, one that provides a new geography of management. Finally, and closer to our times, what we now call globalization—and which we too often reduce to a concoction of fads and slogans—inheres in a fundamental change in the spatiality of capital (Trouillot 2001a). In short, modernization has everything to do with political economy, with a geography of management that creates *places*: a place called France, a place called the third world, a place called the market, a placed called the factory or, indeed, a workplace.

If modernization has to do with the creation of place as a relation within a definite space, modernity has to do with the projection of that place—the local—against a spatial background that is theoretically unlimited. To put it differently, modernity has to do not only with the relationship between place and space but also with the relation between place and time. For in order to prefigure the theoretically unlimited space—as opposed to the space within which management occurs—one needs to relate place to time, or, better said, to address a unique temporality, that is, the position of the subject located in that place. Thus, modernity has to do with these aspects and moments in the development of world capitalism that require the projection of the individual or collective subject against both space and time. It has to do with historicity.

I will further expand on that argument by discussing the work of Reinhart Koselleck (1985) and by discussing features of Caribbean history. For now, we may note as markers of modernity historical moments that both localized the individual or collective subject while opening its spatial and temporal horizons and multiplying its outside references. The invention of private life in the Renaissance and the accompanying features noted by Chartier (1993) and others, such as the spread of silent reading, of personal journals, of private libraries, the translation of the Bible in vernacular languages, the invention of the nation and national histories, and the proclamation of the United States Bill of Rights, can all be read as key moments in the spread of modernity. Closer to our times, the global production of desire, spurred by the unification of the world market for consumer goods (Trouillot 2001a), expands further the geography of imagination of which modernity is part.

This last example is telling. That this global production of desire, as a moment of modernity, parallels globalization as a moment in the spatial history—and thus the management—of capital does suggest that although modernity and modernization should not be confused, they are inherently intertwined. Indeed, one could take the two lists of markers that I have just suggested, extend them appropriately, and draw lines across them that spell out this inextricability. From the printing press to silent reading, from the political rise of the bourgeoisie to the expansion of individual rights, from the elusiveness of finance capital to the elusiveness of global desires, the geography of management and the geography of imagination are intertwined. Just as the imaginary projection of the West constantly refuels managerial projects of modernization, so is modernization itself a condition of possibility of modernity.

Historicity and Alterity:
The Modern as Heterology

As part of the geography of imagination that constantly recreates the West, modernity always required an Other and an Elsewhere. It was always plural, just like the West was always plural. This plurality is inherent in modernity itself, both structurally and historically. Modernity as a structure requires an other, an alter, a native—indeed, an alter-native.

Modernity as a historical process also created this alter ego, as modern as the West, yet otherwise modern.

If we follow the line of argument drawn from Reinhart Koselleck (1985) that modernity implies first and foremost a fundamental shift in regimes of historicity, most notably the perception of a past radically different from the present and the perception of a future that becomes both attainable (because secular) and yet indefinitely postponed (because removed from eschatology), we come to the conclusion that modernity requires a localization of space. Koselleck does not reach that conclusion himself, yet those of us who claim that modernity requires a geography of imagination (Mudimbe 1988; Trouillot 1991) are not necessarily at odds with his analysis. For as soon as one draws a single line that ties past, present, and future, and yet insists on their distinctiveness, one must inevitably place actors along that line. In other words, not everyone can be at the same point along that line. Some become more advanced than others. From the viewpoint of anyone anywhere in that line, others are somewhere else, ahead or behind. Being behind suggests in and of itself an elsewhere that is both in and out of the space defined by modernity—*out* to the extent that these others have not yet reached that place where judgment occurs, and *in* to the extent that the place they now occupy can be perceived from that other place within the line. To put it this way is first to note the relation between modernity and the ideology of progress (Dussel 1993), between modernity and modernism, but there is more to the argument.

In his treatment of modernity, Koselleck insists upon historicity— that is, in part, a relation to time of which the chronologization, the periodization, the distanciation, the increasing speed and range of affective relations from hope to anxiety help to create a new regime. But if he is correct, as I believe he is, this new regime of historicity requires also a localization of its subject. Time here creates space. Or more precisely, Koselleck's historicity necessitates a locale, a *lieu* from which springs this relation to time. Yet, by definition, the inscription of a lieu requires an Elsewhere—a space of and for the Other. That this space can be—indeed, often is—imaginary merely suggests that there may be more continuities than we think between the geography of imagination of the Renaissance and that of the Enlightenment.

Within that geography, elaborations of a state of nature in Hobbes, Locke, or Rousseau, as varied as they indeed are between and across these authors, emerge as alternative modernities—places, locales against which we can read what it means to be modern. Rousseau is the clearest on this for two reasons. First, he is not a modernist. He does not believe in either the inevitability or the desirability of linear progress. Indeed, critics wrongly accuse him of naïveté vis-à-vis the noble savage and earlier stages of human history. Second, that critique notwithstanding, Rousseau explicitly posits his state of nature as a structural and theoretical necessity of which the historical reality is largely irrelevant. He needs that fictional time to mark his own space as a modern one. Later observers will be less perceptive. Indeed, as the line that ties past, present, and future gets more acute and more relevant, as both the momentum behind it and the goal to which it aspires become clearer—otherwise said, as teleology replaces eschatology—from Condorcet to Kant and from Hegel to Marx, the place assigned to the Other may fall not only within the line but also *off* the line. Hegel's dismissal of Africa and Marx's residual "Asiatic" mode of production—maybe his most unthought category—are exemplars of a hierarchy of spaces created through a relation to time. Not only does progress and its advance leave some people "behind" (an elsewhere from within), but increasing chunks of humanity fall off its course (an elsewhere on the outside but that can only be perceived from within). In short, the temporal-historical regime that Koselleck associates with modernity creates multiple spaces for the Other.

If that is so, modernity necessitates various readings of alterity, what Michel de Certeau calls an heterology. The claim that someone—someone else—is modern is structurally and necessarily a discourse on the Other, since the intelligibility of that position—what it means to be modern—requires a relation to otherness. The modern is that subject which measures any distance from itself and redeploys it against an unlimited space of imagination. That distance inhabits the perspectival look to and from the painted subject in Raphaël or Titian's portraits. It fueled the quarrel of the Ancients and Moderns in Louis XIV's France. It is crucial to Baudelaire's (re)definition of modern art and poetry as both recognition and rejection of time.

Baudelaire's Shadow

Idiosyncratic as it may, the case of Baudelaire suggests in miniature the range of silences that we need to uncover for a critical assessment of modernity that would throw light on its hidden faces. As is well known, Baudelaire had just turned twenty when his stepfather forced him to embark for Calcutta. He went only as far as Mauritius and Bourbon (now Réunion), then part of France's plantation empire. That trip inspired—and may have seen the first drafts of—many of the poems that would later be published in *Les Fleurs du Mal*. Back in Paris, Baudelaire entered into a relationship with a "mulatto" actress, better known as Jeanne Duval, widely said to be of Haitian descent. Although Baudelaire's liking of dark-skinned females seems to have preceded that liaison, his tumultuous affair with the woman he called his "Black Venus" lasted over twenty years, during which she was for him a major source of poetic inspiration.

Only recently has the relationship between Duval and Baudelaire become a central object of scholarly research.[2] Emmanuel Richon (1998) points out that Baudelairian scholarship has not even bothered to verify the most basic facts about Duval, including her actual origins. The many sketches of Duval by Baudelaire and other portraits, such as Edouard Manet's "La maitresse de Baudelaire couchée," only confirm her constant presence in his life. Many visitors recount entering the poet's place and finding him reading his unpublished poetry to Jeanne. Literary scholarship has attributed some of Baudelaire's work to a "Jeanne Duval cycle" while insisting on her role as "femme fatale" and relishing the assertion that Duval infected Baudelaire with syphilis. Richon, who demolishes that assertion, convincingly argues that the opposite was more likely.

However, the main lesson of Richon's work goes beyond biographical rectification. His claim that the Indian Ocean trip, and especially the relationship with Duval, fundamentally shaped Baudelairian aesthetics suggests that Baudelairian scholarship may have produced what I call a "silence of significance" through a procedure of banalization. Well-known facts are recounted in passing, yet kept in the background of the main narrative or accorded little significance because they "obviously" do not matter (Trouillot 1995). Yet can it not matter that Baudelaire was living a racial taboo in the midst of a Paris sizzling with arguments for and against the abolition of slavery and the equality of human races? Slavery was abolished in Bourbon and other French possessions less than seven years after he had been there and while he was enthralled in his relationship with Duval. Can it not matter that the eulogist of modernity was also Jeanne Duval's eulogist?

The issue is even more intriguing in light of Baudelaire's own disdain for the modernization—here, the concrete management of places and populations by the French state, republican and imperial as it was—that was a condition of possibility of his own modernity. As in Rousseau, Baudelaire's relation to time, a hallmark of his modernity, does not imply a blind faith in either the desirability or the inevitability of progress. Indeed, Baudelaire is resolutely antimodernist (Froidevaux 1989). His modernity is founded upon the search for a furtive yet eternal present. The past has no legacy; the future holds no promises. Only the present is alive. With Baudelaire, we are thus quite far from either side of the quarrel between the Ancients and the Moderns and from Koselleck's regime of historicity. Baudelaire's historicity is indeed a new brand.

How interesting, then, that this new brand of modernity also leads to "the spatialization of time" (Froidevaux 1989:125). Baudelaire's escape from chronological temporality is space—more specifically, the space of the Elsewhere. Here again, time creates space, and here again, space generates a heterology. Literary scholars have long noted the importance of themes and metaphors of space and of travel, as well as the role of exoticism, in Baudelaire's poetry. While we should leave to specialists the task of mapping out further the many locations in a geography of imagination that links space and time, the Here and the Elsewhere, routine and exoticism, we may want to provoke them in finding out the extent to which the modernity of Baudelaire, the critic, establishes itself against the background of an ethereal Elsewhere that Baudelaire, the poet, inscribes somewhere between Jeanne's body and the islands of the Indian Ocean?

Differently Modern: The Caribbean
as Alter-Native

I have argued so far that modernity is structurally plural inasmuch as it requires an heterology, an Other outside of itself. I would like to argue now that the modern is also historically plural because it always requires an Other from within, the otherwise modern, created between the jaws of modernity and modernization. Here again, that plurality is best perceived if we keep modernity and modernization as distinct yet related groups of phenomena with the understanding that the power unleashed through modernization is a condition of possibility of modernity itself. I will draw on the sociohistorical experience of the Caribbean region to make that point.

Eric Wolf once wrote in passing but with his usual depth that the Caribbean is "eminently a world area in which modernity first deployed its powers and simultaneously revealed the contradictions that give it birth." Wolf's words echo the work of Sidney W. Mintz (1971a, 1974a,b, 1996, 1998), who has long insisted that the Caribbean has been modern since its early incorporation in various North Atlantic empires. Teasing out Wolf's comments and drawing from Mintz's work, I want to sketch some of the contradictions from the Caribbean record to flesh out a composite picture of what I mean by the "otherwise modern."

Behold the sugar islands from the peak of Barbados's career to Cuba's lead in the relay race—after Jamaica and Saint-Domingue—thus roughly from the 1690s to the 1860s. At first glance, Caribbean labor relations under slavery offer an image of homogenizing power. Slaves were interchangeable, especially in the sugar fields, which consumed most of the labor force, victims of the most "depersonalizing" side of modernization (Mintz 1971a). Yet as we look closer, a few figures start to emerge that suggest the limits of that homogeneity. Chief among them is the slave striker, the one who helped decide when the boiling of the cane juices had reached the exact point when they could be transferred from one vessel to the next.[3] Some planters tried to identify that moment by using complex thermometers. Yet since the right moment depended on temperature, on the intensity of the fire, on the viscosity of the juice, and on the quality of the original cane itself and its state at the time of cutting, other planters thought that a good striker was much more valuable than the most complex technology. Indeed, the slave who acquired such skills would be labeled or sold as "a striker." Away from the sugar cane, especially on the smaller estates that produced coffee, work was often distributed by task, thus allowing individual slaves at times to exceed their quota and to gain additional remuneration.

The point is not that plantation slavery allowed individual slaves much room to maneuver in the labor process; it did not. Nor is the point to conjure images of sublime resistance. Rather, Caribbean history gives us various glimpses at the production of a modern self—a self producing itself through a particular relation to material production—even under the harshest possible conditions. For better *and* for worse, a sugar striker was a modern identity, just as being a slave violinist, a slave baker, or a slave midwife (Higman 1984; Debien 1974; Abrahams 1992:126–30).

That modern self takes firmer contours when we consider the provision grounds of slavery. Sidney Mintz (1974b) has long insisted on the sociocultural relevance of these provision grounds, small plots in which slaves were allowed to grow their own crops and raise animals on the margins of the plantations on land unfit for the main export crops. Given the high price of imported food, the availability of unused lands, and the fact that slaves worked on these plots in their own free time, these provision grounds were in fact an indirect subsidy to the masters, lessening their participation to the reproduction of the labor force.

Yet Mintz and others—including myself—have noted that what started as an economic bonus for planters turned out to be a field of opportunities for individual slaves. I will not repeat all these arguments here (Trouillot 1988, 1996, 1998). Through these provision grounds, slaves learned the management of capital, the planning of family production for individual purposes. How much to plant of a particular food crop and where, how much of the surplus to sell in the local market, what to do with the profit involved decisions that required an assessment of each individual's placement within the household. Thus the provision grounds can be read not only as material fields used to enhance slaves' physical and legal conditions—including at times the purchase of one's freedom—but also as symbolic fields for the production of individual selves by way of the production of material goods.

Such individual purposes often found their realization in the colonial slave markets, where slaves—especially female slaves—traded their goods for the cash that would turn them into consumers. Here again, one can only guess at the number of decisions that went into these practices, how they fed into a slave's habitus, how they impacted on gender roles then and now in the Caribbean. Individual purposes also realized themselves through patterns of consumption from the elaborate dresses of mulatto women to the unique foulard that would distinguish a slave woman from another one. The number of ordinances regulating the clothing of nonwhites, free and enslaved, throughout the Caribbean in the days of slavery is simply amazing. Their degree of details—for example, "with no silk, gilding, ornamentation or lace unless these latter be of very low value" (Fouchard 1981:43), is equally stunning. Yet stunning also is the tenacity of slaves who circumvented the regulations and used clothing as an individual signature.

Moreau de St.-Méry, the most acute observer of Saint-Domingue's daily life, writes: "It is hard to believe the height to which a slave woman's expenses might rise. . . . In a number of work gangs the same slave who wielded tools or swung the hoe during the whole week dresses up to attend church on Sunday or to go to market; only with difficulty would they be recognized under their fancy garb. The metamorphosis is even more dramatic in the slave woman who has donned a muslin skirt and Paliacate or Madras kerchief" (in Fouchard 1981:47). Moreau's remarks echo numerous observations by visitors and residents of the Americas throughout slavery's long career.

If modernity is also the production of individual selves through patterns of production and consumption, Caribbean slaves were modern, having internalized ideals of individual betterment through work, ownership, and personal identification to particular commodities. It was a strained and harsh modernity, to be sure. Otherwise modern they were—yet still undoubtedly modern by that definition.

One could argue—although the argument is not as easy as it seems—that the selves on which I just insisted may have existed elsewhere without the forced modernization imposed by colonialism. I would readily concede that point if it leads to the realization that the modern individual self claimed by North Atlantic consciousness is not unique to the

North Atlantic. At the extreme opposite, one could also argue that the detached individual self is only a fiction of the North Atlantic geography of imagination, an ideological by-product of the internal narrative of modernity. Surprisingly, perhaps, I am even more willing to concede that point. Indeed, in either case, the central issue is not that of an allegedly modern individual subjectivity—whatever that may be—but the insertion of that subjectivity into a particular regime of historicity. Clothing as individual signature may be as old as human society. So may be the production of identity through labor. At any rate, I doubt that these two features—or any of the markers usually claimed to signify the rise of the modern self—first obtained as such in Renaissance or post-Renaissance Christendom. Intellectual and art history, literature, and philosophy may have misled us in overrating these individual attributes of the modern self to the detriment of the historical context within which these selves were fashioned. François Hartog (1980) sets the projection of alterity as the context for self-identification as far back as Herodotus. Horkheimer and Adorno (1972) see in Odysseus the precursor of the modern subject. Closer to ground, Ariès and Duby (1988) and their collaborators in the *History of Private Life* project effectively extend notions of privacy or even intimacy back into the Middle Ages. I suspect that with similar data, one could make as potent discoveries outside of Christendom, thus relativizing the narrative that makes the modern individual self such a eurocentric product.[4]

Yet again, necessary as this revisionist narrative is, it is not the central issue. Too often, critics of eurocentrism flesh out their arguments in terms of chronological primacy. They spend much energy demonstrating that such-and-such a feature claimed by North Atlantic narratives to have been a European first could actually be found elsewhere before European presence. The mistake here is to forget that chronological primacy is itself a central tenet of North Atlantic imagination. That is, the value of being the first comes from a particular premium on time, a specific take on historicity. The existence of certain social features outside of Europe matters less than the inscription of these features in social and political regimes *then* and much less even than the inscriptions of these same features—as found in Europe then—in North Atlantic narratives *now*. From that perspective, the modern self may be less a matter of the content of an individual subjectivity than that of the insertion of that subjectivity into a particular regime of historicity and sociopolitical management. On that latter issue, the most crucial one in my view, the Caribbean story is most revealing.

Modern historicity hinges on both a fundamental rupture between past, present, and future—as distinct temporal planes—and their re-linking along a singular line that allows for continuity. I have argued that this regime of historicity in turn implies an heterology—that is, a necessary reading of alterity. Striking, then, is the fact that Caribbean history as we know it starts with an abrupt rupture between past and present—for Europeans, for Native Americans, and for enslaved Africans. In no way could the enforced modernization imposed by colonization be perceived by any of the actors as a mere continuation of an immediate past. This was a New World for all involved, even for those who had lived within it before it became new to others.

For indeed, the consciousness that times had changed, that things were falling apart and coming together in new ways, was both inescapable and yet inseparable from the awareness that others were fundamentally different—different in where they came from, in the positions they occupied along any of the intersecting hierarchies, in the languages they spoke, in the costumes they wore, in the customs they inhabited, in the possible futures they could envision. The sensibility to time and the recognition of heterogeneity associated with modernity are inescapable here. Indeed, they have been central themes of Caribbean scholarship (Trouillot 1992, 2001b).

Here again the slave quarters are telling. There was imposed the sudden discovery of a common African past but also the awareness that this commonality barely covered fundamental differences. One could not address that other next door, who looked so strikingly similar, without using a language derived at least in part from that of the masters. Was not that as modern as the vulgate version of the Bible? More modern than the quarrel between seventeenth-century French intellectuals as to whether the king's engravings were best written in French or in Latin? If the awareness of one's position in history not just as an individual but as part of a group and against the background of a social system brought to consciousness is a fundamental part of what it means to be modern, the Caribbean was modern from day one—that is, from the very day colonialism imposed its modernization. If the awareness of sociocultural differences and the need to negotiate across such differences are part of what we call modernity, then the Caribbean was modern since at least the sixteenth century—that is, from day one of North Atlantic modernity. But if that is so, the chronological primacy of the North Atlantic falters.

Yet chronology here is only an index. My goal is not to replace North Atlantic chronological primacy over the rest of the world with a Caribbean chronological primacy over other colonies and postcolonies. To be sure, historical particulars made the Caribbean, for better and for worse, the area longest under European control outside of Europe itself and the only one where Europeans moved as if it was indeed empty land, *terra nullius*, to be fashioned along modern lines. To be sure, now-dominant North Atlantic narratives—reflecting the international reach of the English language, the expansion of Protestantism as a variant of Christianity, and the spread of Anglo-Saxon and Teutonic sensibilities—reduce the crucial role of Portugal and Spain in the creation of the West. To be sure, a related emphasis on the Enlightenment and on the nineteenth century and the downplaying of the Renaissance as a founding moment also lead to a neglect of the role of the Caribbean and Latin America in the production of the earliest tropes associated with modernity, a chronological amnesia that crucially impedes our understanding of the North Atlantic itself (Trouillot 1991, 1995; Dussel 1993).

Yet I want to insist that the lessons learned from the Caribbean are applicable elsewhere. As a historical process inherently tied to modernization, modernity necessarily creates its alter-native in Asia, in Africa, in Latin America—in all these areas of the world where the archetypal Caribbean story repeats itself with variations on the theme of destruction and creolization. Modernity creates its others—multiple, multifaced, multilayered. It has done so from day one: *we* have always been modern, differently modern, contradictorily modern, otherwise modern —yet undoubtedly modern.

I don't want to conclude with this pun on Bruno Latour's famous title, however tempting a *bon mot*. In *We Have Never Been Modern*, Latour (1993) suggests that the North Atlantic's "modern constitution" rests on a divide between scientific power, meant to represent things as they are, and political power, meant to represent subjects as they wish to be. Latour sees the formulation of this divide (science/politics, object/subject, nature/culture) as the impossible dream of modernity, since the world so neatly divided is actually made of hybrids. Nevertheless, Latour does admit, almost in passing, that blind faith in this divide also makes the moderns invincible. I am interested in this invincibility. Latour's witty title could be misread as to imply that we could have been modern according to definition. But if modernity is as much blind faith in this narrative as its global consequences, we have long been modern, except that the *we* here is not only the North Atlantic but also the hidden faces of modernity necessary to North Atlantic hegemony—if not invincibility.

Ultimately, however, that modernity has long obtained outside of the North Atlantic is only a secondary lesson from the Caribbean savage slot, a conclusion that still makes us what is there to be explained. Yet is the alter-native really what is there to be explained? Is the puzzle the female slave who used her kerchief as individual signature, or the laws that repeatedly tried to curb her individual expression? Is the puzzle the resilience of the creolization process under slavery, or the expectation that enslaved Africans and their descendants would be either a tabula rasa or mere carriers of tradition (Trouillot 1998)? In short, is not the puzzle within the West itself?

The Caribbean story as I read it is less an invitation to search for modernity in various times and places—a useful yet secondary enterprise—than an exhortation to change the terms of the debate. What is there to be analyzed further, better, and differently is the relation between the geography of management and the geography of imagination that together spurred and underpinned the development of world capitalism. And in the context of that reformulation, the Caribbean's most important lesson is a formidable one indeed. For that lesson, as I see it, is that modernity never was—never could be—what it claimed to be.

Notes

1. Belonging to that class does not depend on a fixed meaning. It is a matter of struggle and contest about and around these universals and the world they claim to describe. For instance, only time will tell if newly popular expressions such as "globalization" or "the international community" will become North Atlantic universals.

2. That relationship provides the thread of Haitian novelist Fabienne Pasquet's *l'Ombre de Baudelaire* (1996), whose title I borrow here.

3. According to Higman (1984:170-72), the head sugar boiler added lime, controlled evaporation, and decided when to strike the sugar at the point of crystallization. He "was depended on by the planters to make correct decisions in what required 'practical chemical knowledge' but remained more an art than a science" (1984:172). Mintz (1985:49-50) who discusses striking at length, notes: "boiling and 'striking' . . . required great skill, and sugar boilers were artisans who worked under difficult conditions" (1985:49).

4. Sometimes the data are there and only the perspective is missing. Reversing the dominant perspective, Sidney Mintz asks: "Who is more modern, more western, more developed: a barefoot and illiterate Yoruba market woman who daily risks her security and her capital in vigorous individual competition with others like herself; or a Smith College graduate who spends her days ferrying her husband to the Westport railroad station and her children to ballet classes? If the answer is that at least the Smith girl is literate and wears shoes, one may wonder whether one brand of anthropology has not been hoisted by its own petard" (1971b:267-68).

References

Abrahams, Roger D.
1992   *Singing the Master: The Emergence of African American Culture in the Plantation South.* New York: Pantheon Books.

Ariès, Philippe, and G. Duby
1988   [Eds.] *A History of Private Life II: Revelations of the Medieval World.* Cambridge, Mass.: Harvard/Belknap Press.

Chartier, Roger
1993   [Ed.] *A History of Private Life III: Passions of the Renaissance.* Cambridge, Mass.: Belknap Press.

Debien, Gabriel
1974   *Les esclaves aux Antilles françaises (XVIIème-XVIIIème siècle).* Fort de France: Sociétés d'histoire de la Guadeloupe et de la Martinique.

Dussel, Enrique
1993   Eurocentrism and Modernity: Introduction to the Frankfurt Lectures. *boundary 2* 20: 65–76.

Fouchard, Jean
1981 [1972]   *The Haitian Maroons: Liberty or Death.* New York: Blyden Press.

Froidevaux, Gérald
1989   *Baudelaire: Représentation et modernité.* Paris: José Corti.

Gaonkar, Dilip Parameshwar
1999   On Alternative Modernities. *Public Culture* 11(1): 1–18.

Glissant, Edouard
1992 [1989]   *Caribbean Discourse: Selected Essays.* Edited by A. J. Arnold. Caraf Books.

Hartog, François
1980   *Le miroir d'Herodote: Essai sur la représentation de l'autre.* Paris: Gallimard.

Higman, B. W.
1984   *Slave Populations of the British Caribbean 1807–1834.* Baltimore, Md.: Johns Hopkins University Press.

Horkheimer, Max, and Theodor W. Adorno
1972   *Dialectic of Enlightenment.* New York: Seabury Press.

Knauft, Bruce M.
2002   Critically Modern: An Introduction. In *Critically Modern: Alternatives, Alterities, Anthropologies* [this volume]. Edited by Bruce M. Knauft. Bloomington: Indiana University Press.

Koselleck, Reinhart
1985   *Futures Past: On the Semantics of Historical Time.* Cambridge, Mass.: MIT University Press.

Latour, Bruno
  1993 [1991]   *We Have Never Been Modern*. Cambridge, Mass.: Harvard
       University Press.

Mintz, Sidney W.
  1971a The Caribbean as a Socio-cultural Area. In *Peoples and Cultures of
         the Caribbean: An Anthropological Reader*. Edited by Michael M.
         Horowitz, pp. 17–46. Garden City, N.Y.: American Museum of
         Natural History Press.
  1971b Men, Women and Trade. *Comparative Studies in Society and History*
         13(3): 247–69.
  1974a The Caribbean Region. In *Slavery, Colonialism, and Racism: Essays*.
         Edited by Sidney W. Mintz, pp. 45–71. New York: Norton.
  1974b *Caribbean Transformations*. Chicago: Aldine Publishing.
  1985   *Sweetness and Power: The Place of Sugar in Modern History*. New
         York: Penguin Books.
  1996   Enduring Substances, Trying Theories: The Caribbean Region as
         Oikoumene. *Journal of the Royal Anthropological Institute* 2(2): 289–
         311.
  1998   The Localization of Anthropological Practice: From Area Studies to
         Transnationalism. *Critique of Anthropology* 18(2): 117–33.

Mudimbe, V. Y.
  1988   *The Invention of Africa: Gnosis, Philosophy, and the Order of Knowl-
         edge*. Bloomington: Indiana University Press.

Pasquet, Fabienne
  1996   *L'Ombre de Baudelaire*. Paris: Actes Sud.

Richon, Emmanuel
  1998   *Jeanne Duval et Charles Baudelaire. Belle d'abandon*. Paris: L'Har-
         mattan.

Rousseau, Jean-Jacques
  1984 [1755]   *A Discourse on Inequality*. Harmondsworth: Penguin.

Trouillot, Michel-Rolph
  1988   *Peasants and Capital: Dominica in the World Economy*. Baltimore,
         Md.: Johns Hopkins University Press.
  1991   Anthropology and the Savage Slot: The Poetics and Politics of Other-
         ness. In *Recapturing Anthropology: Working in the Present*. Edited by
         Richard G. Fox, pp. 17–44. Santa Fe, N.M.: School of American
         Research Press.
  1992   The Caribbean Region: An Open Frontier in Anthropological The-
         ory. *Annual Review of Anthropology* 21: 19–42.
  1995   *Silencing the Past: Power and the Production of History*. Boston: Bea-
         con Press.
  1996   Beyond and below the Merivale Paradigm. Dominica: The First 100
         Days of Freedom. In *The Lesser Antilles in the Age of European Ex-*

pansion. Edited by Stanley Engerman and R. Paquette, pp. 230–305. Gainesville: University of Florida Press.

1998   Culture on the Edges: Creolization in the Plantation Context. Special issue, "Who/What is Creole?" Edited by A. James Arnold. *Plantation Society in the Americas* 5(1): 8–28.

2001a   The Anthropology of the State in the Age of Globalization: Close Encounters of the Deceptive Kind. *Current Anthropology* 42(1): 125–38.

2001b   The Caribbean. In *International Encyclopedia of The Social and Behavioral Sciences.* Edited by Neil J. Smelser and Paul B. Baltes. London: Elsevier Science.

2002   Adieu Culture: A New Duty Arises. In *Anthropology Beyond Culture.* Edited by Richard G. Fox. Berg Press.

PART III

Eight

On Being Modern in a Capitalist World

Some Conceptual and

Comparative Issues

Donald L. Donham

In 1999, I published a book *Marxist Modern: An Ethnographic History of the Ethiopian Revolution*. In manuscript form, the first part of the title had been *Vernacular Modernities*. During the last stages of writing, I changed the title because I had become increasingly wary of the recent proliferation of uses of the notion of modernity. Having taken on so many different (and sometimes contradictory) meanings, the concept seemed to me to have lost analytical edge. In the absence of definition, an invocation of modernity, or indeed postmodernity, functions as a sort of performative: what it effects for the person who utters it—and the effect is gained simply through the utterance—is placement within a supposed theoretical avant-garde. Ironically, to invoke modernity or its aftermath nowadays has itself become a claim to be fresh, to make a new beginning—in other words, to be modern.[1]

As I pondered such issues, it seemed that there was a key difference between the adjective, "modern," and the noun, "modernity." The adjective points toward ethnographic and historical specification—local peoples have their own ideas about what is modern, and these are contextually dependent and exist to be discovered, not assumed by theoretical definition. It was Ethiopian people's own notions of the modern that I was most interested in highlighting and analyzing, for the course of the Ethiopian revolution could hardly be understood without them.

In contrast, the noun, "modernity," pointed in other directions. It suggests a way of thinking or a state of being, whether for individuals or societies, and, I believe, an implied theory about such a way or state. Once the adjective has been transposed into the noun, modernity floats

much more easily above the ground of ethnographic and historical specification. And floating, it has a tendency to colonize theoretical space,
to gather about it all sorts of assumptions. In this context, it is perhaps too easy to appear innovative when all that is entailed is a certain
inexactness.

Bruno Latour (1993) has argued that theories of modernity are
merely the West's misrecognition of itself, the assumption of a way of
knowing that claims a kind of Archimedian independence from culture
and history. If, as Latour claims, "we" in the West have never been modern in this sense, then the corollary—radical in relation to some recent
work—is surely that "they" haven't been either. On this reading, the
current proliferation of the concept of modernity and particularly the
tendency to pluralize it may not be as helpful as it once appeared.

To illustrate this tendency, let me briefly consider the journal *Public
Culture*, which recently published an issue on "alter/native modernities," one of four of what it called its millennial quartet. The other three
volumes were devoted to globalization, cosmopolitanism, and finally
"millennial" capitalism (of these currently topical issues, only capitalism required a doubling of the adjective, millennial). In the editorial
introduction to the first volume of the set, Carol Breckenridge claimed
that the phrase "alter/native modernities" was coined by Arjun Appadurai in the mid-1980s. She went on to explain:

> Alternative modernities is a concept that refuses singularity, while
> it recognizes the disjuncture and the uneven terrain where simi-
> larity and difference meet. Without an apparatus to describe a wide
> range of cosmopolitan cultural forms and the processes that shape
> them, how can we describe the postcolony as anything other than
> a site of mimesis for Western modernity? (1999:viii)

This passage contains a number of assumptions that might be examined, but in the present context, the one I would like to draw attention
to is the evident anxiety about representing the non-West as a *copy* of
the West. The solution to this perceived problem is to pluralize and to
pun on the notion of "native."

Such an approach appeals undoubtedly to the dominant structure of
thought and feeling within anthropology, the stress on the value of
relativizing. The difficulty in the present case is that this move implicitly smooths out what are in reality vast differences in power and wealth
in what must be seen today as an interactive global system. By pluralizing and relativizing, it suggests that each modernity is on an equal foot-
ing. In this way, the embarrassment of the copy is kept at bay, for each

modernity (like each culture in the traditional formulation) is, at base, incommensurable with others.

In this essay, I would like to take another tack. I want precisely to highlight differences in global power as variously placed peoples appreciate them and suggest that *in this context,* the notion of the copy—with all its love and hate—goes straight to the heart of what might be called the modern predicament. What does it mean to copy? In much of modern Western thought, the copy is necessarily the secondary, the inherently inferior, that which can never embody the value of the original. To appear to do so is in fact fraud. But as modernisms have replaced one another, the distinction between original and copy has been blurred. In Walter Benjamin's famous essay, "The Work of Art in the Age of Mechanical Reproduction" (1969), the increasing availability of the copy begins to diminish the "aura" of original works of art, and Jean Baudrillard (1994) has proposed that a diacritical mark of our present is that the very distinction between original and copy has vanished—as we are left only with the simulacrum.

As with many other aspects of what has been variously called modernity, the "original" notion of the (modern) copy may have received its characteristic definition, not in Europe, but at the colonial interface (see Mitchell 2000). Homi Bhabha (1994:86) has written revealingly on what he calls colonial mimicry, "the desire for a reformed, recognizable Other, as a subject of a difference that is almost the same, but not quite." Almost white, but not quite. Almost civilized, almost democratic, almost . . . but not quite. Here, we can appreciate the hall-of-mirrors effect that the modern notion of the copy sets in train—one in which colonized peoples begin to copy models of capitalist rationality, only to have that fact (and the supposed necessary incompleteness of their emulation) taken as the ideological ground for continued domination.[2]

The notions just sketched appear to be an indispensable component of the modern. Outside the capitalist core, local constructions of the modern typically involve attempts to mold the future by the application of reason—usually by copying strategies that have worked, or that have appeared to have worked, elsewhere.[3] The motive for copying is precisely an appreciation of gaps in wealth and power in an unequal, and for that reason, threatening, world. As capitalist media have increasingly connected the haves and the have-nots of the global order, the (local) appreciation of uneven development has grown keener and more complexly layered, combining admiration and delight with loathing and rejection.

In order to analyze these processes, I suggest we need (1) cultural analyses of the modern that are set within (2) an appreciation of the pattern of capitalist development. In the rest of this essay, I am going to attempt to unpack these assertions and to push beyond positions that I myself set out in *Marxist Modern* and Jean Comaroff and John Comaroff argued in volumes 1 and 2 of their *Of Revelation and Revolution* (1991, 1997).

Part of the rationale for comparing these books is that both projects are about the effects of Western missionaries on local African cultures and political economies, and both take up the question of the modern. I am going to argue that neither study makes as clear as it might what I shall call the dialectic between the modern and capitalism. My book, by focusing so intently on Ethiopia—which was about as remote in the 1970s as it was possible to be from capitalist production—does not make clear how, nonetheless, the wider shape of the global order conditioned Ethiopian notions of the modern. Comaroff and Comaroff, on the other hand, appear to misread black South African notions of the modern as an unconscious surrender to capitalist hegemony and so assume too close a relationship with capitalism.

In what follows, I use and recontextualize materials both from my book and from a critique of Comaroff and Comaroff that I have recently published (Donham 2001). In doing so, my aim is to push toward a clearer, comparative approach to modernity and capitalism—an approach in which neither of these megaterms collapses into the other but in which both are seen as intertwined in recurring ways in recent world history.

Orientations and Definitions

What do I mean by "modernity"? I myself have already slipped from the adjective to the noun. To respond, I would point out that I do *not* mean a state of being, whether for a society or an individual, about which a theory can be developed. Rather, what I would like to indicate by the term is a local public sphere in which at least some actors invoke notions of the modern in claims to power. To invoke the modern involves a particular rhetorical stance and a way of experiencing time and historicity, with a certain structure of progressive expectations for the future. The past is separated from the present and expectations are reoriented to the future. Modernity, then, as I am using it, is the space in which notions of the modern are articulated.

But modernity thus configured is hardly a homogeneous space, for the notion of the modern typically produces reactions and refusals, what I have called antimodernisms. At one level, these appear as total rejections of progress and reason, often being clothed in religious worldviews called fundamentalist, but at other levels, antimodernisms turn out to be much more complex and ambivalent copies of certain aspects of modernisms. Finally, the notion of the modern also creates the semantic space in which ideas of tradition are constructed and reconstructed. Tradition is the domain outside of the modern—that which the modern continually threatens and replaces. Tradition cannot exist without the modern. What I am calling modernity is, then, the discursive space in which an *argument* takes place, one in which certain positions continually get constructed and reconstructed.

Here I am inspired by the German historian Reinhart Koselleck (1985), who has described the genesis of a modern experience of time in European history. Until well into the sixteenth century, the dominant European mode of temporalizing (and thus casting expectations for the future) was provided by the grand narrative of the Bible—the prophecies of what was to come: Christ's Return, the Final Judgment, the End. Control over this future, Koselleck argues, undergirded the stability of the Roman Church. All prophecy about the future had to receive the authorization of the church, so that those who did not, like Joan of Arc or Savonarola, ended up at the stake. In this discursive context, the metanarrative of biblical prophecy provided a static framework in which all events were fitted—in which the End was constantly expected on the one hand and continually deferred on the other.

According to Koselleck, the Reformation destroyed this way of experiencing time. Gradually the future opened up—not as a culmination of a predetermined sacred story, but as an empty, secular, and essentially unknowable space, one that had to be thought of in terms of probabilities rather than prophecies. In this new space, human beings, through their own rationality, could act on their own society. Progress was the result of this rationality. The French Revolution was the first great event experienced with this view of time. Robespierre declared in 1793, "The progress of human Reason has laid the basis for this great Revolution, and the particular duty of hastening it has fallen to you" (cited in Koselleck 1985:7).

So to sum up, I argue that the notion of the modern involves a particular way of experiencing history, a way that reorients expectations toward the future, an essential unknowable future, one open to the application of human reason. The modern, however, rarely goes unopposed. It was precisely the French Revolution that inspired the formation of the great Christian missionary societies in Britain at the beginning of the 1800s. These Christians (many of whom would find their way to South

Africa, as I shall point out later) read the Revolution not as the application of reason to human history, but as the eruption of dire events that fulfilled biblical prophecies that the End was near. In order to allow for the completion of these, according to the Bible, Christians had to take the Word of Christ to the very ends of the earth so that he could return and bring history to a close. What I am calling "modernity" is, then, from the very beginning, a radically heterogeneous affair.

Let me turn to "capitalism." Here I can be briefer, for I do not believe that the basic outline of Marx's analysis has been substantially improved on. Capitalist production involves abstract value in the form of capital on the one hand and embodied labor power on the other. The capitalist buys labor power and sets it to work with a particular technology, and at the end of the process, the capitalist controls the surplus or profit. But capitalists are in competition with one another, and this competition continually drives the adoption of more efficient technologies. By adopting a more efficient means of production, the capitalist controls more profit vis-à-vis his inefficient competitors. The market itself eventually weeds out inefficient capitalists (they go bankrupt), and through this process of what Joseph Schumpeter was later to call "creative destruction," capitalist progress ensues.

In this way, technological advancement is built into the very structure of capitalist relations. Unevenness of economic development inevitably results, along with a continual churning of social conditions. As Marx and Engels (1978:476) said, "All that is solid melts in the air."

Now, we can immediately appreciate the elective affinity between an economic system in which change is inbuilt—in which technological progress is required—and a way of experiencing historicity that focuses on the future. In this context, it is hardly an accident that notions of the modern—that is, aspects of people's lives that count as "up to date," "on the cutting edge"—become a cultural obsession. The "new" is something that capitalism *has* to produce.

But what I'm calling the public sphere of modernity is hardly confined to the capitalist sectors of the global order. Indeed, the most intense forms of modernisms often occur precisely outside its boundaries, as people realize their "backwardness" and yearn to appropriate the power and wealth of other places. Thus, the first communist revolution occurred, not as Marx believed it would, in the developed heartland of capitalism but in fact on its semiperiphery, in Russia. And during the twentieth century, from China to Ethiopia, modernist revolutions have occurred in even more remote areas of the world capitalist system. Antimodernist movements, too, are probably strongest outside the developed capitalist core.

The Ethiopian Revolution

With these orienting statements, let me turn to my book on Ethiopia (Donham 1999). As I have said, capitalism hardly presented itself as a problem in Ethiopia. Rather, I was much more concerned to develop a way of understanding Ethiopian notions of the modern and how they were narratively constructed and copied from other world examples. At one point in the analysis, I ended a chapter with the assertion, echoing Geertz, "it's stories all the way down, stories of stories of stories."

But clearly I had gotten a little carried away with my own rhetoric. A little reflection would have revealed that the kind of stories that were taken up in Ethiopia was in fact conditioned by Ethiopia's particular place within a global system dominated by capitalism. In order to clarify this conditioning, I would like to review three questions:

(1) Why was the Ethiopian revolution of 1974 apparently the only so-cial revolution that Africa has seen so far?
(2) Why did almost all Ethiopian revolutionaries take up Marxism in 1974?
(3) Why were peasant revolutionaries in the south almost all from evan-gelical Christian backgrounds?

First, why did the only African social revolution occur in Ethiopia? It should be clear that I am using a restrictive definition of revolution, one that stipulates a concurrent change in class relations that takes place with a transformation of the state. Neither, by itself, qualifies as a social revolution. For example, the Industrial Revolution entailed a change in class relations but not necessarily the state, while numerous changes in the state have occurred without a transformation in class relations. True social revolutions are comparatively few, and Ethiopia constitutes the only African case of which I am aware—one that compares with the French, Russian, and Chinese examples.

Why only Ethiopia? The answer revolves, I believe, around the fact that Ethiopia was the only African country not colonized by Europeans. (I'm leaving aside Liberia as a special case.) After the Battle of Adwa in 1896, the Italians were confined to their colony of Eritrea, and Ethiopia developed independently for most of the twentieth century. One ironic consequence of this proud fact was that Ethiopia was more isolated from the world capitalist system than the European colonies that surrounded it, and therefore enjoyed little of the technological progress that came with colonization. This situation recalls the old adage that the only situation worse than being exploited is *not* being exploited.

By the 1950s and 1960s, educated Ethiopian elites were becoming painfully aware of their economic "backwardness" compared to colonies like Kenya (and "backward" was exactly the word they used). And increasingly, these Ethiopians used the image of the European past, and feudalism in particular, to understand their present economic and political order—which they blamed for Ethiopia's lack of progress. This consciousness of the unevenness of capitalist development was, then, absolutely essential in the processes that led to Ethiopian revolution. Elsewhere in Africa, decolonization led to political struggles that generally united African elites with peasants against European colonists. In Ethiopia, in contrast, struggles from below eventually transformed both the structure of the state and the entire class structure as peasants pitted themselves *against* the Ethiopian elites whom they blamed for the country's backwardness.

In sum, it was Ethiopia's peculiar position within the global political economy—its political independence combined with economic backwardness—that prepared the way for the revolution.

My second question is why did almost all Ethiopian political actors after 1974 become Marxists. It is essential for the reader to understand that no organized Marxist party "made" the Ethiopian revolution. Rather, it was the other way around: the revolution would finally make a Marxist party. In the process, factions competed, fought, and killed one another in a massive wave of terror after 1976, but virtually all of these factions saw themselves as Marxists. Why?

Again, one has to understand Ethiopia's particular placement in relationship to cold war alignments after the 1950s. There were at that time two grand narratives of progress in the world: the story of the West with liberal capitalist development and individual freedom versus the emancipatory narrative offered by the Soviet Union as a kind of modernist trumping, one that promised to beat the West at its own game, to usher in progress, development, and freedom in a future that even the West was destined to join.

Haile Selassie was one of the most adept African leaders in exploiting Western fears of the movement of communism into Africa, and during the 1950s and 1960s, Ethiopia received more U.S. foreign aid than the rest of the continent combined. By the beginning of the 1970s, there was then an indelible link in the minds of educated Ethiopians between the old Ethiopian so-called feudal elite and what came to be termed "American imperialism." As up-and-coming educated Ethiopians began to blame the old elite for backwardness and lack of progress, they associated all those things as well with North American narratives and policies. Rejecting their place within a stratified and uneven world pushed

young, educated Ethiopians toward the Marxist metanarrative of progress and development. According to one Ethiopian political actor during
the time:

> [Marxism] generated mass hysterical loyalty. . . . Many did not
> read about it, but that was beside the point. They were obsessed by
> it. Most accepted it as true even before they read about it, and
> when they did read they found the "self-evident" truth. (quoted in
> Donham 1999:126)

This brings me to my third and final question, why did almost all
peasant revolutionaries in the south come from evangelical Christian
backgrounds? This to me is the most fascinating of my three questions
and illustrates what I see as a characteristic dialectic of modernity. It
involves a story of the formation of a so-called faith mission, the Sudan
Interior Mission (SIM) in Canada at the end of the nineteenth century,
the placement of missionaries in southern Ethiopia by the 1930s, and
the formation of a strong indigenous church in many areas of the south
by the 1960s.

Here, let me highlight the connection between narratives of the modern and antimodern among the missionaries and the structure of world
capitalism. The SIM originated as an interdenominational movement in
North America that eventually took on the label of "fundamentalism"
by the 1920s. A reaction against modernist forms of Christianity that
attempted to bring the Bible "up to date," to harmonize the scriptures
with science and progressive knowledge, the SIM situated itself as explicitly "antimodernist," a phrase they themselves used. The Bible for
SIM fundamentalists was the inerrant Word of God. And it was the
Bible that commanded Christians to take God's Word to the ends of
the earth, so that Christ could return and bring the grand narrative of
the Bible to a close.

Not only did the SIM fundamentalists understand the Bible as literally true, they developed a narrative reading of the scriptures that up-
ended modernist forms of temporal expectations. For modernist, so-
called postmillennialist Christians, the world was getting better and
better. Eventually a millennium of peace and harmony would be reached,
after which Christ would return. But for fundamentalist, premillennialist Christians, by the early twentieth century, the world was in fact getting worse and worse. As the situation irreversibly deteriorated, Christ
would return—any day now, according to the signs of the times—*before*
the millennium, not after. Christ's sudden intervention in history would
mean salvation for the blessed few but damnation for the sinful many.

Perforce, the leaders of premillennialism did not believe that they could do anything to change the overall shape of history. Yet their view of a foreordained future hardly led to a quietism—indeed, if anything, it led to the reverse: an increased anxiety and urgency, an escalating commitment to oppose apostasy wherever it occurred, and most particularly for the events I am interested in, an enlarged emphasis on evangelicalism and foreign missions.

An altogether remarkable process occurred as capitalism went into crises in North America after 1929. Almost all the mainline Protestant denominations drew back from foreign missions as the level of church contributions declined. But the premillennialist SIM flourished, and indeed began to send more missionaries to Africa than all the other Protestant groups combined. How, in the context of the one of the great economic crises of the West, were they able to do so?

Part of the answer is that premillennialist readings of the Bible prepared believers for bad times. The world was running downhill as the devil went from triumph to triumph. Crisis, sin, and decay all went together. But the devil's apparent victories were only apparent and should, in fact, be read as "signs of our time"—signs that Christ would return to earth, any day now—at which point the living would be declared forever saved to heaven or forever condemned to hell. Before Christ could return according to prophecies in the Bible, his Word had to be distributed to the ends of the globe. In this way, the experience of crisis and adversity was transformed by a narrative of eventual triumph of Christian faith. By the 1930s, as the North American economy went into deep depression, supporters of the SIM, sensing the end of time, gave more and more to foreign missions—as a result of which the first batch of missionaries arrived in Ethiopia.

Once in Ethiopia, the history of how local peoples, largely those in the south, were converted to evangelical Christianity is a complicated story (one that involves the peculiar way that the Maale religion, for example, indexed spiritual success by signs of outward material success). Here, I want to highlight the fact that what had been intensely antimodernist in the North American religious context became, in fact, hypermodernist in the local Ethiopian social context. Consider only the biblicism that the missionaries brought to southern Ethiopia, their emphasis on the Bible as the inerrant word of God. To North Americans, this doctrine protected religion from the modernist claims of science. Whatever science professed to know, all that anyone *really* needed to know was the Bible.

In the context of southern Ethiopia, however, an emphasis on the Book had entirely different meanings and consequences. In Ethiopia, being able to read the Bible (and hence other books) in a society in which no one else could, separated one not from modernity—far from it—but from tradition. After the 1940s, the missionaries were required to use to the national language, Amharic, both in preaching and in Bible publishing. For southerners, being literate in Amharic opened a whole new world of the nation, courts, newspapers, and radio—in short, all the trappings of the Ethiopian modern.

To skip to the early 1970s, then, we can see why it was that evangelical Christian converts in the south, already local modernists, became the revolution's main supporters. They had already separated themselves from tradition, they were aware that missionaries came from vastly technologically superior societies compared to their own, and they had already begun to dream about "progress." As the revolution burst on the scene, they enthusiastically took up the project of destroying tradition, sometimes as ruthlessly as their French, Russian, and Chinese counterparts. Evangelical Christians, far out of proportion to their numbers in the population, dominated the leadership of new revolutionary institutions by 1975.

In sum, while Ethiopia had little capitalist production within its borders, nonetheless, its placement within a stratified global system—the outlines of which Ethiopian actors were intensely aware of—provided the essential ground on which local notions of the "modern" were constructed. In the particular case of Ethiopia, local modernisms led to profoundly anticapitalist results, as the Ethiopian revolution unfolded and the state socialized the economy.

Development of Capitalism in South Africa

Let me turn now to South Africa and to the work of Comaroff and Comaroff, *Of Revelation and Revolution* (1991, 1997). Ethiopia and South Africa are interesting cases to juxtapose. Ethiopia, as I have pointed out, was on the very periphery of global capitalism during the twentieth century. South Africa, on the other hand, lay at the other extreme for the African continent. South Africa was the area of Africa most intensely colonized—not only colonized but settled as well. White settlers from Europe, ancestors to the Afrikaners, began arriving as early as the seventeenth century, and missionaries to the local "heathen" soon followed. In the nineteenth century, the discovery of diamonds and then gold suddenly dropped the most advanced forms of finance capital in the world in the middle of the South African subsistence economy. Eventually, mining was to provide the motor for the only industrial revolution on the African continent.

South Africa furnishes, then, a very different case compared to

Ethiopia. Comaroff and Comaroff could hardly ignore capitalism. Indeed, it became the primary object of their explanatory quest. To begin,
Comaroff and Comaroff, like myself, notice that the missionaries (whatever their intentions) furnished the primary sites for local constructions
of the modern, from architecture to dress to medicine. In volume 1 of
Of Revelation and Revolution, they tended to homogenize such modernist claims into "*a* culture," set in opposition to traditional Tswana culture, but by volume 2, they point out that "modern" and "traditional"
are, as I have tried to present them here, mutable rhetorical stances
within a recurring argument, constructed in mutual interaction.

So far, our two analyses are similar. But Comaroff and Comaroff then
assert that it was actually such constructions of the modern in South
Africa that inducted blacks into an unconscious capitalist hegemony—
even before the discovery of diamonds or gold, even before capitalist
enterprises:

> Long before the advent of mining and manufacture in South Af-
> rica . . . evangelists strove to instill the routines and dispositions
> of wage work, the pleasures of consumption, the enclosed proprie-
> ties of the domestic estate, the cleavage between the public and the
> private. (1997: 33)

After the analysis I have just presented of Ethiopia, this argument is
a striking one. In the case of Ethiopia—admittedly, more than a century
later—modernist notions were used to produce a profoundly anticapitalist social order. But in the case of South Africa, Comaroff and Comaroff
argue that vernacular modernisms led, "almost inevitably" they say, to
capitalist hegemony. They assume that to copy missionaries from the
capitalist West was inevitably to be led down the capitalist path. But
was it?

I would suggest that the missionary successes that so impress Comaroff and Comaroff—in domains from money to medicine—were real
ones, but what the missionaries were successful at was exemplifying the
notion of the modern, not necessarily of instilling capitalist hegemony.
We gain, I believe, greater insights into the attractions of the new for
the Tswana when we place, as Comaroff and Comaroff did not, Afri-
kaner farmers, the Boers, into the historical and material picture. The
land-hungry Boers were, after all, the major threat to the Tswana at the
time. In such a context, what the religion of the British missionaries
appears to have offered some Tswana was both protection against the
Boers and a kind of modernist trumping, a symbolic end run around
their most pressing enemies at the time—for the British missionaries

considered not just the unconverted Tswana but also the Boers as "back-ward."

That the missionaries played such a role, that they became in Stray-er's (1978) phrase "mediators of modernity," is an ironic result, for in many ways, the missionary movement itself was a rejection of mod-ernism at home, at least in religion. As I have mentioned, both the mission societies studied by Comaroff and Comaroff were established partly in reaction to the French revolution—that founding event of European modernism. As Comaroff and Comaroff show in volume 2 of *Of Revelation and Revolution* (1997), missionaries, whatever their reli-gious commitments, would play a crucial role in the development of Tswana vernacular modernisms. But just because the conversation about the modern began before, and took place alongside, the development of capitalism in South Africa does not mean that it was an aspect necessary for the shape that the latter took.

In the conclusion to volume 2, Comaroff and Comaroff anticipate this objection:

> What would have happened, we have been asked, had Protestant missions never established themselves among Southern Tswana? Would not the same processes have occurred, if more brutally, as a result of colonial capitalism alone? (1997:409)

The Comaroffs' reply:

> The question is useful, but not for the obvious reasons; rather, be-cause it underscores how we differ from those who would see colo-nialism primarily as a product of political and/or economic forces, forces merely qualified by cultural factors. In our view, it is always to be understood, *at once,* as economic and cultural, political and symbolic, general and particular. (1997:409)

But this is not the issue. Let us accept that any social formation must be understood as "at once" economic and cultural. The question before us involves the historical weighting that an analyst must give each in par-ticular contexts.

Comaroff and Comaroff weight Protestant Christianity very heavily indeed: "Proletarianization was an almost inevitable consequence of the Noncomformists' economic revolution and the beliefs that informed it" (1997:187). It was, Comaroff and Comaroff contend, "dialectically en-tailed" (2001:156) in South African capitalism:

We have tried to show, after Weber, just how integral to early British industrial capitalism was Christian political economy, and vice versa. Subtract Protestantism from the equation and capitalism, if it had evolved at all, would have been something altogether different, something perhaps more like the various capitalisms that developed beyond, if not independently of, western Europe. We would argue the same for colonial capitalism in nineteenth-century South Africa. (1997:409)

I would suggest a counterhypothesis: There was *no* capitalist hegemony in South Africa initiated by the missionaries or others during the nineteenth and for most of the twentieth century. Consider briefly what such would have required: that black laborers would have considered the selling of their labor power as only a part of the givens of their social world. To become so enmeshed in capitalist categories requires a forgetting or a suppression of the memory of the processes of primary accumulation in which workers are separated from the means of production, most especially land. In South Africa, this process did not go on behind social actors' backs, nor did it occur through the unseen hand of the market. It was perpetrated by the state for all to see and was enforced by naked coercion: The 1913 and 1936 Land Acts were "blatantly discriminatory instruments of dispossession by which black South Africans were deprived of direct access to 87 per cent of the land area of South Africa" (Murray 1992:287). To assume that early twentieth-century Southern Tswana accepted this as only a part of the hegemonic, the "taken for granted," is difficult.

To sum up, there is probably some form of elective affinity between capitalism and modernist notions of the future as empty and therefore susceptible to rational calculation. But Comaroff and Comaroff go too far when they assert that the second in and of itself prepared the way for capitalism in South Africa. That process seems much more fraught, much more shot through with contradictions.

Conclusion

World systems theory of the 1970s was a single-mindedly and perhaps simplifyingly economic and political enterprise. In the 1990s, the work of Appadurai (1996) and others has talked instead of cultural flows, of cosmopolitanisms, and alter/native modernities. But this more recent work has sometimes been carried out remarkably innocent of the hard edges of global economic and political reality. This is indicated no more starkly than in the currently popular notion that the power of the state has somehow recently declined as such in the so-called postmodern era.

Our world is one of jarring juxtapositions, it is true. A few months ago, the minister of information and culture for the Taliban in Afghanistan announced that the monumental statue of Buddha in Bamiyan was being destroyed, as required by Islamic law. "The head and legs of the Buddha . . . were destroyed yesterday. . . . Our soldiers are working hard to demolish the remaining parts. They will come down soon. . . . it's easier to destroy than to build" (*New York Times*, 4 March 2001, p. 6). Without a globalized capitalist and media-saturated world, it is doubtful that Afghan soldiers would be working so hard on such a project.

In this essay, I have attempted to argue that to understand incidents such as Bamiyan—or the 11 September 2001 attack on the World Trade Center in New York City, which took place after this essay was first written—we need to attend to people's own notions of the modern, their copies and anticopies. At points, recent cultural theory has obscured these interactions as much as it has elucidated them. The attraction of the modern (and of the antimodern) becomes clear only when such ideas are placed within the context of global capitalism—with all its gaping differences in power, wealth, and life chances. It is such gulfs that produce the ambivalence contained in modern copies—that curious, sometimes explosively reversible mixture of love and hate that currently motivates the relationship between the globally poor and globally rich.

Acknowledgments

I would like to thank the audiences at three universities at which this chapter was first presented as a paper—after the original panel organized by Bruce Knauft at the American Anthropological Association meeting in San Francisco. Each time, I learned something new and was able to expand my analysis. The three include my own university, Emory, as well as the University of California at Davis and the University of Bergen. This article includes material that has appeared in my 1999 book and in an extended critique of work of Comaroff and Comaroff on South Africa (Donham 2001; see also the Comaroffs' response in Comaroff and Comaroff 2001). The justification of bringing these materials together here is to compare and contrast the Ethiopian and South African cases.

Notes

1. To appreciate more of this performative effect, let me note parenthetically an opposite case, a concept whose utterance currently locates one not on the frontier of knowledge and insight, but in a supposedly superceded past—with what has been left "behind." A reference to plain capitalism probably accomplishes this effect in the most efficient way possible at present.

2. The notion of the copy outlined above may be a dominant within global capitalism. But it is not the only possible cultural construction of the act of imitation, and it would be useful to have more materials about the variety of ways that differently placed persons have seen the act of copying.

3. Sometimes, it is the "West" that is copied, but not always and perhaps not even ideally. Rather, for many parts of the marginalized world today, it is the apparently successful example outside the West that is critical. For Ethiopian intellectuals in the early twentieth century, Japan, and for Ethiopian revolutionaries in the mid-1970s, China. Japan and China were potent symbols for Ethiopians precisely because they were *not* the West but were assumed to have been successful in amassing power and wealth on a scale to compete with it.

References

Appadurai, Arjun
    1996   *Modernity at Large: Cultural Dimensions of Globalization.* Minneapolis: University of Minnesota Press.

Baudrillard, Jean
    1994   *Simulacra and Simulation.* Translated by Sheila Faria Glaser. Ann Arbor: University of Michigan Press.

Bhabha, Homi K.
    1994   Of Mimicry and Man: The Ambivalence of Colonial Discourse. In *The Location of Culture,* pp. 85–92. London: Routledge.

Benjamin, Walter
    1969   The Work of Art in the Age of Mechanical Reproduction. In *Illuminations.* Edited by Hanah Arendt, pp. 217–52. New York: Schocken.

Breckenridge, Carol A.
    1999   Editor's Comment on Querying Alternativity. *Public Culture* 11(1): viii–x.

Comaroff, Jean, and John L. Comaroff
    1991   *Of Revelation and Revolution, Volume 1: Christianity, Colonialism, and Conscious in South Africa.* Chicago: University of Chicago Press.

Comaroff, John L., and Jean Comaroff
1997   *Of Revelation and Revolution, Volume 2: The Dialectics of Modernity on a South African Frontier.* Chicago: University of Chicago Press.
2001   Of Fallacies and Fetishes: A Rejoinder to Donham. *American Anthropologist* 103: 150–60.

Donham, Donald L.
1999   *Marxist Modern: An Ethnographic History of the Ethiopian Revolution.* Berkeley: University of California Press.
2001   Thinking Temporally or Modernizing Anthropology. *American Anthropologist* 103: 134–49.

Koselleck, Reinhart
1985   *Futures Past: On the Semantics of Historical Time.* Translated by Keith Tonbe. Cambridge, Mass.: MIT Press.

Latour, Bruno
1993   *We Have Never Been Modern.* Translated by Catherine Porter. New York: Harvester Wheatsheaf.

Marx, Karl, and Friedrich Engels
1978   *The Marx-Engels Reader.* Edited by Robert C. Tucker. New York: Norton.

Mitchell, Timothy
2000   The Stage of Modernity. In *Questions of Modernity.* Edited by Timothy Mitchell, pp. 1–34. Minneapolis: University of Minnesota Press.

Murray, Colin
1992   *Black Mountain: Land, Class and Power in the Eastern Orange Free State, 1880s to 1980s.* Washington, D.C.: Smithsonian Institution Press.

Strayer, Robert W.
1978   *The Making of Mission Communities in East Africa: Anglicans and Africans in Colonial Kenya, 1875–1935.* London: Heinemann.

Nine

Alternative Modernities or an Alternative to "Modernity"

Getting Out of the Modernist Sublime

John D. Kelly

How will the current quest for a theory of alternative modernities look fifty years from now? Perhaps the pluralization of modernity will be strikingly reminiscent of the pluralization of "civilization" fifty years ago, in the post–World War II paradigm of Great Traditions and modernization. Starting in the 1940s and 1950s, European colonial empires were retooled into allegedly self-determining, formally symmetric nation-states in what was sometimes called a "new world order." Anthropologists and other scholars conceptualized the collapse of colonial civilizing missions by diffusing and then redoubling the civilizing process. The civilizing process diffused into a plurality of great histories of advancing, advanced civility. Then all civilizations were aligned with "tradition" against "modernity," a new era of progress that simultaneously ennobled and naturalized the new world order. Looking at decolonization and seeing modernization, area studies and comparative civilization programs ultimately failed to fathom much about the cultures of European colonialism, the dynamics of decolonization and the predicaments of postcoloniality. Now, conceptions of alternative modernities proffer a culturally coeval globe wherein globalization can densely and coherently blend without homogenizing. The idea of "alternative modernities" appears to allow for study of a nonteleological globalization. My principal concern is that the concept of "modernity" is still so hard to ground and so easy to float, in this guise increasingly, even exponentially. "Modernity" is still undefined and in fact undefinable. It is sublime.

Against a sublime, something so big, significant, and awesome that it

cannot be defined or described, but only evoked, the Bakhtinian anti-
dote is a grotesque, an inextricably embodied, living reality, undisguis-
ably ugly and undeniably fertile. Alternatively, one sublime can subsume
or replace another, as modernity did civilization. Modernity now con-
fronts alternative modernities, over the virtual wreckage of postmodernity. I resist the imputation that we must accept one sublime or another.
It is easy, now, to ridicule ethnographic research from the nineteenth
century and the early twentieth century that argued endlessly about
"civilization" but had little of substance to say about European empires.
By the late twentieth century, research on colonial societies has come to
take the ugly realities of European empires far more seriously than alleged necessities or inevitabilities of civilizing process. A hundred years
from now, when our successors read our volumes of research and argument about "modernity" and the "alternative modernities," will they be
moved by our sublime visions of vast historic processes? Or will they be
more interested in why we haven't paid more attention to something
that really isn't sublime at all: United States power since World War II?

Much social theory since World War II has sought the commanding
heights of modernity, has sought to map its most objective underlying
structures and uncover awesome secrets in its subjective predicaments.
I'm suggesting that this project might be as intellectually limiting as
was the quest to really know civilization at the height of European imperial power, that even an ethnographic project relentlessly reconsidering modernity a posteriori can still become trapped in a modernist sublime. I will define the terms "sublime" and "grotesque" more closely,
will discuss the rise of the modernist sublime, and will review in detail
strong arguments from Marilyn Ivy and Aihwa Ong for conceptions of
"alternative modernity" as a framework for future scholarship. But I
want to begin, for comparative purposes, with a self-appointed British
imperial famous for the relentlessness of his probing of European imperial morality. I want first to show you the power of a sublime conception
by showing how "civilization" organized and limited the apperceptions
of a famous observer of colonial extremes.

Civilization and Joseph Conrad

"The concept of civilization," observed Norbert Elias in his history of
manners, "has often been used in a semimetaphysical sense and has remained highly nebulous" (1978:223). This semimetaphysical nebulous-
ness, this sublime character, aided in the almost mythic deployment of
concepts of civilization in European colonial history, a deployment Elias
also observed:

John D. Kelly

260

In 1798, as Napoleon sets off for Egypt, he shouts to his troops: "Soldiers, you are undertaking a conquest with incalculable consequences for civilization." Unlike the situation when the concept was formed, from now on nations consider the *process* of civilization as completed within their own societies; they see themselves as bearers of an existing or finished civilization to others, as standard-bearers of expanding civilization. Of the whole preceding process of civilization nothing remains in their consciousness except a vague residue. Its outcome is taken simply as an expression of their own higher gifts . . . And the consciousness of their own superiority, the consciousness of this "civilization," from now on serves at least those nations which have become colonial conquerors, and therefore a kind of upper class to large sections of the non-European world, as a justification of their rule, to the same degree that earlier the ancestors of the concept of civilization, *politesse* and *civilité*, had served the courtly-aristocratic upper class as a justification of theirs. (Elias 1978:50)[1]

But what happened, then, when an intellect with the acumen and experience of a Joseph Conrad probed at those justifications linking "civilization" to colonial conquest?

In *Heart of Darkness* (1899), Joseph Conrad describes brutality beyond the world of civility and brutality within the hearts of men.[2] He means men, in a gendered construction as well as a universalistic one. The men are particularly attracted to the darkness, its violent sensual freedom, its detestable, fascinating "utter savagery" (1963:6). The civilized women of Conrad's novella, notably the "Intended" of Kurtz, are described by Conrad's narrator Marlow as "out of it—completely. They—the women I mean—are out of it—should be out of it. We must help them stay in that beautiful world of their own, lest ours get worse" (1963:49). Marlow lies to Kurtz's Intended when she asks for Kurtz's last words, when she wants "something—to—to live with" (1963:79), seeking meaning out of the death of the man who went farthest into the heart of darkness. Marlow tells her that her name was spoken on Kurtz's dying breath, keeping secret from her the whisper that Marlow in fact still heard the dusk itself repeat: "the horror," etc. Gendered light and darkness run through Conrad's novella. We could, but won't, pry under the anxiety revealed in the difference between Marlow's certainty that the women "are out of it" and his resolution that they "should be out of it," Marlow's possibly ambivalent anxiety to keep women in the dark (i.e., the light), about what the men are about. Noting these gendered complexities but leaving them aside, I want to look at something more superficial here, something obviously everywhere in this text: Conrad's commitment to the sublime chronotope of civilization.

Conrad is often read and taught as a critic of colonialism. Such readings, I think, commonly overstate Conrad's intentions, and in ways of interest to us here. Conrad felt revulsion for the ubiquitous, cruel violence of the upriver stations. But did he have any aspiration to stop it? Marlow is telling his cautionary tale, on a ship, to the other members of a new, puny, colonial company, a captive audience of novices awaiting only the tide on the Thames to begin their own new colonial venture. And Marlow is quite willfully going too, more than a small problem for any anticolonial moral to the story. Marlow's first words, sitting on deck surveying the edge of London at dusk, suggest both how inevitable and necessary he reckons colonization to be: " 'And this also,' said Marlow suddenly, 'has been one of the dark places of the earth' " (1963:5). Marlow's thoughts before his story are in praise of the Romans who civilized Britain, "men enough to face the darkness" (1963:6). Conrad was no reformer, as Michael Taussig (1987) has pointed out. The same issue was taken into Conrad's theology in a remarkable commentary on Conrad published by American H. L. Mencken in 1917: Conrad "grounds his work firmly upon this sense of cosmic implacability . . . The exact point of the story of Kurtz, in 'Heart of Darkness,' is that it is pointless . . . Conrad makes war on nothing; he is pre-eminently *not* a moralist. He swings, indeed, as far from revolt and moralizing as is possible, for he does not even criticize God. . . . One might even imagine him pitying God" (1963:162–63).

Pitying God because the darkness is as real as the light, and inscribing a testament to the dark's profound attractions, is not the same as denying the reality of the light. Conrad believed in civilization, at least in the sense that he took the premise of a civilizing process extremely seriously, even as he looked into the dark. And we do not; we do not, I argue, take the idea of civilization seriously. That is why it has become so easy to misread the morals of Conrad's tales. Does not the image of a wild interior and exterior original nature, civilized by a process ongoing, seem as dubious to most of us as it seemed inexorable to Conrad? What we are far more likely to imagine inexorable is not civilization or civilizing missions, but modernity. (Or in volumes such as this, perhaps, alternative modernities.) We take the chronotope of modernity, not civilization, seriously, and for the two-word version of my essay, too seriously. If we take modernity as seriously as Conrad took civilization, our criticism will neglect truly alternative possibilities. Thus my title, with apologies to Arturo Escobar (1995) and his call for alternatives to development. I hope not for alternative modernities but alternatives to "modernity" as a chronotope necessary for social theory.[3]

Sublimes and Grotesques:
Political Imagery, Locations, and
Objective Possibilities

I speak in my title of "getting out of the modernist sublime." This is a project I recommend for social theory. The sublime, as I draw the concept from the aesthetic theory of Bakhtin and others is a conception of something beyond beauty that art can aspire to depict or at least evoke.[4] The sublime, especially, is something that has to be evoked, not described, because sublime subjects are beyond actual delimitation, "things" such as God or terror, nature, justice, or love. Bakhtin was skeptically fascinated by the centripetal dynamics that cement sublime aesthetics to official, elite classes, the powers of sublime imageries to constitute and consolidate authority whether in Christian sacraments commemorating Christ's sacrifices for Gospel or in Soviet sanctifying commemorations of the people and sacrifices of Revolution. His skepticism led him to reexamine and no doubt to romanticize the forms of life and of art that provided the most robust answers and antidotes to sublime, ritualized solemnities, the counterdiscourses that gathered and quickened the centrifugal forces that always also operated in real social fields, discourses that had the capacity to engage sublime aesthetics without surrendering to them in aim or object. His favorite was the grotesquery of the comic novels of Rabelais, as capable of corrosive parody of the Church's divines as they were protected by their vulgarity from easy incorporation as an alternative theology of divinity itself. If, as I argue here, we reside now within a modernist sublime, what we need is more than alternative modernities: we need a grotesque that can speak far more groundedly about the ways and means of contemporary power. Mindful, also, of the convention of Borges that the best surprise endings are given away early, I don't mind repeating that what we need now, as an alternative to modernity, is an ethnographically fleshed understanding of the largest, though eminently unsublime, grotesque of our age: American power.

> Beyond the narrow scope of this dispute there was a wider problem
> of principle: could manifestations such as the grotesque, which did
> not respond to the demands of the sublime, be considered art?
> (Bakhtin 1984:35)

Can social theory do without sublime concepts that appear to have what Benjamin Lee Whorf once called "cosmic scope of reference"

(1956:61)? This wider problem of principle for social theory is intrinsic to my inquiry here. A good case could be made that, for all that debates in social theory can be pitched for example as relativisms versus universalisms, historicisms versus universalisms, realisms versus universalisms, and so on, in fact, at some level, any social theory relies on premises of universal scope of reference, and any plausible social theory also has dimensions that are historicist or at least evolutionary, that are relativist or at least cognizant of locality. To be more concrete as we approach the question of so-called modernity, any social theory implicitly or explicitly will punctuate global time. The alternative to modernity I will delineate here is also a punctuation of global time, in fact one that splits the period of modernity down the middle, and denies that the present moment has yet itself clearly constituted any equivalent watershed. But my claim is that the punctuation of global time I want to offer is of a different character—in short, not sublime but grotesque. The global time I depict has a monster in its midst—in fact more than one, a British Empire commanding half the world's industrial capital in an age of European empires, an age much dependent on sublime conceptions of so-called civilization, and later, American power, in our age, much taken by its own so-called modernity. The global time I depict has these monsters of manifold influence not because it has to, but because it does, a frank appeal not to necessities dialectical or otherwise, but to a real material and cultural history.

Punctuating global time by way of figures of manifold influence rendered grotesque rather than sublime means operating with global referents that do not, intrinsically, "respond to the demands of the sublime," as Bakhtin put it. It means not having a social theory with human history centered (let alone culminating, as so many dialecticians would have it, let alone ultimately, finally culminating, as for the "end of history" crowd) on the societies being analyzed, but rather with centers, peripheries, and boundaries that do not establish finalities or horizons of meaning. From my own Bakhtin-inflected Weberian point of view, this is a great virtue.

Max Weber exempted no concepts from his dictums concerning the contingencies as well as the necessities of ideal types. Ideal types make description possible, Weber argued, isolating in the infinitude of social phenomena the dimensions of potentially greatest meaning to us. Good research will always be driven by ongoing estimations of significance as well as by ongoing efforts to measure the objective adequacy of claims. Weber argued, I think correctly, that the infinity of phenomena contrasted with the changing finitude of perspectives and questions guarantees that no theory could ever be final. This positions the sublime aspect of reality beyond final capture even by our own (and his own) most sublime conceptions, and casts doubt on sublime conceptions, especially when they strive for finality.[5]

> The cultural problems which move men to form themselves ever anew and in different colors, and the boundaries of that area in the infinite stream of concrete events which acquires meaning and significance for us, i.e., which becomes an "historical individual," are constantly subject to change. The intellectual contexts from which it is viewed and scientifically analyzed shift. The points of departure of the cultural sciences remain changeable throughout the limitless future. (Weber 1949:84)

Weber's analytics do not correspond on every point with Bakhtin's. Where Weber pins much political concern on the potentials for objective specification by particular social scientific concepts, and hopes, for example, to specify what is exceptional about the rationality of the European Enlightenment by way of harnessed deixis, describing it as a rationality somehow uniquely "this-worldly," Bakhtin expects the most important conceptualizations to come in larger chronotopic wholes and expects every authoritative discourse to focus such deixis centripetally, to see itself as " 'this world' (that is, the established world, which it is always profitable to serve)" (Bakhtin 1984:262). Here, I find Bakhtin more persuasive both about the referents of "this world" and about the importance of criticism of chronotopic wholes, yet still, with Weber, commit to the premise that in social science, estimation of objective adequacy as well as significance is always of ongoing importance. To refocus something I have already said, then, from my own Bakhtin-inflected Weberian point of view, it is a great virtue to orient our research to grotesque rather than sublime coordinates, especially considering political dimensions of research aims and objects.

The appearance of sublime significance in such things as "civilization" —or, I submit, "modernity"—might well point no further than the centripetal swirl of historically temporary centers of power, when seen from a greater distance. If we need better ways to understand actual powers in history, especially those of greatest significance now, it strikes me highly unlikely that we will find them by way of such terms. Can you have a social theory that specifically abjures sublime significances for its social facts? Probably only, under contemporary conditions, by explicitly seeking one, since to do so is to challenge premises of the extant genre.

Another brief belletristic foray can help clarify the difference between civilization and modernity as chronotopes, that is, as space-times of possibility for the location of agents, actions, and events. Consider what happens to light and darkness in the move from the imagery of Conrad to that of V. S. Naipaul in *An Area of Darkness*, a 1964 account of travel in India. To Naipaul, too, the light resides in Europe, and the darkness in the now ex-colony.[6] But the etiology of darkness and light is reversed: civilization, via civilizations, has morphed into tradition, perhaps great, but definitely binding, enthralling, entrapping, encasing, sacralizing into stasis. The world that is free is not the uncivilized but the modern. Civilization transformed into tradition chokes off the light of enlightenment. A dubious great divide alterity is sustained, but the terms are quite consequentially altered, especially in the location of freedom and natural, "whole" behavior.

This shift goes beyond individual writers; we can glimpse one dimension of its institutionalization in the changing ways academic disciplines are privileged in government. In the era of United Nations, decolonization, and United States power, economists have become important advisors on policy. More than any other kind of social scientist, economists walk a revolving door between academy and government, shaping policies with their powers to model the rational choices of agents portrayed as simply free to choose. In the high days of the British Empire, Economics was not the necessary discipline. Whether the cadets of the imperial civil service needed training in Political Economy was debatable and debated, as debatable as it now is whether policy makers need knowledge of history. But before the era of the United Nations, the bureaucrats of empire were not all or even mostly Political Economists. But many of them were historians. The British Empire was sequined with Elphinstones, governors of colonies who also became preeminent historians of the places they governed. And many of the historians of the first rank, the Mills and Macaulays, were also high officials in the home government. In their view, social and political reality was essentially historical, and it took knowledge of history, perspective on history of civilization, and familiarity with such things as the history of Roman law, to formulate policy well.

To summarize then, even when Conrad knew well and portrayed vividly the mundane as well as the sublime horrors of the civilizing mission, the limits of his critique lay in the inevitability he projected—we too were once dark, more's the pity for everyone. Conrad could be no more than postcivilized, ambivalent about civilization as a reality, because he believed after all that civilization was a real process. Conrad's relationship to civilization was thus as profound, and binding, as that of the postmodernisms to modernity. But our topic is not postmodernism, but rather modernity and alternative modernities. Let us look closer at "modernity," the sign and concept.

Modernity and the Modernist Sublime

How, specifically, is "modernity" a sublime conception? Let us consider a recent description of it:

> What I mean by the modern—as if one could simply define it—indicates not only urban energies, capitalist structures of life, and mechanical and electrical forms of reproduction . . . the problem of the nation-state and its correlation with a capitalist colonialism . . . a global geopolitical matrix from the mid-nineteenth century on. It indicates as well the changes effected in identities and subjectivities, through the emergence of individualism and new modes of interiority; in relationships to temporality, through the emergence of "tradition" as the background against which progressive history could be situated; and in institutional procedures, through what Foucault has called individualization and totalization: bureaucratic rationalisms, Taylorized modes of production, novel forms of image representation, mass media, scientific disciplines. In their historical specificity, these modes, procedures, and apparatuses constitute a discursive complex which I think of as modern. (Ivy 1995:4–5)

Pity the social scientist taking a definition such as this as a means to decide whether, say, India in 1857 or Hawaii in 1897 is or is not part of any modernity or alternative modernity. The sublime nature of the discursive complex here described is not merely my allegation. It is explicitly declared at the outset: "What I mean by the modern—as if one could simply define it—indicates not only. . . . " Modernity, we are told, cannot actually be defined, or at least it cannot be simply defined. Even "what I mean" can only incompletely be told, by a list prefaced by "not only," a list encompassing and juxtaposing matters economic, material, psychological, informational, institutional, and political, all asserted to be part of one complex but without any serious effort to portray causal links of items with very uneven historical and social distribution in fact.

I think that you will find this kind of acknowledgment and disclaimer, or something similar, in most sophisticated discussions of any actual modernity.[7] Ivy strikes me as extreme in the extensive honesty of her sublime evocation, and also in the explicitness of her exploitation of the capacity of the sublimely undefinable object to contain unresolved relationships and flat-out contradictions. A footnote attached to the penultimate quoted sentence here is: "The names of Marx, Weber, Freud, Foucault, and Habermas (not necessarily in that order) hardly need to be invoked as the essential theorists of modernity" (Ivy 1995:5, n. 9). Some aspects of this construction of modernity are accidental. Other scholars of modernity confront a Foucault with a Habermas, a Marx with a Weber, rather than composing them as all essential theorists without any necessary order. But as Dean C. Tipps showed devastatingly in his famous and trenchant 1973 review of theories of modernization, neither multifactorial open sets nor single-process focused theories of modernity work well. Theories that connect modernity and modernization to a single "critical variable" and a single type of social change (e.g., capitalism and industrialization) will either blur the specificities and complexities of this underlying causal complex by associating it with all the other connoted connections of "modernity," or else reduce "modernity" to a synonym of the critical variable (Tipps 1973:203–5). We are left, then, with what Tipps called "dichotomous" approaches, finding "modernity" in multifactorial open sets and vague claims that a great divide is ineluctably already crossed. Here, Tipps argued, "the attempt by modernization theorists to aggregate in a single concept disparate processes of social change which rather should have been distinguished has served only to hinder rather than facilitate their empirical analyses" (1973:222). Is it any different for more recent studies of "modernity"?

"Modernity" the word is actually a strange one. Its history is interesting. Jacques Le Goff's research for his encyclopedia article on the concepts of "Antique" or "Ancient" and "Modern" led him to the following conclusion:

> The term *modernity* was coined by Baudelaire in his article "The Painter of Modern Life," which was written around 1860 and published in 1863. The term gained currency primarily in literary and artistic circles during the second half of the nineteenth century, and was later revived and much more widely used after World War II. (1992:40)

"Modern" the adjective has a much longer career of robust, common usage, especially as the antithesis of "ancient."[8] One finds occasional instances of respect for modern things and even for modern people, "the moderns," in such radical writings as those of Francis Bacon in the 1500s. But the identification of something as modern generally carried a pejorative connotation well into the nineteenth century (as argues Raymond Williams 1976).

But again let us be more superficial and notice the obvious. "Modern," the adjective, is a comparative adjective, a kind of shifter. Bacon's moderns live in the fifteenth century, well before most, but hardly all, the stuff in the list of the components of Ivy's "discursive complex." Bacon's moderns lived well before electrical or even most mechanical forms of reproduction, for example, let alone Taylorized modes of production, but were highly entwined with, and reflecting upon, their own version of urban energy, bureaucracy, and scientific discipline. Le Goff and many others distinguish between modernism and modernity; one could argue Bacon was a modernist not yet in a modern world (though he would dispute it, preferring to place himself as balancing the Ancients and Moderns). But this begs the question we really should consider after observing that "modern" is a shifter. Whether something is modern or not shifts according to context.

Leaving aside the modernness of Bacon in his time versus ours, consider the high-speed optical switches that Lucent Technologies was recently desperate to "modernize," having bet wrongly on a new generation designed to maximize information volume per cost unit rather than switching speed. Switches that were unknown ten years ago can be called "traditional" in contemporary newspaper business pages, not modern anymore. But more important, they could still be considered, simultaneously, the essence of the new, modern information age in almost any other context. It is not adequate to grant the individual material objects, these switches, careers in which they gradually or abruptly lose their modernness, nor even to reckon absolutely that they had and lost modernness as a type of technological device, because depending on context of comparison, depending on which frame of temporal comparison is invoked, the same switch, or automobile, or bucket is either and both the quintessence of modern technology or clearly, indisputably obsolete.

What, then, can we possibly be talking about when we rely on the word "modernity," this dressed-up sign of laterness, to specify a location for any social phenomenon?

Many scholars have emphasized that the referent of "modernity" varies dramatically according to ethnographic and historical context (including the essays by Foster and by Donham in this volume). Several of the essays in this volume show that much can be learned by tracking the content of culturally constituted modernities and modernisms in various contexts of usage. When these contexts are advertising campaigns spanning a region, or a national radio system, the centripetal connections of institution and ideology can stabilize and ramify these phenomena in their constituted "localities." What is rendered is not so

much a modernity as a locality—these are issues concerned with what
Arjun Appadurai (1996) has aptly termed "production of locality." It
seems to me that the only way to describe these phenomena without
rendering their "modernity" quaint in its locality is to be able to figure
the global in a space-time not dependent on, like, you know, actual modernity. The indisputable ethnographic phenomena of variation in the
content of so-called modernity is no mystery, from the outset, when we
realize that the very concept is built from a comparative adjective, a
shifter, that it always and inevitably includes the semiotic incompleteness of deixis despite its paradoxical declaration of a state of being. Or
as Le Goff recognized in 1977, "Ultimately, modernity can designate
anything at all" (1992:49).

In his abstract for the session that has led to this volume, Bruce
Knauft wrote of "alternative modernities" as an "intentional oxymoron." My point here is that in the hands of a Baudelaire, at its origins, the word and concept of "modernity" was once itself an intentional oxymoron, the "-ity" part, constitutive of a state or condition of
being, hitched to a temporal shifter. The modernists in the world of art
deliberately engineered a modernist sublime and declared it grand and
ineluctable. They engineered their modernist sublime as deliberately,
and by the same method as, for example, the Madhyamaka Buddhists
led by Nagarjuna in the first century or so CST (Christian Standard
Time) constituted a semiotic sublime. To refer to a reality whose existence they expected to be entirely, contingently relative to the appara-
tuses of active semiotic attachment, the Madhyamaka relied on a word,
Sanskrit *tattva*, that combined *tat*, "this" or "that," and *tva*, "ity" or
"ness," reality, the "thatness," the "thisity," a reality inextricably constituted by continuing acts of referential engagement. They knew why
they were calling reality *tattva*. Baudelaire understood the deliberate,
sublime paradox of describing an era accepting of ineluctable change as
a modernity. But somewhere along the line we social scientists began
using the word without noticing much of anything strange about it. To
reiterate the formal point, the concept of a modernity, especially when
taken to name an era of global history, is as intrinsically paradoxical as
would be a yesterdayity, afterity, nowity, or, I hesitate to invite, lateity,
postity, or neoity, possible concepts not intrinsically stranger than modernity. (Consider also, for example, "contemporaneity," still used and
recognized as a shifter.)

Thus there is reason why the language had the shifter adjective
"modern" for a long, long time, and the clear idea of "Moderns" as
advocates for modern things, even "modernists" and "modernism," for
a long time, but no conceptualization of "modernity" until the second

half of the nineteenth century, as the art world instituted self-conscious modernism. "Modernity" rose to real ubiquity after World War II in a much denser net of institutional articulations. Only then did the modern unmoor from modernism and fully move from experienced utopia (and dystopia) to become the semimetaphysical, nebulous ideology of a completed, lived, free, and final "modernity" (cf. Elias on civilization and Napoleon, above),[9] America's grace and a telos not dangerous for the downtrodden. Civilizations were not only relativized, earnestly, in repudiation of colonizers' arrogance, but also refashioned as traditions, great and otherwise, material for the building of new nations and modern states. Decolonization was narrated as modernization.

How do we get out of the modernist sublime? It strikes me as unlikely that a postmodernism as such can resolve the problem. The addition of "post" enabled the modernists of the late twentieth century to again paint themselves masters of their own sublime, at the cost of having to live within it. "Alternative modernities" seeks a new departure.

Commensurably Incommensurable, by Nature or by History? Alternative Modernities and American Power

I cannot give you an adequate account of the history of discussion of alternative modernities. If the concept first emerged outside of anthropology, it is news to me; within anthropology, as far as I can tell, it emerged especially within discussions of contemporary Asia. Lisa Rofel, whom many would credit, herself credits Arjun Appadurai (Rofel 1999:287, n. 10). I want to devote most attention here to Aihwa Ong's powerful recent argument for study of alternative modernities, an argument for sharply distinguishing the conception of alternative modernities from theories of postcoloniality. But to raise a key issue, let us start not with Ong's argument but with another passage from Marilyn Ivy's ethnography of modernity and phantasm in Japan. Ivy's subtle 1995 ethnography clearly launches the concept of alternative modernities in all but name and includes an elaborate discussion, already, of what will probably be a crucial issue for most theories of alternative modernity: commensuration.

> What I want to underline, however, is the co-occurrence—the coevalness—of the problem of Japanese modernity with that of modernities elsewhere, and the shared temporality that implies.
> That coevalness does not imply the collapsing of differences. . . .
> Neither, however, would I want to insist on the radical nature of

Japanese difference. . . . If Japan is incommensurable, it is incommensurable in ways commensurate with other modern nation-states in the historical specificity of its modern entanglements. (Ivy 1995:5–6)

If Japan is incommensurable. It is still, a big "if." Incommensurability is an extremely strong concept. Most scholars would probably recognize it as a key to Thomas Kuhn's theory of the limits to progress in scientific research, why revolutions in research are only cumulative from the perspective of the reigning paradigm. The argument for incommensurability will probably never stop irritating the blustering advocates for the possibility of final theory, who tend not to notice that it has been entirely abandoned by many in science and technology studies, most notably Bruno Latour. Sadly, we face another case of paradigms lost, as one branch of cultural studies builds on foundations being actively undermined in their discipline of origin. Why would Ivy, who has good reasons, want a Japanese difference neither absolute nor reducible, incommensurable but in ways commensurate, commensurate precisely in something she calls "historical specificity," but a historical specificity of something (commensuratedly, after all) generic, a "modern nation-state"? What Scylla and Charybdis drive Ivy to such adroit tacking? No doubt, she steers us past both the rocks of eurocentrism disguised as universalism, and also the whirlpool of orientalism. But will commensurate incommensurables really float for the long hauls?

To make a long story short, Latour (1988) argues persuasively that the claim of incommensurability founders on its underestimation of the acts of will in all determinations of similarity and difference. Things cannot be similar or different in or for themselves, before all deliberation of scale, salience, and mode of measure. The calibration of such determinations is also, always, a matter of translations with multiple possibilities and inevitable drifts as well as accumulating strengths of interest. The constitution of refusals to translate, to commensurate, to render transparent or even graspable, is far better recognized, argues Latour, as a precipitate of will built into design than as a fact of nature or any other fatality.

This position actually fits well with Ivy's argument, and we can restate Ivy's argument in Latourean terms. Before we do so, a simple ethnographic example out of Fiji, a place I know well. Readers of the dominant local newspapers, English language, have in the aftermath of the coups of 1987 been confronted with a new political party. Gone is the Alliance Party, the party that had claimed to represent all of Fiji's so-called communities but was increasingly the vehicle of the indigenous or ethnic Fijian chiefs. Emerging out of the Great Council of Chiefs, or at least out of its majority faction, came a new political party, the Soqosoqo ni Vakavulewa ni Taukei. Quite a break in self-representation in the predominant local newspapers, from "Alliance Party" to "Soqosoqo ni Vakavulewa ni Taukei." The English-language media at first relied on translations of the party name, "Fijian People's Party" or "the Fijian Political Party." But this dominant party's chiefly leaders made clear that its title was actually untranslatable. English could not do it justice, and Fiji's post-Coups press has settled on referring to it as the Soqosoqo ni Vakavulewa ni Taukei, or, 99 percent of the time, as the SVT. Can we not see, plainly in such an example, the difference between uncommensurated and incommensurable, and the play of will and power in the management of translation, transparency, and authority?

So if we assert the existence of commensurate incommensurabilities, who is doing the commensurating, and then spotting and declaring the absolute limit to its own power to commensurate in the face of other sovereign wills? If each incommensurable modernity is mysteriously correlate with the sovereignties alleged to modern nation-states in "historical specificity," then who pulled off this particular intentional oxymoron, making all the modern nation-states commensurate precisely in their historical specificity? These may seem like rhetorical questions, but I don't actually think they are. I think someone actually did commensurate the planet into a congeries of nations and states largely settled into nation-hyphen-states, making nations the paramount real order-giving units and developing an explicit doctrine that natural order is sustained when and only when an actual nation has an actual state and vice versa. This project of U.S. foreign policy was largely realized during the Truman presidency.

In 1945, before the Truman Doctrine became the explicit name of American global policy, Harry Truman stood in San Francisco, at the end of the Big One and the outset of our era, and announced the end of war in the form of the United Nations. No more wars allowed, neither between nations nor states, and henceforth only self-determination (recall, by the way, the monopoly on the means of coercion he then wielded in his capacity as U.S. president, and recall his demonstrated capacity to use it). In what historians of decolonization have recognized as a transformation of stunning rapidity (see, e.g., Louis 1977), the European empires were rapidly recalibrated with varying degrees of resistance (British least, French most) into multiple nation-states in the new format. Set those nations free—to imagine themselves mere communities, with a need, a nature, and a destiny to develop, not to conquer or rule anyone else, horrors, but rather, as the term of the era crystallized it, free to modernize. Modernity, it was discovered by the august social scientists, was something the so-called West had had for a long time (not merely civilization, which was the arrogance of the imperial traditions).

Of course it wasn't just Truman. Decolonization on the American plan did not generate the anticolonial energies of a Gandhi or Kenyatta; in fact, of course, it straitjacketed them (see also Scott 1999 on the promises and failures of the Bandung conference). Even among the Americans, Truman was not the main force in the composition of explicit policy. Unquestionably, the Roosevelt White House planned more of what was then widely discussed as "the new world order," a phrase widely circulating in the 1940s and deliberately revived by George Bush senior's speechwriter Richard Haass for a president then in search of "the vision thing." The idea of a perpetual peace has much deeper roots, including many Enlightenment-era European schemes for concerts and leagues of symmetrically constituted states mutually recognizing and respecting each others' sovereignties. These schemes were mostly utopias and ideals, aspirations for civilization. Before the rise of the UN world, only Herderian extremists in European social theory saw intrinsic connections between nations, nature, and peace; nature was more generally thought red in tooth and claw, even before the rise of Social Darwinisms, nations as willful pursuers of their destinies. And only in the UN world was imperial sovereignty outlawed, civilizing missions scorned, sovereignty declared viable *only* as the self-determination of a nation. Then, were nations imagined in turn to be mere communities, longing only to be free (cf. Anderson 1983; Kelly and Kaplan 2001). Truman could confidently condemn the "totalitarian" designs of fascists and communists (rendering sinister all desires to raise the level of civilization, converting them to conspiracies to enslave by imposed social order) and contrast their evil to the natural desires of nations for peace and freedom. Henceforth, no other destinies could manifest legitimately for nations or states, except the natural benefits of freedom.

To briefly pull together a few broader themes: "modernity" and the "nation-state" share a startling intellectual career. Both become ubiquitous after World War II, "modernity" spreading widely in intellectual usage, "nation-state" emerging virtually out of nowhere (the term "nation-state" appeared in no major dictionaries of the English language before the 1950s; see Kelly and Kaplan 2001). And both terms, circulating in a vast transatlantic scholarly consortium, were solemnly recognized the cornerstones of centuries of practice in the West, never mind those pesky empires, providing a great continuity of European and American "historical specificity" at the very moment when the Americans, allied with those still colonized, were actually dismantling the European empires. Critics of United States power are right to speak of neoimperialism in all of this, but as a translation, this has its costs. To paint the victors with the uniform and arms of the vanquished helps greatly in reconfiguring their virtues as a grotesque. But neoimperialism cannot wholly clarify our view of the strategies, tactics, and weapons that really won the war and set the terms of global peace, including especially what Al Gore and George W. Bush were in remarkable recent agreement upon, what Gore termed "strategic humility."

Alternative Modernities, or an
Alternative to Modernity

Some argue (e.g., Foucault [1970] in *The Order of Things*) that a modern era began sometime before the twentieth century and that it is, by the late twentieth century, in crisis. As we have seen and as we will discuss, others have more recently suggested instead that alternative modernities have emerged in our world, comparable and coeval but not wholly commensurable. I am not seeking a dialectical synthesis here, but more skeptically an alternative to both of these approaches. And while I am skeptical enough of "modernity" as the cardinal punctuation of global time to be interested in other alternatives to modernity,[10] I am really, obviously, offering only one alternative to modernity myself in this essay. I am suggesting that contemporary cultural initiatives, local and global, be situated in their relations with and against a grotesque actuality, the American plan for the postwar world, not with, against, post, or alternative to "modernity."

This alternative gives great weight to the end of an era of European empires (empires imagining European civilization as a singular achievement) and the onset of an era of decolonization of these empires. It leads me to real interest in Aihwa Ong's argument against the continuing global significance of postcoloniality, her location of an emergent alternative modernity of a transnational Chinese public in what she calls a "post postcolonial era" (1999:35). Ong engages the project of postcolonial critics from Said, Bhabha, Spivak, Hall, and Gilroy to Guha, Chatterjee, and Chakrabarty with a combination of respect and skepticism. She has respect for the intentions and accomplishments of these theorists in confronting Western power, when they insist on the continuing importance of colonial history and its consequences for once-colonized societies. But she is more profoundly skeptical. She is skeptical about the applicability of postcolonial theory to East Asia, especially contemporary East Asia. But further, she is skeptical that any postcolonial theory, as a global theory, can ever decenter the West, can ever undertake Chakrabarty's goal, one she highly admires, of parochializing Europe (Chakrabarty 2000). Ong writes, "The loose use of the term 'the postcolonial,' then, has had the bizarre effect of contributing to a Western tradition of othering the Rest . . . in many areas of the world, we must move beyond an analysis based on colonial nostalgia or colonial legacies" (1999:34–35), especially toward the positioning of "countries," as she puts it, in the global political economy.

Leaving aside whether a global political economy is up to the task, also, of tracking the dynamics within and between structures of forces and relations of coercion, forces and relations of communication, etc., I want to focus here on Ong's resolution of the Chakrabartian problem: how to parochialize the West.

> It appears that unitary models of the postcolonial and of modernity are ascendant at a time when many Asian countries are not interested in colonialism or in postcolonialism . . . and are in the process of constructing alternative modernities based on new relations with their populations, with capital, and with the West. (1999:35)

So "countries" have emerged as agents of collective will, taking a large initiative to construct something alternative. Of course, Ong will not leave these collective agents as "countries," but will have much to add concerning the imaginaries and agencies of transnational subjects, vital issues first explored by Appadurai and others. The initiative, precisely in the emergence of collective agents not self-determining tamely within the template of the nation-state, is obviously an unanticipated development for those inhabiting the Truman Doctrine world of natural markets, nations, and states, guarantors of peace in freedom and modernity. Ong is right to insist that these transnations, as Appadurai has also argued, are something new under their sun. But where, exactly, is their sun in Ong's formulation? She still accepts the sublime depictions: a West, with a collective, long-standing modernity, with which the new relations will be made. Like Ivy, Ong wants the contemporary modernities to be coeval and not even "bipolar" with the West. She suggests

> a method that considers how nation-states, in shaping their political economies and in discursively representing themselves as moral-political projects, while borrowing extensively from the West, also

seek to deflect the West's multiple domination. We must go beyond treating "multiple modernities" as formations that are merely reactive to Western capitalism. Instead, we can examine the national and localization processes that actively negotiate new relations to capital. (1999:36)

From a Bakhtinean, dialogical point of view, the anxiety about portrayal of agency as reactive is misplaced, since effectively no discourse is Adamic, truly capable of setting its own terms and relations. More important, then, is the location of capitalism, not merely as "Western capitalism," the possibility that the initiatives of the Chinese transnation involve new relations with capital not reducible simply to new relations with the West. This is both important and no doubt true. But to really parochialize Europe, and to really undermine American "strategic humility," we need more than a plurality of alternative coeval initiatives. The vaguely quiescent symmetry of such a vision of self-determination is straight Harry Truman and refracts the distribution and delimitation of sovereign powers that the new world order found natural. We need to ask about the West with the acuteness that we ask about the East, as in whether it exists. Or, if it is as dead as Nietzsche's god, when did it die? Wasn't that East–West thing a map of civilizations on a Eurasian land mass? To really parochialize Europe, I think it is time to force upon the Americans the kind of credit for initiative and rupture, recommensuration of global space-time, that Ong and Appadurai provocatively anticipate to be coming again with the world of transnational publics.[11] Thus, a softer version of my thesis would be simply that America, too, fashioned an alternative modernity. But I resist the symmetries that such commensuration implies, and I think it important to note how the Americans preferred to find themselves, humble but, we are reminded, strategically so, merely one nation-state in a modern, united globe-full.

Locating globalization and the nation-state in a modernity, whether or not its core is capitalism, grants each an unmerited inevitability. The same planning sessions—Bretton Woods, Dumbarton Oaks, San Francisco, all sites in the United States—that generated the United Nations planned much of the new financial organization of the world after World War II. Out of these conferences and others, and first of all out of the halls of American government from the late 1930s to 1945, came the blueprints for the institutions that replaced a very different imperial European financial order with what the Americans called "multilateralism," breaking down schemes of so-called bilateral preference, schemes that not incidentally had supported specifically imperial finances in privileged relations between colonies and colonizers. Out of the halls of the government of the United States in the 1940s came a World Bank, an International Monetary Fund, and an International Trade Organization, later reconstituted as the World Trade Organization. Out came a new kind of global treaty titled General Agreement on Tariffs and Trade. The United States held enormous leverage over a ravaged Europe in deep need of capital yet already in vast debt to the United States, and used it to shove the end of imperial finance down the Europeans' throats. Only the Communists, who had a plan of their own that was arguably about neither civilization nor modernity, resisted joining the new economic institutions for about forty years.

The globalization of finance, which vastly extended its domination of industry in the fashion much better understood by Veblen than by Marx, began as a deliberately anti-imperial, anti–Great Power dimension of the American's plan. Locating it in a global modern sublime will not get us far enough in understanding how to oppose it as a real, contemporary global nemesis. Nor will celebrating the integrity and dynamics of alternative modernities be enough, especially when they are, quite palpably, remobilizing relations to finance, markets, and transnational institutions of representation and even coercion, not on an alternative planet, but on the one real one where the capacity of formal symmetries of freedom and difference to renew and extend substantive injustice is becoming increasingly manifest. To celebrate, and especially to anticipate, symmetric alternative modernities is to ratify the Truman Doctrine translated into a new social scientific sublime.

An Eavesdropping Coda

Much of what interests me here can be illustrated differently by a fragment of an interview, an interview about something the interlocutors agreed to call "modern civilization," yet viewed very differently.

> The tendency in modern civilization is to make the world uniform. Calcutta, Bombay, Hong Kong and other cities are more or less alike, wearing big masks which represent no country in particular.

> Yet don't you think this very fact is an indication that we are reaching out for a new worldwide human order which refuses to be localized? . . . We are gradually thinking now of one human civilization, on the foundation of which individualities will have great chance of fulfillment. The individual, as we take him, has suffered from the fact that civilization has been split up into separate units,

instead of being merged into a universal whole, which seems to be the natural destiny of mankind.

I believe the unity of human civilization can be better maintained by the linking up in fellowship and cooperation of the different civilizations of the world. (Chakravary 1961:106)

This text is not recent. It is not influenced by Ulf Hannerz on creolization or Appadurai on production of locality, nor even by Robert Redfield or Milton Singer on Great Traditions and modernization. As some clues might suggest, notably the reliance on civilization as the master concept (insistently pluralized by one of the interlocutors),[12] it comes from before World War II—in fact, from Geneva in 1930. The interlocutors are Rabindranath Tagore and H. G. Wells. It is Tagore, the Indian poet and public intellectual, who insists on plural civilizations in the face of Wells's prediction of a new, worldwide human order, one universal civilization as the natural destiny of mankind. Civilizations are to be cherished, to the poet, not traditions creating an area of darkness. Wells, by 1930, is no longer a science fiction writer but in fact author of world histories and polemics about future necessities. Wells is one of Britain's leading advocates for what he called "democratic socialism," a political idea whose ghost, I think, still haunts us. By 1930, Wells was on the verge of crystallizing the phrase "new world order" as the name of what he thought was inevitably coming, though he hoped for an actual world government (see also Wells 1940). Neither Wells nor Tagore used the word "modernity" even once. But it is the same debate that we are called to have. Human civilization versus different civilizations, modernity versus alternative modernities. It is not a new debate. And it is the wrong debate.

If our choices are singular or plural modernity, we will, inevitably, find ways to have both moments, theoretically. After the war, the philologists found their plural civilizations within one humanity, and the social scientists found their great traditions and their singular modernity. If we find a singular modernity, there will also be a vocabulary for its variations; if we have alternative modernities, there will be a vocabulary for their commensuration, coevalness, symmetry. We are, in fact, closer, far closer, to grasping the dynamics of ascendancy and challenge to United States power in our age than were our predecessors to understanding the anticolonial movements and decolonization process undertaken in and around so many of their field sites. But pace the powerful arguments of Aihwa Ong and others, I think to get farther on the former, we still need more attention to the latter. To understand present transnational initiatives within and in some ways against a world of allegedly sovereign nation-states ensconced in a silent array of global institutions forcing multileveled economic globalization, we do not need a better theory of "modernity." In fact, the modernist sublime is vital to the occlusion, by sublimation, of the specificities of recent global history. To better understand the transformations of the mid–twentieth century and the strategic humility of United States power, we should get out of the modernist sublime.

Acknowledgments

This chapter began as a paper for a session titled "Inflections of modernity" at the 2001 annual meetings of the American Anthropological Association. Thanks to all the participants and several people from the audience at the session for comments, especially to discussants Elizabeth Povinelli and Jonathan Friedman. Bruce Knauft's careful editorial reading has improved the manuscript in many ways, as have comments from Edward LiPuma and Robert Foster. Jeffrey Bennett provided extremely useful and wide-ranging commentary not only about this argument, but also about Mannheim and about the multiple roots of European modernism and the vicissitudes of its engagements with its opponents, much more than could be incorporated, let alone done justice, here; we will have to await his own works. This article draws extensively on Martha Kaplan's and my recent joint work on decolonization and the nation-state. Martha Kaplan has read and improved every draft. All faults are my own. I have made no attempt to expand this article to address events of 11 September 2001 and after, events that make these issues all the more urgent.

Notes

1. To Elias, the flaw in the self-perception of the colonizers is not that they believe themselves products of a civilizing process, but that they imagine themselves finished. In the final analysis, Elias actually seeks a factual, scientific understanding of the civilizing process, as the fuller rendering of the first quotation makes clear: "The concept of civilization, as the first chapter of this volume shows, has often been used in a semi-metaphysical sense and has remained highly nebulous until today. Here, the attempt is made to isolate the factual core to which the current prescientific notion of

the civilizing process refers" (1978:223–24). Elias in fact wants to use the reality, as he sees it, of civilizing process to confront and critique "the modern image of man" (1978:259).

2. I take it for granted that readers are familiar with the basic story of *Heart of Darkness*. If not, a simple outline: a man named Marlow narrates the story of his trip upriver deep into the interior of Africa, to find and bring back a brilliant man named Kurtz who has abandoned his work for their company and apparently gone native, gone mad, or both. Kurtz dies on a bed on Marlow's ship shortly after Marlow finds him.

3. For those unfamiliar with it, "chronotope" is a term coined by Russian literary critic Mikhail Bakhtin (see especially 1981). It refers to the premises about space-time intrinsic to and constitutive of genres of text. Bakhtin contended that powerful premises about possible contents make genres possible, from various kinds of lists to treaties to novels, and that all genres operate on the basis of premises about the relations between text, audience, and the qualities of the stuff in the texts. While the history of genres is the history of changes in their premises and possibilities, there are also characteristic premises for each about kinds of things, events, and relationships that are possible and impossible to depict. For example, characters experiencing events are possible in novels in a way that differs from most kinds of lists. Different chronotopes project different kinds of possible space-time, with different relations to the audience; for example, epics set human heroes in motion through events of extreme significance in past times more important than the audiences' present, while novels can be set in "the present," or in an accessible past or future, while utopias imagine other, unreal places and times, and so on. My concern is of course what we do, must, and can imagine necessary for our own social theory: the chronotopes we presume and depend on.

4. The others here would include Immanuel Kant and Edmund Burke, but less Kant than would perhaps be canonical. Determining conditions of possibility for art and life out of his own speculations about what is a priori, Kant rendered pursuit of the sublime a heroic and inevitable mission for specifically modern aesthetics. Lyotard's postmodernism (1984:77–81) kidnaps the Kantian heroism for his own guys, allegedly less "nostalgic" in their commitment to present the unpresentable. He observes "an amazing acceleration" as generations of modern artists challenge each other's rules; I am reminded of Marx's survey in "The German Ideology" (1978:147) of the "revolutions" in philosophy among the young Hegelians: "Certainly it is an interesting event we are dealing with: the putrescence of the absolute spirit." To be clearer, my skepticism is neither whether art can or should endeavor to provoke various forms of recognition and reaction to sublime conceptions, nor whether much in fact separates various projects in sublime aesthetics in self-consciously modern art. But I am skeptical that pursuit of the sublime has a unique or even privileged relationship with either art or modernism, something that anyone who can reflect upon their

knowledge of the history of religion should strongly come to doubt. Similarly, my skepticism rests especially with the "should," when the question is whether social scientists can and should pursue the sublime in their own works.

5. Ironically for me, Weber was of course also an important theorist of the modern. But note how his famous claim in the first sentence to his introduction to the comparative sociology of world religions includes the perspectival opening that specifically warns against finality, a warning renewed by the late skeptical "(as we like to think)" that has frustrated so many readers: "A product of modern European civilization, studying any problem of universal history, is bound to ask himself to what combination of circumstances the fact should be attributed that in Western civilization, and in Western civilization only, cultural phenomena have appeared which (as we like to think) lie in a line of development having *universal* significance and value" (Weber 1958:13). Weber sees only "a product of modern European civilization" bound to be concerned with this (alleged) Western exceptionalism in, precisely, development of universal significance, whose appearance of universal significance and value might or might not survive its time and place. And of course, note that it is civilization, not modernity, that Weber sets his modern Europeans within.

6. The imagery comes in most obviously in the final chapter, the long flight back to Europe, daybreak in Beirut, morning in Rome. "Light was coming . . . the tarmac was glazed and cool. Beyond it was a city which one knew to be a city, full of men as whole as these who . . . drove up in electric lorries to unload luggage: laborers, menials, yet arrogant in their gait, their big bodies and their skills. India was part of the night: a dead world, a long journey." Impressed by these whole, big-bodied men of the light, yet feeling homeless among them, even in London, Naipaul closes his journey with reflections on his attenuating connections to the "dead world" of his travels. "How could I admit as reasonable, even to myself, my distaste, my sense of the insubstantiality and wrongness of the new world [of light] to which I had been so swiftly transported. This life confirmed that other death; yet that death rendered this fraudulent. . . . The world is illusion, the Hindus say. . . . I saw how close in the past year I had been to the total Indian negation, how much it had become the basis of thought and feeling. And already, with this awareness, in a world where illusion could only be a concept and not something felt in the bones, it was slipping away from me. I felt it as something true which I could never adequately express and never seize again" (1981:279–81). The horror, etc., is here not in what India lacks, but what it has held on to. The British Raj in India "was a clash between a positive principle and a negative; and nothing more negative can be imagined than the conjunction in the eighteenth century of a static Islam and a decadent Hinduism" (1981:220).

7. To consider another example, one from far afield, see T. J. Clark's magisterial history of modern art, *Farewell to an Idea*: "As for the word 'modernity,'

John D. Kelly

282

it too will be used in a free and easy way, in hopes that most readers know it when they see it" (1999:4). Clark goes on to identify aphorisms such as Valery's: "The modern contents itself with little" that, Clark writes, "seems to me to sum up this side of modernity the best." Thus we see both the acknowledgment, that modernity will not be clearly or rigorously defined, and the disclaimer, the "seems to me" personalizing of the vantage or perspective taken. Acknowledging that he is taking a "minority view," Clark also tries to give a finite organizing logic to his cluster of features, resorting to what Tipps (1973) would characterize as a "critical variable" conception of modernity and modernization. "I should say straight-away that this cluster of features seems to me tied to, and propelled by, one central process: the accumulation of capital, and the. . . . " (Clark 1994:4). Foster (this volume) provides a deliberately nonsublime "modernity." His critical variable definition, focused on time-space distanciation, will admit, for example, urban China to "modernity" sometime before the year zero in Christian Standard Time, a kind of objective outcome that might provoke fruitful new questions, but an outcome that Clark et al. are clearly not prepared to grapple with.

8. But we should qualify Le Goff's claim that Baudelaire actually coined the word "modernity": the *Oxford English Dictionary* cites instances of usage of "modernity" in English from 1753 and one even from 1627. But almost all of these had the sense of the modernness of character of a person or object, not of a whole space-time in the state or condition of modernness, as when "Macrobius is no good author to follow in point of Latinity, partly on account of his modernity" (anonymous, 1796), or "Here is a modernity, which beats all antiquities for curiosity" (Horace Walpole, 1753). Baudelaire's argument is no doubt a touchstone for discussion of a modernity in the sense of an inhabited space-time chronotope, a total social condition.

9. Here I am remembering, also "ideology" and "utopia" in Mannheim's sense (Mannheim 1936), a useful rubric that nevertheless, as many have said, oversimplifies histories of genres and their connections to social positions and movements. Reliance on grotesque historical coordinates can produce grounds for critical politics that need not rely on utopian imagery or other sublimes.

10. I recognize that many scholars, including other contributors to this volume, are interested in reconsidering "modernity" within a specifically Marxist dialectic as part of the history of capitalism. Reexamining the history of capitalism, and looking for specific connections between discourses of "modernity" and "modernization" and developments in the forces and relations of production, distribution, and consumption, are projects many have undertaken in complex ways that I will not review, let alone join in on, here. To be clear, my own approach would be Weberian, not tying all history to an underlying dialectic of forces and relations of production. There are many good, open questions about how to configure the actual history of capitalist production in its complex, uneven connections to forces and rela-

tions of coercion, and forces and relations of communication—forces and relations that are, in my view, not simply reducible to or dependent upon those of production, as Weber argued long ago (on production and coercion see, e.g., Weber 1978:913 ff.). To expect, instead, that "modernity" or "modernities" are fetishes with a single grand secret, to expect that they would best be explained by an underlying total-social reality of capitalism, late post neoliberal or whatever, is to trade in one sublime for another.

11. In fact, both Ong and Appadurai note clearly their distinct personal experiences of a modernity or a West that was American rather than British in character (Ong 1999:29; Appadurai 1996:1–2). Ong also notes the significance for East Asian intellectuals of "an American reformulation of Western bourgeois thought," notably Rostow's (1960) modernizationist tract *Stages of Economic Growth* (Ong 1999:81). Yet on the same page, one can track the slow settling of Western modernity back into a unity as she concluded that narratives of Asian modernity contain elements from "Western discourses" (plural) and negotiate against "Western domination in the world" (reunified).

12. Braudel (1980) traces to 1850 the emergence among scholars of the term "civilizations" in the plural. He perceives thereafter a complex of European theorizing about both civilization as a singular process and differences between civilizations (as well as both singular and plural discussions of "culture"), a complex he wishes to extend in his own work. The first European pluralizings of the conception of civilization served both for the unending comparisons especially of France and England, but also East and West (in the wake of growing skepticism of the oriental Renaissance image of the East as the West's earliest origin), and not least, comparison of civilizations ancient and modern. While civilization, in the singular, cannot be said to have disappeared, my impression is that in the wake of the mid–twentieth century "new world order," it lost its "metaphysical" (cf. Elias 1978) or sublime reality, precisely as modernist sublime ramified, as "modern civilization" became "modernity."

References

Anderson, Benedict
   1983   *Imagined Communities: Reflections on the Origins and Spread of Nationalism.* London: Verso.

Appadurai, Arjun
   1996   The Production of Locality. In *Modernity at Large*, pp. 178–99. Minneapolis: University of Minnesota Press.

Bakhtin, M. M.
   1981   Forms of Time and of the Chronotope in the Novel. In *The Dialogic Imagination*, pp. 84–258. Austin: University of Texas Press.

1984   *Rabelais and His World*. University of Indiana Press.

Braudel, Fernand
1980   The History of Civilizations: The Past Explains the Present. In *On History*, pp. 177–218. Chicago: University of Chicago Press.

Chakrabarty, Dipesh
2000   *Provincializing Europe: Postcolonial Thought and Historical Difference.* Princeton, N.J.: Princeton University Press.

Chakravary, Aniya
1961   *A Tagore Reader.* Boston: Beacon Press.

Clark, T. J.
1999   *Farewell to an Idea: Episodes from a History of Modernism.* New Haven, Conn.: Yale University Press.

Conrad, Joseph
1963 [1899]   *Heart of Darkness.* Edited by Robert Kimbrough. New York: Norton.

Donham, Donald L.
2002   On Being Modern in a Capitalist World: Some Conceptual and Comparative Issues. In *Critically Modern: Alternatives, Alterities, Anthropologies* [this volume]. Edited by Bruce M. Knauft. Bloomington: Indiana University Press.

Escobar, Arturo
1995   *Encountering Development: The Making and Unmaking of the Third World.* Princeton, N.J.: Princeton University Press.

Elias, Norbert
1978   *The History of Manners.* Volume 1 of *The Civilizing Process.* New York: Pantheon Books.

Foucault, Michel
1970   *The Order of Things: An Archaeology of the Human Sciences.* New York: Vintage.

Foster, Robert J.
2002   Bargains with Modernity in Papua New Guinea and Elsewhere. In *Critically Modern: Alternatives, Alterities, Anthropologies* [this volume]. Edited by Bruce M. Knauft. Bloomington: Indiana University Press.

Ivy, Marilyn
1995   *Discourses of the Vanishing: Modernity, Phantasm, Japan.* Chicago: University of Chicago Press.

Kelly, John D., and Martha Kaplan
2001   *Represented Communities: Fiji and World Decolonization.* Chicago: University of Chicago Press.

Latour, Bruno
    1988   *The Pasteurization of France.* Cambridge, Mass.: Harvard University
            Press.

Le Goff, Jacques
    1992 [1977]   Antique (Ancient)/Modern. In *History and Memory.* By
            Jacques Le Goff. New York: Columbia University Press.

Louis, William Roger
    1977   *Imperialism at Bay: The United States and the Decolonisation of the
            British Empire, 1941–1945.* Oxford: Clarendon Press.

Lyotard, Jean-Francois
    1984   *The Postmodern Condition: A Report on Knowledge.* Minneapolis:
            University of Minnesota Press.

Mannheim, Karl
    1936   *Ideology and Utopia: An Introduction to the Sociology of Knowledge.*
            New York: Harcourt, Brace and World.

Marx, Karl
    1978   The German Ideology: Part 1. In *The Marx-Engels Reader.* Edited
            by Robert C. Tucker, pp. 147–200. New York: Norton.

Mencken, H. L.
    1963 [1917]   Joseph Conrad. In *The Heart of Darkness.* By Joseph Conrad.
            Edited by Robert Kimbrough. New York: Norton.

Naipaul, V. S.
    1981 [1964]   *An Area of Darkness.* New York: Vintage Books.

Ong, Aihwa
    1999   *Flexible Citizenship: The Cultural Logics of Transnationality.* Dur-
            ham, N.C.: Duke University Press.

Rofel, Lisa
    1999   *Other Modernities: Gendered Yearnings in China after Socialism.* Berke-
            ley: University of California Press.

Rostow, Walter W.
    1960   *The Stages of Economic Growth: A Non-communist Manifesto.* Cam-
            bridge: Cambridge University Press.

Scott, David
    1999   *Refashioning Futures: Criticism after Postcoloniality.* Princeton, N.J.:
            Princeton University Press.

Taussig, Michael
    1987   *Shamanism, Colonialism and the Wild Man.* Chicago: University of
            Chicago Press.

Tipps, Dean C.
    1973   Modernization Theory and the Comparative Study of Societies: A
            Critical Perspective. *Comparative Studies in Society and History* 15:
            199–226.

Weber, Max
1949   "Objectivity" in Social Science and Social Policy. In *The Method-
ology of the Social Sciences*, pp. 50–112. New York: Free Press.
1958   Author's Introduction. In *The Protestant Ethic and the Spirit of Capitalism*, pp. 13–31. New York: Scribners.
1978   *Economy and Society*. Berkeley: University of California Press.

Wells, H. G.
1940   *The New World Order: Whether it is Attainable, How It Can be At-
tained, and What Sort of World a World at Peace Will Have to Be*. New
York: Alfred A. Knopf.

Whorf, Benjamin Lee
1956 [ca. 1936]   An American Indian Model of the Universe. In *Language,
Thought, and Reality*, pp. 57–64. Cambridge, Mass.: MIT Press.

Williams, Raymond
1976   *Keywords: A Vocabulary of Culture and Society*. New York: Oxford
University Press.

Ten

Modernity and Other Traditions

Jonathan Friedman

Modernity is an increasingly popular and confused term of reference, one that has not been an object of anthropology as such until quite recently. The reason for this is in itself worth discussion. Sociology, of course, has had lots to say on the issue, and many of the major debates in an earlier period were very much focused on the issue of the transition itself and its possible meanings. *Gemeinschaft* to *gesellschaft,* status to contract, tradition to modernity, evolution and development were all part of a general understanding of the transformation of European societies and of the world as a whole. The modern in this perspective was envisaged as a series of states-of-the-world: individualism, market, liberty, and democratic government; briefly, the model of a society, a civil society made up of free individuals whose activities were organized within the framework of a state ruled by an elected government, whose goals were individual self-fulfillment and whose alterity implied a secular existence where religiosity and all cultural identity were relegated to a private predilection bereft of public influence. This notion was not the product of empirical investigation but of a quite general act of self-reflection, one that sought to delimit the specificity of an emergent condition. So we are squarely in the realm of identity talk, of categories that might immediately be designated as ideological or even mythical. Modernity, like one of its metonyms, the French Revolution, is a myth of contemporary Europe—a charter of a social order rather than an aid to its understanding. This is partially true, of course, and it is a major problem in much of the literature on the subject. On the other hand, we have taken it upon ourselves in the West to claim analytical distance to ourselves, to be able to come to a self-understanding via rational critique and empirically grounded research. This may also be a particularly self-congratulatory myth, but I shall accept its value for the time being, as nothing has come along to replace it.

The recent plethora of writings on the subject of modernity, clearly depicted in Bruce Knauft's introduction to this volume, poses serious questions as to what it is we are supposed to be talking about. His critique of Harvey's neglect of "economic and political histories of non-Western peoples—including their engagements with and resistances against capitalism" is where anthropology can be said to have encountered this primarily sociological discussion. It might be countered in good relativist terms that modernity is a product of European capitalist society, a cultural specificity, a "tradition" that is inapplicable to the understanding of non-Western societies. Now this implies further questions that have never been asked in a clear fashion. Are the different Western polities similar with respect to their "cultures?" If so, is this a product of a common or convergent history, a capitalist history for example, producing similar social and cultural transformations? If what is called "modernity" is the product of these transformations, then are all social formations subject to the same kind of trajectory? Or might we assume another more structuralist position in which modernity comes in varieties, the latter the products of particular historical articulations of capitalist development in differing initial conditions? This would produce French, English, and American modernities, as well as Indonesian, Japanese, and Chinese modernities. These are big questions that are not easily assumed or taken for granted in discussing alternative modernities or alternative relations to a single modernity. They cry out for more precision, for an elucidating of perspectives rather than yet another plunge into the murky waters of this discourse.

I shall in the following briefly indicate what appear to be the problems that have yet to be solved in such discussions, as well as suggest what one might be doing in constructing a viable discursive arena.

In the chapters here, as noted by Knauft, there is a virtual grab bag of terms listed, if not united, under the term "modernity." Individualism, nation-state, imperialism, and capitalism, whether millennial or just plain capitalism, are all points of reference for numerous discussions. We shall return to the laundry list since it is not only a reflection of the indeterminacy of the term but also has been a symptom of more theoretical sociological works (Giddens 1990; Friedman 1994:214–27).[1]

The uses of the term in recent anthropological texts seem to arrange themselves along a set of varying contours.

1. Modernity is very often defined as the contemporary—for example, the existence of witchcraft today as an expression of the modernity of witchcraft (e.g., Geschiere 1997). The latter is modern because it is part of a process organized within the global capitalist world of today, not of yesterday. This notion has no particular content, no specificity. It is a mere temporal category of presupposed disjunction and it is often conflated and confused with more substantive understandings of the term.

2. Modernity can refer to the leading sector or region of the world, understood in hierarchical terms, as a center/periphery structure or as empire. It includes the center of the "system," the West and the Others, the peripheries and subperipheries that are defined and then define themselves in relation to the modern. The modernities described in this version are primarily relations to a postulated modern, something that exists in another part of the world, the subject of either emulation or rejection.

3. Modernity is simply the set of modern products, or the products of capitalism, the products of the center as well. The latter is present metonymically, in the form of commodities and images, from haute couture to CNN or visions of "modern life." Many write of modernities in other parts of the world as a relation or representation of or discourse on these metonymies.

4. Our own approach is to understand modernity as a cultural space, a regime of social experience. This approach is closer to Trouillot's chapter in this book and is rooted, of course, in both older and more recent sociological discussions.

Examples of these usages, not mutually exclusive, are most common in recent anthropology. In the vast literature on developing areas, we are usually faced with situations that combine what are assumed to be modern phenomena in situations that anthropologists are or were wont to define as "radically" other, nonmodern, traditional. Thus in this volume, Foster refers to some of the large body of work that has come from Papua New Guinea in which money, the state, and other powerful persons, and "development" are interpreted in terms of categories that are clearly not part of the accompanying baggage of these Western "concepts." But rather than analyze them emically in the context of local categories, he instead invokes Giddens's concept of "trust" as a means of denoting the points within a social field where contradictions may occur. The fear of Lever Brothers soap in Africa . . . rumors that it was made of human baby fat can thus be compared to the fear of dioxins in

Coke and milk products in Belgium. But of course, here, the interpretation is based on very different premises. Dioxins are artificial chemicals found in herbicides. They are feared because they represent biologically deleterious substances as such. The presence of human baby fat in soap is clearly the product of a different kind of activity linked to an interpretation of white savagery and linked to the force of evil embedded in this particular process of production. Of course, they are both just stories, but the categorical assumptions that motivate them are quite different. This issue is *not* dealt with by Foster. The question one might ask here is to what extent modernity and contemporaneity are being conflated. Englund and Leach (2000), who go to great lengths in criticizing the notion of modernity in anthropology, demand just this, a stronger ethnographic analysis, claiming that much of the current discourse on modernity in anthropology simply supplants other people's categories of experience with our own, or, in their terms, with a meta-narrative of modernity.[2]

Similarly, the chapters by Spitulnik and Wardlow in this volume deal with relations to what is defined by the anthropologist as western modernity. Spitulnik, writing of Zambia, goes to language use itself and thus avoids what she sees as the more ethnocentric use of the term "modernity" as simply progress. She finds a great deal of local variation: a progress-oriented modernity, a consumption-oriented modernity, a stylistically oriented modernity, and a temporally clocked modernity. But in all of the specificity, it is not clear that we are talking about the same kind of phenomenon, as Spitulnik herself notes. Desire for the things or the life, objectified in images of the West, does not require the term "modernity." On the contrary, it is the analysis of such desire that can provide insight into the nature of this assumed phenomenon. Wardlow (this volume) demonstrates clearly the way in which relations to Western goods reproduce in transformed ways local gender relations and local interpretations of objects. This is a question of cultural assimilation, in part or in toto. The things of the outside world are integrated into the life processes of the local social order.

Donham (this volume) links discourses of modernity to the logic of capitalism. Modernity becomes a discursive space within which representations of the modern, the anti-modern, and the traditional are constructed in confrontation with one another but still linked to a common set of properties.

> So, what I am calling modernity is, in essence, the discursive space
> in which an argument takes place, an argument in which certain

positions continually get constructed and reconstructed. (Donham 2002:6)[3]

Revolutions are linked to local dreams of progress, images of a future. He also argues against the usage of the nominal form, modernity—as opposed to modern, which is a clearer relativizing term.

Donham's "modern" is equivalent to my own use of the term "modernist" when he refers to the relation to centers of world power, but he is, as seen above, aware that modernity is a specific field of discourse produced within capitalism, one that leads to his suggestion that opposing representations might best be seen as complementary aspects of a single matrix—an approach that I have myself suggested (Friedman 1994). Donham appropriates Latour's argument that modernity is a self-mystification of the fact that "we have never been modern" which implies that any notion of *alternative modernities*, must be rejected. Here he scores important points against the popular image of culturally determined capitalisms and modernities suggested by Comaroff and Comaroff and others. He makes an important distinction in this analysis between modernity as a discourse produced within capitalism and relations among peripheries of the world system and its centers which represent, for the former, a possible future life, a life filled with the paraphernalia of those centers, including everything from computers to democratic ideals.

Donham's analysis of the Ethiopian revolution is contextualized by the relations of underdevelopment in which elites are acutely conscious of a difference that they desire to overcome. Marxism developed as the basis of antiroyalism, but, more importantly, missionary-imported millennial Christianity originated a relation to the future that could be dubbed revolutionary. It is noteworthy that this church was traditionalist at home in North America (i.e., against adapting to modernizing changes). In Ethiopia, it is, on the contrary, modernist. This is no paradox, of course, since fundamentalism represents a more general modernism with respect to economic development, individualism, etc. And of course it is a product of the "developed world." What is modernist in one place may be reactionary in another in terms of internal discourses of the different places, but fundamentalist Christianity is not, in its various forms, traditionalist in general, only with respect to certain forms of social control. Otherwise Victorian morality would have to be dubbed reactionary, and it often is so dubbed. This is a confusion of contemporaneity and modernity since the particular degree to which capitalist penetration dissolves moral and other forms of social control and community is not identical to the politics of "progress." Otherwise, neoliberalism is as progressive as women's liberation, and socialist ideology is fundamentally reactionary.

In Donham's argument, the modern is used as a relative term that is affiliated with aspects of capitalist reality. Modern is the way it is in the center of the system. Here the issue of alternative is less important than the set of relations within which representations of the future are produced. Modernity captures the temporal orientation to something that may already exist somewhere else. His reference to the word, then, is closer to the notion of modernism, a strongly developmentalist future orientation. This is the representation of a center periphery relation in a temporal register, the very core of evolutionary thinking.

In these cases, we must reiterate our question. Is this alternative modernity in action—that is, the integration of things and images from our part of the world into their lives? What is the nature of this integration? The argument for the existence of a global modernity is overturned in these examples, unless one redefines modernities as the contemporary. This has been clearly understood by a number of contributors to this volume. What is the ethnographic situation in which the issue arises? It is an anthropology that has finally eschewed all attempts to block out what is not part of the contemporary situation in those parts of the world that have been incorporated into the Western realm of economic processes and structures of administration. The latter has often been admitted only as context, and the anthropological journey has often been envisaged as a passage from our world into theirs. The last part of the trip is one that moves from the colonial or Western or "modern" sector out there into native territory, where true ethnography of the other can be practiced without the interference of the larger context.[4] But once we admit this larger context as part of the field, are we necessarily including the other in our social field, our life world, where they become increasingly like us via increasing contact with the things, concepts, and structures of our world, the virus of modernity?

This perspective represents a strong tendency in the retooling of the anthropological gaze. Kelly (this volume) infers something of this sort in his questioning of the very use of the term "modernity," but his approach is that of the doctor in search of symptoms. Yes, alternative modernities are like the alternative civilizations of the last century which were transferred into the relativistic culture concept of American anthropology in this century. Without discussing the facts of the argument, it is important not to forget the nature of the problem—one that is more serious than whether we are not reproducing the same old imperial categories with each new reformulation of perspective. It is not enough to identify the existence of the "imperial" gaze. The problem is the properties of the gaze itself and its pivotal position in all of these formulations. Alternative modernities assume variations on some invariant theme or set of themes. While in a previous era there was plenty of free room for the existence of profound differences in the structures of social life, this kind of difference has been eliminated from the current version of the gaze. The anthropology of the colonial and the postcolonial are among the popular products of the recent change of perspective. But in this shift, there has been a tendency to replace the categories of the people we study by extensions of our own categories. Otherwise, the question of alternative modernities would not have been so easy to pose in the first place.[5] This is where the entire discourse of modernities merges with the discourse of globalization. And it is all still part of an implicit evolutionary paradigm. Primitive and traditional become a more general expression of radical differences which have become increasingly less radical and have even disappeared into a single globalized reality.

There are many takes on this, some more historical than others. The notion that the world is all modern, then, is an expression of an implicit understanding that we are all part of the same global cultural process. The alterity of modernities is the result of a new set of mixtures of previous difference with contemporary sameness diffused now across the face of the earth. Thus, there is a set of new differences in this world, but these are not clearly delimited. They are often simply the fact of colonial and postcolonial administration, of Nikes, of a great number of social changes that dot what was once a world of more absolute difference. It is the same kind of alterity that characterizes the difference between France and England as modern nation-states. It is a combinatorial modernity in which the alternative forms are all variations on the same basic themes, "structures of common difference" as Rick Wilk (1995) has put it.

Whose Modernities?

Alternative modernities are invariably about a certain representation and practice of a dependency relation, a social construction of peripherality —but how is modernity understood in the centers themselves? This must ultimately return us to the earlier sociological discussion, which was more focused on the content of the term than on its connotative function with respect to those defined as peripheral to its existence. This does not mean that the sociological literature offers a solution to our problem, since it partakes of much of the list, like the nature of other discussions. We might begin by dropping the necessary assumption that modernity is a concept and maintain it simply as a word that has and does refer to a cluster of phenomena that may or may not be systematically related to one another. I shall suggest below that they do hang together and that it is in uncovering the nature of the configuration that we can contribute to an understanding of the apparent resonance of the term. We can begin with the list itself (Friedman 1994):

Individualism
Public/private division
Democracy
Nation-state
Enlightenment philosophy/critical rationality
Capitalism
Global economy/imperialism
Modernism/developmentalism/evolutionism

These terms are not of the same logical type. "Individualism" and "global economy," for example, relate to different orders of reality, but this does not exclude the possibility that they might be systemically related in material terms. A substantial issue in many of the chapters of this volume is how people relate to the image of the modern, or to the modern as the empty sign of the world's centers. But this is a different issue. It is, as we have suggested, a relation to something that is already defined as modern—that is, the West and a set of items that represent the latter. This is a formal rather than a substantive relation. Any item can be chosen as a subject for discussion, for appropriation as part of a particular "modern" identity, but the logic that links the terms is largely irrelevant. The alternative modernities concept is compatible with the laundry list of terms because they are integrated as signs into other forms of life, other strategies. The atomization of the list allows a hybrid approach to the issue, as indicated in Knauft's introduction to this volume. Because no logic, no structured field, is stipulated, it becomes all too easy to conflate contemporaneity and modernity, as reflected in the following passage from this book's introduction, concerning Robert Foster's chapter.

> Crisp, red, twenty-kina currency notes that depict the head of a boar now combine ritual efficacy and monetary value. Here is the antithesis of the colonial exotic that projected native people thinking that money was merely pretty paper. Instead, Anganen play quite actively and consciously with meanings of money and performative enactment. They directly engage the importance of cash

with the importance of ritual. The creative fusion of these divergent "modern" and "traditional" elements does not deny one for the other. Instead, Foster's analysis reveals a capital ritual in which becoming healthy and becoming modern can hardly be disentangled or reduced to a residuum of something else.

Are these two things, traditional and modern, combined in the sense of remaining separate and contiguous, or is something else going on . . . ritual efficiency and monetary value? OK, but how are these articulated? If the schema relating good health and being modern and dependent on the accumulation of wealth is dominant, then it might be argued that this schema is structurally similar to former cultural schemes with the mere addition of new terms. If it can be shown that the schema is a single structure of integration (i.e., that new elements are assimilated to the same set of relations), then the issue of modernity is largely vitiated —that is, if the structure is not "modern." This also begs the entire question of the modern as such, but the issue need not arise as long as the term (i.e., its content) goes unscrutinized. It is in order to clear up this problem that we need to return to the issue of modernity "at home," where the term has, of necessity, come under serious scrutiny.

The Logic of Modernity

Do the terms in the list above have anything to do with one another? I have argued that, in fact, they are aspects of a unitary process that inflects them all in a particular way (Friedman 1994). The advance of commercial capitalism generated a dissolution of larger sodalities over several centuries. This advance itself was predicated on the formation of a European-centered world market from the fifteenth century. It enabled a new form of differentiation by wealth in which the individual accumulation of capital/abstract wealth was paramount. This reconfigured class structure in such a way that a bourgeoisie increasingly became the most powerful group in society. With the gradual demise of the aristocratic model of fixed status, consumption became a primary means of social self-definition. The eighteenth century marks the first consumption revolution in Western European history (McKendrick et al. 1982). Lord Chesterfield's famed correspondence with his son deals with the problem of confronting increasing numbers of people whose status is unclear, because socially unmarked, and the necessity of creating a personal space secure from public encroachment. The private sphere emerged in the same period, a sphere of the "*négligé*" where the self was free from the imposed and increasingly unclear roles of the public sphere. But more importantly, the core principle of this change is the fracture of the person into a private subject and a public identity.

From this fracture springs the well-known experience of alterity. Alterity, the founding dynamic of modernism, is an understanding of the world in which identity is reduced increasingly to social role, achieved rather than ascribed, temporary, and even alienated from the subject. The nation-state is a political formation that depends on the dissolution of older sodalities and communities and the individualization of a territorial population enabling the state with some effort to resocialize it into a new kind of identity based on "citizenship" rather than subject status. Democratic forms of politics make increasing inroads in the state as the nation/people become the only source of sovereignty with the demise of the aristocracy. This entire development is dependent in its turn on capitalist economic growth, which in its turn is dependent on the formation of larger economic and therefore political arenas than the territory of the state itself. The formation of imperial systems is the foundation of the entire development, as it is in the center of empire that the social transformation leading to modernity occurs. The success of this process produces a new social identity, one in which the national society itself is placed within the center of the larger imperial process. This creates a center/periphery organization of the world, but in the circumstances of individualization and the disintegration of theologically based cosmologies such as the Great Chain of Being. If mobility depends on individual success, the latter can readily be understood as a process of development. If this modality of experience is transferred to the larger society and even to nature, the result is evolutionism, the ordering of the world in terms of degrees of developmental success. This is, then, a future-oriented cosmology which becomes generalized to all domains, natural history, social history, and individual development, and which is the core of modernism.

This is no mere expression of a relativity, of a contemporaneity that requires its complementary opposite—tradition, the primitive, or whatever. This would be to conflate the term "modernity" with its specific cultural content. I shall suggest here that there is a real content to the notion of modernity, one that can only be understood in terms of a set of complementary parameters. The latter generate tendencies to the structuring of an identity space, one in which traditionalism is just as modern as modernism, primitivism, and postmodernism. All of these can be understood as expressions of the parameters of the space. The graphic that I have made use of for a couple of decades (figure 10.1) consists of a number of simple dichotomies that define four end points, or polarities. The latter are ideal types that only exist tendentially in

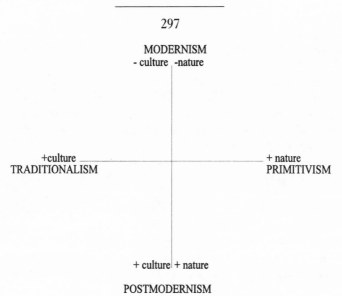

Figure 10.1. The identity space of modernity

reality. Thus, the modernist pole, the dominant in most of the history of modern capitalism, repudiates both the natural and the cultural as conceived of, respectively, as libidinous and superstitious. It defines itself as rational, universalist, and progressive. The traditionalist pole repudiates nature but not culture, investing itself in the authority of cultural models and in cultural models of authority and social order. The primitivist pole rejects the cultural as the essence of authority, in the sense of authoritarian order, of control and repression, and invests itself in the primordial, creative, and libidinous capacities of "Natural Man." The postmodernist pole rejects only the modernist pole, investing in both nature, understood as the immediacy and creativity of the natural state, and holistic wisdom as opposed to scientific knowledge. While postmodernists are primarily modernity's cynics, primitivists are represented by many youth movements and pop culture, and in the early part of the century, by the primitivist intellectual movement. Modernists are distributed among the rationalist elites, political and economic, and traditionalists represent the great majority of those who have opted for roots, ethnic and religious.

If these poles define the limits of the space, they do not determine its dynamic, which depends on the larger social and political economic context. The way people identify over time is a function of global systemic processes. The contemporary period of hegemonic decline is a period of increasing polarization within this space, in which traditionalism is clearly on the rise—and massively so—while modernism is increasingly weakened. Where the future fades, people tend to invest in the past. The result is ethnification and cultural fragmentation, at least in the lower half of the social order. At the top, a congery of modernist and post-modernist elites become the new cosmopolitans. This represents a certain folding in upon itself of the identity space, so that modernist and postmodernist identifications become increasingly fused in spite of their contradictory natures.[6] This is New Age modernism, revolutionary neoliberalism, and other "doublethinks" so common in Third Way ideologies that have brought political elites from right and left into the *Neue Mitte* (the German term for "Third Way").

If the schema illustrated in figure 10.1 can be understood as a set of interwoven processes, all of which are dependent on the degree of intensity of capital accumulation and commodification of the social field, then modernity can be understood as a structure in the structuralist sense—not a fixed form, but a set of properties of a series of interconnected dynamic processes. This further raises the issue of historical conditions, and here I would immediately suggest that modernity is a transhistorical structure that has appeared in several times and places, always a product of a similar set of processes of commercial capitalist accumulation. It can be said to have appeared in classical Greece, continuing into the Hellenistic, and then Roman eras before disappearing, but there are also tendencies in certain periods of Chinese and Indian regional history, and in the Arab world during the Middle Ages. The degree of individualization and "alterity" has, of course, varied, just as have other tendencies, such as democracy, the nation–state, rationalist philosophy, and science. This is related to differing political–historical contexts. These similarities are clearly worth investigation. Thus, in one sense, we have certainly never been modern, insofar as these tendencies have never worked themselves out to their logical conclusions in any historical period. On the other hand, the tendencies themselves are of the same order, and it is here that we may speak of a family of phenomena that harbor similar structural dynamics.

Modernity is, in this argument, the *cultural field of commercial capitalism, its emergent identity space.* This implies that the question of so-called alternative modernities would have to be reframed. The alternatives within modernity are aligned within the same space of features. And it is because of these invariant features that we can speak, if we so desire, of alternative modernities. But this is not the case if the cultural field is organized in terms of other basic features. Thus, the fact that one desires Western goods does not have anything to do with modernity as such. This is emphatically so if the desire itself is structured in terms of the logic of a very different kind of social world. Cargo cults in this sense are totally focused on what appears *to us* to be the modern, but this ignores the internal order of this relation, the intentionalities involved, and what these objects mean in the lives of those who desire them. Ethnographic analysis is too often glossed into or replaced by a ready-made interpretation based on the experience of the observer. Trouillot (this volume) suggests something along these lines in proposing that modernity lies in the historical formation of a specific kind of social existence that includes elements such as private life, human rights, the nation, and alterity, but his stress on this latter term as the experience of historical rupture is in my terms a partial characterization that enables him to suggest that the colonial "Caribbean was modern from day one." It can certainly be argued that the establishment of slave societies was an historical process that transferred Africans from their worlds to a universe constituted by European design and that this was the creation of a new kind of order in the colonized territories. But the tendencies toward the realization of a modern cultural space as discussed above were quite limited, depending on the strength of the transformative process of a basically dual economy and on the degree to which other forms of social reproduction could be established or reconstituted in the periods of economic decline. It is in Europe and other centers of capitalist accumulation that the process of commodification, the deepening dissolution of other forms of sociality, led to an increasingly dominant modernity that is only partially emergent in the historical Caribbean. Whether the latter qualifies as a variant of modernity in the terms referred to above depends on how the threshold is defined. The latter is arbitrary, of course, as are all definitions, but the issue of where to place the threshold is itself founded on the understanding of a definite set of processes that determine the degree to which a modern identity space has been spawned.

I would suggest that this structural approach might help make sense of the otherwise quite confused issue of alternative modernities that is current in anthropological discussions. Instead of immediately utilizing the term "alternative modernities," it might make more sense to first ascertain the nature of relevant parameters. In all cases that I have encountered, the issue is one of confrontation, articulation, and subsumption of other parts of the world by expanding capitalism, and modernity seems to be taken along for the ride, as if it were part of the baggage itself and not an emergent product.

300

The Ideological Basis of "Alternative" Modernities

There is an interesting ideology that links the use of the term "modernity" to a notion of historical discontinuity. It is based on the very acceptance of the evolutionary character of the term, so that to even insinuate that modernity is a rather restricted phenomenon can be construed as racism. This fear of association with such discrimination has led to an even stronger bond between "modernity" and "contemporaneity," one that is clearly illustrated by recent discussions of the "modernity" of witchcraft.

Geschiere's (1997) work on sorcery in Cameroon is an excellent example of the problem that arises when applying notions like alternative modernities. Here, there is an agenda. Geschiere would like to insist that contemporary sorcery is modern. This implies that all of the properties of the latter that display some historical continuity are subsumed within this new category and are thus assimilated to the modern. He thus creates precisely that discontinuity that has been the hallmark of Western notions of the modern. What is the same and what is different? For Geschiere, the objects and actors are different, but the mode of going about identifying others and the central issue of wealth accumulation and inequality is admittedly part of the "old" logic. However, it is the introduction of new objects and actors that is crucial. This implies that potlatching with sewing machines is not potlatching, but modern potlatching, something entirely new. And what is new is what is introduced from the outside, implying that the "foreign" played no role in the past. Now if, as in the Congo region, the highest ranked prestige goods need to be exotic, and if their value is a sign of a political status relation to the outside world, then there ought always to be a tendency to import new things into the internal cycles of exchange and dominance. The application of a term such as "modernity" flattens out a more complex articulation of different kinds of structure that may indeed coexist but which are nevertheless of different orders. This kind of critique was made of modernization theory by Marxists decades ago.

Geschiere writes clearly that there are "traditional" elements in modern sorcery after he castigates others for entertaining such dangerous ideas (2000:23). His modern tale is as follows: X arrives in town without money to buy food . . . he joins a tontine (*famla*) and contracts a debt that has to be paid by offering one of his kin. "Or si la notion de dette en sorcellerie n'est pas neuve, elle acquiert de nouvelles dimensions en étant en rapport direct avec le *famla*" ["Now even if the notion of debt in sorcery is not new, it takes on new dimensions in relation to the *famla*] (2000:24). What is apparently new is the linkage to the labor of others, to the capitalist process. But what is changed in all of this? As he says himself, "le discours de la sorcellerie s'articule si facilement aux changements modernes" ["the discourse of sorcery so easily articulates with modern changes"] (2000:24). What is new are the new commodities introduced by the world market: "biens hautement convoités parce que devenus les symboles mêmes de la vie 'moderne': maisons 'en dur' équipées de frigidaire, de télévision et de tout ce qui rend la vie moderne agréable; voitures de luxe (Mercedes, ou maintenant Pajero), etc." ["highly coveted goods because they have become the very symbols of 'modern' life: solidly built houses equipped with refrigerators, televisions and all that renders modern life so agreeable; luxury cars (Mercedes and now Pajeros), etc."] (2000:24). What is the real problem here? Could it be that the term "modern" is being forced on the situation to be understood? Are these symbols of modern life for those who acquire them? Or are they symbols of modernity primarily for us? Are we dealing with a notion of modern as we have defined it above, as a structure of experience, or are these things modern in the sense of foreign prestigious items that demonstrate wealth in a particular local scheme of representation linking wealth, health, and power? Geschiere answers this by warning us that to use the word "retraditionalization," as Chabal and Dalloz (1999) do, is dangerous because this new imaginary is the product of "un effort concerté pour participer aux changements modernes, voire pour les maîtriser" ["a concerted effort to participate in modern social changes and even to control them"] (2000:225). There is nothing to indicate that this engagement has to do with the content of modern life. On the contrary, the "modern" appears in all of his own and other ethnographic material to be appropriated to other schemes of interpretation and practice. Geschiere himself admits that the mode in which the logic of sorcery is applied in the contemporary situation is continuous with the past. He suggests, in the final analysis, that it is the closed/open nature of sorcery, its flexibility with respect to its objects, that is its resonant base for modernity.

The argument is often framed in singular terms. We are today in the modern world, so everyone who is part of this in the material sense—that is, part of world capitalism—is part of modernity as well. All the rest is variation on this single theme. This is a contorted version of Fabian's call to accept the contemporaneity of the contemporary rather than classifying it as radically other in the sense of temporally past. But in Geschiere's version, modernity is conflated with contemporaneity. There is a world of difference between material contiguity and interaction that is orchestrated by the world system, and the cultural and social articulations that order such contiguity and interaction in ongoing social lives. There is no contradiction between material unification and the continued existence of separate social worlds, even where they are very much transformed. The denial of continuity coupled to the assertion of the radical otherness or specificity of the modern expresses a kind of politically correct approach to difference. Oh yes, they can be very different—but they are differently modern.

This is the problem in the work of Comaroff and Comaroff as well, where "occult economies" are associated with globalization, or as it is now termed, "millennial capitalism." The occult is a reaction to the onslaught of the world economy and not a phenomenon that might have its own internal logic. The enemy here is some straw man notion of *tradition*, interpreted as the fixed, essentialized culturalist imprisonment of the "other" in a local unchangeable world, the world of traditional anthropology, which at last is being revolutionized by this new "afterology" (Sahlins 1999). While admitting that there are clear continuities, the fact that it is happening here and now and in a new context ordered by the contemporary changes of the capitalist system makes it entirely different. This is *our* problem, perhaps, *our* millennialism, our desperate need to project ourselves into the future and take "them" with us, with the feeling that we are indeed entering a new world of cybercapitalism and virtual accumulation. But this is, in fact, more of an academic impression than a revolutionary prophecy. After all, even for those enthusiasts of the brave new world who have boarded the train, the "revolution" is one made by capital, and not by those who would oppose it. Capitalism has not changed in its general tendencies to the deepening of commodification, the increase in the rate of accumulation of fictitious capital relative to real accumulation, the increasing lumpenization of large portions of the world's population. All these processes are abetted by the new high technology, but they are certainly not its cause, and if anything, they are the symptoms of a capitalism in dire straits, a situation quite predictable from the logic of the system (Friedman 1999, 2000, 2001; Hirst and Thompson 1996; Harvey 1989; Wallerstein 1979). If there is something new here, it is the strange air of radical identity or self-identity among those intellectuals who are both representatives of the privileged classes and translators of ordinary liberalism into the language of radicalism.

But there is more here than meets the eye. What is it that seems to embarrass anthropologists in admitting that the world might consist of mere variations on modernity? It would seem to be the claim that somehow modernity is about rationality and that magic is therefore some-

thing that belongs to our past and to traditional society. When arguing for the global prevalence of "modern" magic, the African "occult
economy" is merely a local variant of a global millennial phenomenon.
Thus, the driving force in this change is globalization itself, the speeding up of circulation of goods, images, information, T-shirts, and cults:
"it is a feature of the millennial moment everywhere, from the east coast
of Africa to the west coast of America." They might well stress the local
forms of this phenomenon: "Once more, however, a planetary phenomenon takes on strikingly particular local form" (Comaroff and Comaroff
1999:291). In one sense, these authors are expressing an awareness that
is very much already present in the media. In another sense, their account jumps directly from the fact of globalization itself to what are
claimed to be magical reactions. Too much to buy, consumer insanity,
understood as the liberation of desire, and not enough money to get it
all, not for the poor masses. This is what produces the occult economy,
the magic of money, the imagination of zombies, and of sorcery.

This is not a new connection, of course. It is a replication of the old
structural functionalist account, but now in a more intensified situation
and with, of course, a new, millennial, vocabulary. The old account also
linked the epidemic of sorcery to the inroads of the market into "traditional" African societies. Sorcery, as Geschiere puts it, is an attempt to
stop the flow of globalization. In the old days, it was an attempt to do
something more particular—for example, to counter the commercializa-
tion of social relations. So what's new, we might ask? A closer account
would have to clarify the fact that it was elders who were accusing their
children or nephews of sorcery as the latter became increasingly independent economically as they became employed in the capitalist sectors
that encroached on these worlds, a process that was explosively evident
in the early colonial period. So even the "modernity" of witchcraft has
a historical continuity. Ekholm Friedman has argued that the kind of
witchcraft/sorcery found in contemporary Congo is, in fact, a phenomenon that dates only to the latter half of the past century—that is, to
colonialism itself, and that before that, it was organized as a chiefly
mechanism of political control over potential revolts by vassals (Ekholm
Friedman 1992). Even while admitting the historical continuity of the
forms of these phenomena, it seems preferable to some, however contradictory, to stress their discontinuity with the past.

The newfangled millennial discourse encompasses the world's differences in a new version of theme and variation. The theme now is capitalism as a cultural phenomenon. A critique of those who would stress
cultural continuity in all of this[7] is revealing with respect to precisely
the contradiction discussed here. We are warned not to retreat into some

form of old-fashioned localism in order to avoid "the "methodological challenge posed by the global moment" (Comaroff and Comaroff
1999:294):

> This move is typically rationalized by affirming, sometimes in an
> unreconstructed spirit of romantic neoprimitivism, the capacity of
> "native" cultures to remain assertively intact, determinedly differ-
> ent, in the face of a triumphal, homogenizing world capitalism.
> Apart from being empirically questionable, this depends upon an
> anachronistic ahistorical idea of culture. Of culture transfixed in
> *opposition* to capitalism—as if capitalism were not itself cultural to
> the core, everywhere indigenised as if culture has not been long
> commodified under the impact of the market. In any case, to re-
> duce the history of the here and now to a contest between the pa-
> rochial and the universal, between sameness and distinction, is to
> reinscribe the very dualism on which the colonizing discourse of
> early modernist social science was erected. It is also to represent
> the hybrid, dialectical historically evanescent character of *all* con-
> temporary social designs. (Comaroff and Comaroff 1999:294)

Who is the culprit? I seem to have been counted in the category by
Meyer and Geschiere (1999), whose position is practically identical to
that of Comaroff and Comaroff and who participate in their quota of
mutual admiration. In the introduction to *Globalization and Identity*, I
am taken to task for precisely this awful crime of continuity:

> He [Friedman] emphasizes that globalization goes together with
> "cultural continuity." This makes him distrust notions like "in-
> vention of tradition" or "hybridization"; instead, one of the aims
> of his collection of articles seems to be to understand the relation
> between the "global reordering of social realities" and "cultural
> continuity" . . . this . . . makes him fall back, in practice, on the
> highly problematic concept of "tradition," which—especially in
> his contributions on Africa—seems to figure as some sort of base-
> line, just as in the olden days of anthropology. . . . Similarly he
> relates the emergence of *les sapeurs*, to "certain fundamental rela-
> tions" in Congo history which "were never dissolved"; as an ex-
> ample of such "fundamental relations" Friedman mentions: "Life
> strategies consist in ensuring the flow of life-force. Traditionally
> this was assured by the social system itself." This is the kind of
> convenient anthropological shorthand which one had hoped to be
> rid of, certainly in discussions on globalization. . . . Friedman's re-
> version to such a simplistic use of the notion of tradition as some

sort of base line—quite surprising in view of the sophisticated things he has to say about globalization—illustrates how treacherous the triangle of globalization, culture and identity is. Relating postcolonial identities to such a notion of "tradition" makes anthropology indeed a tricky enterprise. (Meyer and Geschiere 1999:8)

The use of the terms "surprising," "treacherous," "tricky enterprise" in reference to my argument for the continuity of core properties of life strategies within the global system strikes me as evidence of a certain terminological nervousness. I do not, of course, make use of the concept of "tradition" at all. I use the word "traditionally" in referring to both a colonial and precolonial past. If this makes anthropology a "tricky enterprise," it would be interesting to know just how. I refer in the article they discuss to the way in which, in spite of the destruction of Congolese polities at the end of the last century under the onslaught of Leopold's Congo Free state, the major transformations reproduced a number of basic structures. This analysis was taken from Ekholm Friedman's work on the subject (1992), which analyzes the way in which transformation actually works, the way in which certain basic logics of being and of life strategies remain intact, even in transformation, and even as the political and much of the social order collapse. This is not in order to oppose culture to capitalism. It is to ascertain the way in which different logics articulate with one another over time. If all of these authors admit that some things don't change while others do, then we would seem all to agree, and yet not so. The reason is related to the way reality is classified. To see an articulation over time is to stress a transformational approach to historical change. To see in every new combination of elements something completely new is to stress discontinuity. Many years ago (Ekholm and Friedman 1980), we suggested that the global/local relation could be understood in terms of a double process: the incorporation of local structures into the reproductive cycles of an expanding capitalist system *and* the cultural assimilation of imported relations, categories, and objects into local strategies. We spoke of two kinds of transformation, one in which local change is endogenously organized but initiated and channeled by global relations, and another in which local structures are simply replaced by those from the dominant power. These two kinds of transformation occur, of course, together, but it is important not to confuse them. In Hawaii, the native population was reintegrated into the imported organizations of American colonial society, from church to school to the entire political structure. Their whole society was replaced. In Africa, colonial institutions did not replace local political structures in this way, and postcolonial African polities can be said to have strongly assimilated the imported formal structures of government. The same can be said to have happened in Papua New Guinea, where the state, while implementing the categories of formal Western organization, enmeshed them within local forms of sociality.[8] Thus, a district governor could describe his activities in terms of distribution to relatives, the accumulation of prestige typical of "big man" activities. Now, of course, big man strategies are themselves an endogenously structured transformation that might be of quite recent date. From my point of view, this is not a question of modernity but a particular articulation of different logics in a particular place. Contemporary, of course. Simultaneous, of course. But this does not mean that people can't live in radically different worlds of experience, of desire, or ways of going about the world.

I have myself discussed this issue in a publication with James Carrier on the subject of *Melanesian Modernities* (1996). In this context, the term is simply a way of marking the fact of participation in a postcolonial set of institutions, but it implies nothing about the way in which this participation occurs. From this vantage point, it would have been more adequate to speak of Melanesian Contemporaneities—a clumsy term indeed, but more to the point. There are many different ways of appropriating Western products, ways that are not contained within Western cultural logics. The potlatching with sewing machines at the turn of the last century referred to above was not a different way of being modern, but a different way of connecting to a larger world. The ultimate and very difficult issue here relates to the limits and nature of such differences, and this cannot be solved by simply stating that people play at different roles in different situations and that therefore the way to understanding is hybridity. The latter concept entirely misses the problem of articulation—that is, how, exactly, differences are integrated with one another.

A Confusion of Terms

Let me return now to the millennial arguments. They stress the modern as hybrid, as evanescent, as unbounded in space and as impossible to characterize in terms of what Comaroff and Comaroff refer to as the dualism of colonial discourse. Here is the heart of their argument for the necessary discontinuity of the modern. The world is one because capitalism is now globalized. And capitalism is thoroughly cultural, apparently equivalent to modernity, although this is never clearly addressed. This means that the world is a collection of specific capitalisms and therefore of specific modernities. In other words, to identify continuity is to deny the absolute contemporaneity and coevalness of the entirety of the world's populations.

I am not in favor of reforming language, but it is important to be able to distinguish among vastly different usages. In order to clarify this for myself, and perhaps the reader as well, let me suggest the following categorization:

1. Modernity as the contemporaneous refers to a situation of integration within the capitalist world economy and to varying degrees within the capitalist world as such.

    The relations to the capitalist world can vary according to the way in which different populations participate in that world, the articulation of different structures of experience, different socialities to one another. Being integrated into global capitalist reproductive process is not equivalent to being dominated by the capitalist logic. It is one thing to plant cash crops in order to gain money incomes, but where these incomes are used to buy pigs in order to give feasts in the context of a big man strategy, then the local form of accumulation of prestige, *while dependent on the larger market, is not organized by it*. Where a big man begins to use his monetary wealth to employ workers instead of gaining people's labor via debt and exchange relations, then we can speak of a tendency to capitalization of social relations. However, in order to move toward category (2) below, capitalist accumulation would have to become dominant within the population so that the big man strategy became a form of prestige only, a symbolic expression of accumulated capital. We note that there is an enormous economy of prestige in capitalist modernity, of course. Otherwise there would be no private universities, no Rockefeller Center, but these entities are direct products of capital accumulation. The generosity of the millionaire does not automatically create pressure for reciprocity, indebtedness, and social dependency. There are other mechanisms for that. Where there is a sphere of social reproduction that is not organized in capitalist terms, external to the capitalist sector, there is a sphere for the production of other forms of identification, sociality, cultural representations.

2. Modernity in the structural sense, as outlined above, refers to the cultural parameters of capitalist experience space, an outgrowth of the commodification of social relations which occurs to various degrees in time and space.

Modernities can vary in terms of the recombination of their basic parameters and in the degree of their realization. This is very much a question of historical change. European modernities represent a set of variants with respect to individualization, the private/public division, modernist ideology, and so on. These variants can profitably be compared to modernities that emerge in certain elite sectors of the third world, in certain classes, in China, Japan, and India, and to earlier historical modernities (in classical Greece, certain periods of ancient Mesopotamia, etc.). These variations, belong to the same family of forms because of certain basic tendencies that they harbor. In all of these cases, I would argue that capital (in the Weberian sense, below) accumulation is dominant in the social reproductive processes. This suggestion cannot be dealt with in full here, but it has been more fully discussed elsewhere (Ekholm Friedman and Friedman 1979; Friedman 2000; Adams 1980; Larsen 1976). I refer here to capitalist accumulation that is a process and that should not be conflated with any notion of social type. A social formation can be more or less transformed as a result of capitalist processes, but the latter is no more nor less than a logic of wealth accumulation—in the most general sense, the conversion of money capital or what Weber called abstract wealth into more such wealth.[9] The relation between this logic and the social reproduction of a particular population generates tendencies toward what I have described as modernity, but these tendencies are worked out to varying degrees and in variable ways insofar as the logic works itself out in different social and cultural contexts. Since there are no examples of societies that have become totally capitalized, and since capitalist reproduction does not dissolve everything, there are plenty of domains that are transformed without being dissolved and reconfigured in capitalist terms. Thus, there are clearly differences in local and national cultures within formations dominated by capitalist accumulation. There are large areas of social existence that are not the products of capitalism, and in this sense, we have never been modern.

It may be useful to refer to alternative modernities, or whatever term might seem appropriate, to characterize a particular form of articulation between peripheral societies in the world system and centrally initiated capitalist processes. These vary along two axes: one, the degree of transformative integration into the global system, and the other, the representations of the center as future, wealth, and well-being, as well as strategies related to such representations. But the primary sense of the term, as the identity and cultural spaces of capitalism, refers to the fundamental aspects of a particular phenomenon whose parameters have been the source of the various fragments that are so often compiled in lists like that referred to earlier: individualism, democracy, capitalism, alienation. The latter have, in their turn, functioned as metonymic referents of the alternative modernities described for the world's peripheries. They mark a peripherality that is emptied of cultural content, wherein the word "modern" is simply our or even their gloss on another kind of relationship, one that is structured by different kinds of experience of the world. Modernity in the former sense, however, can be understood as a kind of "tradition," a particular cultural configuration with a long history and full of its own magic and fetishism, as Marx demonstrated long ago. Much of the discourse that I have criticized here is wittingly or unwittingly based precisely on an opposition between modernity and tradition. Otherwise, the use of the term to describe the globalized world has no sense, nothing with which it can be contrasted. I have argued that this very opposition is itself a product of the logic of modernity, the logic of temporal differentiation, of development. Those who so adamantly claim modernity for the entire world are inadvertently replicating that which they so enthusiastically claim to escape.

Notes

1. Friedman (1994:214–27) contains a detailed critique of Giddens's atomistic laundry-list definition of modernity.

2. It is noteworthy that none of the replies to this article entertain a sustained critique of just this point. Whether or not the local is constituted, practiced, stable, or unstable, it is the locus of cultural production via the emergence of habitus.

3. In my discussion of modernity as an identity space, I suggest some similar terms as parameters for such a space.

4. The critique of this search for the native is not new, of course, and was the hallmark of Gluckman and the researchers of the Rhodes Livingstone Institute.

5. It is significant that while Foster argues for the existence of such modernities in terms of precisely an articulation of the Western with the indigenous, Spitulnik questions the "analytical power" of a term that is so variable in its meaning.

6. The identity space itself is best understood as a topological surface which

is also variable in form, capable, as indicated here, of folding in on itself in certain conditions.

7. No names are mentioned, interestingly enough, but the straw man would seem to be Sahlins, who is one of the few anthropologists to have explicitly attacked the globalizers.

8. This does not, of course, imply that the transformation is *generated* by internal dynamics. On the contrary I would argue that the "big-manization" process is probably related to significant changes in regional and global contexts—for example, the breakdown in the exchange systems linking highlands and lowlands combined with the introduction of massive amounts of shell valuables and/or money from the West. On the other hand, the tendency to the emergence of "fighting with food" is probably a much older process, one that may have well oscillated from such feasting to control over the flow of prestige goods (Persson 2000).

9. This notion is opposed to the generally accepted Marxist notion, which includes the wage relationship as central. We have argued that the wage relationship is only one of the possible ways in which capital can reproduce itself on an expanded scale, one that becomes increasingly generalized in industrial capitalism but that is not the core of its logic. Following Weber, I define capital simply as abstract wealth, which thus provides for a structural continuity between the various forms of historical capital accumulation. Marx himself is quite aware of this, and it plays a crucial role in his analysis of capitalist reproduction in its most sophisticated versions, in volume 3 of *Capital* and in the *Theories of Surplus Value,* where fundamental contradiction of capitalist reproduction is that between fictitious accumulation and real accumulation—that is, the fact that capitalism is driven by a need to convert money into more money, and the way this simple logic bogs down in the necessity of passing through production and its realization on the market. It would be simpler, of course, to simply speculate. The logic of mercantilism is *the logic* of accumulation before it penetrates and reorganizes the labor process, a penetration that is reversing itself in the current period.

References

Adams, R.
  1980   Anthropological Perspectives on Ancient Trade. *Current Anthropology* 15: 239–58.

Chabal, P., and J.-P. Dalloz
  1999   *L'Afrique est partie. Du désordre comme instrument politique.* Paris: Economica.

Comaroff, Jean, and John L. Comaroff
  1999   Occult Economies and the Violence of Abstraction: Notes from the South African Postcolony. *American Ethnologist* 26: 279–303.

Donham, Donald L.
   2002   On Being Modern in a Capitalist World: Some Conceptual and
          Comparative Issues. In *Critically Modern: Alternatives, Alterities,
          Anthropologies* [this volume]. Edited by Bruce M. Knauft. Bloom-
          ington: Indiana University Press.

Ekholm Friedman, K.
   1992   *Catastrophe and Creation: The Transformation of an African Culture.*
          London: Harwood

Ekholm Friedman, K., and Jonathan Friedman
   1979   "Capital," Imperialism and Exploitation in Ancient World Systems.
          In *Power and Propaganda: A Symposium on Ancient Empires.* Edited
          by M. J. Larsen, pp. 41–58. Copenhagen: Akademisk Forlag.
   1979   Towards a Global Anthropology. In *History and Underdevelopment.*
          Edited by L. Blussé, H. L. Wesseling, and G. D. Winius. Leiden:
          Center for the History of European Expansion.

Englund, Harri, and James Leach
   2000   Ethnography and the Meta-Narratives of Modernity. *Current An-
          thropology* 41:225–48.

Foster, Robert J.
   2002   Bargains with Modernity in Papua New Guinea and Elsewhere. In
          Critically Modern: Alternatives, Alterities, Anthropologies [this vol-
          ume]. Edited by Bruce M. Knauft. Bloomington: Indiana Univer-
          sity Press.

Friedman, Jonathan
   1994   *Cultural Identity and Global Process.* London: Sage.
   1999   Class Formation, Hybridity and Ethnification in Declining Global
          Hegemonies. In *Globalization and the Asia Pacific: Contested Territo-
          ries.* Edited by K. Olds, P. Dicken, P. Kelly, L. Kong, and H. Yeung,
          pp. 183–201. London: Routledge.
   2000   Concretizing the Continuity Argument in Global Systems Analysis.
          In *World System History: The Social Science of Long Term Change.*
          Edited by R. Denemark, J. Friedman, B. Gills, and G. Modelski,
          pp. 133–52. London: Routledge.
   2001   The Paradoxes of Real Existing Globalization: Elite Discourses
          and the Grassroots. In *Images of the World,* pp. 52–65. New York:
          UNESCO.

Friedman, Jonathan, and James G. Carrier
   1996   [Eds.] *Melanesian Modernities.* Lund Monographs in Social Anthro-
          pology No. 3. Lund, Sweden: Lund University Press.

Geschiere, Peter
   1997   *The Witchcraft of Modernity: Politics and the Occult in Postcolonial
          Africa.* Charlottesville: University of Virginia Press.
   2000   Sorcellerie et modernité: Retour sur une étrange complicité. *Poli-
          tique Africaine* 79: 17–33.

Giddens, Anthony
   1990   *The Consequences of Modernity*. Stanford, Calif.: Stanford University
           Press.
Harvey, David
   1989   *The Condition of Postmodernity: An Enquiry into the Origins of Cul-
           ture Change*. Cambridge: Blackwell.
Hirst, P., and G. Thompson
   1996   *Globalization in Question*. Cambridge: Polity.
Larsen, M. J.
   1976   *The Old Assyrian City State and its Colonies*. Copenhagen: Akade-
           misk Forlag.
Kelly, John D.
   2002   Alternative Modernities or an Alternative to "Modernity": Getting
           Out of the Modernist Sublime. In *Critically Modern: Alternatives,
           Alterities, Anthropologies* [this volume]. Edited by Bruce M. Knauft.
           Bloomington: Indiana University Press.
Knauft, Bruce M.
   2002   Critically Modern: An Introduction. In *Critically Modern: Alterna-
           tives, Alterities, Anthropologies* [this volume]. Edited by Bruce M.
           Knauft. Bloomington: Indiana University Press.
Marx, Karl
   1974   *Capital*. Volume 3. London: Lawrence and Wishart
   1976   *Theories of Surplus Value*. London: Lawrence and Wishart
McKendrick, Niel, John Brewer, and J. H. Plumb
   1982   [Eds.] *The Birth of a Consumer Society*. London: Europa Publica-
           tions
Meyer, B., and P. Geschiere
   1999   [Eds.] *Globalization and Identity: Dialectics of Flow and Closure*. Ox-
           ford: Blackwell
Persson, J.
   2000   *Sagali and the Kula*. Lund: Lund University Dissertations in Social
           Anthropology.
Sahlins, Marshall D.
   1999   Two or Three Things that I Know about Culture. *Journal of the
           Royal Anthropological Institute* 5: 399–421.
Spitulnik, Debra A.
   2002   Accessing "Local" Modernities: Reflections on the Place of Lin-
           guistic Evidence in Ethnography. In *Critically Modern: Alternatives,
           Alterities, Anthropologies* [this volume]. Edited by Bruce M. Knauft.
           Bloomington: Indiana University Press.
Trouillot, Michel-Rolph
   2002   The Otherwise Modern: Caribbean Lessons from the Savage Slot.
           In *Critically Modern: Alternatives, Alterities, Anthropologies* [this vol-

ume]. Edited by Bruce M. Knauft. Bloomington: Indiana University Press.

Wallerstein, Immanuel
1979   *The Capitalist World-Economy*. Cambridge: Cambridge University Press.

Wardlow, Holly
2002   "Hands-Up"-ing Buses and Harvesting Cheese-Pops: Gendered Mediation of Modern Disjuncture in Melanesia. In *Critically Modern: Alternatives, Alterities, Anthropologies* [this volume]. Edited by Bruce M. Knauft. Bloomington: Indiana University Press.

Wilk, R.
1995   Learning to Be Local in Belize: Global Systems of Common Difference. In *Worlds Apart: Modernity through the Prism of the Local*. Edited by Daniel Miller, pp. 110–34. London: Routledge.

Contributors

Donald L. Donham is Professor of Anthropology and currently Director of African Studies at Emory University. His interests center on the method and theory of ethnographic description in a globalized capitalist world, and he has done extensive field research in both Ethiopia and South Africa. He is the author of *Marxist Modern: An Ethnographic History of the Ethiopian Revolution* (1999), *Work and Power in Maale, Ethiopia* (2nd ed., 1994), and *History, Power, Ideology: Central Issues in Marxism and Anthropology* (1990).

Robert J. Foster is Associate Professor and Chair of the Department of Anthropology at the University of Rochester. His current research interests include globalization, material culture, and comparative modernities. He is the author of *Materializing the Nation: Commodities, Consumption, and Media in Papua New Guinea* (Indiana University Press, 2002) and *Social Reproduction and History in Melanesia: Mortuary Ritual, Gift Exchange and Custom in the Tanga Islands* (1995), and editor of *Nation-Making: Emergent Identities in Postcolonial Melanesia* (1995).

Jonathan Friedman is Directeur d'études at the École des Hautes Études en Sciences Sociales in Paris and Professor of Social Anthropology at the University of Lund, Sweden. His interests include global system history and global/local articulations, ethnicity and indigenous movements, and Southeast Asia and Polynesia. He has done fieldwork in Hawaii since the late 1970s. He is the author of *Cultural Identity and Global Process* (1994), and editor of *Consumption and Identity* (1994),

System, Structure and Contradiction in the "Evolution" of Asiatic Social Formations (1998), and *PC Worlds: An Anthropology of Political Correctness* (forthcoming).

Ivan Karp is the National Endowment for the Humanities Professor of Liberal Arts and Director of the Center for the Study of Public Scholarship at Emory University. His research interests include social organization and social change, African systems of thought, and the ethnography of museums. He has edited *African Philosophy as Critical Inquiry* (with D. A. Masolo, Indiana University Press, 2000), *Museums and Communities: The Politics of Public Culture* (with Christine Kreamer and Steven Lavine, 1992), *Exhibiting Cultures: the Poetics and Politics of Museum Display* (with Steven Lavine, 1991), and *Personhood and Agency: The Experience of Self and Other in African Cultures* (with Michael Jackson, 1990).

John D. Kelly is Associate Professor of Anthropology at the University of Chicago. His research interests include social theory, historical anthropology, knowledge and power in early historic India, and colonial and postcolonial Fiji. Together with Martha Kaplan, he has published articles on dialogical social theory and the book *Represented Communities: Fiji and World Decolonization* (2001). Another coauthored book is near completion: *Laws Like Bullets: On Colonial Law and Its Consequences.* His volume *A Politics of Virtue: Hinduism, Sexuality, and Countercolonial Discourse in Fiji* was published in 1991.

Bruce M. Knauft is Samuel C. Dobbs Professor of Anthropology and Director of the Vernacular Modernities Program at Emory University. His research engages broad issues of critical theory with ethnographic and historical specifics—in Melanesia and more generally. His interests include the articulation between subjective orientations and political economy in relation to religion, violence, gender, sexuality, and governmentality. His books include *Exchanging the Past: A Rainforest World of Before and After* (2002), *From Primitive to Post-Colonial in Melanesia and Anthropology* (1999), *Genealogies for the Present in Cultural Anthropology* (1996), *South Coast New Guinea Cultures: History, Comparison, Dialectic* (1993), and *Good Company and Violence: Sorcery and Social Action in a Lowland New Guinea Society* (1985).

Lisa Rofel is Associate Professor of Anthropology at the University of California, Santa Cruz. Her current research addresses sexuality, citizenship, and globalization. Her book is titled *Other Modernities: Gendered Yearnings in China after Socialism* (1999).

Debra A. Spitulnik is Associate Professor of Anthropology at Emory University. Her research spans the fields of linguistic anthropology, sociolinguistics, media anthropology, media and nationalism, and comparative Bantu linguistics. Her current book project, *Voicing the Nation: Verbal Art and the Public in Zambian Talk Radio,* investigates the discourse styles and public-sphere functions of one of the most popular radio programs in Zambian history. Her forthcoming book is *Media Connections and Disconnections: Radio Culture and the Public Sphere in Zambia.*

Michel-Rolph Trouillot is Professor of Anthropology at the University of Chicago. He has written extensively on the Caribbean, globalization, historical apologies, and the production of concepts and categories in the human sciences. His books include *Silencing the Past: Power and the Production of History* (1995), *Haiti: State against Nation* (1990), and *Peasants and Capital: Dominica in the World Economy* (1988).

Holly Wardlow is Assistant Professor of Anthropology at the University of Toronto. Her publications include research on gender and modernity, the impact of mining in Papua New Guinea on gender ideologies, the changing practices and meanings of bridewealth, and sexual and reproductive health.

Index